The Psychology of Meditation

Peter Sedlmeier

The Psychology of Meditation

Varieties, Effects, Theories, and Perspectives

Library of Congress Cataloging in Publication information for the print version of this book is available via the Library of Congress Marc Database under the LC Control Number 2022931601

Library and Archives Canada Cataloguing in Publication
Title: The psychology of meditation : varieties, effects, theories, and perspectives / Peter Sedlmeier.
Names: Sedlmeier, Peter, author.
Description: Includes bibliographical references.
Identifiers: Canadiana (print) 20220162662 | Canadiana (ebook) 20220162719 | ISBN 9780889375765 (softcover) | ISBN 9781616765767 (PDF) | ISBN 9781613345764 (EPUB)
Subjects: LCSH: Meditation. | LCSH: Meditation—Psychological aspects. | LCSH: Meditation—Therapeutic use. | LCSH: Mindfulness (Psychology)
Classification: LCC BF637.M4 S43 2022 | DDC 158.1/2—dc23

© 2022 by Hogrefe Publishing
www.hogrefe.com

The authors and publisher have made every effort to ensure that the information contained in this text is in accord with the current state of scientific knowledge, recommendations, and practice at the time of publication. In spite of this diligence, errors cannot be completely excluded. Also, due to changing regulations and continuing research, information may become outdated at any point. The authors and publisher disclaim any responsibility for any consequences which may follow from the use of information presented in this book.

Registered trademarks are not noted specifically as such in this publication. The use of descriptive names, registered names, and trademarks does not imply, even in the absence of a specific statement, that such names are exempt from the relevant protective laws and regulations and therefore free for general use.

The cover image is an agency photo depicting models. Use of the photo on this publication does not imply any connection between the content of this publication and any person depicted in the cover image.

Cover image: © goo.gl/73nyq6 – iStock.com with overlay of Figure 3.2 (The Buddhist Noble Eightfold Path)

PUBLISHING OFFICES
USA: Hogrefe Publishing Corporation, 44 Merrimac Street, Suite 207, Newburyport, MA 01950
Phone +1 978 255-3700; E-mail customerservice@hogrefe.com
EUROPE: Hogrefe Publishing GmbH, Merkelstr. 3, 37085 Göttingen, Germany
Phone +49 551 99950-0, Fax +49 551 99950-111; E-mail publishing@hogrefe.com

SALES & DISTRIBUTION
USA: Hogrefe Publishing, Customer Services Department,
30 Amberwood Parkway, Ashland, OH 44805
Phone (800) 228-3749, Fax (419) 281-6883; E-mail customerservice@hogrefe.com
UK: Hogrefe Publishing, c/o Marston Book Services Ltd., 160 Eastern Ave., Milton Park, Abingdon, OX14 4SB
Phone +44 1235 465577, Fax +44 1235 465556; E-mail direct.orders@marston.co.uk
EUROPE: Hogrefe Publishing, Merkelstr. 3, 37085 Göttingen, Germany
Phone +49 551 99950-0, Fax +49 551 99950-111; E-mail publishing@hogrefe.com

OTHER OFFICES
CANADA: Hogrefe Publishing, 82 Laird Drive, East York, Ontario, M4G 3V1
SWITZERLAND: Hogrefe Publishing, Länggass-Strasse 76, 3012 Bern

No part of this book may be reproduced, stored in a retrieval system or transmitted, in any form or by any means, electronic, mechanical, photocopying, microfilming, recording or otherwise, without written permission from the publisher.

Printed and bound in the USA

ISBN 978-0-88937-576-5 (print) · ISBN 978-1-61676-576-7 (PDF) · ISBN 978-1-61334-576-4 (EPUB)
https://doi.org/10.1027/00576-000

Contents

Preface IX

Part 1: Varieties

    Chapter 1: What Do People Do When They Say They Meditate? 3

    Chapter 2: What Is Mindfulness? 23

    Chapter 3: Traditional Classifications of Meditation Techniques ... 43

    Chapter 4: Western Attempts at Classifying Meditation Techniques 61

    Chapter 5: Why Do People Meditate? 71

Part 2: Effects

    Chapter 6: Effects of Meditation for Healthy Practitioners 85

    Chapter 7: Effects of Meditation in Clinical Settings 121

    Chapter 8: Hot Topics in Meditation Research 145

Part 3: Theories

    Chapter 9: Traditional Theories of Meditation 173

    Chapter 10: Western Explanations 211

Part 4: Perspectives

    Chapter 11: Perspectives on Meditation Research 231

References 255

About the Author

Peter Sedlmeier is professor of psychology at Chemnitz University of Technology, Germany. He mainly teaches research methods and cognitive psychology. Apart from the psychology of meditation, his current areas of interest include intercultural research, time processing, and computer modeling of cognitive and statistical processes. He has been practicing meditation for more than 20 years, mostly Zen, interspersed with some extended excursions into the Theravada world, and some experience in yoga meditation and transcendental meditation (TM).

Preface

The present volume attempts nothing less than to give a state-of-the-art summary of what we currently know about the psychology of meditation. Of course, one volume cannot possibly summarize everything, and as an author I had to make some difficult choices, but the aim of this work is to give a representative overview of what psychological science has achieved so far in this area, as well as which problems are still around. One could say that the main point of the book is to prepare the reader for the suggestions for future research given in the last chapter.

There is much confusion in meditation research about what meditation is, how it is embedded in various practicing contexts, and why people meditate at all. Therefore, this book puts an emphasis on clarifying these questions in Part 1, on the varieties of meditation. Chapter 1 describes the vast diversity of meditation techniques, and Chapter 2 deals with the notoriously problematic issue of *mindfulness*, which is often (wrongly) thought of as synonymous with *meditation*. Chapters 3 and 4 look at meditation in its respective contexts – traditional and Western, respectively. And Chapter 5 reviews the astonishingly few attempts at finding out why people begin to meditate at all and why they stay with it.

Part 2 of the book deals with the effects of meditation. Meanwhile, an incredibly large number of studies have examined the effects of meditation, and it seems that no end is in sight for the exponential growth curve of the number of publications. This forced me to rely mainly on meta-analyses (and even meta-syntheses – that is, summaries of meta-analyses). Chapter 6 gives an overview on the very varied research on the effects of meditation on more or less healthy practitioners. Many more studies have been conducted on the effects of meditation for practitioners from clinical populations, which are reviewed in Chapter 7. There are some exciting new trends in the topics for meditation research, such as the use of meditation apps, adverse outcomes of meditation, differential effects of different practices, and the impact of spirituality and ethics. These are dealt with in Chapter 8.

The usual order of presentation in books on a given scientific topic is to begin with the theory part and then present and discuss the empirical evidence in light of the theories. This book does it the other way round, and there is a justification for that: So far, the bulk of meditation research has been conducted with little or no theoretical background. To be sure, there are *theories of meditation*, and they will be summarized in Part 3 of the book. Chapter 9 presents my understanding of the psychological aspects of four main traditional approaches: Samkhya-Yoga, early Buddhism, Advaita

Vedanta, and Zen. Western attempts at explaining why and how meditation works are reviewed in Chapter 10.

As mentioned above, all of this – that is, a summary of the varieties, the effects, and the theories of meditation – can be seen as a preparation for the last part of the book, presenting perspectives on meditation research (Chapter 11). For seasoned meditation researchers, it might be that not that much in the book will really be new. However, I am not aware of any other book that takes so many pains to prepare the argument that meditation research definitely needs to be improved – regarding which, some suggestions will be offered here. Measured by the number of publications, meditation research is already a success story, but its real success hinges on how well we *understand* the psychology of meditation. Such a profound understanding, which would express itself in a good theory (or in several good theories), will certainly help to improve the practice of meditation. But it also has the potential to reach far beyond meditation research proper, to the enrichment of our understanding of consciousness and cognition.

Although this book officially has only one author, it is in fact the product of many people's efforts who contributed in one way or another. As this is a book on meditation, I begin with my teacher AMA Samy, thanking him for all I learned from him. Many aspects of what is covered in this book only became much clearer to me (still with some room for improvement though) by discussing them with fellow meditators, meditation teachers, and researchers interested in meditation. Some of them deserve special mentions and thanks: Ven. Angulgamuwe Ariyananda, Britta Biedermann, Matthijs Cornelissen, William van Gordon, Carl Hooper, Caroline Jones, Sonali Marwaha, Ven. Nanasiri, Bhikkhuni Agga Nani, Veerachart Nimanong, Ulrich Ott, Ramakrishna Rao, and Ajahn Suphan. I owe much to my friend K. Srinivas who sadly passed away so prematurely. While I was on sabbatical at Pondicherry University, India, he, being a philosophy professor himself, opened the door to Indian philosophy for me. Without him, there would be no Chapter 9 in this book (at least not as it looks now).

Colleagues and students who give critical feedback on one's writings are an indispensable part of scientific work, at least for those persons whose first-draft versions of papers and books are usually far off from how they ideally should look. I am one of those persons. Therefore, I was very fortunate to receive help from many people who read some chapters of the book and provided me with valuable and sometimes (most importantly!) very critical feedback. My thanks to Britta Biedermann, Anna-Nora Fenske, Eva Henschke, Frank Heydel, Carl Hooper, Stefan Ibold, Helmut Kunkel, Ulrich Ott, and Vivien Röder. I am especially indebted to Ritesh Mariadas, Karin Matko, and Isabell Winkler, who looked through most if not all of the chapters. My heartfelt thanks to them all!

The book would not exist had not the folks from Hogrefe encouraged me to write it. I would like to thank especially Robert Dimbleby and Lisa Bennett, who brought the project on its way and accompanied me throughout, as well as Irina Rau for her careful production work and Timothy DeVinney for his excellent copyediting.

Peter Sedlmeier

Part 1
Varieties

Chapter 1
What Do People Do When They Say They Meditate?

Meditation grows your brain, enhances empathy, reduces blood pressure, boosts the immune system, reduces anxiety and depression, is the ultimate pain killer, increases positive emotions, and makes you more intelligent. This is just a small sample of the effects of meditation you can read about on the Internet (e.g., Chowdhury, 2019; Dimitrov, 2019; Miller, 2021; Rana, 2021). So, it might indeed be a good idea to meditate, and I will come back to the evidence for these claims in later chapters of the book. But what should you actually do to achieve all these benefits? Such advice sounds like you just have to know what meditation is and then practice it. This uniform view of meditation is also what researchers in the West have mostly adhered to, so far, although some early work already made clear that meditation is far from being a uniform practice (Goleman, 1977; Naranjo & Ornstein, 1972; see also Oman, 2021).

When you ask meditators what they do when they say they meditate, their answers are, however, quite diverse. For instance, when we asked experienced meditators from various traditions and looked into the literature, we eventually obtained a list of 309 different meditation techniques (Matko et al., 2021a). These many techniques are of course not totally different, and Chapter 4 presents a classification system based on these 309 techniques, along with the results of other researchers' attempts to classify meditation techniques. In Chapter 3, we will also have a look at traditional classifications. However, before a summary of the many techniques of meditation, some selected examples should help convey an impression of the huge variety to be found in the meditation landscape. We will see that basically anything can be an object of meditation, but that meditation focuses mostly on bodily or mental processes. We will see that meditating often means observing something or being aware of some process, but it can also mean mentally influencing the body or mind, generating emotions, performing some action repeatedly, moving in a specific way, or combining several of these.

Watching the Breath

The most commonly used object of meditation is the breath. It accompanies us through our whole life, and we can easily observe it. A basic practice is to just place all one's attention on the coming and going of the breath. Hereby, one can focus on the sensation the air creates when passing the nostrils. One may explore where exactly in the nostrils (opening, further inside, or higher up the sinuses) this sensation is perceived most accurately. Usually, between the end of the out-breath and the following in-breath, and also between the end of the in-breath and the following out-breath, breathing is suspended for a moment. This halt should also be noted. The aim is to be clear and calm and not tense while being aware of the breath, but also to do so without relaxing too much, i.e., to the point of falling into a sluggish state (see, for example, Ricard, 2011, p. 76).

Watching the breath at first sounds easy, but when you try it, you will probably notice that your mind wanders very quickly. For instance, if you want to stay with perceiving the sensation of the breath at the opening of the nostrils, it may be difficult to do that for an extended period of time because the sensation is so faint. This will improve with practice, but to strengthen the feeling it may help to watch the feeling in cold weather – for instance, when you leave your home on an icy winter day. You might also want to watch the feeling when your breath is very short as, for instance, when you run or work out.

Over time, meditation teachers have devised innumerable specific ways to watch the breath. For an illustration, one can again have a look at some of the variations proposed by Matthieu Ricard, a very experienced monk and scholar who was mainly trained in one of the Tibetan Buddhist traditions (Ricard, 2011, pp. 70–81). An easy way of watching the breath is to count it (please note that counting itself comes in many variations – you can, for instance, vary the number up to which you count, whether you count at the end of the out-breath or the beginning of the in-breath, or both). Then you could "fill" the in- and out-breath by mentally repeating 1, 1, 1, 1, 1, ... during the course of an in-breath (the number of repetitions depending on the length of the breath), and 2, 2, 2, 2, 2, ... during the course of the next out-breath, and do that until you arrive, say, at 10, 10, 10, 10, 10, ... and then begin again. Another variation consists of filling the breath with mentally expressed wishes such as "May all beings be happy," while breathing out, and "May all their suffering be dispelled," when breathing in. Breathing can also be "filled" with mantras, see the section Repeating Words or Sentences, in this chapter).

For some, it might be easier to watch the effect of breathing instead of the breath itself – the place to look at for that could be your abdomen, which rises with the in-breath and falls with the out-breath. Here is an instruction from the tradition of Vipassana advocated by Mahasi Sayadaw (Mahasi, 1991, p. 5. Please note that "Sayadaw" is not a name but a title – literally "royal teacher" – commonly used in the Burmese Theravada monk tradition, referring to a senior monk or an abbot of a monastery):

> Try to keep your mind (but not your eyes) on the abdomen. You will thereby come to know the movements of rising and falling of it. If these movements are not clear to you in the beginning, then place both hands on the abdomen to feel these rising and falling movements. After a short time the upward movement of exhalation will become clear. (Mahasi, 1991, p. 5. Reprinted here with permission from the Buddhist Publication Society.)

The two examples from Ricard and Mahasi already illustrate that basic meditation techniques may be hard to separate into totally distinct categories: The breath can be used to better concentrate on thoughts or wishes ("May all beings be happy"), or the concentration on body movements (rising and falling of the abdomen) can be used to better attend to the breath. This mixture of techniques is also evident in practices in which the breath is not only watched, but also partly influenced. These and similar ways of observing the breath can be found in all major traditional approaches to meditation, as well as in newly developed ones.

Watching Body, Thoughts, and Emotions

Breathing is, of course, also a bodily process, but because of its central role in all traditions of meditation, it has received an opening section here of its own. If you have tried such an approach to staying with the breath and could not, you may feel some negativity. This would be a good opportunity to switch to a different object of meditation: observing your negativity. Maybe you notice that there is some pressure in your stomach– you could then observe this pressure. You might think "I have not had such a pressure before": Observe this thought. Just to sit and observe whatever comes up and let it go again is a basic exercise. It can be found in most Buddhist forms of meditation, but also in many other contemplative traditions as well as in secular approaches. Staying open to all that happens, sometimes termed *open awareness* is, at least for most beginners, much more difficult than to watch the breath. This is probably why some meditation teachers recommend restricting open awareness to bodily processes (e.g., Sheng-Yen, 2002).

Body Scan

Some variants of what is currently known as Vipassana meditation (for some variations, see Chapter 3), as well as newly created secular approaches such as mindfulness-based stress reduction (MBSR), recommend moving the awareness of bodily processes systematically through the whole body (e.g., Hart, 1987; Kabat-Zinn, 1990; Mahasi, 1991), a technique often called a body scan. The exact ways a body scan is performed vary. For instance, in the approach made popular by S. N. Goenka (see Hart, 1987, p. 92), attention is systematically moved through the whole body, from feet to head and back. Doing that, practitioners are advised not to search for or avoid particular types of sensation. Instead, in moving through the body, they should just observe all physical sensations as they occur naturally.

"Waiting" and Labeling

There are even practices in which meditators "wait" to notice a specified bodily process appear. For instance, in the above-mentioned approach to Vipassana developed by Mahasi Sayadaw (e.g., Mahasi, 1973), meditators are to be constantly aware if their meditation posture "tilts," and every time it does, they are to progress one bead on their prayer beads. In this tradition of Vipassana, it is also common practice to silently label everything that comes up, as exemplified in the following instruction by Mahasi:

> If you imagine something, you must know that you have done so and make a mental note, imagining. If you simply think of something, mentally note, thinking. If you reflect, reflecting. If you intend to do something, intending. When the mind wanders from the object of meditation which is the rising and falling of the abdomen, mentally note, wandering. Should you imagine you are going to a certain place, note going. When you arrive, arriving. When, in your thoughts, you meet a person, note meeting. Should you speak to him or her, speaking. If you imaginarily argue with that person, note arguing. If you envision or imagine a light or colour, be sure to note seeing. A mental vision must be noted on each occurrence of its appearance until it passes away. (Mahasi, 1991, p. 7. Reprinted here with permission from the Buddhist Publication Society.)

The practice of labeling whatever comes up in consciousness is also part of many other approaches to meditation, such as in some varieties of Zen (e.g., Samy, 2005).

Consistently Focusing on an Object

Consistently focusing on an object is already described in early Hindu and Buddhist texts, such as the *Yogasutras* or the *Vimuttimagga*. For instance, the *Vimuttimagga* (Path of Freedom), which dates to the 1st century CE and is ascribed to the Sri Lankan Theravada monk Upatissa, tells how to practice such focused meditation. Here is a description of how to concentrate on a so-called earth *kasina* (a disc made of clay that represents the element of earth), referred to in the modern translation of the text as *mandala*:

> When the yogin dwells on the *mandala*, he should not open his eyes too wide nor shut them entirely. Thus should he view it. If he opens his eyes too wide, they will grow weary, he will not be able to know the true nature of the *mandala*, and the after-image will not arise. If he faces the *mandala* closing the eyes fast, he will not see the sign because of darkness, and he will arouse negligence. Therefore, he should refrain from opening his eyes too wide and closing them fast. He should dwell with earnestness on the *mandala*. Thus should the yogin dwell (on the *mandala*) in order to gain fixity of mind. As a man looking at his own face in a mirror sees his face because of the mirror, i.e., because the face is reflected by the mirror, so the yogin dwelling on the *mandala* sees the sign of concentration which arises, because of the *mandala*. Thus should he take the sign by fixing the mind through even gazing. Thus one takes the sign through even gazing. (Upatissa, 1961, p. 73. Reprinted here with permission from the Buddhist Publication Society.)

This text talks also about one effect that can be expected from a prolonged practice of concentration, the arising of a "sign" (*nimitta* in Pali), a kind of secondary meditation object, whose nature depends on the primary object of meditation (for background information, see Brahm, 2014; Pa-Auk, 2000). Apart from kasinas, there are many other possible objects of concentrative meditation, foremost among these, again, is the breath (for a collection of such objects mentioned in early Buddhist texts, see Shaw, 2006). Which object a (monastic) meditator should concentrate on has been extensively written about by the medieval Sri Lankan monk Buddhaghosa (2010). Most of these techniques are still practiced in Theravada monasteries, and a selection of them can also be found in contemporary approaches to meditation. These include such unlikely candidates such as the sound of silence (Sumedho & Amaro, 2007) or the smile (Brasington, 2015).

Influencing Breath and Body

If beginning meditators try to observe their breath, they usually find that it changes: It becomes shorter, longer, or less regular just by concentrating on it. But some breathing techniques aim to achieve exactly this: modifying the breath. It has long been known that deep meditative states are connected with slowing down the breath considerably and making it almost imperceptible. Thus, it seems plausible that this connection also works the other way round: If I slow down my breath or make it almost imperceptible, deep meditative states may result. And indeed, watching the breath in a systematic way is supposed to have exactly that effect (e.g., Catherine, 2011; Pa-Auk, 2000).

Utilizing the Breath

In classical yoga (see Chapters 3 and 9) the cultivation of the breath (*pranayama*) is an essential part of the practice, often performed together with bodily postures (*asanas*). There, it is usually not regarded as meditation proper but as a preparation for it. But many meditation techniques in other spiritual traditions incorporate the breath as a help to concentrate on mantras (holy syllables, words, or groups of words), objects, or as a means to influence the sensations and processes in parts of the physical or the *subtle body* as postulated in ancient Indian theories. (Different traditions have different views about additional bodily components of a fine material level. The best-known of these is probably the Chinese *qi* system, which is, for instance, referred to in acupuncture and *qigong*; see, e.g., Liang & Wu, 2006.) Many meditators probably have had the experience that pain vanishes after some time if they mentally direct their breath into the respective region of the body. As already mentioned, a simple way of using the breath to influence bodily processes is to slow it down to achieve a state of relaxation or, if practiced intensively, a state of deep tranquility.

Concentrating on Energy Centers and Energy Flow

A further way of influencing the body consists of concentrating on body parts that are supposed to relate to subtle matter or energy centers, as well as on the energy flow that connects them. As already mentioned above, an influence is postulated in several spiritual approaches as, for instance, qigong (see also the section Other Forms of Meditative Movement, in this chapter) or several forms of yoga (e.g., Flood, 1996). Energy centers also play a role in Buddhist traditions. For instance, in Zen, some practitioners concentrate on the *tanden*, situated below the navel (e.g., Kushner, 2018).

Several systems of yoga give a central role to a similar form of subtle body that is said to contain energy centers or *chakras*. The main chakras, thought to be aligned along the spine, are, for instance, to be activated in kriya yoga (introduced in 1920 to the US by Paramahamsa Yogananda), by having life force (*prana*) flow through them (Yogananda, 1950). The most common chakra system consists of seven main chakras – six major ones and a seventh energy center that has a special status (e.g., Flood, 1996). Often, the energizing activity starts from the lowest, the *muladhara* (root) chakra situated at the root of the spine and goes up through the *svadhishthana* (navel) chakra, the *manipura* (solar plexus) chakra, the *anahata* (heart) chakra, the *vishuddha* (throat) chakra, the *ajna* (forehead) chakra (often regarded as the seat of the "third eye"), and the *sahasrara* (crown) chakra, which is regarded as the highest spiritual center of the subtle body. These chakras (or variations thereof) also play a central role in other Hindu (e.g., kundalini yoga) or Buddhist (tantric) approaches (Feuerstein, 2001). Similar energy centers that can be influenced in meditation are assumed in Sufism (e.g., Ernst, 2000, p. 107).

Repeating Words or Sentences

Repeating a holy word or mantra is the basic technique in *transcendental meditation* (TM), which was brought to the West by the Hindu teacher Maharishi (meaning "great teacher") Mahesh Yogi (see Shear, 2006; for details about TM, see also the section Transcendental Meditation, in Chapter 3). Other approaches to meditation in the Hindu context propose the use of generally available and meaningful mantras (see Gonda, 1963, for an overview). The mantra is often seen as a vehicle to transcend the mind and experience the divine.

Mantras From the Hindu Tradition

The most well-known mantra is the holy syllable *Om*, which is often combined with additional words such as *Om Namah Shivaya* (adoration offered to Lord Shiva). Another common mantra is the Hare Krishna mantra dedicated to the Hindu god Vishnu and his consort. This *maha-mantra* (great mantra) consists of the names of Krishna's consort Radha (Hare) and names for two avatars of Vishnu (Krishna and Rama):

Hare Krishna, Hare Krishna
Krishna Krishna, Hare Hare
Hare Rama, Hare Rama
Rama Rama, Hare Hare.

Probably the most highly esteemed mantra, especially by Indian practitioners, is one that stems from the *Rig Veda*, one of the earliest Indian philosophical texts, and is known as *Gayatri mantra* or as *Savitri mantra* ("savitur" in the mantra refers to Savitri; diacritical marks are omitted):

om bhur bhuvah svah
tat savitur varenyam
bhargo devasya dhimahi
dhiyo yo nah pracodayat

Gayatri is the name of the Vedic meter in which the verse is composed (Staal, 1986), and Savitri is often referred to as an ancient (male) deity who is connected to the Sun, but the famous yogi and sage Sri Aurobindo claims that *she* "is the Divine Word, daughter of the Sun, goddess of the supreme Truth who comes down and is born so save" (Aurobindo, 1995, Author's note). Both the Hare Krishna mantra and the Savitri mantra are often chanted (sung aloud in a group). There are numerous – often quite different – translations, but usually the Savitri mantra is only recited in Sanskrit (one translation can be found in Goodall, 1996, p. 3: "We meditate on the lovely light of the god, Savitṛ: May it stimulate our thoughts"), and occasionally it is also used in other yogic techniques – for example, for determining the length of breath control (Feuerstein, 2001, p. 209).

The Indian meditation teacher Eknath Easwaran, who lived and taught in the US, proposed a method of silent daily mental repetition of one or more somewhat longer passages of text that meditators can choose freely from any mystical tradition (e.g., Buddhism, Christianity, Judaism, Hinduism, Islam, or Daoism). He asserted that the focused repetition of these text passages improves concentration and helps in spiritual transformation (e.g., Easwaran, 2013). In addition, he recommended using shorter mantras all through the day whenever possible.

Mantras in Other Spiritual Traditions

Continuously repeating such short mantras whenever everyday life allows for it is not only found in Hindu approaches (where they are often referred to as *namajapa* or *japayoga*) but also in meditative forms of the Kabbalah (Judaism; e.g., Kaplan, 1982), Sufism (Islam; e.g., Ernst, 2000; Schimmel, 2014), and in Christian forms of meditation (e.g., Pennington, 2006; Utterback, 2013), and the similarities are well recognized across religions (e.g., Molleur, 2009; Unno, 2002; Wong, 2010). For instance, in Sufism, the name of God (*Allah*) or the sentence "la ilaha illa Allah" ("there is no deity but God") is repeated, and in the Christian Orthodox church, meditators repeat the Jesus Prayer or Prayer of the Heart. It consists of the name of Jesus or some variations thereof such as "Lord Jesus Christ" or, a long form, "Lord Jesus Christ, Son of God, have mercy on me, a sinner" (Hovorun, 2019). Often practitioners use prayer beads, a practice that is also common in Hindu and Buddhist practices, where they are referred to as *mala* or *japamala* (Ramkrishna Das, 2003; Vandana, 1992). Because of its connection to spiritual and religious texts and prayer beads the rosary is also sometimes seen as a meditation technique (Bryan, 1991).

A further Christian meditation technique stemming from medieval Christian mysticism has been proposed by the American Trappist fathers Thomas Keating, William Meninger, and Basil Pennington: the *centering prayer*. Here is an instruction by Pennington (2006, p. 250):

1. Choose a sacred word as the symbol of your intention to consent to God's presence and action within.
2. Sitting comfortably and with eyes closed, settle briefly and silently introduce the sacred word as the symbol of your intention to consent to God's presence and action within us.
3. When you become aware of thoughts, return ever so gently to the sacred word.
4. At the end of the prayer period, remain in silence with eyes closed for a couple minutes.

Anthony de Mello, an Indian Jesuit and meditation teacher, even suggested partly secular forms of *namajapa*, such as "1, 2, 3" (de Mello, 1984). However, some of his suggestions apparently went too far for the Catholic Church.[1] Finally, a recent approach to mantra meditation includes mantras from traditional Hindu approaches but is also open to mantras from different spiritual traditions (Bringmann et al., 2020).

Contemplating Phrases or Short Passages of Text

Whereas mantra meditation mostly involves a nondeliberative awareness of a word or sentence, often as a means to connect to some deity or to some

---

[1] The Congregation for the Doctrine of the Faith (headed by the former Cardinal Ratzinger, who was later Pope Benedict) came to the conclusion that some of de Mello's positions were "incompatible with the Catholic faith and [could] cause grave harm" (see http://www.vatican.va/roman_curia/congregations/cfaith/documents/rc_con_cfaith_doc_19980624_de mello_en.html). However, the set of associated practices called *sadhana* is still used widely today in Christian-run meditation centers around the world.

form of cosmic consciousness, there are other approaches to meditating with phrases or short passages of text that also include investigation, deliberation and contemplation. Prominent among these are the approaches of Advaita Vedanta and Zen (see Chapter 9). Maybe the most famous of these phrases is the question "Who am I?" introduced by Shankara, the founder of Advaita Vedanta, and recommended by Ramana Maharishi, a famous Indian Yogi. Struggling with this question should help to realize one's true Self. There are four principal phrases in Advaita Vedanta, the so-called mahavakyas (great sayings) taken from different *Upanishads* (late Vedic Sanskrit texts). One of these is *Tat tvam asi* ("You are that"), meaning that the true essence or origin of everything (*tat* - which refers to *sat*, the "existent") is what every individual (*tvam*, "you") is (*asi*, "are"; Goodall, 1996, pp. 136–137).

Even more importance is given to the contemplation of phrases in Zen practice (mainly Rinzai Zen), in which practitioners are given so-called *koans* for the same purpose (Heine & Wright, 2000). A famous koan, the first case in a collection called *Mumonkan* (often translated as "Gateless Gate") is this: "Does a dog have Buddha-nature or not?" Chao-chou replied, "No!" (that answer given by Chao-chou, Japanese name "Joshu," is often rendered in Japanese as "mu" or Chinese, "wu," even in translations). On first sight, this answer contradicts the most fundamental tenet in Zen, which says that Buddha-nature (or the true Self) is innate in all sentient beings, but it is supposed to provide a jolt to the practitioner's ordinary way of thinking (Buswell, 2006, p. 78). Contemporary Zen teachers not only use the traditional koan collections but also person-specific ones or fundamental questions of life such as "What is the purpose of life?" (e.g., Kjolhede, 2012).

Cultivating Positive Emotions

Emotions can also be the target of meditation. Prominent among them are the so-called *brahmaviharas* (divine abodes), also called the four immeasurables: loving kindness, compassion, empathetic (or sympathetic) joy, and equanimity.[2] Their cultivation plays an important role in Theravada Buddhism, and the medieval Sri Lankan teacher Buddhaghosa dedicated the whole of Chapter 9 of his famous *Visuddhimagga* to this topic (e.g., Buddhaghosa, 2010). Also, Patanjali's *Yogasutras* mention the cultivation of

---

2 These are the original Pali and Sanskrit terms for reference: Four immeasurables: *appamanna* [Pali], *apramana* [Sankrit], loving kindness: *metta* [Pali], *maitri* [Sanskrit], compassion: *karuna* [Pali and Sanskrit], empathetic joy: *mudita* [Pali and Sanskrit], and equanimity: *upekkha* [Pali], *upeksha* [Sanskrit].

brahmaviharas as a meditation technique (Book I, Verse 33; see Chapple, 2008; Feuerstein, 2001). Another tradition they play an important role in is Tibetan Buddhism (Ricard, 2011; Wallace, 2006), and also some Zen teachers recommend this practice (e.g., Nhat Hanh, 1985; Samy, 2002).

The general idea is to not only experience these emotions once in a while but to learn to live within them or, in other words, to make them one's natural way to interact with the world.[3] Initially these positive emotions might be easily mixed up with their "near enemies": loving kindness with affection that includes attachment, compassion with pity, empathetic joy with enthusiasm, and equanimity with indifference. One might now think: "Okay, loving kindness, compassion, and empathetic joy can be regarded as emotions, but equanimity, isn't that just their absence?" In response, the meditation teacher and scholar Alan Wallace (2006, p. 67) argues that equanimity is in fact the basis for developing the other three (see also Ricard, 2011, p. 112). Equanimity works as an antidote to two tendencies we all carry with us, which are seen as causes for an unsatisfactory life: *craving* (wanting to have or keep something) and *aversion* (wanting to get rid of something).

Cultivating the Brahmaviharas

Let us have a look at how these four emotions can be developed. There are different ways, and frequently practitioners use their breath and their visualizations, which let them direct these different kinds of affection to themselves or to others. The first two steps, for each of the brahmaviharas, often consist of focusing on oneself, and then on somebody one likes. Classically (in the Theravada tradition), four phrases are used for the loving kindness cultivation that express the wish to be (1) free from danger, (2) mentally and (3) physically happy, and (4) be well (Salzberg, 1995, p. 37).

In other traditions, meditation teachers use many different forms. Matthieu Ricard, a teacher in the (later) Tibetan Buddhist (Vajrayana) tradition, whom we have already met, suggests for the second step (the one directed to somebody one likes) to imagine a young child who approaches you. You imagine the child looking at you joyously, confidently, and full of innocence. You imagine caressing the child and let yourself be entirely pervaded by the feelings of a love that wishes for nothing more than the child's well-being spread through you. This loving kindness should then be cultivated, sustained, and nourished (see Ricard, 2011, p. 109).

---

3 According to some authors, the brahmaviharas should not be seen as emotions themselves but as cognitive processes that give rise to emotional experiences, e.g., Gilbert et al. (2019). However, for practical purposes, this distinction should not make much of a difference.

After that, practitioners let their loving kindness flow to somebody "neutral" and then to somebody they do not like. Sometimes, in a fifth step, it is recommended to radiate one's loving kindness to the whole world. A traditional form of doing so is to send loving kindness (Pali: *metta*) to the 10 directions (east, southeast, south, southwest, west, northwest, north, northeast, above, and below). The German scholar and Theravada monk Anālayo (2019a) argues that this meditative radiation into the 10 directions is the original form of the practice, and that the current form of directing the intentions (e.g., "may you be happy") to selected individuals, proceeding from oneself to somebody one likes, to a neutral person, and finally to a difficult person was added later. More recent formulations for where to send one's loving kindness include, for instance, "all living beings, "all creatures", "all females", "all males"; and these can be combined with any directions such as "may all females to the east be happy" (Salzberg 1995, p. 101).

But what if even the first step does not work? What if you do not like yourself? Tsoknyi Rinpoche, a Tibetan lama, argues that in this case it does not make sense to practice loving kindness meditation: If you do not like yourself, you will not be able to like others (Tsoknyi, 2013; note: "Rinpoche" is a honorific title used in Tibetan Buddhism – meaning "precious one" – to show respect for distinguished teachers). But there are ways out of this dilemma: You can learn to like yourself by just watching yourself: your breath, your body, your emotions and thoughts (see above). The Vietnamese Zen master Thich Nhat Hanh (e.g., Nhat Hanh, 1985; Nhat Hanh & Anh-Huong, 2016; note: the name "Thich," meaning "of the Shakya clan" – that is, of the clan the Buddha belonged to – is given to Vietnamese monks and nuns as their "family name" to show affinity with the Buddha) recommends walking meditation (see below) especially to make contact with one's difficult emotions and to learn to accept them and oneself, and finally learn to like oneself.

How to practice compassion meditation? The practice here also usually starts with oneself with phrases such as "May I be free of my pain and sorrow" and "May I find peace." Some practitioners prefer talking to themselves in the second person, for example: "May you be free of your pain and sorrow." As with the loving kindness meditation, compassion is then directed toward somebody one likes, then to a neutral person, and then to somebody one does not like. And sometimes, again, compassion is spread over the whole world. The same procedure is used for empathetic joy meditation, starting again with the intention to experience joy about one's own qualities, successes, and happy events.

The practice for equanimity is somewhat different. Here, traditionally, one starts with a neutral person (because this is considered to be easiest) and holds a sense of this person in one's mind, internally reciting "All beings are the owners of their karma. Their happiness and unhappiness depend upon their actions, not upon my wishes for them." Other possible phrases can include the wish that we all accept things as they are or the thought that one wishes others happiness while acknowledging that we cannot make choices for them (for an overview see Salzberg, 1995, pp. 193-194).

After that, the usual sequence for equanimity meditation is benefactor, friend, enemy, oneself, and all beings (benefactors play a central role in the monastic context because monks and nuns could not survive without them). Again, there are many variations in the exact instructions. Some meditation teachers recommend that one view the world from the perspective of another person (e.g., Wallace, 2006, pp. 71-72).

Tonglen

The Tibetan Buddhist practice of *tonglen* (giving and taking) also uses loving kindness and compassion but relies on a different technique. In this technique, meditators exchange suffering for happiness by using their breath. Here is an excerpt of the instruction for one's own suffering suggested by Lama Palden Drolma ("vajra" means indestructible or diamond and refers to the indestructible diamond-like true nature. The term "vajrayana" refers to the "diamond vehicle," and is often regarded as synonymous with Tibetan Buddhism):

> Get in touch with any aspect of your suffering and open to loving-kindness and compassion for yourself. Work through any issues that arise, such as unworthiness. See your suffering as black smoke, and breathe it into your heart chakra. As soon as the smoke touches the vajra, let a lightning bolt of brilliant white light transform the suffering into awakened love, compassion, and healing energy. Breathe out this white light, awakened love, into yourself sitting in front of you.
>
> Repeat this process again and again, synchronizing the meditation with your breath. Imagine your ordinary self filling with white light, which is awakened love. This light alleviates suffering and brings about awakening. Imagine yourself becoming gradually healed, illuminated, and awakened. (Palden Drolma, 2019, p. 137. From the book *Love on Every Breath*. Copyright © 2019 by Lama Palden Drolma. Reprinted with permission by New World Library. Novato, CA. www.newworldlibrary.com)

The tonglen practice, like all related practices, is thought to break the spell of self-centeredness: It takes on the suffering of oneself and others and is supposed to transform and dissolve it through altruistic love and compassion, so that meditators will be naturally inclined to behave in a compassionate manner (Ricard, 2011, p. 119). One might even consider the Jesuit *contemplation to attain love* as a variation of the cultivation of positive emotions. Although in that practice, love is foremost directed to God, while also including cultivating love of our neighbors (Ganss, 1992, p. 183).

Establishing a Love Relationship With a Deity

In some approaches to meditation, to be found in several world religions, practitioners nurture romantic love for a personalized deity. This devotional love is free from expectations and anxiety but, despite its spiritual nature, is not seldom described as erotic and ecstatic, and is in most cases expected to culminate in a mystical union. The central aim of this love relationship is to fully give up one's false ego and thereby attain liberation.

Bhakti Marga

The most prominent spiritual path (marga) that seeks to establish such a love relationship is probably the bhakti marga (path of devotional love), already mentioned in one of the most important Hindu texts, the Bhagavad Gita (commonly dated to the 2nd century BCE).[4] The Bhakti movement includes many varieties in which the personal god (or goddess) varies with the devotee. It might best be expressed by looking at the poems by some famous devotees who often were also famous poets. Here is the beginning of a poem by Mirabai, a Rajput female poet and devotee of the god Krishna, who lived in the 16th century:

> My body is baked in the fever of feeling.
> I spend my whole time hoping, friend.
> Now that he's come, I'm burning with love –
> shot through, shameless to couple with him, friend.
> (Hawley, 2005, p. 107. Reprinted here with permission from Oxford University Press.)

And here are the beginnings of two other poems by the mystic and poet-saint Kabir, a devotee of the god Ram, who lived in the 15th and 16th century and drew from both Hindu and Muslim (Sufi) sources:

---

4 It is one of the three (or four) main margas or ways of yoga described there; the others being *jnana yoga* (path of knowledge) and *karma yoga* (path of work or virtuous action); and sometimes also *dhyana yoga* (path of meditation) is added to these three (Goswami, 2015).

> Is there a life without the love of Ram?
> Go and throw it in the fire!
> (Hawley, 2005, p. 292. Reprinted here with permission from Oxford University Press.)

and

> Say Ram, Ram; think of Ram;
> and you will find great fortune.
> (Hawley, 2005, p. 300. Reprinted here with permission from Oxford University Press.)

A more contemporary figure in the Bhakti movement is A. C. Bhaktivedanta Swami Prabhupada (born Abhay Charan De; died 1977) who founded the Hare Krishna movement.

Sufi Mystic

Probably the best-known mystic and poet in the Sufi world was Jalaluddin Rumi (13th century), and here is one of his poems:

> Love is here like the blood in my veins and skin
> He has annihilated me and filled me only with Him
> His fire has penetrated all the atoms of my body
> Of "me" only my name remains; the rest is Him.
> (Vaughan-Lee, 2006, p. 227)

Christian Contemplation

Also in Christianity, there are examples of contemplatives (mainly monks and nuns) who have practiced love meditation of this kind. One of the most well-known is Teresa of Avila (16th century). She also was a prolific writer who produced both poems and prose. Here is an excerpt from her autobiography, which describes a vision (according to her created by the Lord) she had as a result of her meditative practice (the "he" in the text refers to an angel):

> I saw in his hand a long spear of gold, and at the iron's point there seemed to be a little fire. He appeared to me to be thrusting it at times into my heart, and to pierce my very entrails; when he drew it out, he seemed to draw them out also, and to leave me all on fire with a great love of God. The pain was so great, that it made me moan; and yet so surpassing was the sweetness of this excessive pain, that I could not wish to be rid of it. The soul is satisfied now with nothing less

than God. The pain is not bodily, but spiritual; though the body has its share in it, even a large one. It is a caressing of love so sweet which now takes place between the soul and God, that I pray God of His goodness to make him experience it who may think that I am lying. (Teresa of Avila, 1904, p. XXIX.17)

Moving in a Specific Way

Meditation can also be practiced in movement. And there are quite a number of ways in which meditative movement can take place. The detailed expositions here will be restricted to walking meditation and the "active meditation" proposed by the famous Hindu meditation teacher Osho, with only brief summaries of some other approaches.

Walking Meditation

The most common way of meditative movement, to be found in many meditative approaches and in many varieties, is *walking meditation*. Some approaches are very strict about how to hold arms and hands, how to move and how fast, and what to concentrate on, whereas others are quite open. For illustration, we will have a look at two instructions, the first one from Jack Kornfield, a Theravada practitioner and teacher who spent many years in a Thai forest monastery (Kornfield, 2008, pp. 122-123):

> To practice, select a quiet place where you can walk comfortably back and forth, indoors or out, about ten to thirty paces in length. Begin by standing at one end of this "walking path," with your feet firmly planted on the ground. Let your hands rest easily, wherever they are comfortable. Take a few deep breaths and then open your senses to see and feel the whole surroundings. After a minute, bring your attention back to focus on the body. Center yourself and feel how your body is standing on the earth. Feel the pressure on the bottoms of your feet and the other natural sensations of standing. Let yourself be present and alert.
>
> Begin to walk a bit more slowly than usual. Let yourself walk with a sense of ease and dignity. Relax and let your walking be gracious and natural, as if you were a king or queen out for a royal stroll. Pay attention to your body. With each step feel the sensations of lifting your foot and leg off the earth. Then mindfully place your foot back down. Feel each step fully as you walk. When you reach the end of your path, pause for a moment. Center yourself, carefully turn around, and pause again so that you can be aware of the first step as you walk back. You can experiment with the speed, walking at whatever pace keeps you most present.

(Reprinted with permission from The Random House Group Ltd.)

The Vietnamese Zen master Thich Nhat Hanh has suggested many walking meditation exercises – here is one of them:

> We can practice walking meditation by counting steps or by using words. If the rhythm of our breathing is 3-3, for example, we can say, silently, "Lotus flower blooms. Lotus flower blooms" or "The green planet. The green planet," as we walk. If our breathing rhythm is 2-3, we might say, "Lotus flower. Lotus flower blooms," or "Walking on the green planet. Walking on the green planet," for 5-5. Or "Walking on the green planet. I'm walking on the green planet," for 5-6. (Nhat Hanh, 2011, in the section *Interbeing*. Reprinted with permission of Parallax Press.)

Nhat Hanh goes on explaining that one should not just say the words but really see the flowers blooming under one's feet, and really become one with the green planet. He also invites practitioners to use their own creativity and wisdom and enjoy the walking meditation.

"Active Meditation" (Osho)

Osho, also known as Bhagwan Shree Rajneesh,[5] argued that especially Westerners might not be able to sit in silent meditation because they are full of negative feelings, emotions, and thoughts that, however, can be discharged by *active meditation*. Osho (2004, pp. 67-68) suggests a 1-hour active meditation that consists of five stages. In the first stage (10 min), practitioners are instructed to breathe chaotically and as fast and hard as possible through their noses, concentrating on their exhalation, until they literally become the breathing. Hereby, they should use their natural body movements to help build up energy. In the second stage (also 10 min), they should let go of everything and "go totally mad." They should take care that their mind does not interfere with what is happening. The third stage (again 10 min) consists of jumping up and down with raised arms, shouting, as deeply as possible, the mantra "HOO!, HOO!, HOO!" When landing, they should do so on the flat of their feet so that it hammers "deep into the sex center," totally exhausting themselves. Stages four and five last for 15 min each. In the fourth stage, practitioners should suddenly freeze in the position they are in and just observe what is happening to them. And in the final stage, they are to celebrate and rejoice with music and dance, with a feeling of gratitude and the idea of carrying their happiness throughout the day.

---

5 He was born Chandra Mohan Jain and "Rajneesh" is a nickname he received in childhood. "Shree" is a honorific title, also used for veneration for deities, "Bhagwan" is an epithet for deity, and "Osho" is also a honorific title of preceptor or high priest, used in several forms of Buddhism.

Other Forms of Meditative Movement

Prostrations are another special form of meditative movements, common in all Hindu and Buddhist practices but especially in Tibetan Buddhism. They might be considered a form of meditation on its own (e.g., Tromge, 1995).

A quite spectacular form of meditation in movement is the *whirling of the dervishes* practiced by the Sufis in the Mevlevi order (going back to the already mentioned Jalaluddin Rumi). The Mevlevis whirl around their body axis counterclockwise. Their arms are extended, their right palms point upward (to receive Divine grace) and their left palms, toward which the dancers gaze, point downwards (to channel that grace to the world). With each full turn, the dancers inwardly chant "Allah" – that is, they also practice some kind of mantra (*dhikr*) meditation. This kind of meditation serves, as do the other Sufi techniques, to lose one's (false) ego and move closer to the Divine (for some more background information on the Mevlevi order and its founder, see Lewis, 2008; Schimmel, 2003).

Also, the Chinese (Daoist and Confucian) tradition knows some kinds of meditation in movement, under the names of qigong and tai chi (Liang & Wu, 1997, 2006).[6] Although the respective exercises can be practiced exclusively for health reasons or as martial arts, their higher sense is to use them to become one with the Dao, the ultimate *Truth* (see also Chapter 9). Both qigong and tai chi postulate a force or energy, *qi*, behind all things in the universe. The flow of qi is often obstructed but can be made to flow freely by practicing suitable body movements, often associated with breathing exercises and visualizations (Liang et al., 1997).

Opening Up

Many spiritual paths in which meditation plays a central role assume that the final goal (enlightenment, liberation, unio mystica, realization, ...) cannot be reached solely by one's own efforts but meditators need help from some higher or divine force (God, cosmic consciousness, Purusha, Brahman, Dao, ...). This idea of opening up to the Divine is probably most prominent in the *integral yoga*, developed by the Yogi and poet Sri Aurobindo and his consort, Mirra Alfassa, also known as *Mother* (e.g., Aurobindo, 1996;

---

6 There are many different approaches to *qigong* and *tai chi*, and "qigong" is sometimes seen as an umbrella term that encompasses tai chi (McCaffrey & Fowler, 2003). There are even recent attempts to subsume all forms of meditation under the heading of qigong (e.g., Chen et al., 2010).

Salmon, 2006). Integral yoga does not prescribe specific meditation techniques. To prepare for opening up, all techniques that might help – such as the ones described in this chapter – can be used as a preparatory step. The main goal of integral yoga is to connect human consciousness to the Divine, not only for oneself but for the whole of mankind. The aspiration of connecting to the Divine can be strengthened by traditional forms of meditation. However, it is even more important to keep open for the feeling of the Divine presence in everyday life – work plays a very important role here – and thus increase the longing for it (Huppes, 2001). Only if meditators open up in this way to the divine consciousness, which is assumed to be already there in every human being, will the barriers between normal and divine consciousness fall.

Conclusion

The present selection of meditation techniques is still very selective, and some forms are currently much more popular than others, although the popularity of techniques varies across regions and communities. But the main aim of this exposition was to make clear that meditation is far from a monolithic concept; and the term "meditation," which derives from the Latin verb *meditari* (to think, contemplate, devise, ponder) might actually be considered a misnomer, at least in the wide sense in which it is currently used because in many meditation techniques, practitioners should rather not think or ponder. In Chapter 8, we will see that different meditation methods might also have different effects, although research on this issue is still in its infancy. Eventually, if we understand more about the mechanisms and effects of different meditation techniques, we may also end up with a more precise terminology. But for the time being, it is probably best to stick with the term "meditation," which will be done in the rest of this book. There is, however, already a competitor term, which is sometimes even treated as a synonym to meditation: *mindfulness*. Mindfulness clearly is the market leader these days, and therefore it deserves a chapter of its own: Chapter 2.

Chapter 2
What Is Mindfulness?

The reader may be wondering why, so far, this work has not covered the subject of *mindfulness meditation*. In this chapter, however, it will become clear that it has already been introduced, but even many scholars in the field, at least those with a psychological background, are unsure about the meaning of the terms "meditation" and "mindfulness." For example, Bond says:

> I do not think that I really understand the distinctions and overlaps between meditation and mindfulness. I have examined the relevant literature to try to identify established and agreed-upon definitions for both terms, but I have not been able to do so for "meditation," although I have found agreed-upon definitions for "mindfulness." ... Psychology has largely adopted the term mindfulness, so it is not surprising that there are agreed-upon definitions for this word. Further complicating the definitional quandary is that "mindfulness meditation" is used freely in the literature, which could imply that this is different from mere "meditation" or "mindfulness." (Bond, 2016, p. 255)

Mindfulness has different meanings in contemporary psychology, and the discussion of what mindfulness is and is not is a prominent topic in scientific journals, both philosophical (e.g., the journal *Contemporary Buddhism*, especially Issue 1, 2011) and psychological (e.g., the journal *Mindfulness*, in many contributions in recent years). The main topic to be dealt with here is, of course, mindfulness meditation – that is, mindfulness as an intervention. But to understand the current confusion, it might also be informative to first have a look at mindfulness as a trait and as a state (see Davidson, 2010). Then, after describing current conceptions of mindfulness meditation, this chapter will discuss the traditional (Buddhist) concept of mindfulness in some detail (for more background information on Buddhist theory, see Chapters 3 and 9).

Mindfulness as a Trait

There are a huge number of research papers dealing with questionnaires that are supposed to measure *trait mindfulness*. But what is trait mindfulness? To find out, let us first have a look at what mindfulness questionnaires measure.

Questionnaires and Findings

To begin with, not all mindfulness questionnaires refer to the context of meditation. For instance, Ellen Langer's (1989) rationally derived theory of mindfulness proposes that a mindful person seeks out and produces novelty, is attentive to context, and is flexible in thought and behavior. This notion of mindfulness was captured in the *Mindfulness/Mindlessness Scale* (MMS) and originally postulated four factors: *novelty seeking, engagement, flexibility*, and *novelty producing*, although later examinations of the construct suggested that a one-factor mindfulness model was superior to other candidate models (Haigh et al., 2011).

However, most mindfulness scales – implicitly or explicitly – make reference to a Buddhist background. Bergomi et al. (2013) give an overview of the respective scales available at that time. From seven validated scales, they identified altogether nine different aspects of mindfulness (actually, they examined eight scales but one of them that measures mindfulness as a state will be discussed in the next paragraph). These aspects were (for sample items and references to the respective questionnaires see their Table 1 on p. 193): (1) observing, attending to experiences; (2) acting with awareness; (3) nonjudgment, acceptance of experiences; (4) self-acceptance; (5) willingness and readiness to expose oneself to experiences, nonavoidance; (6) nonreactivity to experience; (7) nonidentification with own experiences; (8) insightful understanding; and (9) labeling, describing.

The number of dimensions considered in the individual mindfulness questionnaires varies from one to five. For instance, the *Mindful Attention Awareness Scale* (MAAS; Brown & Ryan, 2003) postulates only one single presence factor relating to attention. A two-factor solution is proposed by the *Philadelphia Mindfulness Scale* (PHLMS; Cardaciotto et al., 2008): *awareness* (but not acting with awareness) and *acceptance*. And the *Five Facet Mindfulness Questionnaire* (FFMQ; Baer et al., 2006) suggests, as the name says, five different aspects of mindfulness: allowing one's thoughts and feelings to come and go without becoming involved or carried away with them (*nonreact*), noticing internal and external experiences (*observe*), attending to one's activities in the moment as opposed to operating on "autopilot" (*actaware*), labeling internal and external experiences with words (*describe*), and accepting and not evaluating one's thoughts and feelings (*nonjudge*).

The factor structures in several of the questionnaires reviewed by Bergomi et al. (2013) did not stand up to replication, and sometimes, new factors with new interpretations were identified in later studies. In a similar overview, including nine meditation-related trait mindfulness questionnaires, Sauer et al. (2013) conclude that most authors seem to agree that mindfulness consists of two distinct factors, *presence* and *acceptance*, but that all questionnaires are in need of improvement. They also identified the MAAS and the FFMQ as the two most often cited instruments, which still was the case some years later (van Dam et al., 2018). For the FFMQ, there already exists a meta-analysis with 148 studies (157 samples) that correlated the five facets with negative affective symptoms (Carpenter et al., 2019). The size of the estimated population correlations differed: *Nonjudge* and *act with awareness* correlated most highly with affective symptoms, followed by the *describe* and *nonreact* facets, but the *observe* facet was not correlated, which the authors interpret as a demonstration of the importance of assessing trait mindfulness in a multidimensional way.

There are also many findings showing that mindfulness training (see section Mindfulness as an Intervention, in this chapter) yields an increase in the scores on mindfulness questionnaires (Khoury et al., 2013; Quaglia et al., 2016; Visted et al., 2015). But similar increases in mindfulness scores are also found as a result of cognitive behavior therapy, and from participating in a tango class (Pinniger et al., 2012). Moreover, the effect sizes vary considerably across different questionnaires (Baer et al., 2019b). It seems that items in mindfulness questionnaires sometimes use the jargon of *mindfulness-based interventions* (MBIs) that may prime response bias (van Dam et al., 2012), and are understood differently by beginning and experienced meditators (Belzer et al., 2013; Grossman & van Dam, 2011). However, Antonova et al. (2015) found no difference between expert Buddhist meditators and a control group on two trait mindfulness questionnaires. To make things even worse, students who smoked and practiced frequent binge drinking exhibited higher mindfulness scores than participants in a mindfulness retreat (Leigh et al., 2005). All this indicates the possibility that more mindful participants (e.g., as result of an extended meditation practice) have lower scores on mindfulness questionnaires than less mindful ones. A potential explanation could be that more mindful respondents have higher introspective accuracy (and therefore recognize their limitations with respect to aspects of mindfulness more easily), for which there is some evidence (Fox et al., 2012). This would mean that the use of mindfulness questionnaires in measuring the effects of some interventions on trait mindfulness might yield contaminated effects. But the really important question here is what mindfulness is or should be defined as.

Theoretical Background

As already mentioned, all or most trait mindfulness questionnaires make a connection to Buddhist theory or at least to other authors who make that connection (for an overview, see van Dam et al., 2018, p. 39). So let us have a look at what this connection is. It seems that the first mindfulness questionnaire was the *Freiburg Mindfulness Inventory* (FMI; Buchheld et al., 2001). The authors, following Amadeo Solé-Leris's 1986 book (Solé-Leris, 1986), which is based on the *Visuddhimagga*, an authoritative 5th-century text on Theravada Buddhism, define mindfulness as "moment-to-moment attentional, unbiased observation of any phenomenon in order to perceive and to experience how it truly is, absent of emotional or intellectual distortion" (Buchheld et al., 2001, p. 6). This definition, which as we will see below (The Traditional Conception of Mindfulness, this chapter) indeed follows early Buddhist sources, does not sound like it describes a trait but rather an activity. However, the authors complement their definition by postulating that mindfulness is an outcome of systematic meditation practice, and that mindfulness has other effects in turn, such as enhanced insight, fresh alertness, curiosity, more accurate perception of inner states and motions, decreased emotional reactivity and negative affect, and a greater sense of compassion. For some of these effects, they cite a well-known Zen teacher: Shunryu Suzuki (Suzuki, 1975). Not surprisingly, the questionnaire also contains items that refer to activities (e.g., "I observe how my thoughts come and go"). One way to reconcile trait mindfulness with mindfulness as an action might be to assume that trait mindfulness is the result of mindfulness practice, which in turn is influenced by trait mindfulness: an interactive relationship, so to speak. However, such a relationship does not seem to be clearly specified in the original Buddhist sources.

Let us now have a look at the theoretical framing for the two most often cited trait mindfulness questionnaires. Brown and Ryan (2003), the authors of the MAAS, briefly refer to the definition of the Theravada monk and scholar Nyanaponika Thera (in this context, "Thera," meaning *elder*, is not a name but an honorific term in Pali, for monks who have spent at least 10 rainy seasons, or years, with the community of monks after their higher ordination): "Mindfulness is the clear and single-minded awareness of what actually happens to us and in us at the successive moments of perception." They also refer to the Vietnamese Zen master Thich Nhat Hanh (whom we have already met in Chapter 1) who says that mindfulness is "keeping one's consciousness alive to the present reality" (Brown & Ryan, 2003, p. 822). But then they go on to postulate a propensity or willingness to be aware and to sustain attention to what is occurring in the present, which they also term "mindfulness," as well as interpersonal and intrapersonal variations in that propensity (Brown & Ryan, 2003, p. 822). Once again, these additions do not seem to be part of traditional Buddhist teachings.

Regarding the other often-cited questionnaire, the FFMQ, Baer et al. (2006) contend that "mindfulness is usually defined to include bringing one's complete attention to the experiences occurring in the present moment, in a nonjudgmental or accepting way" (p. 27), but they do not explicitly refer to any Buddhist source. Note that this definition, in comparison with the former ones taken from the Buddhist literature, has already been "augmented" by the inclusion of acceptance. In addition, the authors cite some founders of MBI programs (e.g., Hayes et al., 1999; Kabat-Zinn, 1982; Linehan, 1993; Segal et al., 2002) and argue that "these interventions conceptualize mindfulness as a set of skills that can be learned and practiced in order to reduce psychological symptoms and increase health and well-being" (Baer et al., 2006. p. 27). The five facets of the FFMQ were the result of exploratory factor analyses of the responses to all of the items contained in the trait mindfulness questionnaires available at that time.

In sum, based on this selective but probably representative choice of sources, it seems that within a few years, the concept of trait mindfulness was created using some loose associations to the original Buddhist notion of mindfulness (see section The Traditional Conception of Mindfulness, this chapter), and then adding in some additional characteristics that resulted from the interplay with practices and results of MBIs. It seems fair to say that, as of yet, the concept of trait mindfulness does not have a firm theoretical basis: It is not really clear what it is, whether it can be summarized as one single construct or a collection of different ones (if so, which ones), and how it differs from other constructs, such as affectivity, curiosity, decentering, mind wandering, or meta-awareness (see also Chapter 10).

Mindfulness as a State

Mindfulness has also been conceptualized as a state. However, this conception of mindfulness has drawn much less attention. So far, there seem to be only three questionnaires for measuring state mindfulness.

Questionnaires and Results

The first state mindfulness questionnaire was built by Brown and Ryan (2003; Study 4) by rephrasing five items from their trait mindfulness scale so that they referred to a specific time (e.g., "I was doing something automatically, without being aware of what I was doing"; "I was rushing through something without being really attentive to it"). Participants had to make their ratings each time they received a pager signal. Brown and Ryan (2003) used both scales, trait and state, to predict some other variables (autonomy, as well as pleasant and unpleasant affect) and found common as well as differential effects. Overall, this questionnaire seems to have been rarely used.

The *Toronto Mindfulness Scale* (TMS; Lau et al., 2006) was constructed by asking participants to reflect on an immediately preceding meditation session and to indicate the degree to which 42 mindfulness items chosen per consensus by the authors described their experience. The final questionnaire consists of 15 items and comprises two factors, termed *curiosity* (e.g., "I was curious to see what my mind was up to from moment to moment") and *decentering* (e.g., "I was more invested in just watching my experiences as they arose, than in figuring out what they could mean").

More recently, Tanay and Bernstein (2013) developed the *State Mindfulness Scale* (SMS). Starting with 25 items, they arrived at a questionnaire with two (correlated) factors: *state mindfulness of mind* (15 items, e.g., "I noticed pleasant and unpleasant emotions") and *state mindfulness of body* (6 items, e.g., "I noticed some pleasant and unpleasant physical sensations").

Research comparing results in trait mindfulness questionnaires and measures of state mindfulness found inconsistent (Tanay & Bernstein, 2013) or little to no relationships between the two constructs (Bravo et al., 2018; Thompson & Waltz, 2007). So, one might argue that a separation between these two uses of the term is justified. In general, MBIs seem to have an effect on state mindfulness, but the measurement of state mindfulness might be plagued with similar difficulties to those of trait mindfulness, especially given an as-yet-nonexistent sound theoretical grounding.

Theoretical Background

Brown and Ryan (2003) do not discuss any specific theoretical foundations for state mindfulness apart from what they mention with respect to trait mindfulness. Lau et al. (2006) cite Kabat-Zinn (1990) as well as some researchers who are themselves on the list of authors for that work. In summarizing these sources, they write that "mindfulness has been described as a non-elaborative, non-judgmental, present-centered awareness in which each thought, feeling, or sensation that arises in the field is acknowledged and accepted as it is" (Lau et al., 2006, p. 1447). Then they go on to say (referring to Bishop et al., 2004) that alternatively, mindfulness can be viewed as a state-like quality that has two components: "(a) the intentional self-regulation of attention to facilitate greater awareness of bodily sensation, thought, and emotions, and (b) a specific quality of attention characterized by endeavoring to connect with each object in one's awareness (e.g., each bodily sensation, thought, or emotion) with curiosity, acceptance, and openness to experiences" (Lau et al., 2006, p. 1447). We will see in section The Traditional Conception of Mindfulness that the second component especially is not fully consistent with the original Buddhist concept. As an aside, astonishingly, Bishop et al. (2004, p. 234) come to the conclusion that mindfulness is "a process of regulating attention" and "a process of gaining *insight* into the nature of one's mind." It is not clear to me how the connection from process to trait and state has been made.

Tanay and Bernstein (2013) refer to what is arguably the most central text on mindfulness (*sati*) the *Satipatthana Sutta,* as well as the later Abhidhamma literature (Bodhi, 2013). In doing so, however, they seem to equate "mental factor" (*cetasika* in Pali; mindfulness, *sati*, is such a mental factor) with "mental ability" (i.e., a trait), which does not seem to be justified even in the Abhidhamma. They also refer to the two-component definition of mindfulness already referred to by Lau et al. (2006).

In sum, although the notion of state mindfulness might be considered to be closer to the original concept of mindfulness than that of trait, the definitions of state mindfulness are also unclear.

A recent attempt to reconcile different notions of mindfulness including traditional ones suggests the decomposition of mindfulness into different dimensions (Lutz et al., 2015). The resulting seven-dimensional framework should then be used as a heuristic for generating and communicating research hypotheses on the cognitive and neural mechanisms presumably underlying mindfulness practices. The three main dimensions along which mental states can be located are *object orientation* (degree to which one is aware of some particular thing), *dereification* (degree to which mental processes are inaccurate depictions of reality), and *meta-awareness* (degree to which current contents of consciousness are explicitly noted). These three primary dimensions are complemented by four more secondary dimensions: *aperture* (broadness of the scope of attention), *clarity* (degree of vividness with which an experience occurs), *stability* (degree to which experience is stable over time), and *effort* (phenomenal impression of how easy one's current mental state is to sustain). For instance, the state of mind wandering is characterized by low to medium object orientation, low dereification (contents of experience are interpreted as accurate depictions of reality), low meta-awareness (absorptive state), narrow aperture, medium clarity, low stability, and low effort (Lutz et al., 2015, Figure 1). This phenomenological matrix of mindfulness-related practices allows for the locating of, for instance, addictive craving, rumination, and several meditation techniques. It might indeed be useful for deriving research hypotheses, but because of its generality, it does not seem to help much in defining mindfulness as a state.

Mindfulness as an Intervention

Mindfulness as an intervention – that is, mindfulness meditation – has been an enormous success story. The single most influential person with respect to introducing mindfulness interventions in the West is certainly Jon Kabat-Zinn who in 1979 created the *Mindfulness-Based Stress Reduction* (MBSR) program at the University of Massachusetts (Kabat-Zinn, 2003). This program proved to be hugely successful (see Husgafvel, 2016), and glancing through the literature, one gains the impression that many scholars in the field equated (and some still do) mindfulness meditation with MBSR. MBSR was originally applied in clinical settings and inspired the development of other treatment regimens that were partly based on it, and are nowadays known as MBIs. But meanwhile, the term "mindfulness meditation" seems to encompass almost every kind of meditation, and MBSR is also used in nonclinical populations although its use in clinics still seems to expand continuously.

The Varieties of Mindfulness Meditation

Mindfulness-Based Stress Reduction

The initial version of the MBSR program had another name, the *Stress Reduction and Relaxation Program* (SR&RP), and consisted of three "mindfulness meditation practices": sweeping (now known as body scan), *mindfulness of breath and other perceptions*, and *hatha yoga postures* (Kabat-Zinn, 1982). Since then, the original program has been augmented and modified in many respects, as can be witnessed on numerous Web pages and books (e.g., Kabat-Zinn, 2009; Stahl & Goldstein, 2019). The standard program taught by thousands of certified trainers worldwide consists of an 8-week workshop with weekly 2.5- to 3.5-hr group meetings and a 1-day retreat (Santorelli et al., 2017). MBSR comprises a collection of practices with cognitive, emotional, and bodily components, stemming from different secular and spiritual backgrounds. In each class, participants are taught informal and formal practices. The informal practices include group discussions and exercises, mindful eating (with a special focus on raisins), mindful speaking and listening, and mindfulness of daily activities. The formal practices consist of focusing on one's breath (several ways), and the practices of open awareness, body scan, yoga postures, walking meditation, and loving kindness meditation.

Apart from the program's superior structure and organization, as well as its relatively short duration and the interesting mix of techniques, the main reason it has flourished so well is probably that it works (see Chapters 6 and 7). Another reason for its success might be that it does not openly refer to any religious or spiritual basis: MBSR is a fully secular meditation program (but see Chapter 8).

Mindfulness-Based Interventions

The MBSR curriculum has become a framework for other, more specific intervention regimens such as *mindfulness-based relationship enhancement* (MBRE; Carson et al., 2004), the *mindfulness-based eating awareness training* (MB-EAT; Kristeller et al., 2006), or the *mindfulness-based art therapy* (MBAT; Monti et al., 2006). But also broader approaches are usually included in the MBI family. Here we will take a brief look at the three presumably most influential of those.

Mindfulness-based cognitive therapy (MBCT; Segal et al., 2013) is based on the MBSR's 8-week program but has been specifically adapted to people with repeated depressive episodes. It combines mindfulness practice with cognitive therapy. However, whereas cognitive therapy includes an effort to evaluate and change thoughts and feelings, MBCT works toward accepting them. Two other widely used MBIs, *dialectical behavior therapy* (DBT; Linehan, 1993; see also Koerner, 2012) and *acceptance and commitment therapy* (ACT; Hayes et al., 2012), are sometimes referred to as *mindfulness-informed interventions* because they place less emphasis on formal meditation practices (Shapero et al., 2018). DBT originally concentrated on the treatment of borderline personality disorder but is now being used for numerous other conditions. The program teaches mindfulness skills, typically in group settings, to develop one's "wise mind" by focusing on three *what* skills (observing, describing, and participating) and three *how* skills (being nonjudgmental, one-mindful, and effective), thereby connecting to the two-component model of mindfulness (Bishop et al., 2004).

ACT is usually provided in an individual therapy setting. It draws strongly on a cognitive behavioral framework, emphasizing commitment and behavior change strategies, but also heavily relies on acceptance and mindfulness strategies. To help clients accept their current circumstances, ACT uses real-life examples and metaphors, which is expected to increase contact with the present moment, thereby decreasing rumination on past deeds and worry about the future.

Other Variants of Mindfulness Meditation

Whereas already MBSR and the MBIs can arguably be classified into distinct categories, the use of the term "mindfulness meditation" has spread far beyond these approaches. It has been used for different forms of Vipassana and Zen meditation (Bowen et al., 2006; Ivanovski & Malhi, 2007), for Shamatha (concentrative) meditation (Zeidan et al., 2010), Tibetan Buddhist practices (Ortner et al., 2007), or simply attending to the breath (Zeidan et al., 2011). Even mantra meditation (transcendental meditation [TM]) is argued to increase mindfulness (Tanner et al., 2009). Such an indiscriminate use of the term may invoke the impression that "mindfulness meditation" (or mindfulness for short) is just a synonym for "meditation." In Chapter 3, we will see that this is not so.

Theoretical Background

Jon Kabat-Zinn's MBSR is a highly eclectic mix of techniques that stem from different spiritual traditions, both Buddhist (Theravada and Mahayana) and Hindu (Yoga and Vedanta). However, the collection of techniques is presented without explicit reference to their origins – in contrast to an earlier, widely ignored proposal by Deatherage (1975). This is, of course, not necessarily a bad thing. On the contrary, the omission of all of the philosophical, religious, and cultural undertones might draw people who otherwise would not at all consider trying out meditation. Kabat-Zinn acknowledges the diversity of MBSR's theoretical and spiritual background but argues that "mindfulness" may be used as an umbrella term (Kabat-Zinn, 2011, p. 290). This might, pragmatically, have been a good decision, as judged from the success of the program, but from a theoretical standpoint, the indiscriminative use of the term "mindfulness" can severely restrict the advancement of our understanding of how meditation works (see Chapters 10 and 11). We will indeed see later (Chapter 8) that different components of MBSR may differ considerably in their effects.

The theoretical background of the MBIs seems to consist mainly of the consensus definitions that also have been used in defining mindfulness as a trait and a state. And sometimes these definitions seem quite circular because, somewhat simplified, the argument runs like this: What is mindfulness? The result of mindfulness meditation. And what is mindfulness meditation? A procedure that increases mindfulness. This is different for other traditional practices, which are also sometimes summarized under the term "mindfulness meditation," such as Vipassana, Zen, and Tibetan Buddhist practices, as well as concentrative approaches to meditation (see Chapters 3 and 9).

The Traditional Conception of Mindfulness

Note that even among Buddhist scholars, there is no full agreement about the original meaning of mindfulness – that is, about what the Buddha meant when using this term (*sati*) in his discourses (e.g., Amaro, 2015; Anālayo,

2019b; Husgafvel, 2016; Levman, 2018; Sharf, 2014; Shonin et al., 2015; this is not, of course, the only issue Buddhist scholars disagree about – in fact, they disagree about many things – see, e.g., Frauwallner, 2010; Gombrich, 2013 – but it seems that most of these disagreements do not have strong implications for meditation practice). However, there seems to be a consensus among Buddhist scholars that the most authoritative source of the meaning of mindfulness in early Buddhism is the *Satipatthana Sutta*, the Buddha's discourse on the four satipatthanas or foundations or establishments of mindfulness (*Majjhima Nikaya* 10).[7]

Let us have a look at the opening proclamation of the *Satipatthana Sutta*, which the Buddha addressed to his followers. It begins by proclaiming that the practice of the four foundations of mindfulness leads all the way to *nibbana* (Sanskrit: *nirvana*) – that is, enlightenment, awakening, or liberation – while, on the way, sorrows, pain, and displeasure are also overcome.[8] And what is the practice? It consists of continuously contemplating, being diligent, clearly knowing (or comprehending), being mindful, and being free from desires and discontent. What changes in the course of the practice are the specific satipatthanas, the body, the feelings (positive, negative, neutral), the mind, and the *dhammas* (e.g., Anālayo, 2003, p. 3). *Dhamma* (Pali) or *dharma* (Sanskrit) is a key concept in Indian religions that has multiple meanings and there is no single-word translation for it. In Buddhism, it can mean "cosmic law," (dependently arising), "phenomena," and "mental constructs cognized by the mind." Here, the last is meant by the term (to get an impression of the great variety of meanings, see, for instance: https://suttacentral.net/define/dhamma). Thus, mindfulness practice is not just mindful awareness but should be accompanied by clearly knowing or comprehending, and it obviously works better if practitioners are diligent and free from distracting ideas and emotions (desires and discontent). This is emphasized by Anālayo (2018a, p. 1050) who argues that in the context of satipatthana meditation, mindfulness might be compared to clear water used

---

7 The *Satipatthana Sutta* is the 10th sutta in the *Majjhima Nikaya*, the "Collection of Middle-Length Discourses," which is one of five *nikayas* [collections] of *suttas* (lit. string, thread, but used to refer to aphorisms or discourses of the Buddha), included in the so-called *Sutta Pitaka* [Discourse Basket]. There are two other *pitakas*, the *Vinaya Pitaka* [Discipline Basket] that mainly contains rules for monastic life, and the later *Abhidhamma Pitaka* [Higher Dhamma Basket] that contains scholastic explanations of Buddhist doctrines (see also Chapter 9). The contents of the *Satipatthana Sutta* can also be found in numerous other (mostly later) suttas (see Anālayo, 2003).

8 The term *dukkha* is often translated as suffering, but a more adequate rendering seems to be something like unsatisfactoriness or displeasure (e.g., Rahula, 1959, Chapter 2). I like especially the definition by Ford (2006, p. 7): "not having what we want, not wanting what we have."

for making a soup. But water alone does not give the soup flavor, which comes from spices and other ingredients, the most important being clearly knowing (*sampajanna*).

To understand the role of this special ingredient, another simile might be helpful:

> The input provided by *sampajañña*, clearly knowing, could be illustrated with the example of yeast, due to which the dough of mindfulness practice can grow into the bread of liberating insight. Without yeast, the dough will result only in flatbread. Yeast on its own, however, will not be nourishing at all. It is when the cultivation of mindfulness comes in combination with the right amount of the yeast of clearly knowing that the tasty and nourishing bread of insight will result. (Anālayo, 2018b, p. 8. Reprinted with permission of Windhorse Publications.)

Regarding the objects of this continuous process of contemplation or awareness: body, feelings, mind, and dhammas, these four satipatthanas are actually categories and may be seen as a map of possible human experiences (Weber, 2017). For instance, body (*kaya*) refers to breathing, postures (walking, standing, sitting, lying), activities, anatomical parts, elements (earth, water, fire, and air), and a corpse in decay. The *Satipatthana Sutta* contains an instruction for each (see Anālayo, 2003, for detailed descriptions).

The second satipatthana, feeling, is not really feeling in the sense we usually understand it but rather a feeling tone or a hedonic tone (*vedana*). It can take three states: pleasant, unpleasant, or neutral. Also, the predominant translation of the third category, mind (*citta*) might be considered a slight misnomer because, according to the sutta, apart from contraction, distraction, narrowness, concentration, and liberation, this category also includes lust and anger. So, at least in part, it is about what we would nowadays term feelings and emotions. And finally, the dhamma category contains the (dependently arising) objects of the mind. These are concepts that are part of Buddhist theory, such as the five *hindrances*, the five *aggregates* (see Chapter 9), and the six *sense spheres*, which, in addition to the five senses, also include the mind. In Buddhist theory, the mind perceives thoughts, and thus the fourth satipatthana prominently includes perceptions and cognitions.

It will be helpful now to briefly recapitulate what the traditional conception of mindfulness is. First, mindfulness is a process or an activity (and not a trait or a state). Second, it does not act alone but should always be accompanied by clear comprehension, which means that it is a conscious process (not an absorptive one). And third, the practice of mindfulness should be directed to basically all aspects of human experiences. The *Satipatthana Sutta* does not fully specify the exact procedures for mindfulness meditation. However, there are two well specified contemporary versions of traditional mindfulness meditation, those of Bhikkhu Anālayo and Akincano Marc Weber – the first with a more monastic and the second with a more therapeutic flavor to it.

Bhikkhu Anālayo's Approach to Mindfulness Meditation

Bhikkhu Anālayo (*Bhikkhu*, in Pali, is a common designation for a Theravada monk and means "beggar" or "one who lives by alms" or, in other words, a monk) is a Theravada monk and Buddhist scholar who bases his profound understanding of the satipatthanas especially on the early discourses (suttas) and not so much on later commentaries. (This has, for instance, an impact on the understanding of the topic of memory as one of the meanings of sati; see, e.g., Anālayo, 2019b; Rapgay, 2019. However, this issue need not concern us here because it does not affect the practice of mindfulness meditation.) After having written two widely well-received books on the theoretical basis of mindfulness meditation (Anālayo, 2003, 2013), he summarized his insights and experiences about the actual practice in another book (Anālayo, 2018b), which is the basis for this present paragraph (Anālayo's meditation instructions are freely available from https://www.windhorsepublications.com/satipatthana-meditation-audio/).

The basic pattern of Anālayo's mindfulness practice is "being in the present, knowing what is happening, and proceeding accordingly" (Anālayo, 2018b). As a result of his scholarly studies, he suggests using seven objects of mindfulness meditation, selected from the four satipatthanas: anatomy of the body, elements of the body, death, feelings, mental states, hindrances, and awakening factors (see Table 2.1).

Obviously, the body is represented disproportionately here, with three of the seven topics – anatomy and elements connected with the body, and death (cessation of breathing). The reason for this is that mindfulness of the body is the easiest way of practicing mindfulness and can be used as an anchor or a grounding to return to. The Buddha used several similes (allegories) to illustrate this point, one being the simile of the six animals as given in the *Chappana Sutta*, which is found in the *Samyutta Nikaya* [Connected Discourses] of the *Sutta Pitaka*. For a translation by Thanissaro Bhikkhu, see https://www.accesstoinsight.org/tipitaka/sn/sn35/sn35.206.than.html. Six different animals (snake, crocodile, bird, dog, hyena, and monkey) are bound together and pull each other in different directions. The strongest one pulls the others in the direction it prefers until it gets tired, and another animal takes over. These animals stand for the six senses (seeing, hearing, smelling, tasting, touching, and thinking). That thinking is considered a perceptive process is probably the most interesting difference between the early

Table 2.1. Mindfulness meditation as taught by Bhikkhu Anālayo (based on the descriptions of the mindfulness practice in Anālayo, 2018b)

Mindfulness meditation (Bhikkhu Anālayo)	
Being in the present, knowing what is happening, and proceeding accordingly	
Contemplation of body	1. *Anatomy:* Body scans of skin, flesh, and bones 2. *Elements:* Body scans concentrating on solidity (earth), humidity (water), heat (fire) and movement/breath (wind) 3. *Death:* Connecting the breath with life (every inbreath could be the last)
Contemplation of feelings	4. *Hedonic tones:* Body scans for pleasant, unpleasant, and neutral feelings (hedonic tones), later extended to nonbodily aspects
Contemplation of mental states	5. *Qualities of the mind:* "How is the mind?" with or without mindfulness, lust, aversion, delusion, etc.?
Contemplation of dhammas	6. *Hindrances:* What are the conditions that lead to the arising and overcoming of sensual desire, anger, sloth and torpor, restlessness and worry, and doubt? 7. *Awakening factors:* Recognizing and cultivating mindfulness, investigation, energy, joy, tranquility, concentration, and equipoise.

Buddhist theory of cognition and contemporary psychology; for more on this, see Chapters 9 and 11. If, however, mindfulness of the body is established, this is like firmly planting a strong post in the ground, and so the animals eventually give up running around and stay beside the post. For his version of mindfulness meditation, Anālayo uses the image of a wheel with seven spokes and mindfulness of the body as the hub of the wheel.

The contemplation begins with body scans of skin, flesh, and bones (anatomy), followed by body scans focused on the four elements. The element of earth refers to the solidity/hardness/resistance of the body parts, the element of water to their liquidity/wetness/cohesion, the element of fire to their temperature/warmth, and the element of wind to motion/vibration/oscillation, and especially the breath. The breath is then connected to life and death; but the skeleton or other stages of decay are also used in the third contemplation. Giving differential attention to the inhalations (connected to the recollection of one's mortality) and exhalation (connected with an attitude of relaxing and letting go) ensures maintaining the practice in a balanced manner. These three contemplations on the body are meant to cultivate a lessening of attachment to the body.

Contemplation of feelings (hedonic tones of pleasant, unpleasant, and neutral) is also first practiced with the help of body scans (one for each of the three tones) and later extended to nonphysical perceptions. It is emphasized that the body is a constant source of unpleasant feelings, especially caused by pain, but also that being in the here and now produces an initially very subtle pleasant feeling that should be cultivated. The continued contemplation of feelings makes the changing nature of feelings more and more prominent, which, in turn, makes them a messenger of impermanence.

Contemplation of the mental states consists of inspecting the qualities of the mind: Is it with or without mindfulness, with or without lust, aversion, or delusion? It also helps to use labels, such as "anger." Eventually it should become clear that the mind constantly changes and also that this is a messenger of impermanence just as the changing nature of feeling tones is.

Whereas the contemplation of the mental states predominantly involves emotional states, the contemplation of dhammas refers to (dependently arising) cognitive phenomena. In early Buddhism, there are several lists of dhammas, and Anālayo uses two of the subgroups of dhammas that are of special importance in the Buddhist way of salvation: the *five hindrances* and the *seven awakening factors*. The hindrances are thought to obstruct the path to liberation, whereas the presence of the awakening factors leads forward on that path. Thus, the contemplation of dhammas is about the type of mind in which liberation can (or cannot) take place. The sixth contemplation examines the conditions that give rise to sensual desire, anger, sloth and torpor, restlessness, and worry, as well as doubt, and also how these five hindrances on the way to salvation can be overcome. And the seventh contemplation initially focuses on the first of the seven awakening factors – that is, on mindfulness, inculcating the qualities of keen interest, and open receptivity, as well as balanced and unbiased observation. When mindfulness is not present, the other six factors lack their foundation. The next three awakening factors – investigation, energy, and joy – are meant to energize the practice, and the remaining three – tranquility, concentration, and equipoise – bring calmness to the practice. The contemplation should arouse and balance the seven awakening factors.

In each of these seven steps, all preceding ones are briefly repeated, and the practitioners are admonished to always come back to the grounding of the body. After each of the specific contemplations, practitioners are encouraged to open all six *sense doors* (eyes, ears, nose, tongue, body, and mind) to be aware of whatever is there. To learn the seven contemplations, Anālayo recommends a period of 7 weeks, one contemplation per week, with the aim of all four satipatthanas eventually becoming an integral part of one's life.

Akincano Marc Weber's Approach to Mindfulness Meditation

Akincano Marc Weber is a Buddhist teacher and psychotherapist who was a Theravada monk in forest monasteries in Thailand and Europe for 20 years. He uses a TV channels simile in his teachings (see below) and translates the satipatthanas into contemporary language (e.g., Weber, 2015a, 2015b, 2017). Table 2.2 summarizes the present author's understanding of his talks. Mindfulness meditation means knowingly relating to one's own experiences that take place in the present moment. He argues that the now (the present moment) is not a point but a somewhat extended period of time and, for illustration, uses the simile of a valley that separates two huge mountain ridges: The present moment is not like the lowest point in the valley but rather the bridge that spans over that lowest part.

According to Weber, all four channels run all through our waking time, and most people are most of the time tuned in to channel IV, the *dhamma channel*, which broadcasts the contents of the mind. There, they are usually swept away by their thoughts and associations without really being aware of what is happening in that channel. He recommends, if possible, to let the thoughts pass by ("play the blue mountain and let the clouds go past") or, if that is not possible, labeling the thoughts and/or switching to channel I. Channel I is the easiest to watch, and focusing awareness on the body is the safest way to make sure that we attend to the present moment. Even if there

Table 2.2. Mindfulness meditation as taught by Akincano Marc Weber (based on his various talks)

Mindfulness meditation (Akincano Marc Weber)	
Relating to one's experiences by knowingly being aware of the present moment: one channel at a time	
Channel I Somatic experience	"Flavors of the body" (heat, cold, soft, warm, itching, pulsing, vibrating, solidity, expansiveness, pain, etc.)
Channel II Hedonic experience	Pleasant, unpleasant, neutral
Channel III Affective experience	"Inner weather" (emotions, impulses of mind, anything that bears some flavor of – not necessarily conscious – intentionality or volition)
Channel IV Cognitive experience	Contents of mind (concepts, images, stuff out of which we make the stories, stuff associatively knitted together)

are problems such as when I actually want to watch the breath and a pain in my knee arises, I can go to the knee, meet it, make it my meditation object: a throbbing pain, hammering pain, does it move inwards or outwards? Investigating the changes often make the pain bearable. And learning to meet pain – that is, the investigation of pain – can bring a lot of stillness, confidence, and personal growth. Also, channels II and III are much more difficult to watch than channel I. For them, Weber makes similar recommendations. If for instance, I experience fear in channel III, he advises that I go to channel I and explore in which part of the body that fear manifests itself and watch that manifestation. So, mindfulness meditation is basically watching and switching your TV channels with full awareness. (One could argue that the picture here is somewhat simplified because the channels obviously affect each other, which does not seem to be really well accounted for in this approach.)

Recapitulation

Back to the main question of this chapter: What is mindfulness? Obviously, there are different answers. Let us start by comparing the oldest answer to the more recent ones. Can mindfulness as conceived in the *Satipatthana Sutta* be regarded as a trait? One could argue that the mindfulness practices described there might eventually lead to measurable changes on a dimension (not specified there) that might be called a trait. We will see in Chapter 9 that early Buddhist theory does not provide for traits of any sort because according to it, all things arise and pass away (the notion of a trait is usually connected to some kind of permanence). But even if Buddhist theory was consistent with the notion of traits, it should have become clear that the usual definition of mindfulness traits in Western (meditation) research is not consistent with what we can read in the *Satipatthana Sutta*. For instance, the *Satipatthana Sutta* does not mention acceptance, which is regarded as a central ingredient in some Western conceptions of mindfulness.

How about mindfulness as a state? One could contend that states (in contrast to traits) are in principle consistent with Buddhist theory, depicting temporary results of mindfulness meditation practice, but also here, the contents used in state questionnaires are at best only partly consistent with the contents mentioned in the *Satipatthana Sutta*. One might, however, think of what states to expect after extended mindfulness practice according to the *Satipatthana Sutta* and devise a questionnaire accordingly. At the moment, many of the constituents of Western definitions of mindfulness as a trait or a state are *not* well connected to Buddhist theory.

And finally: Are contemporary practices to mindfulness meditation (MBSR and MBIs) consistent with the traditional notion of mindfulness? Some parts of MBSR, such as the body scan or mindful eating, certainly are, whereas others, such as yoga postures or group discussions, certainly are not. For others, such as focusing on one's breath and practicing loving kindness meditation, it depends: If they are done with the aim of deepening concentration (moving toward absorption), they are not, but if these techniques are used to cultivate awareness of the processes involved, they are. We will see in Chapter 9 that Buddhist theory advocates two families of meditation techniques: one (often termed *samatha* meditation) that should deepen concentration and lead to absorptive states, and another (often called *vipassana* meditation) that should lead to insight. Although the former is often seen as a preparatory help for the latter, only the latter can be regarded as mindfulness meditation in a strict sense. In MBIs, the proportion of techniques that could be seen as mindfulness techniques in the *Satipatthana Sutta* sense is even lower: "Current employment of mindfulness in health care and education, in spite of some degree of affinity, does not really qualify as an implementation of the four establishments of mindfulness" (Anālayo, 2019c, p. 611).

We have seen that there is a sizeable discrepancy among the uses of the term "mindfulness" even within contemporary meditation research, and that none of the recent uses of the term fully coincides with its traditional meaning. A good illustration for the confusion, or rather the incoherent mixture, can be found in a recent article that summarizes the effects of mindfulness on event-related potentials (Verdonk et al., 2020). In this summary paper, secular mindfulness practices, Vipassana, Zen, and Buddhist meditation (!) are all treated alike. Moreover, the authors treat differences in trait mindfulness in the same way as differences between meditators and non-meditators.

The concept of mindfulness as it now stands is a loose story or, maybe, a set of several somewhat less loose stories. But how much does that matter in terms of the usefulness of the respective instruments and procedures? Maybe not so much. One has to keep in mind that all psychological traits, prominently among them various accounts of intelligence or the Big Five personality traits, are in the end just conventions, which have proven to be useful. The main difference between such established traits and mindfulness as a trait is that the former are theoretically well founded whereas mindfulness is not (yet). (A close look at other commonly used constructs also sometimes reveals that their theoretical foundations are still shaky; e.g., Hommel et al., 2019.)

One solution to the present problematic situation might be to disentangle the different meanings of the term and work on developing a theoretical basis for differently termed aspects currently all subsumed under the heading of mindfulness (e.g., Hadash & Bernstein, 2019). A possible starting point could be the already existing scales (see section Mindfulness as a Trait), which can be summarized in at least nine categories (Bergomi et al., 2013). The task still to be done would be to connect these potential traits to a good theory of meditation, which, unfortunately, as I will argue in Chapter 10, is also still missing. However, in the long run, it might be more promising – as Lutz et al. (2015) suggest – to abandon the concept of mindfulness as a trait altogether and concentrate instead on the notion of mindfulness as a state, especially if short-term effects should be examined (e.g., Magee & Biesanz, 2019). Anyway, one would probably not lose much in conceiving traits as a stable succession of states.

As to the use of the term "mindfulness meditation" for a variety of meditation techniques or collections of such techniques (as in Verdonk et al., 2020), I think a continued indiscriminate usage of the term has the potential to impede an advancement of our understanding of how and why meditation works (see also Chapter 10). We will see in Chapter 8 that different techniques referred to by that label indeed may have vastly different effects.

In sum: It appears that the problem of mindfulness (in all three varieties: trait, state, and activity or intervention) is not so much the result of the discrepancy between contemporary and traditional conceptions but the inconsistency in how it is defined, measured, and implemented as a meditation practice. One way to proceed for the latter could be to examine in more detail what the basic meditation techniques are, and especially, in which combinations they are usually practiced. These questions will be addressed in more detail in the next two chapters – separately for traditional (Chapter 3) and Western (Chapter 4) approaches to meditation.

Chapter 3
Traditional Classifications of Meditation Techniques

In Chapter 1, we looked at meditation practices in isolation to get an impression of the huge diversity of these practices (we will come back to that issue in Chapter 11). Chapter 2 made clear that contemporary "mindfulness meditation" usually comprises whole packages of meditation techniques (to be described in more detail in Chapter 4). The same holds for traditional approaches to meditation. If meditators practice, say, kundalini yoga, Vipassana, Zen, or some other approach in the traditional way, the important issue is whether the whole package of meditation techniques included in the respective tradition leads them to their goal – that is, to liberation, enlightenment, or salvation. However, meditation teachers seem to have always also paid attention to single components of the respective packages to instruct students according to their needs. For instance, the Buddha suggested (in the *Metta Sutta*[9]) to fearful monks that they practice loving kindness meditation to overcome their fears (e.g., Ko Lay, 1990, p. 127); the medieval *Visuddhimagga* advises monks to choose meditation objects according to their temperaments (Buddhaghosa, 2010); and Zen practitioners may be assigned quite different techniques according to their aims and meditation experiences (Kapleau, 2000). Some of these choices of techniques that meditation teachers make might be "prescribed" by their tradition, but others might come from systematic "single-case studies" – that is, from their own experiences of what works for whom. To find out more about what works for whom (and in which context) should be an important aim of meditation research. So, it seems worthwhile to ask what techniques are contained in traditional approaches to meditation. This chapter will look at just a small selection of traditional approaches. But already this glimpse will reveal that even meditation traditions that go under the same name may comprise quite different collections of meditation techniques, depending on specific subgroups or teachers.

Traditional approaches to meditation are all embedded in a religious or spiritual context that also includes ethical and moral guidelines. In fact, in

---

9 One version of this sutta can be found as No. 9 in the first collection of discourses (*Khuddaka-Patha*) of the *Khuddaka Nikaya* ("Minor Collections").

the Abrahamic religions (Judaism, Islam, and Christianity), the context is a dominant presence, and meditation, as a principal practice within the respective tradition was, and is, practiced only by a minority. Nonetheless, even in these traditions, the meditative part always includes several techniques. For instance, Hovorun (2019) argues that meditation in Eastern Orthodox Christianity includes the techniques of the contemplation of sins, the contemplation of the Divine Light (seeing God as uncreated Light), the Jesus Prayer, and hesychasm (ceaseless prayer with complete silence of mind and the reunion of mind with heart). Also in Judaism, meditation comprises several techniques such as a mantra-like practice (reciting difficult divine names in a precise, prescribed manner), guided imagination, oneiric (dream) questions, concentration, recitation of verses, longing for the divine (thereby eventually nullifying the self), and the transformation of daily actions into meditative practice. Thereby, different schools (led by different rabbis) recommend different collections of practices (Persico, 2019). Similarly heterogeneous collections of techniques can be found in Sufism (e.g., Chittik, 2008; Geoffroy, 2010).

Whereas in the Abrahamic religions, meditation always was a marginal phenomenon, in the Daoist (Taoist) religious practice, it plays an important role, and here as well, it comprises several different techniques. Komjathy (2019) and Roth (2015) describe five such (in part quite complex) techniques: *apophatic meditation* (losing bodily awareness and removing all thoughts from consciousness), *ingestion* (incorporating terrestrial and celestial energies), *visualization* (using different objects such as celestial bodies or gods), *inner observation* (a practice influenced by and similar to *satipatthana* meditation, see Chapter 2), and *internal alchemy* (refining the mundane self into an immortal being). Note that there are many varieties of Daoist practices, such as Daoist qigong (e.g., Liang & Wu, 2006), but all comprise several different meditation techniques.

Undoubtedly, the two religious traditions in which meditation had and continues to have a very central place are Hinduism and Buddhism. There are numerous schools of meditation both in Hinduism (e.g., Flood, 1996) and Buddhism (e.g., Harvey, 2004), and it is impossible here to do justice to even a representative sample. One also has to say that the concept of meditation as commonly understood nowadays in the West is alien to both traditions because the *path to liberation* (*sadhana*) is always a combination of many practices of which only some can be referred to as meditation. One Pali term that might be considered close to "meditation" is *bhavana* (bringing into being), which refers to mental or spiritual exercises aimed at cultivating mental states conducive to attain *nibbana* (e.g., Gethin, 1998, p. 174). Here, we will concentrate on a few typical approaches in each tradition, with which the author has had at least some personal acquaintance. For each approach, we will also briefly consider the context in which the respective meditation techniques are embedded. The main purpose of the following paragraphs is to make clear which components the selected approaches consist of. Why they are supposed to work – that is, the underlying psychological theories – will be discussed in Chapter 9.

Hindu Classifications

"Hinduism" is an umbrella term for many religious and spiritual traditions that reach back to the most ancient Indian scriptures, the so-called *Vedas* ("veda" means "knowledge"; Feuerstein, 1998), dated between 3500 BCE and 1200 BCE (estimates differ; see Frawley, 2001; Klostermaier, 2006). However, the real basis for Hindu approaches to meditation, including their contexts, was not the *Vedas* themselves. Instead it consisted of several interpretations thereof, usually termed "philosophical systems" or just "systems." Two of the six main systems, *Yoga*, and *Vedanta* ("end of veda") are the theoretical basis for the two approaches briefly discussed in the next two paragraphs: yoga meditation and transcendental meditation (TM).

Yoga Meditation

There are numerous approaches referred to as "yoga" (see Phillips, 2009), but here we will refer to the traditional form closely connected to the system of Yoga, sometimes called classical yoga (Feuerstein, 2006), with Patanjali's *Yogasutras* (for translations, see Phillips, 2009; Whiteman, 1993; Woods, 1998) as its most authoritative text. The *Yogasutras* are most likely to have been written by several authors between the 2nd century BCE and the 5th century CE (Dasgupta, 1997; Flood, 1996). They are also central to later schools of yoga (Feuerstein, 1998; Phillips, 2009). The *Yogasutras* describe an eightfold path (Figure 3.1) that eventually should lead to liberation, which in this context is specified as the attainment of pure consciousness (see Rao & Paranjpe, 2008; Sedlmeier & Srinivas, 2016; and Chapter 9).

The first two limbs of the path, here rendered as *ethics* and *inner spiritual discipline* (Sanskrit: *yama* and *niyama*), contain rules for right living with others and right living with oneself. These are followed by body postures (*asanas*) and breathing exercises (*pranayama*) that prepare the yogi for the meditation exercises to come, although some breathing techniques are sometimes already regarded as meditation techniques (e.g., Paul et al., 2007; Seppälä et al., 2014). Also, the control of the senses (*pratyahara*) – that is, procedures (often using the breath) for preventing sensory informa-

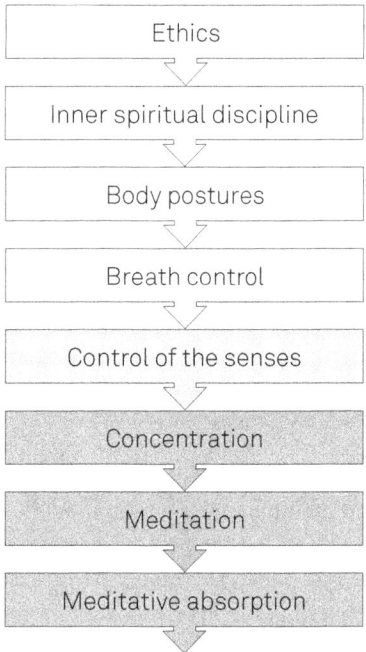

Figure 3.1. The eight limbs of the classical yoga path. Reprinted with permission from "Psychological theories of meditation in early Buddhism and Sāmkhya/Yoga" by P. Sedlmeier & K. Srinivas (2019), in M. Farias, D. Brazier, & L. Mansur (Eds.), *The Oxford handbook of meditation*, Oxford Handbooks Online, p. 11. https://doi.org/10.1093/oxfordhb/9780198808640.013.27

tion from entering the mind – can be seen as a meditation technique. The central meditation techniques are contained in the last three limbs. Concentration (*dharana*) should be permanently held on a given object while avoiding all other thoughts, although the meditator is still aware of the act of themselves doing it and of the object of meditation. There are many choices of objects (see Sivananda, 1945; Vishnu-Devananda, 1995). In the next limb, often rendered as *meditation* or *contemplation* (*dhyana*), the awareness of the act of meditating disappears. Finally, in *meditative absorption* (*samadhi*), the meditator, with the awareness of themselves dissolved, becomes one with the object of meditation.

In sum, one could describe the central meditation techniques of the eightfold yoga path as variants of concentrative meditation. But the four books of the *Yogasutras* also contain more advice on how to meditate, such as practicing the *brahmaviharas* (loving kindness, compassion, sympathetic joy, and equanimity – YS 1.33; see Chapple, 1990, p. 64). Other techniques consist of devotion to a personal god (YW 1.23), or of practicing disinterestedness (YS 1.12), or mantra meditation (YS 1.27–29). Similar (but sometimes quite different) varieties of meditation techniques can also be found in other variants of yoga (Feuerstein, 1998, 2006). Recently, a variant of the eightfold path, *meditation-based lifestyle modification* (MBLM), with mantra meditation as the basic meditation technique, has been proposed by Bringmann et al. (2020, 2021a).

Transcendental Meditation

Maharishi Mahesh Yogi and his *transcendental meditation* (TM) were introduced in Chapter 1 (see the section Repeating Words or Sentences), as an approach that prominently uses mantra meditation. The Maharishi's teacher was a legitimate successor in the *Advaita Vedanta* (nondualistic Vedanta) lineage, founded by the sage-philosopher Shankara (8th century; see Flood, 1996). However, his own career was a bit unusual because due to his membership of the cast of scribes (he worked as a scribe for his guru), he could not become a monk (only Brahmins can). Nonetheless, 5 years after his guru's death, he began teaching without proper authorization in line with the Advaita Vedanta tradition (Lowe, 2011; Lucas, 2014; Williamson, 2010). This nonconformity might also be witnessed in his focusing on the method of mantra meditation, whereas in Advaita Vedanta, mantra meditation is usually not prominent, and Advaitins practice many other techniques, collectively referred to as the "knowledge path" (*jnana marga*; see Dasgupta, 1997, pp. 489–490, Paranjpe & Rao, 2008, pp. 275–276, Raju, 1985, p. 407; see also Chapter 9). It did help the movement that the Beatles had spent some time at the Maharishi's ashram in India and later helped to spread the message in the West. The TM movement claims that only specific mantras stemming from Advaita Vedanta can be used, which are based on a secret selection procedure. It seems, however, that this "secret procedure" is nothing but a systematic selection from a set of words given out by age (Williamson, 2010, p. 88), or age and sex, depending on the specific teacher training course the TM teacher has attended. (A detailed list of mantras and a verbatim description of the (secret) initiation procedure can be found at https://anatomiadaconsciencia.files.wordpress.com/2019/03/tm_mantras.pdf.)

Indeed, TM is an exception, insofar as it relies mainly on only one meditation technique, although there is a program for advanced meditators that teaches the so-called *TM-Sidhi* techniques. This program is based on the *Yogasutras* and purports to teach practitioners to, among other skills, levitate, read minds, and become invisible (Lowe, 2011, p. 63). (In contrast to Yoga, in which the whole third book of the *Yogasutras* deals with obtaining *siddhis* [supernatural powers], in *Advaita Vedanta*, there is no special emphasis on the siddhis; although, because the *Yogasutras* are recognized as a valid source of knowledge, they are not excluded either; Raju, 1985). However, these advanced techniques seem to be nothing but an extension of the basic procedure, a set of sutras (words or phrases) that are to be mentally repeated twice every 15 s after doing a 20-min session of TM, with a pause of 15 min in between each repetition (see http://minet.org/mantras.html). What separates TM from secular mantra meditation is the context – for example, reciting sutras and performing rituals (e.g., *pujas*) with clear connections to *Advaita Vedanta* (a description of the rituals can be found at https://anatomiadaconsciencia.files.wordpress.com/2019/03/tm_mantras.pdf).

Buddhist Classifications

Buddhism also has a classical path to liberation, again consisting of eight limbs: the *Noble Eightfold Path* (for some background information, see Rahula, 1959, Chapter V). To indicate that the eight limbs do not have to be progressed through in a definite order, they are often depicted in a spiral or circular form (e.g., Harvey, 2004, p. 71). And indeed, it is still open to discussion in which order the path should be traveled (Gombrich, 2013, p. 109). Figure 3.2 shows the eight limbs divided into three parts.

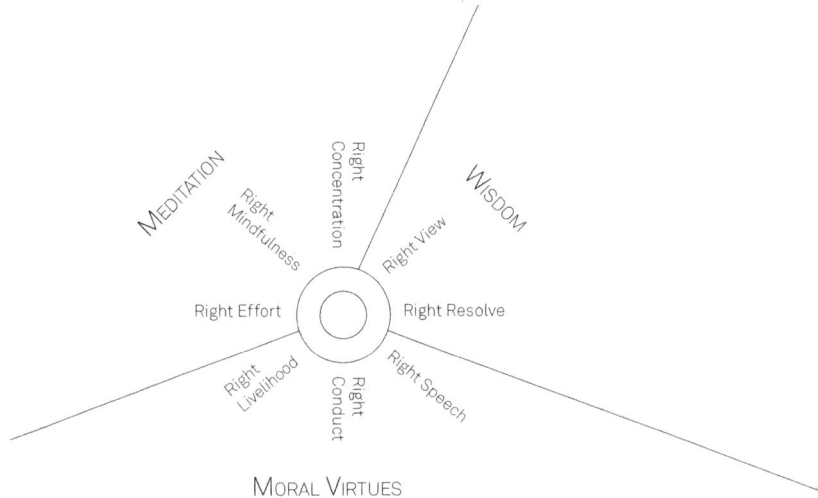

Figure 3.2. The Buddhist Noble Eightfold Path. Reprinted with permission from "Psychological theories of meditation in early Buddhism and Sāmkhya/Yoga" by P. Sedlmeier & K. Srinivas (2019), in M. Farias, D. Brazier, & L. Mansur (Eds.), *The Oxford handbook of meditation*, Oxford Handbooks Online, p. 4. https://doi.org/10.1093/oxfordhb/9780198808640.013.27

Only the moral virtues part, consisting of *right speech, right conduct,* and *right livelihood*, does not entail meditation techniques but is nonetheless regarded as necessary on the path. In the wisdom part, *right resolve* includes the cultivation of the attitude of not expecting anything for one's deeds and the practice of nongreed and nonhatred, as well as loving kindness and compassion meditation. The other limb in the wisdom part, *right view*, stands for developing insight into the true nature of the world, including some basic Buddhist teachings such as the *Four Noble Truths* (see Chapter 9). Also, these two limbs can be seen as meditation in a wider sense.

Traditionally, the meditation part consists of the two *meditation limbs* – *right mindfulness (samma sati)* and *right concentration (samma samadhi)* – but many scholars also count *right effort* in that part. Right effort deals with how to deal with *unwholesome mental states*, especially aversion of any kind (hatred, anger, resentments). If these aversive states are already there, right effort should be used to appease them, and it should also prevent them from arising at all. The best way to do so is cultivate *wholesome states*, such as generosity, kindness, and wisdom. One could argue that this is related to what is nowadays known as loving kindness or compassion meditation (e.g., Salzberg, 1995).

In Chapter 2, we have already seen what the second collection of meditation techniques, right mindfulness, consists of. The mindfulness techniques described in the *Satipatthana Sutta* are also contained in many forms of *vipassana* (Sanskrit: *vipashyana*, literally "special seeing," but usually translated as "insight") meditation (see next paragraph).

The last meditation limb of the Noble Eightfold Path contains right concentration, with the aim of cessation of apperception and feeling. The respective techniques consist of continually concentrating on a given object such as the breath, a mantra, a visual object, and many other choices of objects (Shaw, 2006).[10] Often, several objects are used, and the selection may either follow a general order (e.g., Gunaratana, 1980; Johansson, 1970), or objects may be chosen to accommodate the special needs of the practitioner (Buddhaghosa, 2010; Kornfield, 2008). This kind of concentrative practice is often summarized as *samatha* (calming) meditation.

There is some (still ongoing) debate among Buddhist scholars about the relative importance and relationship between mindfulness meditation and concentrative meditation, often referred to as vipassana and samatha, respectively (for summary, see Gethin, 1998, pp. 198–201). Samatha practice can lead, at least in part, to very pleasant experiences, which are classified

---

10 In Chapter 1, we have already touched on the fact that over the course of concentrative meditation, the original object is often replaced by a more subtle one, termed a *nimitta* [sign] that arises during the practice (e.g., Brahm, 2014).

into several *jhana* (Sanskrit: *dhyana*) states (see Chapter 9). Some scholars argue that this is what is innovative and distinctive about early Buddhist meditation and a path to liberation in itself (e.g., Bronkhorst, 1993; Arbel, 2015). However, most scholars see samatha practice – taken over by Buddhists from preexisting Indian yogic practices – as a very helpful prerequisite for vipassana practice, which, in their opinion is the real innovation of the Buddha (e.g., King, 1980). Most Buddhist scholars seem to be of the view that samatha meditation does not in itself suffice to reach liberation but is a good preparation for vipassana practice, which then leads to *nibbana* (Sanskrit: *nirvana*; see, e.g., Anālayo, 2003; M. Batchelor, 2016; Gombrich, 2006; Gunaratana, 2015). We will see that this is also the view held in different approaches to Vipassana meditation. To accentuate the twofold meanings of (1) "vipassana" as a synonym for mindfulness meditation (second-to-last limb in the Noble Eightfold Path) and (2) "Vipassana" as a Buddhist approach to meditation, the two terms are rendered in different cases [lower case for mindfulness meditation and upper case for the meditation approach(es)]. Also in Zen, the second Buddhist approach described here, we will encounter both mindfulness and concentrative meditation.

Vipassana

Practitioners of Vipassana often assume that their meditation practice stems from Burma (which is correct) and that there is only one kind of Vipassana (which is incorrect). Indeed, there are numerous forms of Vipassana (for overviews, see Cousins, 1996; Kornfield, 1988; van Oosterwijk, 2012), but here we will concentrate on the three that are currently most popular – those of Mahasi Sayadaw (Mahasi, 1973), U Ba Khin and his student S. N. Goenka (Hart, 1987), and Pa-Auk Sayadaw (Pa-Auk, 2000). According to Anālayo (2012), all three of these variants of Vipassana can be traced back to the early discourses in the *Sutta Pitaka*, in particular to the *Satipatthana Sutta*. However, despite claims to the contrary, it is unclear how far back the respective traditions really reach (see Melnikova, 2014). Considering the epoch when the founders, Mahasi Sayadaw (1904–1982), U Ba Khin (1899–1971), and Pa-Auk (born 1934) were (and are) active, all of these approaches, in their current versions, may be fairly recent.

Mahasi Sayadaw

The most distinctive element in Mahasi's approach to Vipassana is to watch the rise and fall of the abdomen, which may have been his innovation (Cousins, 1996, p. 42). His method involves the maintenance of mindfulness and clearly knowing over extended periods of time with very little sleep (Mahasi, 1991). Usually, sitting and walking meditation are practiced alternatingly. In walking meditation, the process of walking is broken down into named stages that are mentally noted and performed very slowly. Mental notes (labeling) and slow movements are an integral part of the meditator's practice. The basic technique in the sitting meditation is to watch the rise and fall of the abdomen (also including labeling), often extended to a kind of body scan that moves meditators' awareness across different points of the body. One could argue that the main meditation technique in this approach consists of applying mental labels to what is experienced throughout meditation practice (which ideally is throughout the waking day), to sharpen clear recognition (Anālayo, 2012, p. 25). Mahasi's approach does without any explicit samatha practice, unlike its two "competitors," described next.

S. N. Goenka (U Ba Khin)

Goenka (1924–2013) was not a monk but a successful Indian businessman, brought up in Burma, who became a wealthy leader of Burma's Indian community. In the 1970s, his teacher U Ba Khin sent him to India to bring the teaching back to its origin (Melnikova, 2014). Meanwhile, Goenka's version of Vipassana is taught in "canned" courses (all instructions are given from audiotapes, although there are teachers who answer questions and give advice). In the first 3 days of the usual 10-day courses, participants practice concentration on the breath, with the aim of calming the mind. This is followed by vipassana practice proper (Hart, 1987). The latter consists of body scan techniques, with an emphasis on feelings (*vedana*). On the last day of the course, meditators are introduced to loving kindness meditation.

Pa-Auk

Of the three Vipassana approaches discussed here, Pa-Auk Sayadaw's is the most traditional, and comprehensive one. It closely follows the *Visuddhimagga* (Buddhaghosa, 2010), a medieval manual of Buddhist practice. This approach to Vipassana puts a strong emphasis on the samatha part. Ideally, the practitioner should have mastered the first four *jhanas* (states of absorption) before starting insight meditation. The preferred object of concentration is the breath, but absorption states can also be reached by using a multitude of other objects such as, for instance, body parts, *kasinas* (typically described as colored disks), or loving kindness (Pa-Auk, 2000). The insight meditation (*vipassana*) can also deal with many objects, including even some not described in the *Satipatthana Sutta*. Note that the object of meditation does not determine whether the practice is a mindfulness technique or a concentrative technique. For instance, both the breath and loving kindness are suggested to be used in both respects.

Recapitulation

All three approaches to Vipassana briefly described here include rituals [such as chanting suttas, elaborate bowing, and taking the "three refuges" – to Buddha, *dhamma* (entire body of his teaching), and *sangha* (initially referred to the monastic community of monks and nuns, but nowadays often includes lay followers of the Buddha as well)] and encompass the following of ethical rules by, for instance, taking precepts. For lay practitioners, these are usually the *five precepts* (refraining from killing, stealing, lying, improper sexual conduct, and consuming intoxicants). All of the Vipassana practices are very intense, and the Mahasi and especially the Pa-Auk approach are most suited for practice in a monastery. Moreover, each of the three approaches includes various, but partly quite distinct, meditation techniques, whereby the specific selection depends on the emphasis given to samatha practice (Mahasi none, Goenka some, and Pa-Auk very much).

Zen

Strictly speaking, the heading for this paragraph should be *Chan* (Chinese), not *Zen* (Japanese), but apparently, the Japanese were more successful in propagating this Buddhist approach to meditation than the Chinese who, after having been exposed to (Mahayana) Buddhist influences from India, established Chan. Chan later gave birth to various lineages summarily referred to as *Zen* in Japan, *Seon* in Korea, and *Thiền* in Vietnam. All of these terms mean the same thing and are abbreviated transliterations of the Sanskrit term *dhyana*. However, there is some justification to mostly using "Zen" here because, if Sharf's (2014) assertion is correct, the two best-known meditation techniques in Zen, *shikantaza* (silent sitting or just sitting) and *koan practice*, are likely Japanese inventions (*shikantaza*) or modifications (koan practice) of the original Chinese meditation techniques. Before we come to these two practices, let us first have a glimpse of early Zen meditation.

In Zen, lineages play a very important role in justifying the special role of teachers, the Zen masters (see Ford, 2006). Therefore, it is no wonder that descriptions of these lineages, such as the Soto Zen Master Keinzan's famous *Denkoroku* (Transmission of the Light) do take some liberties with historical truth (see the Introduction in Cook, 2003; McRae, 1986, 2003). Early Chan history (6th to 8th centuries), as laid down by some of its leading figures, "have much to say about competing Chan schools and ideologies but little to offer in the way of concrete descriptions of practice" (Sharf, 2014, p. 934). However, there are indications that at least initially, actual practice did not deviate from Theravada practice so much, although the theoretical background differed considerably (Gregory, 1986; see also Chapter 9). For instance, Zhiyi (Chih-i; lived 538–597), who was not a Chan master himself (he was actually the founder of another important Buddhist sect, then *Tendai* – see Chappell, 1987) but very influential in the development of Chan (Bielefeldt, 1986, p. 133), proposed, among other techniques, counting the breath, keeping attention on the breath, controlling desire, contemplation (visualization) of the whole body, and contemplation of the mind itself (Cleary, 2005, p. xix).

The *Treatise on the Essentials of Cultivating the Mind* (*Hsiu-hsin yao lun*), attributed to Huineng (Hung-jen), the sixth Chinese Zen patriarch,[11] and his students, summarizes the Zen teachings around the year 700 and also contains some meditation instructions. Here are some examples of the teachings (translations by McRae, 1986; note saṁsāra is the cycle of death and reincarnation, and the aim of all Buddhist practice is to escape this "realm of birth and death," which is achieved when *nirvana* is reached):

> Do not try to search outside yourself, which [only] leads to the suffering of saṁsāra. Maintain the same state of mind in every moment of thought, in every phase of mental activity. Do not enjoy the present while planting the seeds of future suffering – [by doing so] you only deceive yourself and others and cannot escape from the realm of birth and death. (McRae, 1986, p. 126. Reprinted with permission of Unversity of Hawai'i Press.)

> Sit properly with the body erect, closing the eyes and mouth. Look straight ahead with the mind, visualizing a sun at an appropriate distance away. Maintain this image continuously without stopping. Regulate your breath so that it does not sound alternately coarse and fine, as this can make one sick. (McRae, 1986, p. 127. Reprinted with permission of Unversity of Hawai'i Press.)

> View your own consciousness tranquilly and attentively, so that you can see how it is always moving, like flowing water or a glittering mirage. After you have perceived this consciousness, simply continue to view it gently and naturally, without [the consciousness assuming any fixed position] inside or outside of yourself. Do this tranquilly and attentively until its fluctuations dissolve into peaceful stability. This flowing consciousness will disappear like a gust of wind. (McRae, 1986, p. 130. Reprinted with permission of Unversity of Hawai'i Press.)

---

11 In the *Denkoroku*, there are 28 Indian Zen patriarchs listed, beginning with Shakyamuni Buddha, before the Chinese lineage starts with Bodhidharma – the first Chinese patriarch, 5th or 6th century CE – who, according to Zen lore, brought Zen from India to China.

These practices might be summarized as practicing equanimity, concentrative meditation (a samatha exercise) and awareness of consciousness (or mindfulness of the mind, a vipassana exercise), respectively.

Another brief Zen meditation manual titled *Principles of Seated Meditation* (*Tso-ch'an i*), attributed to a monk named Ch'ang-lu Tsung-tse, was probably written around the turn of the 12th century (see Bielefeldt, 1986, for the following). This work also refers to the already mentioned Zhiyi but differs considerably from it. For instance, it recommends keeping the eyes half open (in contrast to keeping eyes closed as is usually recommended in Theravada practice), to simply observe thoughts as they arise, which will eventually lead to a state of samadhi (the mind becomes unified). When leaving the samadhi, it suggests maintaining meditative calm at all times. However, Tsung-tse did not see samadhi as an end in itself. He assumed that wisdom (*prajna*) already exists in the mind and is uncovered when the surface fluctations of thought are calmed (Bielefeldt, 1986, p. 139). Other meditation techniques recommended in early sources include focusing on the image of a single Buddha, and thereby recognizing the identity of that Buddha with the Absolute Reality (*Dharmadhatu*), and on one's own mind. Other objects recommended are the numeral "1" (to experience a sense of unlimited space), or an image of the disk of the sun (a metaphor of the true, enlightened mind within us all).

In sum, whereas Chan monks in public distanced themselves from the ancient (Theravada) practices of samatha and vipassana, the meditation techniques used seem to have been not so much different, although they increasingly involved an assumption not to be found in early Buddhism. This assumption is variously called "Buddha nature," "True Self," "Old Fellow," or "Undying Lord of the House" (Cook, 2003, p. 11) or, in other words, "the existence of an eternal, imperishable self, that is, buddhahood" (Zimmermann, 2002, p. 82; see also Chapter 9). Let us now come back to the two most distinctive meditation techniques in Zen.

Shikantaza

Here, some readers might have expected that meditation techniques would be divided between Soto and Rinzai Zen, the two most important (out of initially many) schools of Zen nowadays. However, this chapter is mainly concerned with meditation techniques, and it seems that the differences between the Soto and the Rinzai schools (as well as other often-referred-to opposites among Buddhist schools) are largely based on sectarian rhetoric. This is nicely illustrated by two anecdotes (Heine, 1990, p. 358): Ta-hui (Japanese: *Dahui Zonggao*), the popularizer of the koan, burned the printing blocks for the famous koan collection *Biyan Lu* (*Blue Cliff Record*; Japanese:

Hekiganroku), which his own teacher Yiin-wu (1063-1135, Japanese: *Engo*) had compiled; and Dogen (1200-1253), the founder of the Soto sect, copied the same text in a single night before returning from China to Japan (important Soto lineages also used koans extensively, e.g., Mohr, 2000, p. 245). Moreover, Hongzhi Zhengjue (1091-1157), a Chinese Chan master who was most influential for the Japanese Soto sect, wrote one of the most famous koan collections, the *Book of Equanimity* (Chinese: *Congron lu*, Japanese: *Shoyoroku*), which is also extensively used by Rinzai schools (Wick, 2005). Further, many teachers in the West are connected in some way or other to the Harada-Yasutani school that explicitly combines Rinzai and Soto (Ford, 2006; Sharf, 1995).

What is shikantaza (just sitting)? Things do not seem to have changed much since the early times of Zen: It is still hard to find exact descriptions of meditation techniques in Zen books. But in trying to make a synthesis from several sources (e.g., Aitken, 1993; Loori, 2013; Kapleau, 2000; Samy, 2002 – all connected to the Harada-Yasutani school) one can arrive at the impression that shikantaza is an open and very flexible version of mindfulness (*satipatthana*) meditation (see Chapter 2). It consists of discarding specific objects and simply watching the six sense doors, with a special emphasis on watching the mind. There is, however, in addition a certain attitude to it, emphasized somewhat differently by different authors. For instance, Yasutani Roshi says that in shikantaza practice, the mind must be firmly planted (like Mount Fuji) but also alert, like a taut bowstring (Kapleau, 2000, p. 61). And Robert Aitken (2015a, 12.69) admonishes: "Just sit facing the empty stage of your mind. Settle into your bones and guts. There are no thoughts, no numbers, and no themes at all." And in the words of the founder of the Soto sect, Dogen Zenji: "Do not think about what is good or evil, and do not try to judge right from wrong" (Uchiyama, 2004, Section 14.22).

Koan Work

We have already briefly touched on koans in Chapter 1. Koans are often stories of an incident between a master and one or more disciples, which involve an understanding or experience of the enlightened mind, usually expressed in a dialogue. Often, only the principal topic, or most essential element or "critical phase" (*hua-t'ou*) is used for extended practice. You probably remember this koan from Chapter 1: "Once a monk asked Chao-chou, 'Does a dog have Buddha-nature or not?' Chao-chou replied, 'No!' ("wu" in Chinese and "mu" in Japanese)." In this case, the critical phrase would be just "no" (or "wu" or "mu") (Buswell, 2006, p. 78).

Here is how Victor Sogen Hori describes koan work on Hakuin's famous "Two hands clap, and there is a sound. What is the sound of the one hand?" in a Rinzai monastery:

> The monk repeats to himself over and over again, "What is the sound of one hand?" constantly posing anew the question to himself. The repetition becomes so ingrained that without conscious effort the *kōan* always rises to consciousness whenever attention is not fixed on anything else. As he drifts off to sleep at the end of the day, the last thing involuntarily drifting through his mind is the *kōan* endlessly repeating itself. And on arising in the morning, the first conscious thought is again the *kōan* continuing its ceaseless repetition from the night before. (Hori, 1994, p. 30)

So far, one could say that koan work is similar to passionate mantra meditation. But it goes further than this:

> In the beginning, the monk seeks for the answer to the koan expecting that the answer will arise someday in his consciousness like an object illuminated by a spotlight. But as he continues to work on the *kōan* and yet still fails to penetrate it, he starts to react to his own inability. He begins to have doubts about the *kōan* practice. He will doubt his own abilities. He may fall into a deep disappointment or depression. He challenges himself to have faith and pushes himself beyond what he thought were the normal limits of endurance and willpower. In this region beyond his normal limits, he panics, turns desperate, becomes frantic. Here all self-consciousness is gone. No longer is there a self constantly watching the self. By such forceful techniques, the Rinzai Zen monastery pushes monks into a state of mind beyond the dualism of ordinary consciousness. (Hori, 1994, p. 30)

According to Hori (1994) the response to the koan is the realization that the monk himself is the koan. To test the understanding of the student, the master checks with requests and questions such as "Cut the sound of one hand into two with one slash of the sword," "Did you hear the sound of one hand from behind or from the front?" and "The sound of one hand – let me hear it too." However, there is also different advice on how to approach a koan. For instance, Wick (2005, p. 5) advises one to think about the koan and ask questions like "What are the people in it saying? What is motivating them? What is motivating you? Which line in the koan is most important?" Such a more intellectually inclined approach might be especially suitable if several hundred koans have to be passed, as is the case in some lineages (Hori, 2006a; Samy, 2013). However, as generations of Zen teachers have stated, koans cannot be grasped merely intellectually, although intellectual understanding may be an important part of the story (Hori, 2006b, pp. 127–129).

Other Meditation Techniques

Usually, students do not begin immediately with shikantaza or koan work but are admonished to practice concentration exercises. These techniques are also practiced by experienced meditators again and again and include centering one's attention in the *hara* (a region approximately four fingers below the navel), practicing different techniques involving the breath, such as counting it or being aware of inhalation and exhalation, as well as being aware of the body (Buksbazen, 2002; Loori, 2013; Kapleau, 2000; Samy, 2002; Sheng Yen, 2006). Another important technique is *kinhin*, meditative walking, usually slow in Soto and brisk in Rinzai (Kapleau, 2000, p. 40). And, of course, all daily activities, including work, meals, or going to the toilet, should be performed in a mindful way. For this, the use of *gathas* (verses) and mantras is recommended (Aitken, 1987). This method is especially put forward by the Vietnamese Zen master Thich Nhat Hanh. He provides gathas for different aspects of formal meditation, but also for all kinds of daily activities, such as for washing your hands, opening the window, beginning to eat, using the toilet, or cutting a flower (Nhat Hanh, 1997, p. 10).

But occasionally, also other techniques such as practicing the brahmaviharas (Samy, 2002; see also Chapter 1) or a special form of mantra meditation – that is, reciting the Buddha's name (Sheng Yen, 2006) or visualizing energy flowing up the backbone (Harada, 2006, p. 7) – are suggested as helpful complements.

Recapitulation

Zen is not uniform. But as in Vipassana, all approaches to Zen include rituals like reciting sutras and bowing; and also walking meditation (kinhin) is practiced by all Zen students. At first sight, reading about Soto and Rinzai Zen, one might have the impression of greatly different practices. However, especially in the West, the original approaches often mingle, and especially in Rinzai Zen, the heterogeneity between different teachers may be as large as that between schools of Zen. Zen has strong similarities to Vipassana practice, especially with respect to mindful living, but the seemingly clear differences between vipassana and samatha are blurred somewhat in shikantaza and koan work.

Conclusion

Some readers may wonder why their favorite school of meditation or schools they find more important than the ones described here have not found any mention. One reason for that is obviously want of space, but another is that the main intention of this chapter is to highlight the heterogeneity of traditional approaches, both between and within them. And, as already mentioned in the beginning of this chapter, a third reason is that the author has stuck to approaches with which he has at least a passing acquaintance. Obviously, all approaches discussed above (and also the ones not discussed) contain not just one but multiple techniques. TM might be considered to come close to a single (main) technique, but that is the only exception I am aware of. The techniques are sometimes rather similar across approaches, and often quite heterogeneous within a tradition. All traditional approaches to meditation are embedded in a religious or cultural background. This background can be noticed in many varieties of rituals, and in ethical and moral rules of living. Using the entire "package" of meditation techniques as offered by a specific school is, of course, fully appropriate for practitioners who have decided to follow that school. They might, however, still be interested in evidence about whether the package works – that is, whether and how much it brings them closer to the aim they connect with meditation, be it enlightenment or "just" getting rid of anxiety or depression. But researchers and scientifically inclined practitioners may be interested in other questions as well.

Do we need the religion or culture part? Religions differ, often dramatically, in their belief systems. So, adhering to the sentence of the excluded middle (something can either be true or not true) not all can be true (for some general limitations of logic in reasoning, see Smith, 2019). Some things might, however, be true to the believer in a different sense, as one might say that characters and stories in famous novels such as *Moby Dick* are true (for a similar point, see Cook, 2003, p. 16). And they might serve a purpose within the approach, such as giving stability, motivation, and encouragement in times of doubt and slackness. Similar questions can be asked about the moral and ethical parts of approaches to meditation. Yet, the ubiquity of quite similar moral and ethical rules across traditions suggests that there might be a strong justification for them being part of these approaches (see also Chapters 8 and 9).

Given the above varieties of practice, what would it mean if a research paper says that Vipassana meditators scored higher on some variable than Zen meditators (or one could exchange these two approaches with any others)? Not much, maybe, because both terms are used in a wide sense, so one would first have to look at the specific packages that have been compared. The composition of given packages certainly matters, given that not all meditation techniques yield the same effects (for which there is evidence, as discussed in Chapters 6 and 8). And then, there is of course the question of whether all techniques in a package are necessary, whether techniques work only in combination with some others, and what specific and potentially different effects single techniques may have.

To complicate things even further, the distinction between concentrative and mindfulness techniques blurs on closer examination. Take for instance the body scan: Is it a concentration or a mindfulness practice? It might be best described as a combination of both. For instance, in the Vipassana tradition according to Mahasi Sayadaw, one has to concentrate on specific points in the body in a given order but then also experience what happens there. Another indication for the interwoven nature of the two kinds of practices might be seen in the fact that the famous *Anapanasati Sutta* (*ana* meaning "inhalation," *apana*, "exhalation," *sati*, "mindfulness") is used as the basis for both concentrative (e.g., Pa-Auk, 2000) as well as mindfulness (e.g., Anālayo, 2018b) practices. These potential complications might be due to long-standing separate traditions that were not much exposed to empirical research. In the West, thousands of studies on the effects of meditation have been conducted (see Chapters 6 and 7), so we might expect a clearer picture in Western meditation research. Whether this is really the case, we will see in the next chapter.

Chapter 4
Western Attempts at Classifying Meditation Techniques

In traditional approaches to meditation, the selection of techniques is usually traced back to some (ancient) authority, a teacher or guru, and is taken for granted. Due to the ascription to authority, there is no need to question the composition of a given "meditation package" or investigate differential effects of different techniques included therein. Often, the teacher might be assumed to know when which techniques should be practiced and by whom, presumably using something like an implicit classification system. However, more and more members of the meditation research community have realized that different forms of meditation are not alike, and what practitioners do when they say they meditate might have specific effects on the results they can expect. One can, of course, still compare whole packages against each other. But apart from the variations within one traditional category – for instance, the heterogeneity of techniques meant when one speaks about Zen or Vipassana (see Chapter 3) – many other factors, such as amount of practice, kind of teacher, personality of practitioner, and other contextual factors have to be taken into account to make sound comparisons.

One way of better understanding the varieties of meditation is to construct more specific classification systems or taxonomies, which is the topic of this chapter. The aim of all classification systems is to further our understanding of the effects of meditation and to improve meditation research. And yet, the idea of meditation as a monolithic category is not yet fully gone.

Meditation as a Monolithic Category

It seems that people from the transcendental meditation (TM) movement initiated one of the first systematic series of studies in the West on the effects of meditation, when, in 1968, they visited Harvard Medical School, asking to be studied. (Even before that, Arthur Deikman had experimented with a concentrative meditation technique he called "experimental meditation." In his view, this technique mirrored what people did in several contemplative traditions, Deikman, 1963, 1966b.) After several unsuccessful attempts, Herbert Benson agreed to conduct the research (Benson & Klipper, 1974). He and his group found a marked stress-reducing effect (Wallace et al., 1971), which he later called the *relaxation response*. Benson concentrated on this response, and also found it when replacing the TM mantra with simple sounds (such as "one"). Moreover, he thought that the initiation ceremony in TM was not necessary, which ended the collaboration with the TM movement (Williamson, 2010, p. 87). Benson claimed that the relaxation response could be elicited by any kind of mantra meditation, including all of the forms developed in different world religions, and by practicing Zen and yoga, as well as "conventional" relaxation techniques such as autogenic training, progressive muscle relaxation, and hypnosis (Benson, 1993). Thus, Benson's conception of meditation seems to have been even more comprehensive (including relaxation techniques) than the huge variety of techniques discussed in Chapter 1. One could argue that this makes sense if all meditation techniques elicit the relaxation response. However, we will see that this is not the case (Chapter 8), and we will also see that there are pronounced differences between the effects of relaxation techniques and meditation (Chapter 6).

The (often implicit) assumption that meditation can be treated as a monolithic category (or that differences between different kinds of meditation do not matter) still lingers in contemporary meditation research. This can be witnessed in attempts to come up with general definitions of what meditation is (for collections of such definitions, see Bond et al., 2009; Matko & Sedlmeier, 2019), and in recent meta-analyses that regard different approaches to meditation as variations of "qigong" (Chen et al., 2012), "mindfulness meditation" (e.g., Verdonk et al., 2020), or "mindfulness-based interventions" (e.g., Klingbeil & Renshaw, 2018).

However, from the beginnings of meditation research, there were attempts to classify meditation techniques, with the anticipation that "there will be both general and specific effects of different types of mediation" (Shapiro et al., 2003, p. 84). Classifications have been drawn along traditional lines, differentiated according to types of meditation, summarized across traditions, differentiated among independent descriptive dimensions, and, recently, by relying on intuitive judgments of expert meditators.

Classifications Along Traditional Lines

Early on, summaries of meditation research used traditional classifications. For instance, there were early meta-analyses concluding that TM had stronger effects than other methods of meditation (Alexander et al., 1991; Eppley et al., 1989; we will see in Chapter 6 that this conclusion was premature). In a later meta-analysis, Ospina et al. (2008) identified five broad categories of meditation practices: mantra meditation, mindfulness meditation, yoga, tai chi, and qigong. In addition, they identified a miscellaneous category that included combinations of different approaches, and a rest category. However, the scarce information about the kind of meditation given in single studies often did not allow for specific categorizations, and therefore, often only TM could be compared with Buddhist approaches to meditation. These Buddhist approaches were most often summarily termed "mindfulness meditation" (e.g., Goyal et al., 2014; Sedlmeier et al., 2012). Except for comparisons of TM with other traditional forms, it is, however, difficult to find studies that use traditional classifications. This makes sense given the huge variety of possible collections of meditation techniques that can hide behind a given traditional term (see Chapter 3). Moreover, there were quite a number of studies that used ad hoc meditation techniques that did not refer to any traditional approach (Sedlmeier et al., 2012).

Classifications According to Types of Meditation

Naranjo (1971) distinguished between three types of meditation, the *way of forms*, including meditation upon external objects such as candle flames, mandalas, koans, questions, and mantras; the *expressive way*, including techniques of letting go of control and being open to inner voices, feelings, and intuitions; and the *negative way*, involving elimination, detachment, emptiness, and centering. In the same book, Ornstein (1971) described two major types of meditation – *concentrative* (which he also termed "turning off" or "shutting down" meditation) and *opening up* – a distinction that in a similar way, was also made by Goleman (1977), who differentiated between the path of concentration (*samatha*) and the path of mindfulness and insight (*vipassana*). He also referred to an integration of these two paths. Further, Goleman based these differentiations on the *Visuddhimagga*, the famous medieval Buddhist meditation manual, already mentioned several times. Similarly, Deane Shapiro extended the "dichotomy" by including a shifting back and forth between the two (Shapiro, 1984), which makes sense because many meditative practices combine the use of specific meditation objects (as in *samatha*) with attending to all impressions within the field of awareness (as in *vipassana*; Eifring, 2016, p. 30).

However, in practical terms, the most influential suggestion regarding the two basic types of meditation stems from Lutz et al. (2008), who used the terms *focused attention* (FA) meditation and *open monitoring* (OM) meditation. These authors deliberately departed somewhat from the original Buddhist notions (see Chapter 3) by conceptualizing meditation as a family of complex emotional and attentional regulatory strategies that can be used for various ends, including the cultivation of well-being and emotional balance. According to the authors, FA meditation entails voluntarily focusing attention on a chosen object in a sustained fashion, and OM meditation involves nonreactively monitoring the content of experience from moment to moment, primarily as a means to recognizing the nature of emotional and cognitive patterns (Lutz et al., 2008, p. 163).

Travis and Shear (2010) added a third component ("automatic self-transcendence") to FA and OM, referring to their interpretation of the advanced stages of TM. Lutz et al. (2008) also mentioned meditation practices that invoke emotional states of empathy and compassion as supplementary practices but did not elaborate on them. In the later literature, however, loving kindness and compassion meditation have been treated as equals to FA and OM meditation (e.g., Fox et al., 2016; Lippelt et al., 2014; Vago & Silbersweig, 2012).

In more recent work, one can often find mixtures of traditional classifications and types of meditation that include several traditions. For instance, Brandmeyer et al. (2019) differentiate between FA and OM meditation, mantra meditation practices, nondual mediation, loving kindness and compassion meditation, and TM. And Pilla et al. (2020) distinguish between mindfulness-based, mantra, kindness-based, yogic, vipassana and samatha, and other meditation.

Arguably the most comprehensive taxonomy of types of meditation techniques stems from Dahl et al. (2015), reproduced here in Figure 4.1. Their intention was to focus on the primary cognitive mechanisms and phenomenological targets of specific forms of meditation, thereby overcoming the limitations of concentrating solely on mindfulness meditation (we will come back to the explanatory part of their model in Chapter 10, in the section Three Families of Meditation Practices). For this purpose, Dahl et al. (2015) propose three "families" of meditative practices: *attentional, constructive,* and *deconstructive*.

The *attentional family* includes practices that are related to the regulation of attention. Dahl et al. (2015) divided that family into practices that involve a narrowing of attentional scope and the cultivation of one-pointed concentration on a single object (FA), and the cultivation of meta-awareness without attending to a specific object (OM). OM is further divided into *object-oriented OM* and *subject-oriented OM*, the latter of which refers to the knowing quality of awareness itself.

The *constructive family* encompasses meditation practices that foster well-being by cultivating virtuous qualities. *Relation orientation* emphasizes harmonious relations with others, whereas *values orientation* refers to ethical frameworks or values. The third subcategory, *perception orientation*, includes practices that aim to alter perceptual habits with respect to sensory objects as well as the subjective perspective itself.

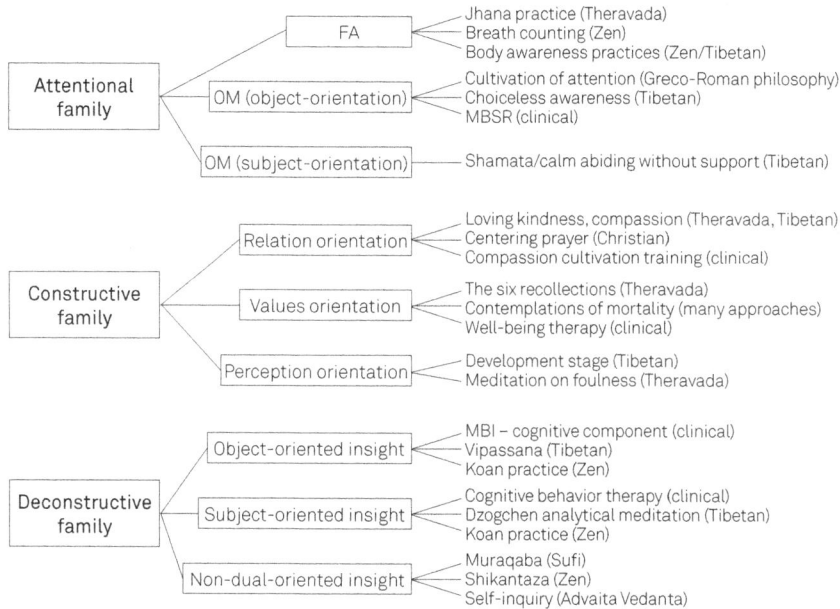

Figure 4.1. Family classification system of meditative practices by Dahl et al. (2015). The number of examples per category shown in the figure is limited here to three techniques each. FA = focused attention; MBI = mindfulness-based interventions; MBSR = mindfulness-based stress reduction; OM = open monitoring. Adapted from Table 1 in Dahl et al. (2015).

Finally, the *deconstructive family* represents self-inquiry techniques thought to elicit insight into the nature and dynamics of conscious experience. This inquiry may refer to objects, such as investigating physical sensations and noting how they are constantly changing (*object-oriented insight*). *Subject-oriented insight* includes practices that inquire into the nature of thought, perception, and other cognitive and affective processes, and *non-dual-oriented insight* practices are designed to reach an altered state of mind "in which the cognitive structure of self/other and subject/object are no longer the dominant mode of experience" (Dahl et al., 2015, p. 519).

Most of the practices listed in the rightmost part of Figure 4.1 should already be familiar to the reader (see Chapter 1). I have not yet referred explicitly to three of the practices listed in Figure 4.1. The *six recollections*, practiced in Theravada Buddhism, consist of the recollections of the Buddha, of the Dhamma, of the Sangha, of one's ethical conduct, of one's liberality, and of heavenly beings (*devas*), which can be seen as part of *sati* practice (Anālayo, 2003, pp. 46–47). *Dzogchen* is a Tibetan contemplative system that includes several practices aimed at recognizing and abiding in "pure awareness" beyond the ordinary dualistic mind (Halkias, 2019). And *Muraqaba*, which may be translated as "constant vigilance" (Geoffroy, 2010) is often used as a summary term for Sufi meditation (several varieties) that includes progressively ordered techniques with the final aim of becoming one with or annihilated in God but is nowadays also used for therapeutic purposes (Azeemi, 2005; Isgandarova, 2019; Omar et al., 2017).

On a closer look, the practices are quite heterogeneous regarding their level of complexity (e.g., compare breath counting with Vipassana), include practices that usually would not be regarded as meditation (e.g., cognitive behavior therapy), and carry with them ambiguities in meaning and categorization [e.g., koan practice is included in both object- and subject-oriented insight practices; and why, for instance, is mindfulness-based stress reduction (MBSR) classified as OM?]. Moreover, there does not seem to be any sound theoretical basis for coming up with these three specific "families." All of these potential caveats notwithstanding, this seems to be the most ambitious and comprehensive Western classification system so far that relies on a combination of types of meditational practices and traditional classifications.

Classifications According to Descriptive Dimensions

Some attempts at classifying meditation techniques ignore traditional categories and types of meditation and rely instead on dimensional descriptions. For instance, Schmidt (2014) proposed a descriptive system with the four dimensions *attention regulation, motivation, attitude,* and *practical context*. This system is meant to constitute a tool for assessing and classifying a given meditation practice, which then can be used for systematic research. To classify a given meditation technique along these dimensions, Schmidt (2014) suggests several assessment tools with both qualitative and quantitative response possibilities that he and his group created. However, he is also open to other ways of measurement. Moreover, not all four dimensions need to be used for a given classification. Here is one of his examples:

> One can imagine that the profile of somebody performing a body-scan (changing focus, focus body, wide attention, mental faculty body-oriented, relaxed strategies with distraction etc.) will be different from metta meditation (i.e., loving kindness meditation) using metta sentences (constant focus, focus mantra, narrow attention, mental faculty emotional, tight strategies with distractions etc.). (Schmidt, 2014, p. 150)

Another classification model that relies on descriptive dimensions has been proposed by Nash and Newberg (2013). For a first classification, the authors use three domains that express the expected effects during the meditation session. *Affective-directed methods* (ADMs) are expected to enhance affective states (examples are loving kindness and compassion meditation). Methods that purport to create an empty state devoid of phenomenological content, a noncognitive and nonaffective state (their examples are TM, Zen, and yoga methods) are classified as *null-directed methods* (NDMs). All remaining methods are by default classified as *cognitive-directed methods* (CDMs). Examples of CDMs are samatha and vipassana. In addition, they use nine descriptive dimensions they call *keys*. These nine keys are illustrated in Table 4.1, using two of their eight example classifications of meditation methods (Nash & Newberg, 2013, pp. 9–11).

The descriptive dimensions of both Schmidt (2014) and Nash and Newberg (2013) sound reasonable, as is the case for the family taxonomy of Dahl et al. (2015), but there seems to be no firm grounding for why exactly these

Table 4.1. A sample comparison between transcendental meditation (NDM) and the Goenka form of Vipassana (CDM), adapted from the taxonomy proposed by Nash and Newberg (Table compiled from information given in the text)

Keys	Transcendental Meditation	Vipassana (Goenka)
Cognitive strategies	Focused concentration, memorization, and visualization	Mindfulness, detached observation, contemplation, and insight
Conceptual and/or physical foci	Mantra (awareness of mantra)	Body (body scan)
Beliefs or special knowledge suggested or required	None	Buddhist teachings
Eyes	Closed	Closed
Static or kinetic	Basic form static, more advanced kinetic form ("Yogic flying")	Static
Silent or auditory	Nonverbal, whereas mantra is repeated silently	Nonverbal
Postural position	Seated comfortably, no strict requirements	Upright seated position, lotus posture if possible
Intrinsic (self-reliant/independent) vs. extrinsic (outside dependent)	Intrinsic	Intrinsic
Control of breathing	Normal breathing	Normal breathing

Note. CDM = cognitive-directed method; NDM = null-directed method.

(and not other) dimensions and categories were chosen. Nonetheless, all three taxonomies are certainly an advantage over earlier classifications relying solely on traditional types of meditation. However, a general limitation of such top-down approaches to classifications of meditation techniques might be the spiritual and/or meditation background of scholars. If these backgrounds are different, chances are that top-down classifications are also different. Recently, a different (bottom-up) approach to classification has been proposed: one that relies on experienced meditators' intuitive judgments.

Bottom-Up Classifications by Experienced Meditators

If experienced meditators are asked to group meditation techniques into categories, they may, especially if they are scholars themselves, be tempted to use their knowledge about meditation traditions and about types of meditation. (There are indications that practitioners tend to become more interested in the spiritual background of their meditation practice, with increasing practice, Sedlmeier & Theumer, 2020.) The result might then not be much different from the classifications and categories discussed above. If, however, these experts were to intuitively judge the similarities of basic meditation techniques stripped of their context, one might get closer to useful classifications. This was the basic idea, we (Matko & Sedlmeier, 2019) pursued in a recent study. But in order to be able to do that, we needed a comprehensive collection of basic meditation techniques. We asked 20 experienced meditators and meditation teachers from different traditions (Hindu, Buddhist, Chinese, and Christian) the following question: "When you meditate, what exactly do you do?" and complemented the respective answers with a comprehensive literature search. This procedure yielded 309 different basic meditation techniques, which were reduced to 50 by following a rule-based selection process that ensured a high degree of heterogeneity (Study 1 in Matko et al., 2021a). In a second study (Study 2 in Matko et al., 2021a), 661 additional experienced meditators (with a mean meditation experience of about 15 years) were asked to indicate how much experience they had with each of the 50 techniques. These ratings were taken as proxies of the popularity of techniques, and then used to reduce the number of techniques to 20. A not-so-large number of techniques was necessary because in the classification study proper (Matko & Sedlmeier, 2019), another sample of 100 experienced meditators (mean meditation experience again about 15 years), were to judge the similarity between all techniques. (For the original $n = 50$ techniques that would have been 1,225 comparisons

$[(n \times (n + 1))/2 - n]$, which only a few participants might have been willing to perform; for 20 techniques, the number of comparisons goes down to a still tedious but manageable 190.) These similarity ratings were then subjected to a multidimensional scaling analysis, which yielded both hidden dimensions and clusters of meditation techniques. The result of this analysis can be seen in Figure 4.2.

This bottom-up procedure yielded two dimensions along which meditation techniques could be classified: *amount of body orientation* (e.g., low in *cultivating compassion* and high in *walking and observing senses*) and *amount of activation* (e.g., low in *sitting in silence* and high in *meditation with movement*). The twenty meditation techniques in Figure 4.2 could be summarized in seven clusters we termed *affect-centered meditation, body-centered meditation, contemplation, mantra meditation, meditation with movement, mindful observation*, and *visual concentration*. Note that these classifications are only partially comparable to the top-down classifications described above.

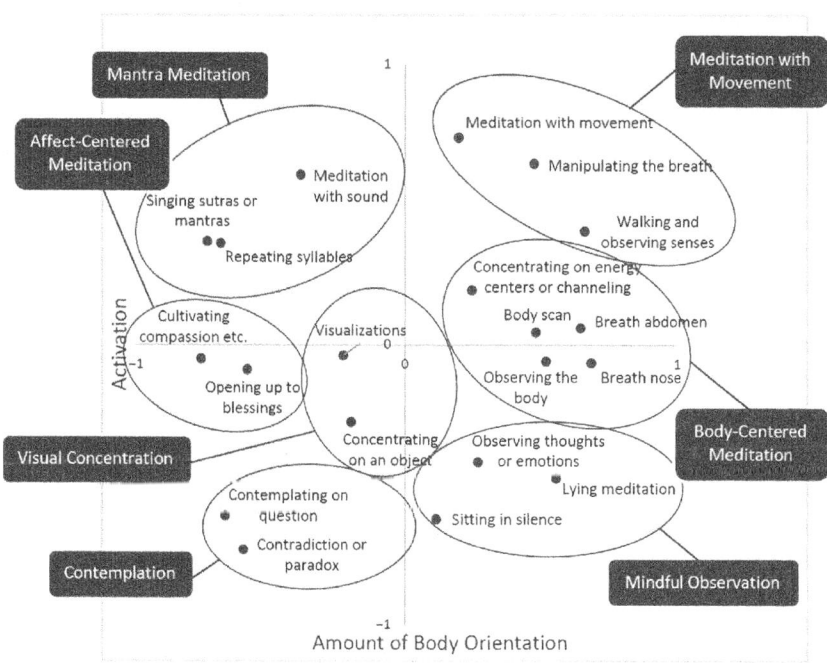

Figure 4.2. Overall multidimensional scaling (MDS) solution, based on average similarity judgments of experienced meditators ($n = 100$) with indicated clusters and labels. Reprinted with permission from "What Is Meditation? Proposing an Empirically-Derived Classification System," by K. Matko and P. Sedlmeier, 2019, *Frontiers in Psychology, 10*, Figure 2. © 2019 The Authors is licensed under CC BY.

Conclusion

Some readers might ask themselves, "Why should these classification attempts be important at all?" If meditators are content with their practice, the research described above would indeed be superfluous for them. However, from many informal conversations, my impression is that usually meditators do not stick with a single practice but may change several times before they stay with a given practice for a longer period of time (see also Sedlmeier & Theumer, 2020; and the "Personal Meditation Journeys" of the authors in M.A. West, 2016). Why the changes? Presumably because meditators are not satisfied with one practice and therefore try another. This could be considered rudimentary single-case research: trying to find the best practice for oneself, by making (informed) comparative judgments. But it would be far better to make judgments about the best meditation practice for oneself right at the beginning. Such judgments certainly involve the aim(s) individuals pursue with meditation (more of that in the next chapter) and personality characteristics, but also specific effects to be expected by practicing specific techniques. To find out about the latter, one first has to decide what "specific technique" means. In the end, one has to find a good compromise between these two extremes: meditation as a monolithic category, and as many types of meditation as there are practices (which would probably mean thousands of them). All of the classification systems described above are attempts to reach such a good compromise.

Apart from these pragmatic deliberations, sound classification systems are, depending on researchers' views, absolutely necessary or at least instrumental for advancing our theoretical understanding of meditation. It seems, for instance, hard to test traditional approaches (like those described in Chapter 3) against each other. First, one always has complex packages, and second, it is often not clear what exactly is contained in the packages (because approaches within a school can be quite different). All of the recent approaches to classification have one thing in common: They are explicit about the techniques used. The best way for meditation researchers to proceed at the moment might be to always give a full specification of the technique used, so that summary analyses can use any existing classification system (or create a new one). Moreover, it might be a good idea to isolate basic techniques and examine their effects not in groups but with single practitioners (more on that in Chapter 11).

Chapter 5
Why Do People Meditate?

In the preceding chapters, we have explored in some detail what people do when they meditate and how their practices can be classified. The huge variety of techniques and classifications, as well as the fact that identical techniques are practiced sometimes with and sometimes without a spiritual and/ or ethical background make it plausible that people may meditate for quite different reasons. As already mentioned several times, traditionally, there is but one reason: liberation, awakening, enlightenment. However, these and other similar terms are very rarely found in contemporary research reports. Therefore, it seems quite unlikely that many participants in a typical study on the effects of meditation pursue such an aim. Even if some do, the number of such studies is huge (see Chapters 6 to 8), and there must be many practitioners who did *not* start meditating with the aim of enlightenment. What then might have been their motivation to begin to meditate? And what keeps them continuing for months or even years?

From the very existence and success of meditation programs with explicitly therapeutic aims (e.g., mindfulness-based stress reduction [MBSR] and the mindfulness-based interventions [MBIs], see Chapter 2), one can deduce that people might use meditation to overcome problems. And one way of overcoming problems may consist in understanding oneself a little better. So, at the outset, one could expect at least a few different kinds of reasons for beginning to meditate: Apart from spiritual or meaning-of-life reasons, people might start meditating for self-help with psychological or, maybe, physical problems, and for learning more about oneself. Early research on the topic indeed centered around these three kinds of reasons. Surprisingly, there are only a handful of studies that have examined why people begin to meditate, so far.

Prespecified Categories of Reasons

It seems that the first systematic study that explored why people meditate was conducted by Deane Shapiro (1992a). He asked 27 individuals (mean meditation experience 4.5 years, mean age 35.6 years) who had signed up for an intensive Vipassana retreat why they had started meditation. The analysis of participants' responses consisted of assigning them to one of three prespecified categories: *self-regulation, self-exploration,* or *self-libera-*

tion or compassionate service. The category of self-regulation (SR) contained reasons such as "to learn to control my stress better," "to become more relaxed," and "to learn to stop my negative thoughts." Reasons categorized under self-exploration (SE) included "wanting to learn more about myself," "wanting to see how my mind works," and "wanting to understand whether this relationship is right for me." Finally, sample reasons for self-liberation or compassionate service (SL) were "wanting to place myself in God's presence," "wanting to deepen my compassion for all living creatures," and "wanting to go beyond my narrow ego" (Shapiro, 1992a, pp. 27–28).

Shapiro regarded the three response categories (he speaks of "goals") as a continuum and expected participants to move along this SR-SE-SL continuum over time. To find out about possible changes, he asked his participants what specifically they hoped to get from the current retreat. He found that there were indeed some changes along that continuum: Whereas 37% of the respondents stated that they began to meditate because they wanted to regulate themselves, only 29.6% pursued the goal of self-regulation in the current retreat. The respective percentages for self-exploration were 22.3% and 25.9%, and those for self-liberation increased the most: from 33.3% to 40.7%. Thus, his tentative conclusion was that with increasing meditation experience, reasons for meditating may shift from self-regulation to self-liberation – that is, toward the traditional goal of meditation.

Carmody et al. (2009) asked 309 participants (mean age 49.5 years) enrolled in MBSR classes about their reasons for beginning to meditate. They used two items each for Shapiro's three categories and had participants rate their importance on a Likert scale from 1 to 5. The two self-regulation items dealt with coping better with stress, pain, or emotions, and feeling better physically and emotionally. The two self-exploration items described increasing self-awareness and self-understanding. And finally, the two self-liberation items were concerned with increased spirituality, wisdom, or insight, and increased peace of mind (Carmody et al., 2009, p. 616). The scores for the two items each were summed up to derive sum scores which all were quite close to the maximum score of 10: 9.34, 8.34, and 8.26, for self-regulation, self-exploration, and self-liberation, respectively. Note that participants in the two studies differed considerably. Whereas Shapiro had asked experienced meditators without explicit health problems, the sample studied by Carmody et al. consisted of participants with, it seems, no previous meditation experience. Moreover, they had stress-related concerns, and about half of them had been referred by their health care practitioner.

In a third study (Pepping et al., 2016), participants (psychology undergrads with some experience in mindfulness meditation) were asked to rate 10 prespecified reasons they had started practicing mindfulness meditation and why they continued with the practice. It turned out that only 37% of the

190 participants (mean age 21.3 years) had an ongoing meditation practice and therefore could answer the second question as well. The top prespecified reasons for both beginning and continuing meditation were (in this order): feel calmer, relaxation, reduce anxiety, and regulate emotions more effectively. Some other prespecified reasons (manage difficult thoughts, concentration, learning and curiosity, and interpersonal relationships) were seen as somewhat less important; and the least important reasons were reducing physical pain, and meditating for spiritual reasons. The only difference between meditators with more or less than 1 year of meditation experience was that less experienced practitioners were more likely to meditate because they wanted to reduce physical pain.

Open Search for Reasons

In the study by Pepping et al. (2016), participants also had the opportunity to give open responses for why they began meditating and why they continued to do so. A qualitative analysis yielded four themes (multiple responses possible): *reduction of negative experiences* (94.7%), *increasing well-being* (31.1%), *introduction by an external source* (28.4%), and *religion/spirituality* (6.3%). Also the analysis of the reasons for continuing practice revealed four themes, highly overlapping with the former: The importance of reduction of negative experiences even increased somewhat (97.8%) and that of well-being increased substantially (to 74.7%). The third category was new: *perception of effectiveness* (18.3%); and religion/spirituality played an even more marginal role (4.2%). Note that only meditators with a continuing practice, about one third of the original sample, responded to the second question. Thus, it is even more surprising that for this selected sample, interest in the religious/spiritual aspects of meditation may have decreased, in contrast to the findings of Shapiro (1992a).

A comprehensive questionnaire developed by Netz and Schmidt has, it seems, not (yet) been published but is briefly described in Schmidt (2014). The authors first collected informal suggestions regarding possible reasons for meditating, from a large number of expert meditators, and derived 58 items from this inquiry. These items were then judged by more than 500 meditators in an online survey. After a first analysis, only 31 of the items were retained, and four factors were derived from those (Schmidt, 2014, p. 148): *well-being, emotion regulation, self-exploration,* and *self-transformation*. These four factors are quite similar to Shapiro's (1992a) suggestions and approximately mirror the qualitatively found themes of Pepping et al. (2016). Correlating the factor scores with meditation experience (in months), the authors found a small positive correlation with self-transformation and a small negative one with well-being, this time consistent with the findings by Shapiro (1992a).

That meditators' spiritual (or secular) background can play an important role in why they begin to meditate is nicely illustrated in a qualitative study by Sparby and Ott (2018). Their participants practiced meditation with an anthroposophical background, and they uncovered themes that were quite different from those suggested previously. These themes were predominantly spiritual and could be classified into three categories: *internal* (inside the subject, e.g., self-realization or initiation), *external* (outside the subject, e.g., duty), and *service* (meditating for something or someone other than oneself, e.g., service to the world and humanity).

Recently, we (Sedlmeier & Theumer, 2020) examined the issue, relying on a two-step procedure (unfortunately, we were at that time unaware of Netz and Schmidt's work described in Schmidt, 2014, which had used a similar procedure). In a first step, we asked experienced meditation teachers from different backgrounds why, in their opinion, their students began to meditate and why they continued. Together with items collected from the literature, we arrived at a list of 77 reasons that were applicable for both beginners and experienced meditators. These items were sent out in a second step to 117 meditation institutions with different backgrounds in Germany. We received 245 responses, with 49 of the respondents having been meditating for less than 1 year ("beginners," mean practice duration 5.4 months, mean age 39.9 years) and 196 for more than 1 year ("experienced meditators," mean practice duration 12.5 years, mean age 47.4 years). As the sample size of the beginners was too small to conduct a factor analysis, we concentrated on exploratory factor analyses (principal component analyses) for the experienced meditators. We analyzed their answers first for why they had begun meditating and then for why they continued to do so. The analysis for the reasons to begin with meditation yielded 11 factors. Thirteen factors were obtained for reasons to continue meditating.[12] In Table 5.1, the factors are ordered according to the explanatory power (eigenvalues) of the factors that summarize the reasons for beginning to meditate (left column). If there was a more-or-less corresponding factor for the reasons to continue meditating, it is placed beside it, and if not, the space to the right is left blank. Sample items for each factor are restricted to the first three (or two, if only two had loadings >.3) with the highest loadings.

---

12 Using the conventional Kaiser criterion, the original number of factors was even higher (18 both for beginning, and continuing meditation), but we restricted our selection to those factors that, after orthogonal rotation, summarized at least two items with factor loadings >.3.

Table 5.1. Factors extracted from principal component analyses of the responses given by experienced meditators (n = 196) for why they began meditating (left) and why they continue to meditate (right). Adapted from Sedlmeier & Theumer (2020, Tables 2 and 4).

Why begin meditating?	Why continue meditating?
Factor 1: Calm down and/or feel better	**Factor 3: Calm down**
Calm down internally	Calm down internally
Relax	Relax
Find good work–life balance	Become more serene
Factor 2: Self-exploration	
Explore not-yet-conscious aspects of my mind	
Understand how my mind works	
Understand why I have certain thoughts and feelings	
Factor 3: Reaction to problems	**Factor 2: Dealing with problems**
Because I am feeling unhappy in my present situation	Deal better with my feelings
Because circumstances in my private life bother me	Because circumstances in my private life bother me
Because I feel that I cannot master the demands of life	Deal better with grief
Factor 4: Open up	**Factor 11: Open up to new insights**
Open up more to my environment	Because I want to deal with alternative views of life
Open up my heart	Become more open to new insights
Accept myself	
Factor 5: Seek spiritual experience and insight	**Factor 1: Spiritual insight/experience**
Seek own spiritual experience	Gain deeper insight into nature of things
Connect to a higher power	Experience altered states of consciousness
Experience altered states of consciousness	Seek enlightenment

Table 5.1. continued

Why begin meditating?	Why continue meditating?
Factor 6: Connecting with nature and self-caring	Factor 13: Enjoy nature
Feel connected to nature	Feel connected with nature
Consciously perceive beauty of nature	Consciously perceive beauty of nature
Give myself more time and attention	
Factor 7: Liberation and compassion	
Practice renunciation	
For the benefit of all sentient beings	
Seek enlightenment	
Factor 8: Mental improvement	Factor 7: Mental development
Improve my intellectual capabilities	Improve professional competencies
Become more creative	Become more creative
Become aware of my potential	Improve my intellectual capabilities
Factor 9: Deal better with problems	Factor 9: Physical problems (plus fear of death)
Deal better with grief	Learn to deal better with physical ailment
Learn to deal better with pain	Sleep better
Learn to deal better with physical ailment	Prevent illness
Factor 10: Personal development	Factor 6: Personal development
Personal development	Personal development
Recognize and remove negative thoughts and beliefs	Experience inner clarity
Make my mind familiar with new positive thoughts and images	Make my mind familiar with new positive thoughts and images
Factor 11: Contentment and clarity	
Experience deep contentment and inner happiness in the present	
Become more open to new experiences	
Experience inner clarity	

Table 5.1. continued

Why begin meditating?	Why continue meditating?
	Factor 4: Care for others, open up
	Have more compassion for others
	For the benefit of all sentient beings
	Contribute to a change in society by meditating
	Factor 5: Self-care
	Be more aware of my body
	Become more sensitive to my current feelings
	Give myself more time and attention
	Factor 8: Unsatisfactory life
	Because my life does not give me fulfillment
	Because I am feeling unhappy in my present situation
	Because I am looking for direction in my life
	Factor 12: Enjoy life
	Enjoy life
	Experience deep contentment and inner happiness in the present

Note. Factors for "Why begin meditating?" are ordered according to explained variance, and sample items according to loadings (only items with factor loadings > 0.3 are retained). Adapted from Tables 2 and 4 from "Why Do People Begin to Meditate and Why Do They Continue?" by P. Sedlmeier and J. Theumer, 2020), *Mindfulness, 11*. © 2020 by The Authors.

The sheer number of factors for both why people began and why they continued to meditate makes clear that reasons to meditate may be much more varied than previously assumed, and this diversity might even increase somewhat over time (13 factors for continuing versus 11 for beginning).

Let us now have a closer look at the results in Table 5.1. First, we can see that there are eight reasons to begin meditation that, in a similar way, also motivate meditators to carry on. Taking the terms from the left column in Table 5.1, the reasons for both beginning and continuing with meditation are to calm down, to react better to problems, to open up, to seek spiritual experiences, to connect better with nature, to support mental improvement, to deal better with problems, and to support personality development. These eight reasons are not equally important for beginners and experienced meditators, as can be seen in the different factor numbers that indicate the explanatory power of the factors (decreases with increasing numbers).

Three factors are specific for beginners: self-exploration, liberation and compassion, and contentment and clarity. Astonishingly, the first two are quite reminiscent of two of the three reasons (self-exploration and self-liberation/compassionate service) identified by Deane Shapiro (1992a) in his study with experienced meditators (see above in the section Prespecified Categories of Reasons). The lower part of Table 5.1 shows five reasons that are specific to continuing meditation. Ongoing meditation practice seems to be seen as helping with the unsatisfactoriness of life (Factor 8) but also as making life more meaningful by caring for others and oneself (Factors 4 and 5). Finally (Factor 12), meditation is expected to enrich life by making it more joyful, a reason that has not been reported before.

The factor structures show how the 77 items, from which we started, can be summarized, and the order of factors shows their explanatory power. Variance explained is, however, not always fully consistent with how important the factors are judged (because variance explained depends on the correlations between variables and not on absolute scores). The latter can be seen by looking at the average ratings for the respective factors (Figure 5.1).

If we only look at the three factors with the highest average approval, we can see that the most important reasons for beginning and continuing meditation might not be so different, after all. Two of these three factors, personal development and calming down, are very important for both beginners and experienced meditators. As already indicated in Table 5.1, the wish for self-exploration (Factor 11: Contentment and Clarity, and Factor 2: Self-Exploration, Figure 5.1, left) apparently is more prominent in the beginning phase of meditation than later on, whereas enjoying life (Factor 12) is seen to be an important benefit of meditation by experienced meditators (Figure 5.1, right).

In sum, it seems that for the meditators in our sample, meditation is not just a tool to overcome psychological and physical problems (Shapiro's self-regulation), gain more insight about themselves (Shapiro's self-exploration), and pursue spiritual aims (self-liberation and compassionate service) but is also used to improve and enjoy life in many ways. This tendency is even more pronounced for long-term meditators.

The differences between beginners and long-term meditators might, however, be larger than our factor-analytical results suggest. After all, in that

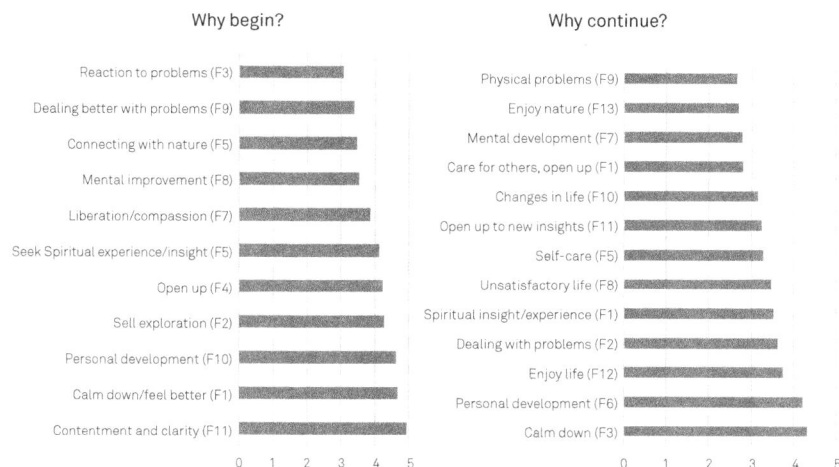

Figure 5.1. Ranking of the factors (F) that summarize reasons for beginning (left) and continuing (right) to meditate, according to their average ratings (rating scales for single items ranged from 1 = *does not apply at all*, to 6 = *applies completely*). Adapted from "Why Do People Begin to Meditate and Why Do They Continue?" by P. Sedlmeier and J. Theumer, 2020, *Mindfulness, 11*, Figures 2 and 4. © 2020 by The Authors.

analysis, the same persons made judgments about why they began and why they continued and all of them *had continued* meditating. We also had administered a short version of the Big Five personality questionnaire. When comparing the sample of beginners (practice less than 1 year) with the sample that was used in the factor analyses, we indeed found some differences: Experienced meditators were more conscientious and less neurotic than beginners (but also older). The former could be practitioners who either dealt successfully with their problems by meditating or never had severe problems anyway, whereas the population of beginning meditators might, in addition, include a group of people who will eventually give up meditating. We also found that the spiritual background mattered: Restricted to the sample of experienced meditators, those with a spiritual (Buddhist) background were less neurotic than those without. Again, the causal connection is unclear.

Conclusion

So far, there is a surprising scarcity of studies having examined why people begin to meditate and why they stick with it. However, even relying on the few available sources, several conclusions emerge. Although Shapiro's

(1992a) original goals of meditation – self-regulation, self-exploration, and self-liberation – play a role in all studies conducted so far (in some they had to play a role because only those reasons were explored), there emerges a much more varied picture from recent research. Instead of being motivated to meditate because one wants to overcome problems, understand oneself better, and reach liberation from the unsatisfactoriness of life, practitioners seem also to pursue many more mundane goals, such as mental development, being more compassionate in everyday life, or just enjoying life more. The motivation to meditate seems also dependent on circumstances of life.

None of the few studies reported above can claim to represent all meditators or even a specified subpopulation. However, some of the results may be used for preliminary speculations. Participants in the Pepping et al. (2016) study were markedly younger than those in the other studies. Only a small percentage of them began meditating for spiritual reasons, and this percentage even decreased in the subgroup of continuing meditators. So, one might expect that overall, only a small percentage of current meditators practice with the aim of enlightenment in mind. The results of the Pepping et al. (2016) study also indicated that many beginners do *not* end up with a regular meditation practice.

In contrast, older (but not old) practitioners (such as the participants in Sparby & Ott, 2018; and the experienced meditators in Sedlmeier & Theumer, 2020) may have tried several options and found one that works for them (and may be a selected sample anyway). Things might be different for persons who mainly come to meditation as a therapeutic intervention (Carmody et al., 2009). A spiritual background, as probably most or all of Shapiro's (1992a) participants had, seems to be motivating. There is some indication that such a background may grow as a result of extended practice (e.g., Schmidt, 2014; Shapiro, 1992a; and tentatively also Sedlmeier & Theumer, 2020), but it could also be that such a (preexisting) background might help with overcoming a drought phase. Anyway, the spiritual background can have strong influences on the reasons to meditate, as evidenced in Sparby and Ott, 2018 (see also Chapter 8).

Be that as it may, the only really strong conclusion from these studies is that there are many different reasons for beginning to meditate and for carrying on the practice. Different reasons to begin meditating might have a strong impact on the effect of meditation. And given the huge variety of meditation techniques explored in the preceding chapters, and indications that not all meditation techniques have the same effects (more about that in Chapters 6 and 8), it seems promising to try to find out more about the match between reasons to meditate and meditation techniques, both for practical and theoretical reasons. If aims and techniques do not match, chances for abandoning the practice increase. So eventually, short screenings, including personality measures, might help to prevent frustration. Especially practitioners with clearly specified goals (other than enlightenment) could choose a technique or an approach that could be custom-tailored to their needs. It would also be interesting to find out how the decision to carry on with meditation practice (or not) depends on personality characteristics, primary reasons to meditate, and meditation techniques (and maybe cultural background). In Chapter 11, we will come back to these issues, but now it is time to have an extensive look at the results of an avalanche of studies on the effects of meditation.

Part 2
Effects

Chapter 6
Effects of Meditation for Healthy Practitioners

In the first four chapters of this book, we have seen that meditation comes in an incredible number of varieties and combinations of techniques, both within religious and secular contexts. Then, in Chapter 5, it became clear that people meditate for a variety of quite different reasons. It seems plausible that the specific technique practiced, whether it is combined with other techniques or not, the context of meditation, meditators' experience, and the motivation to meditate, all influence what one can expect as outcomes. In addition, meditators' personalities might have a sizeable impact on the effects of meditation. We will see in Chapters 9 and 10 that both Eastern and Western theoretical approaches allow for differential predictions of these determinants of meditation outcomes. Unfortunately, so far, most studies have been conducted with little or no theoretical background. This is why this book first reports the effects of meditation before it treats the theoretical approaches (which, in most cases, did *not* underlie the studies). In summarizing the effects of meditation, we will largely omit the effects of very short interventions (e.g., Feldman et al., 2010) and usually not include effects measured directly after meditation because such effects may be quite short-lived, unreliable, and open to many alternative explanations (e.g., Sherman & Grange, 2020).

Meanwhile, thousands of studies have examined the effects of meditation. Searching for the term "meditation effects" in Google Scholar in October 2020 yielded more than half a million hits. This does not, of course, mean that these many studies have in fact examined the effects of meditation, but even if only a small percentage of the references refer to empirical studies, this would still mean a sizeable number of results. This vast number of studies is clearly observable in the avalanche of meta-analyses on the topic that have been produced in recent years. A selection of these will be discussed in this chapter and, to an even larger extent, the next. However, the dominantly atheoretical approach and the concomitantly high arbitrariness of empirical research has carried along with it an uncritical use of the term "meditation" and led to examining a vast diversity of dependent measures without differentiating much among different techniques and other potentially influential factors. Nonetheless, several distinctions can and have been made even in early summary papers and meta-analyses, and more so in later ones. An obvious distinction is the type of dependent measures. We will see that basically any kind of dependent measure commonly used in psychological research has also been tried out in meditation research. Also, methodological issues such as whether studies used randomized designs or not, have usually been considered in meta-analyses (amazingly, a sizeable number of meta-analyses still include pre-post group designs without a control group, which have very low internal validity), as well as the effects of meditation experience. Moreover, approaches to meditation have been distinguished, albeit at a rather coarse level. And finally, a distinction that will characterize this and the next chapter is that between results for practitioners who more or less exclusively meditate for therapeutic reasons and those for whom this is not the case: clinical versus nonclinical populations. It might be hard to draw a clear line between clinical and nonclinical populations (what is normality?), but there are good reasons to look separately at the effects of meditation for these two kinds of populations.

Why Distinguish Between Clinical and Nonclinical Populations of Meditators?

There are two main arguments for why results from clinical and nonclinical studies should be treated separately. The first says that traditionally, meditation was meant only for mentally strong and healthy practitioners, and the second holds that effects for meditators from clinical and nonclinical populations might be caused by different mechanisms, and therefore effect sizes might not be comparable.

The Tradition Argument

Traditionally, meditators did not focus on reducing psychological or bodily problems; their real aim was usually salvation, liberation, enlightenment, unio mystica, nirvana, etc. as the final goal of each respective way. Of course, we cannot exclude the idea that also in ancient times, some salvation seekers suffered from mental problems and were just not pathologized by their fellow people and their teachers. But the chances are that, if this were a widespread condition, the traditional sources would contain mentions of it, which does not seem to be the case. This also does not exclude the possibility that experienced meditators – most prominently the Buddha – were counseling people in need.

Meditators pursuing the traditional path usually were (and are) aware that this is not an easy task. The difficulty of such paths can be evidenced in the rules of living in the respective (often monastic) communities. These rules were (and are) quite hard to follow for people used to every-day life conventions (e.g., the 227 rules for monks and the 311 rules for nuns in the "Patimokkha" part of the *Vinaya Pitaka* in Theravada Buddhism, see Bomhard, 2013). Moreover, most of these salvation seekers were (and are) probably aware of the hardship and potential problems awaiting them on their way (e.g., Kornfield, 1979; Mahasi, 1973; Tsong-Kha-pa, 2000). Teachers in all traditions, but especially in those with a very close relationship between teacher and student, were therefore quite selective, as exemplified here for one tradition:

> According to the Tibetan tradition, an unsuitable vessel can be dirty (full of emotional and mental confusion), turned upside down (inaccessible to instruction), or leaking (incapable of retaining the transmitted wisdom). The teacher is admonished not to waste the precious teaching (*dharma*) on a student who is an unsuitable vessel. (Feuerstein, 2001, p. 17)

A similar selectivity existed also in other traditions (see Feuerstein, 2001), and examples of it or of the teachers' testing attitudes can be found in many anecdotes and stories. Here is an especially drastic example (Cook, 2003, pp. 154–155). According to Zen legend, Dazu Huike, who eventually became the second Zen patriarch in China, wanted Bodhidharma, the first patriarch, to teach him. Huike had stood in the snow outside Bodhidharma's cave all night until the snow reached his waist. However, even after that demonstration of his commitment, Bodhidharma refused to teach him, saying, "How can you hope for true religion with little virtue, little wisdom, a shallow heart, and an arrogant mind? It would just be a waste of effort." (Cleary, 1999, p. 126). Finally, Huike, to prove his resolve, cut off his left arm and presented it to Bodhidharma as a token of his sincerity. Such behavior might in our times be interpreted as insane. But for one, it seems that one has to be cautious with the historical truth of Zen stories (see Chapter 9); and this story has to be interpreted in its historical context and is usually seen as showing Huike's great determination (and not as exhibiting a mental problem). Only after this act he was accepted as student. Even in recent times, some Zen monasteries in Japan still have quite harsh admission procedures meant to screen out nonsuitable applicants, as vividly described by Nonomura (2008). In sum, traditionally, the path of salvation – with meditation as its central part – was generally seen as better suited for healthy people with a strong determination to walk that path.

The Methodological Argument

Daniel Goleman and Richard Davidson, two distinguished meditation researchers, differentiate between levels of meditation practice (Goleman & Davidson, 2017, p. 3). They call the traditional practice the Level 1 path. At Level 2, practice is still deep but parts of the original Asian source (e.g., living as a monk or yogi) have been left behind. At Level 3, they place practices such as mindfulness-based stress reduction (MBSR) and transcendental meditation (TM; see Chapters 2 and 3); and finally, Level 4 is, according to Goleman and Davidson, characterized by using meditation apps or practicing easy-to-use commercialized mindfulness techniques. As can be concluded from the studies discussed in Chapter 5, many beginning meditators whose practice Goleman and Davidson (2017) would probably mainly locate at Levels 3 and 4, search for help with their problems and not for spiritual salvation. Meditation as a therapeutic tool visibly entered the scientific literature only in the late 1970s (Perez-De-Albeniz & Holmes, 2000), led particularly by proponents of the TM and later by the "mindfulness movement" initiated most prominently by Jon Kabat-Zinn (1990, 2003). Meditators from nonclinical and clinical populations presumably have (on average) different backgrounds and different motivations. These differences could have a strong impact on the effects of meditation.

Even if effect sizes for meditators from both populations were comparable in size, this would not necessarily mean they were also comparable in meaning. Imagine, for instance, a very anxious or very depressed person. What happens if this person just waits for some days? Chances are that anxiety and depression decrease on their own, an effect often termed spontaneous remission or (in statistical terms) regression toward the mean. If one assumes that patients begin their treatment (meditation in this case) when they are feeling really bad, this would mean that the measured effects of meditation could be strongly exaggerated. Now imagine such a person having to learn a new technique under these unfavorable circumstances. Learning might be severely impeded and, if at all successful, take considerably longer than for a nonanxious and nondepressed person. This should especially be the case if the meditators are to direct their attention to their anxiety and depression, as is the case in many variants of mindfulness meditation. Thus, if clinical studies exhibit effects comparable to those obtained with healthy practitioners, this would not necessarily mean that the effects are really comparable, but they could be a combination of reduced effects and spontaneous remission (enlarged effects). But motivation and discipline might also be higher in patients than in healthy people who just want to "try out" meditation. In any case, mixing the results, as in meta-analyses that average out effects from both populations, might yield a distorted picture.

Therefore, we will start with the default view that the more generalizable effects of meditation are those shown by practitioners from nonclinical populations. The respective results from studies with meditators in clinical contexts will be dealt with in Chapter 7. Chapter 8 will then give a brief overview of further selected effects; and some very specific effects concerning experienced meditators will be discussed in later chapters, along with the respective theories to which these effects relate to.

General Psychological Effects

The most comprehensive meta-analysis for healthy (nonclinical) adult practitioners still seems to be our own (Sedlmeier et al., 2012), which summarizes studies from the 1970s through September 2011. Of the 595 studies identified for that period, only 163 could be included, partly due to severe methodological problems in the remaining ones. The first surprise in summarizing these studies was the sheer number of different dependent measures. Even after combining very similar measures, we still came up with 133 codes. As this seemed not feasible for further analysis, we reduced these 133 codes to 21 categories. It turned out that effects in book chapters (almost entirely stemming from studies run by members of the TM movement) were systematically larger than those in journal articles (see also Sedlmeier et al., 2014). Therefore, to avoid confounding the impact of meditation with publication outlet, we analyzed only the remaining 125 studies published in journal articles. Figure 6.1 summarizes the results. The largest effect ($\bar{d}=0.98$) was found for dependent measures that referred to improvement in interpersonal relationships, and the smallest ($\bar{d}=0.06$) to "neutral" personality measures, such as extraversion, conservativeness, or sociability.[13] The confidence interval crossing the null effect (Figure 6.1) indicates that meditation did not have a reliable effect on these "neutral" personality measures but yielded positive effects on all other outcomes (the higher the effect d, the more positive the effect, irrespective of the original coding of the variables).

Looking at the magnitudes of specific effects shown in Figure 6.1, one can get the impression that there was a tendency (with several exceptions) for emotional variables (i.e., state anxiety, negative emotions, and neuroticism) to score the highest, followed by attentional and cognitive varia-

---

[13] Effect sizes should always be interpreted in the specific context. Even across psychological areas, average effect sizes differ considerably (Schäfer & Schwarz, 2019). If there is no clear standard of comparison yet, as is the case in meditation research, often the traditional conventions introduced by Jacob Cohen (1988) are used – small: $d=.2$, medium: $d=.5$, and large: $d=.8$ (d is a standard deviation unit).

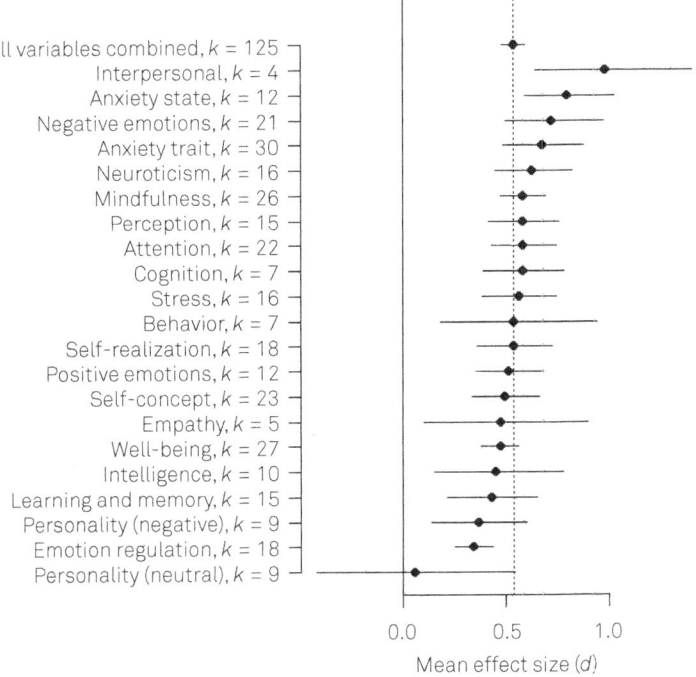

Figure 6.1. Effect sizes (*d*) averaged over *k* studies (out of 125) for different dependent variables. The vertical dotted line indicates the overall effect size of $\bar{d} = 0.54$, and error bars show 95% confidence intervals. Data have been modified (original "*r*"s transformed into "*d*"s). Adapted from Sedlmeier et al. (2012).

bles (i.e., mindfulness, perception, attention, and cognition), with personality variables (i.e., self-concept, intelligence, and negative personality) exhibiting the lowest effects. Neuroticism and trait anxiety could, of course, also have been grouped under negative personality. Keeping them as separate categories was a pragmatic decision because of the relatively large number of studies that reported effects for these variables. The number of other specific negative personality variables was too small to warrant further analysis, and therefore these variables were summarized in one category. Note that all outcomes except "neutral" personality traits can be conceived in a positive–negative dimension, and therefore one may conclude that meditation has generally positive effects on healthy practitioners. (Whether increasing or decreasing scores can be interpreted as positive depends, of course, on the variable in question. For instance, low anxiety and strong attention would both be considered positive, and high anxiety and weak attention negative.) Is this a stable finding? There are at least two ways to find an answer to this question. First, one has to check whether the effect is due to meditation or to some other factors correlated with meditation practice, and second, as always in science, findings need to be replicated.

Active Controls and Replication

If meditation groups are compared with conventional control groups, which was mostly the case in the studies included in Sedlmeier et al. (2012), the effects identified might be due to relaxation, positive thinking, cognitive training, or just social factors such as meeting regularly with a group of people one finds sympathetic, or a multitude of other potential factors. (Please note, conventional control groups were not uniform. In the extreme form, they might be waitlist controls, while other conventional control groups just met and, for instance, listened to talks or watched a movie. However, none of them contained any interventions that could be expected to yield effects similar to those of meditation.) To control for such potential confounding variables, so-called active control groups are increasingly used in meditation research. At this point, it makes sense to recall that Herbert Benson had argued that meditation is nothing but a relaxation response (Benson, 1993; see also Chapters 4 and 10). If that was the case, the effects of meditation should not exceed those of relaxation trainings. Similar arguments could be made for other active control groups – for instance, the effects of meditation could be equated with cognitive training of some sort. Of the 125 studies in our analysis, 16 had used such active control groups (some studies more than one). Figure 6.2 shows that, excluding the variable self-realization, meditation looks to be more than cognitive training [Well-being (cog) and Neuroticism (cog)] and relaxation (all other comparisons). However, effects are comparatively smaller (compare Figure 6.2 to the respective effects in Figure 6.1). This might indicate that meditation encompasses elements of both relaxation and cognitive training. Effect sizes for meditation groups compared with active controls ranged from $\bar{d} - 0.61$ (state anxiety) to $\bar{d} = 0.23$ (self-realization).

To examine whether the effects found in Sedlmeier et al. (2012) could be replicated, we conducted a follow-up meta-analysis covering the years 2011 to 2015, again concentrating on psychological effects of meditation for healthy adults (Sedlmeier et al., 2018). Because it was clear from the results of the previous meta-analysis that effects for conventional and active control groups differ substantially (compare Figure 6.1 and Figure 6.2), this time, we analyzed effects separately, for the two types of comparisons (Figure 6.3). Of the 65 studies that could be included in the analysis, 54 used conventional controls, whereas 16 used active ones (some studies did both).

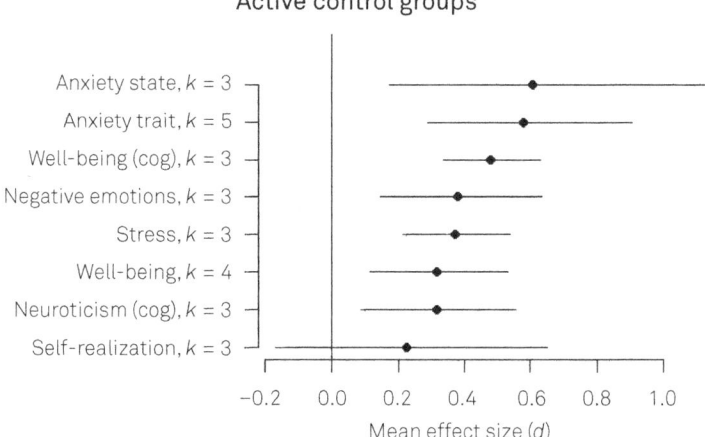

Figure 6.2. Effect sizes (d) averaged over k studies with active control groups (out of 16, multiple comparisons possible) for different dependent variables. Error bars show 95 % confidence intervals; (cog) = cognitive training. Data have been modified (original "r"s transformed into "d"s). Adapted from Sedlmeier et al. (2012).

At a first glimpse, the overall effect of $\bar{d}=0.56$ for comparisons with conventional controls is quite comparable to the overall $\bar{d}=0.54$ in Sedlmeier et al. (2012), in which most studies compared meditators with conventional control groups. As before, the effects do not vanish when meditation groups are compared with active controls that had received, for instance, attentional or educational training or different forms of relaxation training (Figure 6.3, below). However, effects for active controls are no longer reliable (lower end of 95% confidence interval covers 0) for state anxiety (which had a rather strong effect in the previous meta-analysis) and trait mindfulness. Turning to comparisons with conventional controls (Figure 6.3, above), we find that even there, state anxiety as well as depression were on average not found to be reliably reduced by meditation. Moreover, other emotional variables (negative emotions and trait anxiety) exhibited rather small effects, in contrast to previous findings.

What could be reasons for this discrepancy? A tentative explanation for the variations in the effects of mindfulness might be the diversity of measures in the different studies (see Chapter 2), which had to be summarized in the meta-analyses. But diversity of measures alone cannot explain all of the other differences. Did anything else change over the years? It seems like one change that might help to explain the variance was the shifting predominance of different approaches in meditation research. Whereas in the 1970s and 1980s, TM dominated research, later, mindfulness med-

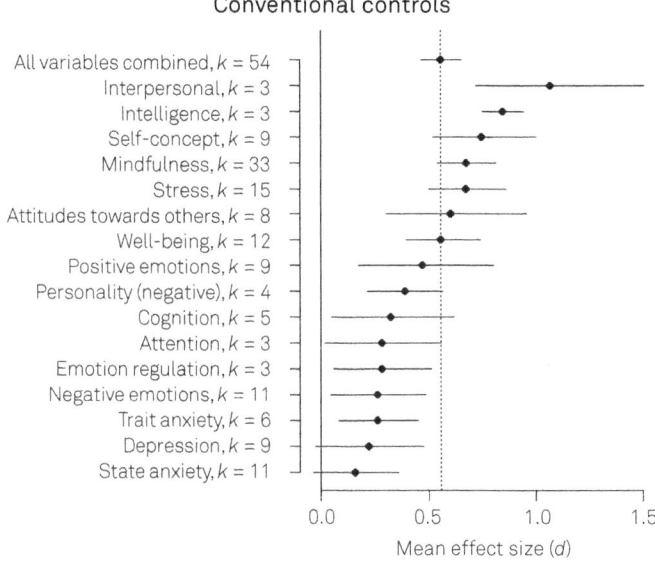

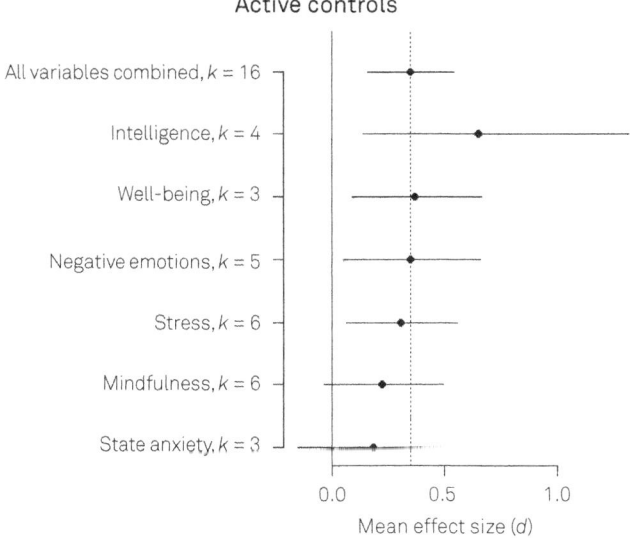

Figure 6.3. Effect sizes (d) averaged over k studies with conventional (out of 54, top) and active control groups (out of 16, bottom) for different dependent variables (multiple comparisons possible). The vertical dotted lines indicate the overall effect size of $\bar{d} = 0.56$ (top), and $\bar{d} = 0.35$ (bottom), and error bars show 95% confidence intervals. Data have been modified (original "r"s transformed into "d"s). Adapted from Sedlmeier et al. (2018).

itation eventually came to be the market leader. Could that have made a difference?

Different Kinds of Meditation

In our first meta-analysis, we could only make a rough distinction between Buddhist-based meditation regimens and TM. The overall mean effect sizes for these two groups of studies were $\bar{d}=0.54$ ($k=46$) and $\bar{d}=0.56$ ($k=36$), respectively (the remaining studies could not be properly categorized because the approaches were either idiosyncratic or numbered fewer than three, which we had set as a limit for meta-analytical examination). However, not all categories of variables were examined by both groups of studies. Figure 6.4 shows the results for the 10 categories that could be compared between these two groups of studies.

Note that several categories of variables were only examined in studies that used Buddhist approaches, such as stress ($\bar{d}=0.75$) and mindfulness ($\bar{d}=0.72$). Keeping that in mind, there are clear differences in effect sizes to be seen in Figure 6.4. Meditators who used Buddhist-based practices improved more with respect to negative personality traits than TM meditators, whereas practicing TM led to more strongly decreased scores in neuroticism and negative emotions. Thus, barring one study, the absence of TM studies in the later meta-analysis might have contributed to the decreased overall effect sizes for emotional variables (Figure 6.3).

In an additional meta-analysis (Eberth & Sedlmeier, 2012), we analyzed the group of Buddhist approaches in a bit more detail, using a set of 39 studies (conventional control groups only) that had a large overlap with the studies in Sedlmeier et al. (2012). The only group of specific Buddhist approaches that reached a noteworthy number of studies was MBSR ($k=17$), so it was compared with all other Buddhist-based approaches combined. In this summary comparison, MBSR clearly did better than the other approaches with respect to well-being. In contrast, other Buddhist approaches combined seemed to increase trait mindfulness more than MBSR did (Figure 6.5).

It seems that awareness of the importance of the specific approach to meditation has increased over time. In our later meta-analysis (Sedlmeier et al., 2018), we found that the authors gave much more detailed information about the respective meditation approaches used. However because the number of studies was not that large, a comparison of effects was only possible by looking at the average effect sizes across studies, irrespective of the specific variables used in those studies, and using only conventional control groups. Thus, the differences between the effects for MBSR and other Buddhist-related approaches to meditation shown in Figure 6.6 must be regarded with some caution, although they might still be deemed informative.

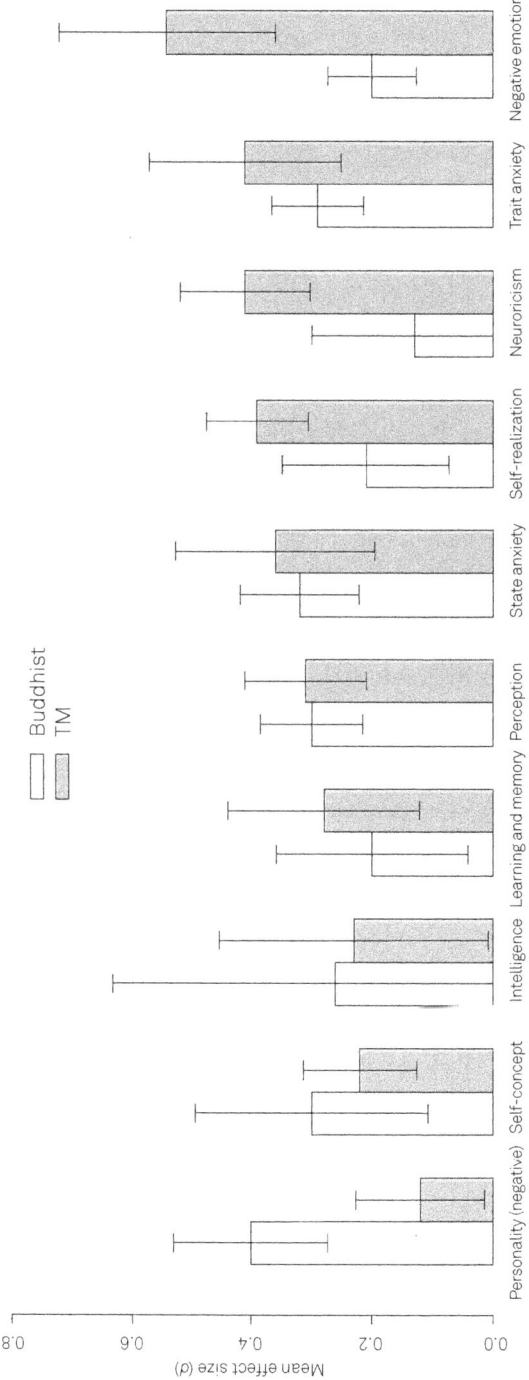

Figure 6.4. Mean effect sizes (d) for 10 variable categories, compared for Buddhist-based approaches and transcendental meditation (TM). Error bars show 95% confidence intervals. Data have been modified (original "r"s transformed into "d"s). Adapted from Sedlmeier et al. (2012).

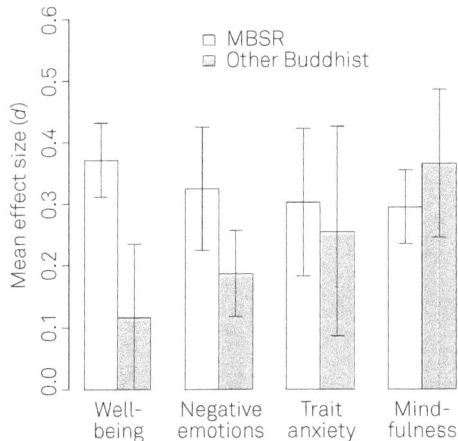

Figure 6.5. Mean effect sizes (*d*) for four variable categories, compared for mindfulness-based stress reduction (MBSR) and other Buddhist-based approaches. Error bars show 95% confidence intervals. Data have been modified (original "*r*"s transformed into "*d*"s). Adapted from Eberth and Sedlmeier (2012).

From the descriptions in Chapters 1 to 3, the reader should be acquainted with most categories in Figure 6.6, except *mixed approaches* (two or more approaches mixed), *strong body component*" (meditation approaches other than MBSR that included a body component such as body scan), and *mindfulness interventions* (ad hoc mindfulness interventions, such as a "mindful breathing training"). Vipassana meditation (different varieties) turned out to have the strongest average effects ($\bar{d}=0.90$), whereas MBSR scored lower than average.

Other Potential Influences

The meta-analyses included both randomized and nonrandomized group comparisons. The usual expectation is that randomized designs yield smaller effects (e.g., because of an initial selection process in nonrandomized designs, members in the meditation groups may be more interested in meditation). However, the differences in effect sizes were negligible in that respect, in all analyses. Another plausible expectation is that the more experienced the meditators, the higher the effects. This was only partially the case in Sedlmeier et al. (2012). For the studies that used matched control groups, effects increased for meditation experience up to 10 years, with the largest gains in the first 4 years, and decreased again after 10 years. For the designs with concurrent randomized control groups, effects only in-

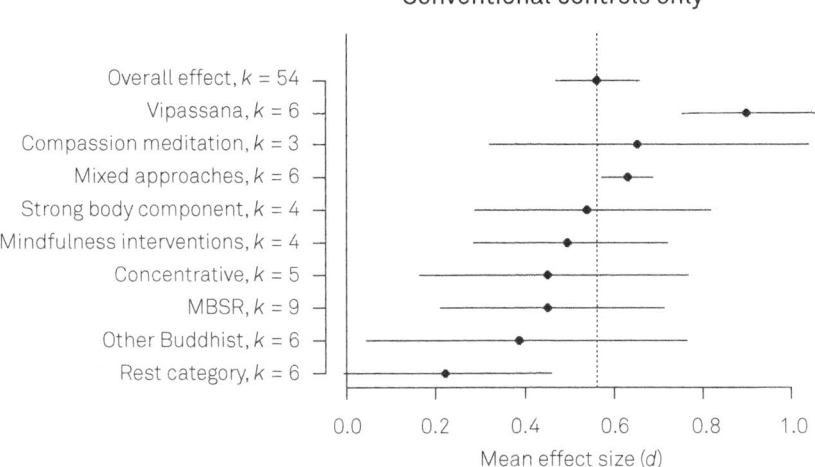

Figure 6.6. Mean effect sizes (d) for different meditation approaches. The vertical dotted line indicates the overall effect size of $\bar{d} = 0.56$, and error bars show 95% confidence intervals. Data have been modified (original "r"s transformed into "d"s). MBSR = mindfulness-based stress reduction. Adapted from Sedlmeier et al. (2018).

creased for the first month. This was different for the studies in Sedlmeier et al. (2018). In those studies, meditation experience had a clear impact on effect sizes for all designs. This difference might be at least in part due to the better quality and greater homogeneity of studies in the more recent analysis. With regards the effect size, there was one partial exception: For the active control groups, effects first diminished from 1 day to about 1 month and then increased again. The most plausible explanation of that pattern seems to be a placebo effect. If practitioners "know" that meditation works, this might have a very strong influence on their judgments and ratings at the beginning, but they may not be able to uphold that belief over several weeks, and thus the initially strong placebo effects would be expected to fade away until the observed effects increased again but this time due to real meditation effects.

Recapitulation

What do the results in these meta-analyses tell us? One has to use some caution in interpreting them because even in the more detailed analyses, effects have been averaged over variables with potentially different outcomes. To begin with, the categories dealt with in these meta-analyses are themselves potentially heterogeneous. A case in point are the many variations of trait mindfulness (see Chapter 2) summarized in a single category. But a similar point can be made for most of the categories of dependent variables dealt with. Even if we assumed that these categories are homogeneous, the effects of meditation on, say, the category "negative emotions" have been summarized over different approaches to meditation, and the effects for, say, MBSR, have been summarized over different categories of dependent variables. There might be some systematicness concerning the relation between a given approach to meditation and dependent measures (and, maybe, also kind of people who practice it). Yet, there is no obvious selectivity of this sort to be observed in the studies that went into the meta-analyses. Thus, at the moment, it seems sensible to assume that the ensuing biases might not be very systematic and not too strong.

Given these assumptions, a first conclusion is that meditation yields generally positive effects for healthy practitioners. These effects are larger than effects of relaxation exercises or cognitive trainings, although meditation might encompass similar mechanisms. There is also a huge variation in the sizes of the effects for different dependent variables, and there are differences in the effects from different approaches to meditation.

However, there is some covariation between meditation approaches and dependent measures. This becomes especially evident if we compare the effect sizes for emotional variables in the 2012 (high) and 2018 (low) meta-analyses. The issue is exemplified in the category "negative emotions" (compare Figure 6.1, Figure 6.3, Figure 6.4, and Figure 6.5). It seems that the difference in effect sizes is at least in part due to a difference in effects between mantra meditation (TM) and (more traditional) Buddhist mindfulness meditation. One plausible explanation for the difference might be that mantra meditation draws the meditator's attention away from negative emotions or anxiety, whereas mindfulness meditation makes them more aware of unpleasant inner processes. And why are the effects of Vipassana so much higher than, say, those of MBSR (Figure 6.6)? The answer to this question might be rather trivial. Vipassana is usually practiced with considerably higher intensity than most other forms of meditation practiced in the West. For instance, in the Goenka method (see Chapter 3), it is recommended that even outside retreats, meditators should practice for 2 hr each day (Hart, 1987).[14] In sum, although these meta-analyses give first answers to basic questions of the psychological effects of meditation for healthy practitioners, they generate many new ones that have partly been addressed in numerous studies since then. A portion of these studies has been summarized

---

14 The effort may pay off though: Harari (2019, pp. 363–364), who himself practices vipassana Goenka style, contends that without meditating regularly for 2 hr each day, he could not have completed his best-selling books *Sapiens* and *Homo Deus*.

in meta-analyses that have examined quite specific groups and used fewer dependent measures that were deemed practically relevant for that group. Some of these meta-analyses have also included studies without control groups (pre-post measurements only). If these could not be clearly separated from control group designs, the respective results are omitted in the following.

More Specific Psychological Results

Meditation in the Workplace

Meditation, or rather mindfulness training Western style, is increasingly deployed in the workplace. Bartlett et al. (2019) summarized the effects from 23 studies. They found beneficial effects for mindfulness ($\bar{g}=0.45$), stress ($\bar{g}=0.56$), anxiety ($\bar{g}=0.62$), psychological distress ($\bar{g}=0.69$), well-being ($\bar{g}=0.46$), and sleep ($\bar{g}=0.26$).[15] For some additional dependent variables that might be considered especially relevant in the context of work, they could not calculate meaningful effect sizes nor draw firm conclusions. This was due to ambivalence in results (for burnout), publication bias (for depression), and insufficient data (for work performance).

There are also meta-analyses that have focused on specific categories of employees. For instance, Dharmawardene et al. (2016) collected studies that examined the effects of meditation (Vipassana, Zen, MBSR, and mindfulness-based interventions, with an average duration of interventions of about 8 weeks) on health care professionals and caregivers. Results for pre-post studies were omitted because of their low internal validity and because they are not comparable to comparisons between controls and meditation groups (because they rely on dependent measures; see Sedlmeier & Renkewitz, 2018, p. 425). Data are taken from the supplementary material provided on the Internet. There was only one dependent measure in common for both groups, self-efficacy, with high effects for both ($\bar{d}=0.72$ and $\bar{d}=0.80$, respectively). Controlled trials of health professionals showed improvements in emotional exhaustion ($\bar{d}=0.37$), personal accomplishment

---

15 Both d and g are standardized mean differences (or standard deviation units). The two measures only differ with respect to how the (pooled) standard deviation is calculated, by which the mean difference is divided: for d, sample standard deviations are used, and for g estimates of population standard deviations, which amounts to either dividing the sum of squares by n or $n-1$, for d and g, respectively (see Sedlmeier & Renkewitz, 2018, p. 293). Thus, g is always smaller than d, but with increasing n, the difference is negligible. It is of note that g and d are frequently mixed up in the literature.

($\bar{d}$=1.18), and life satisfaction ($\bar{d}$=0.48). Caregivers improved in depression ($\bar{d}$=0.49), anxiety ($\bar{d}$=0.53), and stress ($\bar{d}$=0.49). Burton et al. (2017), summarizing the effects of mindfulness-based interventions for reducing stress among health care professionals, found an effect of $\bar{d}$=0.73 (transformed from original $\bar{r}$=0.342), which was even a bit larger than the $\bar{g}$=0.55 found by Khoury et al. (2015) for a nonselected sample of healthy adults.

In sum, with the possible exception of personal accomplishment, which yielded very strong effects, effect sizes were in the same range as those found in previous meta-analyses of meditation effects for heterogeneous adult samples.

Meditation in Schools

Several meta-analyses have summarized the effects of mindfulness-based interventions carried out in schools. The first of these (Zenner et al., 2014) considered studies published until October 2012 and found small effects for study-relevant variables (emotional problems: $\bar{g}$=0.19, stress: $\bar{g}$=0.39, factors of resilience: $\bar{g}$=0.36, and third person ratings: $\bar{g}$=0.25), with the exception of cognitive performance ($\bar{g}$=0.80) (effects for pre-post comparisons performed only on the meditation group were again omitted). Rather small effects were also found in a more recent meta-analysis (Carsley et al., 2018). Effects aggregated over the categories of mental health (anxiety, depression, stress) and well-being (k=21 studies) amounted to $\bar{g}$=0.24. These effects were slightly larger for students in late-adolescence (15-18 years), if external advisers (and not the teachers) conducted the mindfulness interventions, as well as for girls. A recent meta-analysis that concentrated on anxiety as the dependent measure (Odgers et al., 2020) found no impact of meditation ($\bar{d}$=0.05), if one outlying value was omitted. These results are consistent with the summary effect of del=0.20 found for nonclinical youth samples not connected to a school context in a meta-analysis by Zoogman et al. (2015).[16]

These are obviously quite small effects as compared with the general adult population, and the difference becomes especially evident when results for students are compared with those for teachers. For the latter, Klingbeil and Renshaw (2018) found effects of mindfulness-based interventions comparable to those in previous meta-analyses (mindfulness: $\bar{g}$=0.70, mechanisms of mindfulness: $\bar{g}$=0.44, well-being: $\bar{g}$=0.43, stress: $\bar{g}$=0.55, with the nota-

---

16 The effect size del is roughly comparable to d and g but is calculated by subtracting the change score – that is, the standardized pre-post difference – of the control group from that of the treatment group. The procedure allows for imputing missing values (see Becker, 1988).

ble exception of classroom climate and instructional practices: $\bar{g}=0.31$). Another meta-analysis on the topic (Zarate et al., 2019) yielded similar results (mindfulness: $\bar{d}=0.94$, stress: $\bar{d}=0.53$, anxiety $\bar{d}=0.52$, burnout: $\bar{d}=0.33$, and depression: $\bar{d}=0.67$).

Overall, it seems that school students (as well as youths in general) profited less from mindfulness-based interventions than teachers, even though many of the mindfulness interventions summarized in the respective meta-analyses were custom-tailored to student needs.

Meditation for Older Adults

Does older adults' (aged 60 or above) cognitive performance improve if they practice meditation or mind–body exercises? This was the question pursued in a meta-analysis by Chan et al. (2019). The short answer was "yes," and the overall effect size, averaged over 41 studies was $\bar{g}=0.34$. However, there were pronounced differences depending on the type of practice and also on the type of cognitive performance looked at. The authors divided type of practice into four categories and found the highest average effect for qigong ($\bar{g}=0.72$), followed by "meditation" (presumably some sort of mindfulness meditation) ($\bar{g}=0.41$), tai chi ($\bar{g}=0.19$), and yoga ($\bar{g}=0.15$). Regarding specific aspects of cognition, qigong did best for short-term memory and executive function, whereas meditation was better for attention, and (very slightly) for working memory. This meta-analysis also included samples of participants with mild cognitive impairment, for whom the effects were somewhat larger than for fully healthy practitioners. In addition, the results indicate that cognitive performance is only markedly improved when the length of exercise program is medium to long (> 12 weeks), exercise frequency is medium to high (3–7 times/week), and duration of an exercise session is not too short or too long (> 45 to ≤ 60 min/session).

In another meta-analysis, Weber et al. (2020) summarized the effects of meditative movements (tai chi and qigong) and other mind–body interventions (yoga and Pilates) on several dependent measures for participants without mental illnesses aged ≥ 59 years. For studies examining the effects of tai chi and qigong, they found a positive impact on quality of life (overall: $\bar{g}=0.42$, physical $\bar{g}=0.27$, psychological $\bar{g}=0.39$, social $\bar{g}=0.31$), depressive symptoms ($\bar{g}=0.16$), fear of falling ($\bar{g}=0.79$), and sleep quality ($\bar{g}=0.46$). Meditative movements yielded generally higher effects than other mind–body interventions, except for depressive symptoms.

It seems that all or most of the studies reviewed used conventional control groups, for which relatively large effects are expected for adult populations. Therefore, a (very coarse) comparison with previous results for healthy adults indicates that overall effects might be somewhat smaller for older people than for heterogeneous groups of adults. There is also some indication that meditation including movements, such as walking meditation, might be more beneficial for older persons than meditation alone (Chan et al., 2019) or movement alone (Weber et al., 2020).

Specific Groups

That meditation is very widespread is evidenced by the fact that meta-analyses have already been conducted for partly quite specific groups of people. Here are three of them.

Tertiary Education Students

There have been several meta-analyses on effects of meditation on tertiary education students. Some of these did not differentiate between healthy and clinical populations (Bamber & Morpeth, 2019; Gonzáles-Valero et al., 2019; Halladay et al., 2019) and are therefore excluded here. However, one meta-analysis summarized 24 research reports that examined the effects of meditation, yoga, and mindfulness on depression, anxiety, and stress in tertiary education students with nonclinical samples, barring one study (Breedvelt et al., 2019). For comparisons with conventional controls, the authors found results comparable to those for the general adult population (depression: $\bar{g} = 0.42$, anxiety: $\bar{g} = 0.46$, stress: $\bar{g} = 0.42$), although effects were small and unreliable if active controls were used for comparison.

Pregnant Women

Dhillon et al. (2017) summarized the effects of 16 mindfulness interventions of 6 to 9 weeks for pregnant women. The majority of these studies used pre-post measurements, but some compared intervention and control groups. For these, the authors found effects for anxiety ($\bar{d} = 0.31$), depression ($\bar{d} = 0.78$), stress ($\bar{d} = 1.23$), and mindfulness ($\bar{d} = 0.57$). However, the few studies that could be summarized varied widely in their effects (e.g., outliers of $d = 2.78$ for depression, and of $d = 4.11$ for stress – the above values are therefore most plausibly strongly exaggerated), and none of the effects except mindfulness were reliable (confidence intervals covered the null effect).

Family Caregivers of Persons With Dementia

Even for such a special group of people, seven randomized controlled trials could be summarized by Liu et al. (2017). The authors found reliable effects (confidence intervals not covering the null effect) of mindfulness interventions for depression ($\bar{d}=0.58$), perceived stress ($\bar{d}=0.33$), and health-related quality of life ($\bar{d}=0.38$), but not for anxiety ($\bar{d}=0.31$), and no effect for caregiver burden ($\bar{d}=0.08$).

The last two groups of people obviously live in a highly demanding setting. The comparatively small effects found might indicate that such circumstances can have a diminishing impact on the power of mindfulness-based interventions.

Prosociality

Kirby et al. (2017) examined the effects of compassion-based interventions with (mostly) nonclinical samples (they did not report results separately for the two groups, but it seems that the results in the clinical studies did not systematically distort the overall effects). The 21 studies identified (2005 to 2017) from all over the world allowed for a comparison of compassion-based interventions with waitlist and active controls. These comparisons yielded substantial effect sizes (first effect size for waitlist controls, second for active controls): self-report measures of compassion ($\bar{d}=0.55/0.55$), self-compassion ($\bar{d}=0.70/0.60$), mindfulness ($\bar{d}=0.54/0.46$), depression ($\bar{d}=0.64/0.62$), anxiety ($\bar{d}=0.49/0.42$), psychological distress ($\bar{d}=0.47/0.40$), and well-being ($\bar{d}=0.51/0.48$). Unfortunately, the authors do not detail which kind of activity participants in the active control groups performed. Further, rather surprisingly, the kind of control groups did not seem to play a big role: Effects for studies with active control groups were only slightly smaller than those for conventional ones. Moreover, it seems that the effects for compassion and self-compassion were not substantially larger than the effects for other dependent measures less related to the training regimen.

Several meta-analyses have looked at prosocial effects of different kinds of meditation. Kreplin et al. (2018) included all 16 studies with healthy practitioners from 2004 to 2015 that examined the effects of meditation (mindfulness-based interventions, including Zen, loving kindness meditation, and compassion meditation, but no approaches with movement) on measures of prosociality. They report effects for compassion ($\bar{d}=0.80$), connectedness ($\bar{d}=0.45$), empathy ($\bar{d}=0.98$), aggression ($\bar{d}=0.22$), and prejudice ($\bar{d}=0.22$). (For the sake of comparison, the original effect sizes (r) were transformed into d values.) Unfortunately, Kreplin et al. (2018) did not differentiate between different forms of meditation.

The effects in another meta-analysis (Luberto et al., 2018) are hard to interpret because they only report effects from 26 studies pooled to include different populations (including studies with children), meditators with different amounts of experiences, different kinds of meditation interventions, and different formats (group and individual practice). Despite that heterogeneity, they performed a fixed effects meta-analysis that assumed the existence of a single underlying population. Their results for comparisons with active controls were $\bar{d}=0.48$ for objective outcomes and $\bar{d}=0.43$ for subjective outcomes of prosociality. Another meta-analysis (Donald et al., 2019) examined the effects of mindfulness meditation (31 studies) on prosocial behavior (self-reports and observer reports). The authors made a distinction between mindfulness-only and mindfulness-plus-prosocial-emotions interventions, and also differentiated between age groups. Overall, they found $\bar{d}=0.53$ for mindfulness-only studies and $\bar{d}=0.51$ for studies that examined the effects of mindfulness interventions augmented by loving kindness or compassion meditation. The results for adults (age 25+) were highest ($\bar{d}=0.68$), followed by those for children (< 12 years: $\bar{d}=0.55$), adolescents (12 to 18 years: $\bar{d}=0.43$), and emerging adults (18 to 25 years: $\bar{d}=0.34$). A recent meta-analysis (Berry et al., 2020) found an overall effect of mindfulness meditation (excluding ethics-cased interventions) of $\bar{g}=0.43$. Looking at different aspects of prosocial behavior, there were marked differences. The effects for compassionate behavior were highest ($\bar{g}=0.55$), followed by less proneness to retaliation ($\bar{g}=0.54$), decreases in prejudice ($\bar{g}=0.46$), and instrumental helping behavior ($\bar{g}=0.27$), and there was basically no effect for generosity ($\bar{g}=0.03$). Interestingly, average effects for comparisons with active controls were even somewhat larger than those with conventional control groups.

The overall picture emerging from these meta-analyses seems to be quite clear. First, loving kindness and compassion meditation might in general be as suited as "pure" mindfulness training to elicit nonspecific effects – that is, effects for nonprosocial-dependent measures. And second, "pure" mindfulness interventions yield increases in prosocial variables that are comparable to those found for specific kinds of prosocially oriented kinds of meditation. Again, we have some indication that mindfulness meditation (possibly including mindfulness-plus-prosocial-emotions interventions) has smaller effects for adolescents than for adults.

Personality as a Moderator

The reader may already have been wondering about the question, how does personality impact meditation effects? Unfortunately, as yet, there seems to be no meta-analysis covering this topic. The main reason for this state of affairs is probably the scarcity of studies. Note that the effect in question here is a moderator effect – that is, the question of how strongly the size of the meditation effect is moderated by the variance in personality variables. To give you a first impression on the topic, I will present some selected results. Individual effect sizes might not be so informative here and are therefore omitted.[17]

In a study of medical and psychology students, de Vibe et al. (2015) examined whether the effects of MBSR on mental distress, study stress, and subjective well-being were moderated by participants' neuroticism, conscientiousness, extroversion, and trait mindfulness [using the Five Facet Mindfulness Questionnaire (FFMQ)]. Students higher on neuroticism profited more in reducing mental distress and increasing their well-being, and those with higher scores on conscientiousness experienced less study stress, as a result of the meditation intervention. Trait mindfulness and extroversion did not show any pronounced moderating effects. Gawrysiak et al. (2017) examined the effects of different facets of trait mindfulness (see Chapter 2) on pre-post effects of an MBSR program on stress, positive affect, and negative affect. They found that lower acceptance and decentering predicted greater decreases in stress; and higher awareness, acceptance, and decentering went along with larger increases in positive affect. Negative affect had higher reductions when participants' awareness was higher, and decentering scores were lower.

Noone and Hogan (2018) administered a guided mindfulness meditation program to psychology students and found that need for cognition had a sizeable impact on how strong the effects of mindfulness meditation were on critical thinking skills: The higher the need for cognition, the higher the improvements. Goldin and Jazaieri (2020) examined the potential effects of many moderator variables on the impact of compassion meditation on improvements in three forms of fear of compassion (for self, for others, and being the recipient of compassion from others). They identified such moderators only for fear of compassion for self: emotion suppression frequency, reappraisal self-efficacy, and perceived stress (but not reappraisal frequency, suppression self-efficacy, or self-esteem).

Personality factors might also determine which kind of meditation people chose, at least initially. Tang and Braver (2020) examined the question of whether personality characteristics predicted preferences for one of "four prototypical mindfulness techniques" – that is, focused attention, open monitoring, loving kindness, and body scan. It turned out that after participants had been exposed to audio-guided instructions for each of the four techniques, preferences for loving kindness meditation were predicted by empathy, whereas preferences for open monitoring were predicted by nonreactivity and nonjudgment (two facets of trait mindfulness, see Chapter 2).

---

17 Note that in this case, effect sizes do not express the effect of meditation but the effect of personality on the size of the meditation effect. Moreover, as studies differ widely in many respects, these moderator effects would not really be comparable across studies.

What can we conclude from this sample of studies? Probably not much in detail because of the vast heterogeneity of variables and procedures. However, at least some strong moderating effects were found in all studies, which makes it plausible to expect a substantial impact of personality on the effects of meditation, in addition to kind of meditation and context.

Recapitulation

A general aspect of many specific meta-analyses reported above is the high level of heterogeneity of the effects, which means that a substantial amount of their variance is *not* explained by the meditation effect alone. (The details have been omitted because the many numbers would have made the text even harder to read. A measure often used in the meta-analyses is I^2, which indicates the amount of variance not explained by sampling error. Higgins et al. (2003) suggest values of 25%, 50%, and 75% as indicators of small, moderate and large heterogeneity. Most effects in the meta-analyses summarized in this paragraph fall into the last category.) Some candidate explanations for the heterogeneity of effect sizes can be dealt with by focusing on more specific groups and dependent variables. Other potential explanations, such as the specific (combinations of) techniques used, the context in which meditation is done, the motivation to meditate, and meditators' personalities might help to reduce the remaining heterogeneity. However, on a coarse level, some tentative conclusions can already be drawn from these results. First, it seems like a meditator's age makes a difference, at least in the mindfulness-based interventions that dominated the empirical research summarized in the meta-analyses. Children and adolescents and, to a lesser degree, older people might not profit as much from mindfulness meditation as do adults up to about 60 years. The 60-year-old cutoff is, of course, not an exact boundary. It only follows the restrictions made in studies about the effects of meditation on older people. So far, it is unclear whether people aged 20 to 60 differ in how well they respond to mindfulness meditation.

Studies that have examined meditation in the context of workplace and schools did not show effects that deviated markedly from that pattern. This age effect might be due to an approximately inverted U-shaped curve of sustained attention across the lifespan (Fortenbaugh et al., 2015), but other explanations are also possible. For instance, it might be more demanding for older people to learn and practice a given meditation technique. Or could it be, for instance, that directing one's attention to unpleasant aspects of one's life, as might often be the case in some forms of mindfulness meditation, is even more unfavorable for young (and maybe also older) people than for adults in the middle age range? If so, education officials might want to think about programs that place an emphasis on meditation techniques that, at least in the beginning, take meditators' attention away from their problems, such as mantra meditation (e.g., Bringmann et al., 2020; Matko et al., 2021b) or meditation in movement. Especially the latter, in combination with some kind of sitting meditation, seems to be better suited for older people than mindfulness practice alone.

Another interesting finding is that it apparently does not make much difference for the effects on prosocial behavior whether the meditation regimen directly addresses loving kindness and compassion or not. In addition, groups of people who might experience higher levels of stress (e.g., pregnant women, family caregivers of patients with dementia) exhibit lower gains. That could be due to the fact that meditation has to be learnt and that this might take more time under stress. And finally, recent studies indicate that personality might be an important moderator variable in examining the effects of sitting meditation. If the current scientific worldview is correct, all of these effects, or at least parts of them, should show correspondences in brain functioning. What do we know about that?

Effects on the Brain

What is an "effect on the brain"? There are several ways of looking into the brain. In the research on the effects of meditation, two methods especially, or rather families of methods, have been used: *electroencephalography* (EEG) and *magnetic resonance imaging* (MRI). EEG records electrical impulses from the nerves in the brain. "Electro" refers to the electrical impulses sent from one nerve cell to another, "encephalo" refers to the brain, and "graphy" refers to the printing of a record. In particular, EEG measures the synchronous and rhythmic electrical activity of thousands or millions of neurons that have similar spatial orientations. These electrical activities or oscillations can be characterized by typical frequency ranges that are associated with different states of brain functioning. Frequency ranges are measured in oscillations per second, a measure called a *hertz* (Hz). For instance, any rhythmic activity between 8 and 12 Hz can be described as *alpha,* and increased alpha *power* (increased amplitudes of alpha waves) is often associated with relaxation. With increasing attention, the rhythmic brain activity usually accelerates. A wakeful attentional state is characterized by a frequency band between 13 and 30 Hz, termed *beta,* and strongly focused attention is often accompanied by very fast oscillations at over 30 Hz, called *gamma* activity. A special analysis of EEG recordings can be used to examine the brain's response to the occurrence or presentation of specific stimuli or events. The brain's response to an event is then called the *event-related potential* (ERP). "Potential" here means a positive or negative deviation from a mean electrical activity of the brain. In contrast to the usual EEG activities, ERPs have very low amplitudes and therefore, stimuli need to be presented repeatedly. From many presentations of a given stimulus, the brain's responses to these presentations are then averaged, whereby the noise is filtered out, and characteristic positive and negative potentials evoked by the stimulus at hand can be seen.

MRI, the other main technique used in meditation research, produces three-dimensional images of brain structures and processes. It relies on magnetically induced changes in the brain: Nuclei of hydrogen (single protons) located in a strong magnetic field interact ("resonate") when exposed to specific high-frequency electromagnetic radiation. The way different brain tissues resonate is the basis for obtaining images of brain structures of people lying in a scanner. If MRI is used for visualizing processes (instead of structures) in the brain, it is called *functional* MRI (fMRI). In comparison with ERPs (the EEG way to map brain processes to a specific stimulus), which occur very quickly after a stimulus has been presented, fMRI measures take some time because they depend on cerebral blood flow (more oxygenated blood, less magnetic distortion and stronger resonance signals). But in contrast to ERPs, they give more exact information about where in the brain activities occur after a stimulus presentation.

Both EEG and MRI can be used to show changes in brain activity during meditation or changes induced by the presentation of a specific stimulus, but they can also be used to detect lasting differences between meditators and nonmeditators. The former (short-term during meditation) kinds of effects are usually termed *state* effects and the latter (long-term lasting differences) *trait* effects (for the same difference with respect to the construct "mindfulness," see Chapter 2). Of course, measurements of states and traits cannot be completely separated because traits may affect states and vice versa. If meditators have, for instance, as a result of their practice, acquired a more relaxed attitude toward daily hassles (trait effect), this should have an impact on how they react to an aversive stimulus (state effect), and the brain activity seen might be a mixture of both effects. On the other side, if brain activity is repeatedly modified in meditation sessions (many state effects), this might have a lasting (trait) effect. In the following, we will try to give a short overview of what is currently known about both state and trait effects of meditation on the brain.

State Effects

Electroencephalography
What happens in the brain during meditation? An early summary (M.A. West, 1980) describes typical changes in the EEG: At the beginning of a meditation session, the amplitude (power) of alpha waves increases and their frequency slows down, and even *theta* waves (4–7 Hz), usually found before falling asleep, may be seen for advanced meditators (e.g., Zen masters, see Chiesa, 2009) who, however, are fully alert. In deeper parts of meditation, there are phases with fast beta and gamma waves (20–40 Hz) that are (in contrast to the normal wakeful state) well synchronized, which can be interpreted as a sign of extremely stable concentration and alertness. These early findings have been corroborated by a later comprehensive summary of EEG studies (Cahn & Polich, 2006): During meditation, there is an increased power in the theta and alpha bands, with a general slowing down (e.g., within the alpha band, lower frequencies predominate), and an increasing synchronicity as well as an increased chance of gamma effects. These effects might be interpreted as showing increasing relaxation that however (usually) does not go hand in hand with increasing drowsiness but on the contrary with increases in attention and concentration. Pronounced gamma effects during meditation have been found for highly experienced meditators (Lutz et al., 2004), which may be connected to mystical experiences (Ott, 2010). In a later meta-analysis (Lomas et al., 2015a) that examined the neurophysiological effects of "mindfulness meditation" (including Vipassana and Zen meditation) on EEG oscillations, mostly with experienced meditators, only two consistent effects were found to some extent: If EEG during meditation was compared with EEG outside meditation with eyes closed, both alpha and theta power was enhanced. No consistent results were found for the other frequency bands. This study was later criticized by Travis (2020) who argued that Lomas et al. (2015a) did not differentiate between alpha1 (8–10 Hz) and alpha2 (10–12 Hz) and also improperly averaged results from different electrode locations, which obscured effects that, according to Travis (2020), would have shown the effectiveness of TM.

Also a special measure, alpha asymmetry (a comparison of alpha activity in the left vs. right hemisphere, especially in the prefrontal cortex) did not show consistent results (Dorjee, 2020). This conforms to the conclusion of Brandmeyer et al. (2019) who reviewed the studies on the oscillatory correlates of meditation: "While EEG has been a key methodology in the neuroscientific study meditation, no clear consensus has emerged pertaining [to] the generalizable effects of meditation on EEG activity" (Brandmeyer et al., 2019, p. 12).

State ERP effects are usually obtained by comparing the evoked potentials during meditation, with those in a period outside of meditation. There is some evidence that during meditation, the processing of auditory stimuli changes (Chiesa, 2009). This is evidenced by changes in early potentials (about 100 ms after the presentation of the stimulus), possibly indicating heightened sensitivity to sounds. Cahn and Polich (2009) examined experienced Vipassana meditators and also found differences in a later potential (about 300 ms after stimulus onset) which was larger for more experienced meditators (a trait effect!). The authors interpret this as reflecting decreased automated reactivity and evaluative processing of task-irrelevant attention-demanding stimuli. Similar effects were obtained by Biedermann et al. (2016) who concluded that low-level attention might be superior in long-term meditators in general. There seems to be some promise in further examining ERPs, especially concerning P3 amplitudes (Atchley et al., 2016). After reviewing ERP meditation research, Dorjee (2020) concluded that the results obtained to date may be indicative of improvements in meditators' control-related facets of attention.

Magnetic Resonance Imaging
Before effects (differences between meditators vs. nonmeditators; or differences during vs. outside meditation) can be compared, one first has to know where to search for such effects. The usual search method is (somewhat mistakenly) also called meta-analysis: *anatomical/activation likelihood estimation* (ALE) *meta-analysis* (e.g., Eickhoff et al., 2009; Turkeltaub et al., 2002). A bit simplified, this method scans the whole brain for nonrandom signals, based on all of the results that go into the summary analysis. So, an ALE meta-analysis can be conceived of as a data preparation method. A conventional meta-analysis is then often performed on the foci where effects have been identified by the ALE analysis. All the meta-analyses on fMRI and MRI mentioned in the following have used that data preparation method.

Boccia et al. (2015) summarized fMRI studies, solely based on ALE meta-analysis (no effect sizes calculated) and found differential activations in brain areas involved in processing self-relevant information, self-regulation, focused problem solving, adaptive behavior, and interoception.[18] The same method was used by Tomasino et al. (2014) who analyzed 18 fMRI studies, from which they generated 26 comparisons, of which 17 concerned Buddhist meditators and 9 Hindu ones (see their Table 1). Their main question

---

18 It is not clear how many independent samples went into this analysis, as their Table 1 indicates that some samples yielded several effect results.

was whether the fundamental difference between Buddhist and Hindu approaches to meditation – that is, the role of mindfulness in Buddhism (*samma sati*; see Chapter 3 in this present work) which is almost entirely missing in Hindu approaches – can also be observed in neuroimaging studies. Indeed, they found a dissociation between anterior and posterior neural networks that might be related to that difference. Buddhist meditation practices might trigger activation in frontal lobe regions associated with executive attention, whereas for Hindu practices, this might be the case for activations in the posterior temporoparietal cortex, which may be associated with different levels of absorption.

In a later summary study, ALE meta-analysis was followed by a conventional meta-analysis. Fox et al. (2016) summarized state effects found in 32 fMRI studies that examined activation differences elicited by tasks or stimuli during versus outside of meditation. They divided the relevant studies according to different meditation styles, the four most important being *focused attention*, *open monitoring*, *compassion or loving kindness*, and *mantra recitation* meditation. Meditators practiced their style of meditation when lying in the scanner. These authors found different activation patterns for different styles of meditation. During meditation, focused attention practice produced higher activity in brain regions that play a part in cognitive control and the voluntary regulation of attention, and lower activity in regions that have well-established roles in mind wandering. Open monitoring showed pronouncedly higher activations in regions connected with voluntary regulation of thought and action and decreased activation in a region associated with self-referential thought. Practitioners of loving kindness meditation had higher activations in regions associated with awareness of bodily sensations and feelings. Meditators practicing mantra meditation displayed increased activations in regions associated with planning and executing voluntary motor actions, in regions associated with speech production, and in ones connected to visual processing and mental imagery. As exemplified above for focused attention meditation, changes could be in both directions and were on average $\bar{d} = -0.59$ and $\bar{d} = 0.74$. Effects were largest for mantra meditation ($\bar{d} = 1.48$, and $\bar{d} = -1.11$) and smallest for loving kindness meditation ($\bar{d} = 0.44$, and $\bar{d} = -0.68$). The only region that was consistently activated for all styles of meditation was a brain region called the *insula* (for its location, see Figure 6.7, lower left). Activations in the insula are usually connected to the monitoring of the body, awareness of respiration, and basic metacognitive monitoring (i.e., monitoring one's own thinking). Taken together, the fMRI effects indicate that different styles of meditation might indeed yield different effects. Recently, Kim et al. (2020), using ALE meta-analysis, summarized 16 fMRI studies solely for compassion meditation. They found seven broad regions, but only one of these, the insula, had previously been identified by Fox et al. (2016) for compassion meditation. Kim et al. (2020) argue that some other regions commonly connected to compassion might not have been found due to the small number of relevant studies.

Moreover, fMRI effects seem to depend on meditation experience: Concentrating on practitioners of mindfulness meditation (in a wide sense), Falcone and Jerram (2018) found in their ALE analysis (21 studies) that novices exhibited effects only in the insula, whereas foci of consistent activity for experienced meditators could also be found in other brain regions.

Trait Effects

How do meditators differ from nonmeditators with respect to long-term effects that can be observed in daily life? Such differences in traits might be regarded as even more interesting than state effects because they can be expected to express themselves not just during or immediately after meditation. EEG trait effects found so far are quite varied and not easy to interpret (Brandmeyer et al., 2019; Cahn & Polich, 2006). Similar to state effects, it appears trait effects in meditators consistently show higher amplitudes in theta and alpha bands and decreased frequency of the alpha band (Lomas et al., 2015a). There are also indications that experienced meditators in three different meditation traditions (Vipassana, Himalayan yoga, and Isha yoga) show higher gamma (60–110 Hz) amplitudes than controls (Braboszcz et al., 2017). These authors also found higher alpha (7–11 Hz) activity in the Vipassana group than in the other two groups. ERP studies have found results that may reflect changes in attentional resource allocation (Brandmeyer et al., 2019).

The picture emerging from MRI studies is more informative. In their ALE analysis, Boccia et al. (2015), mostly comparing meditators with controls (8 studies, 10 comparisons), found structural brain modifications in areas involved in self-referential processes such as self-awareness and self-regulation. A more comprehensive (traditional) meta-analysis summarized long-lasting meditation effects in meditators' brains by comparing brain structures of meditators and matched samples of nonmeditators (Fox et al., 2014). In contrast to the fMRI studies mentioned above, meditators did *not* meditate during MRI measurements. Figure 6.7 shows the main findings summarized over 21 studies (overall $\bar{d} = 0.46$). Effects were consistently found for eight areas, two for white matter pathways (white dots in Figure 6.7) and six for gray matter regions (gray dots). Gray matter regions are primarily associated with processing and cognition, whereas white matter pathways predominantly serve the coordination of communication between brain regions. The authors argue that the regions indicated in Figure 6.7 can be related to psychological traits or processes. For instance, the respective parts of the frontal cortex (i.e., rostrolateral prefrontal cortex) might signify enhanced meta-awareness following meditation practice; the insula and the somatomotor cortices have been related to body awareness; changes in the hippocampus could indicate differences in memory abilities; the anterior cingulate cortex is known to be related to emotion regulation; and the superior longitudinal fasciculus and corpus callosum are involved in intrahemispherical and interhemispherical communication. Taken together, the results of this meta-analysis indicate that meditation might indeed yield long-lasting changes in the brain. This is also the conclusion of Luders and Kurth (2019), who summarized the results of 12 studies on global, regional, and local effects of meditation on brain structure.

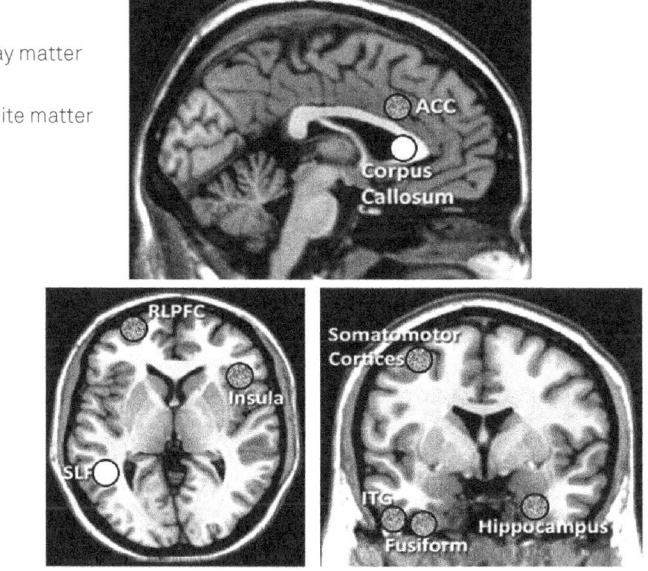

Figure 6.7. Consistent brain structure differences between meditators and matched controls (regional labels are approximate). Gray circles depict gray matter regions, and white circles white matter pathways. ACC = anterior/mid cingulate cortex; ITG = inferior temporal gyrus; RLPFC = rostrolateral prefrontal cortex; SLF = superior longitudinal fasciculus. Adapted from "Is Meditation Associated With Altered Brain Structure? A Systematic Review and Meta-Analysis of Morphometric Neuroimaging in Meditation Practitioners," by K. Fox et al., 2014, *Neuroscience and Biobehavioral Reviews, 43*, Figure 1. © 2014 by Neuroscience and Biobehavioral Reviews.

Recapitulation

The results summarized above indicate that meditation can have substantial effects on the brain. However, brain effects do not speak for themselves. They always need a (psychological) interpretation, which might be termed the *mapping problem* – that is, the problem of mapping brain processes and structures to psychological states and traits. Such interpretations (e.g., what does it mean if gamma waves are more pronounced during meditation or if meditators have thicker insulas?) rely on previous empirical findings, mostly in other research areas, and on theories about brain functioning. Such theories about what brain processes and structures mean psychologically have changed over time, and experts are still far from reaching a full consensus on this (Tang et al., 2015).

An indication of the lack of a good theory concerning the mapping problem becomes evident if one looks at how the regions of interest are selected in meta-analyses of MRI and fMRI studies. The main method to do so, the ALE meta-analysis, starts at the results and not with a theory. This procedure might lead to inconsistent findings (cf. Fox et al., 2016, vs. Kim et al., 2020) and to a severe selection bias that in turn could yield a systematic overestimation of effects (Vul et al., 2009; Vul & Pashler, 2012). Moreover, several relatively subjective decisions have to be taken during MRI and fMRI analyses before one obtains the usual colorful pictures, and each of these steps can bias the results. A drastic example of potential misinterpretations in fMRI research is reported by Bennett et al. (2009, 2011). These authors examined a dead salmon and found that fMRI signals indicated that it still was able to recognize human emotional reactions very well.

Since there is a general lack of longitudinal brain studies, another problem is that it cannot yet be decided whether changes found in the brain are due to meditation (or some other practice such as doing sports, making music, or speaking more than one language) or due to preexisting differences between long-term meditators and controls. Such longitudinal studies might, however, not be expected soon because of the many practical difficulties involved in conducting them (Luders & Kurth, 2019).

Despite these limitations, the evidence for a systematic impact of meditation on the brain is substantial. First, meditation has general effects on the brain that can be connected to positive changes in psychological variables, and second, different methods of meditation differ in their effects (although it might take some time to find out what exactly the differences are). Moreover, meditators' experiences also seem to have a noticeable impact on brain measures. In fact, most of brain studies have been conducted with experienced and very experienced meditators, in contrast to the bulk of psychological studies that have mostly examined meditation interventions in the range of weeks. Despite that restriction for comparisons (we do not know yet how crucial this difference is), the findings of brain studies generally conform with the findings on the psychological effects of meditation summarized above.

Additional Selected Effects

Peripheral Physiological Effects

It seems that, so far, evidence for the impact of meditation on peripheral physiological effects such as *cardiac indices* and *galvanic skin response* is very scarce. Especially from the latter, no firm conclusions can be drawn, and for high-frequency heart-rate variability, which seems to be the most-researched measure in the field, findings are inconclusive (Dorjee, 2020).

Meditation and Blood Pressure

Summarizing previous reviews on the effects of TM on changes in blood pressure, Ooi et al. (2017) concluded that TM can potentially lower systolic blood pressure (SBP) by ~4 mm Hg and diastolic blood pressure (DBP) by ~2 mm Hg. This is a modest effect when compared with antihypertensive drugs (SBP: ~10–15 mm Hg, DBP: ~8–10 mm Hg) but comparable to other blood-pressure reducing lifestyle interventions such as weight loss, relaxation therapies, alcohol reduction, reduced sodium intake, exercise, and coffee reduction. In their meta-analysis, Shi et al. (2017) compared effects of TM with non-TM meditation interventions and differentiated between ambulatory and nonambulatory blood pressure monitoring (ABPM and non-ABPM). In 14 of the 19 studies included, the control groups received some form of health education, which might not really count as an active control. For ABPM and SBP they found a mean reduction of 2.49 mm HG ($k=3$ studies, not reliable) for TM and 3.34 mm HG ($k=4$) for other meditation approaches. The respective figures for DBP were 4.26 mm HG for TM and 2.91 mm HG for the other approaches. The effects for non-ABPM measurements were larger for SBP (TM: 5.57 mm Hg, $k=9$, other: 5.09 mm HG, $k=4$) but not for DBP (TM: 2.86 mm Hg, $k=7$; other: 1.99, $k=3$).

Meditation and Aging

There is some research (no meta-analyses yet) indicating that meditation might slow down the aging process, as evidenced both by psychological and neurological studies. Gard et al. (2014) analyzed 12 studies that examined the effects of meditation on age-related cognitive decline (effects on attention, memory, executive function, processing speed, and general cognition). They concluded that meditation interventions for older adults may indeed slow down cognitive decline. Complementary evidence comes from brain research. Luders et al. (2015) and Villemure et al. (2015) found a slowing down of gray matter atrophy in meditators, and Luders et al. (2011) as well as Laneri et al. (2016) found that white matter aged more slowly in meditators than controls, as well. Especially interesting is a study by Luders et al. (2016) who used a machine-learning algorithm trained to identify anatomical correlates of age from MRI pictures (Franke et al., 2010) to compare experienced meditators with matched controls. They found that meditators' brains were estimated to be on average 7.5 years younger than those of the age-matched controls.

Effects on the Genome

A number of studies have addressed the question of whether meditation has an effect on telomere length. Telomeres are regions of repetitive DNA sequences at each end of a chromosome, which protect these ends from deterioration or from fusion with neighboring chromosomes. Short telomeres are associated with proneness to diseases (e.g., Kalson et al., 2018), worse health outcomes (e.g., Starkweather et al., 2014), and earlier death (e.g., Wang et al., 2018). Schutte et al. (2020) identified 11 studies (with $k=12$ effect sizes) that compared meditators (MBSR, loving kindness meditation, and Zen meditation) to controls. After excluding one study with a huge effect of $g=5.60$ they found a small average effect (longer telomeres) of $g=0.16$. However, if meditators were compared with active comparison groups ($k=8$ studies), the effect dropped to $g=-0.06$. This is consistent with findings showing that, among other interventions, endurance exercises or high-intensity interval exercises also yield longer telomeres (Werner et al., 2019). So, the small effect of meditation on telomere length may be due to some aspect that meditation has in common with other activities such as sports, which could, for instance, be a stress-reducing effect (Alda et al., 2016). Apart from direct effects on the genome, there are some indications that meditation might have effects on gene expression and epigenetics (Venditti et al., 2020).

Conclusion

Although the above overview of empirical evidence is certainly not complete, it should help give a good picture of the current state of affairs concerning the effects of meditation on (relatively) healthy practitioners. Most of what is presented is summary evidence (meta-analyses and reviews) but still some inconsistencies can be identified. Despite this, the results allow for drawing some quite strong conclusions.

Meditation Works
Evidence from examining psychological effects, effects on the brain, and even effects on the genome converge on one central message: Meditation works. And the evidence also suggests that the effects are overwhelmingly positive (we come to negative effects in Chapter 8).

Meditation Is Not (Only) a Relaxation Training
We do not yet know whether effects similar to those caused by meditation might also be caused by other activities such as playing a music instrument, practicing some sports, or learning another language. However, comparisons of results for conventional versus active control groups yield strong evidence that meditation is more than relaxation (and more than the cognitive trainings used in some active control groups). In Chapter 8, we will see that some meditation techniques in fact do not produce relaxation.

Effects Vary Considerably
Differences between meta-analyses summarizing (roughly) comparable studies on psychological effects and summaries of brain research exhibit a degree of heterogeneity that far exceeds the variation to be expected by sampling error alone. This means that there must be additional systematic factors that influence the size of the effects. Some of these have already been identified: type of meditation, meditator's age, and amount of meditation practice.

Different Types of Meditation Have Different Effects
As might be expected from looking at the huge variety of meditation techniques (Chapters 1 to 4), different types of meditation do indeed seem to have different effects. Results in some meta-analyses indicate that, for instance, mindfulness techniques – that is, directing one's attention to possibly unpleasant inner experiences (e.g., watching one's anxiety) – might, at least initially, lead to lower effects than directing one's attention to external objects such as a mantra. There are also indications that older adults

gain additional benefits if their meditation practice includes (but is not restricted to) meditative movements (this might also hold for adolescents – as yet, there seems to be no empirical basis for drawing strong conclusions).

Somewhat surprisingly, there were no pronounced differences between the effects of prosocially oriented meditation techniques (loving kindness and compassion meditation) and other forms of Western mindfulness meditation, even for prosocial dependent variables. This might in part have been due to the fact that loving kindness and compassion meditation are often subsumed in the same category of "mindfulness meditation" in meta-analyses. But it might, of course, also be due to similar effects for prosocially and nonprosocially oriented meditation techniques. This issue can, however, be easily clarified by either making more precise differentiations in summaries of previous research (if that is possible), or in new research directed to that question.

To make sound comparisons between types of meditation, all context variables need to be matched as closely as possible. Research doing this is in its nascent stage (see Chapter 8). The basic conclusion that different types of meditation have different effects can be safely deduced already from existing research on psychological and brain variables. What the differences are exactly is, however, still a largely open question.

Age Makes a Difference
The results of meditation studies in schools especially, indicate that adolescents and adults benefit differently from mindfulness meditation. It is still unclear what leads to the smaller effects for adolescents (and probably) older adults.

Demanding Context Makes a Difference
Groups of people who temporarily live in a more demanding context (at least on average), such as family caregivers or pregnant women, exhibit somewhat smaller effects of meditation than comparable adults. This might be due to fewer resources for learning the meditation technique, but as of now, the issue is still unresolved.

Meditation Takes Time
Some early results (e.g., Sedlmeier et al., 2012) notwithstanding, the results of meta-analyses indicate that practitioners do need some time for meditation effects to unfold. It seems that a meditation practice that lasts less than 1 month might have only very transient effects. One week or even 15 min of

"meditation" cannot be expected to work well. If such mini-interventions show effects, chances are that they are of the placebo variety or short-lived state effects. Unfortunately, most studies in the Western mindfulness paradigm do not allow examination of this issue more thoroughly because most training regimens last around 8 weeks. It would be necessary to do more longitudinal studies.

In sum, although one can safely assume that meditation has many beneficial effects for healthy practitioners, the findings summarized above create more questions than they answer. Overall, results point at the necessity to be much more specific when looking at the effects of meditation. Apart from factors for which there is preliminary evidence of a systematic impact on meditation (type of meditation, age, demanding context, meditation experience), one probably also needs to have a closer look at meditators' motivations and personalities. Including all of these factors is still, however, only the second-best solution. A better solution would be a good theory that allows for precise predictions (see Chapters 9 and 10 for several attempts). In Chapter 11, we will come back to the question of how meditation research might be improved.

Chapter 7
Effects of Meditation in Clinical Settings

This chapter gives an overview of the vast literature on the therapeutic effects of meditation. The very existence of these effects may have been a major door opener for meditation research into mainstream psychology journals, although numerous studies are still published in very diverse (and sometimes rather obscure) outlets. Given the vast number of publications, it does not make sense to report on single studies. Instead, we will focus on meta-analyses. But even the number of meta-analyses on this broad topic is remarkably high, so much so that some of these meta-analyses have been summarized in *meta-syntheses* – that is, syntheses of meta-analyses.

Meta-Syntheses of Meditation Research

The very existence of recent meta-syntheses indicates that research on the effects of meditation targeting clinical variables has strongly expanded in recent years and probably will continue to do so in the future. Here we will briefly summarize the results of three meta-syntheses, in chronological order. The meta-synthesis by Gotink et al. (2015) who summarized 23 (out of a total of 153, already back then!) meta-analyses on the effects of MBSR and MBCT is not included because that article was later retracted by the *PlosOne* editors (the authors did not agree), mostly due to methodological problems (see https://journals.plos.org/plosone/article?id=10.1371/journal.pone.0215608). The other three summaries dealt with here had different foci. The first focused on the effects of meditative movement therapies, the second on health outcomes – that is, on a selection of dependent variables – and the third attempted to summarize the effects of mindfulness-based interventions (MBIs).

Meditative Movement Therapies

Kelley and Kelley (2015) summarized 10 meta-analyses on the effects of meditative movement therapies (yoga, tai chi, and qigong) on health-related quality of life, in patients with breast cancer, schizophrenia, low back pain, heart failure, and diabetes. They found vastly different mean effect sizes across meta-analyses, ranging from $\bar{d}=0.18$ to $\bar{d}=2.28$. The large average effects in some of the meta-analyses were partly due to outliers that had a strong influence because of the relatively few studies included in some single meta-analyses. These results indicate that meditative movements are probably beneficial, but due to the huge heterogeneity in meditation techniques and clinical conditions, not much else can be concluded from this meta-synthesis.

Health Outcomes

In their meta-synthesis of the effects of meditation on health, Rose et al. (2020) initially identified 103 meta-analyses, of which 16 did not examine health outcomes. Health outcomes were categorized into mental health (any outcome that reflected cognitive, emotional, or social well-being, and issues such as anxiety, depression, quality of life, and stress), health behaviors (any health promoting or deteriorating activities, such as smoking), and physical health (objective measures of body fitness, such as blood pressure, blood sugar, hemoglobin, pain, irritable bowel syndrome, and insomnia). After excluding meta-analyses that did not consist of randomized controlled trials and meta-analyses that had a high overlap in the studies they included, they arrived at their final number of 28 meta-analyses, of which they classified 19 as *clinical only* and 9 as *clinical and nonclinical*. If a meta-analysis reported several outcomes (average effect sizes), as 26 of the 28 did, the average of these outcomes was taken.

The overall effect was $\bar{d}=0.5$, and there was no variation between the clinical only and clinical and nonclinical samples, and none for published and unpublished studies, but there was some variation in effect sizes depending on the type of health outcome and the type of meditation (see Figure 7.1). For instance, the mean effect for physical health (averaged over $m=3$ meta-analyses) was somewhat larger than the average overall effect, but the large 95% confidence interval for that effect indicates high heterogeneity (Figure 7.1, top). The category "various" ($m=11$ meta-analyses) indicates the effects of a mix of several of the three types of health outcomes.

Rose et al. (2020, p. 509) argue that "mindfulness," focused attention, and yoga are three major forms of meditation and find that yoga has the largest effect (Figure 7.1, bottom), although this effect (it is not clear from the text, what exactly is meant by "yoga") has a very high heterogeneity. Again, the category "various" includes several types of meditation.

Most of the therapeutic regimens summarized in this meta-synthesis probably stem from Western approaches to meditation, and therefore, the

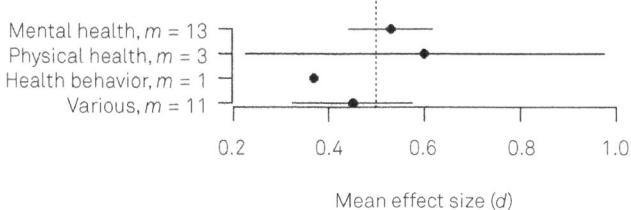

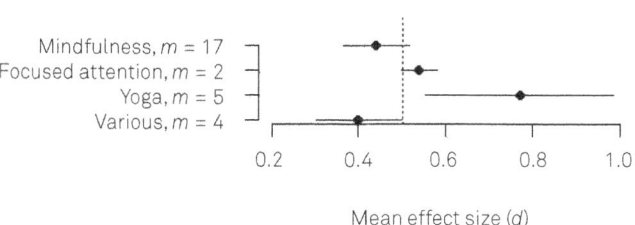

Figure 7.1. Effect sizes ($\bar{d}$) averaged over m (number of meta-analyses, out of 28) for different types of health outcomes (top) and different types of meditation (bottom). The vertical dotted lines indicate the overall effect size of $\bar{\bar{d}} = 0.5$, and error bars show 95% confidence intervals; the length of the 95% confidence interval legs has been calculated by $1.96 \times (SD/\sqrt{m})$. Based on Table 1 in Rose et al. (2020).

variation of the kinds of meditation should be expected to be substantially smaller than in the studies with healthy participants reviewed in the last chapter. Nonetheless, Figure 7.1 still indicates substantial differences in effect size for the three (very coarse grained) categories of meditation and outcomes.

It would have helped if there had been more fine grained categories, such as how meta-analytic effects are divided up among both type of outcome and type of meditation. Moreover, some more information about which effect sizes were averaged in which category might have been helpful because the range of the average effects of the 28 meta-analyses was quite large ($Range_d = [0.16, 0.98]$; Rose et al., 2020, p. 511). However, even if one assumes some publication bias, the substantial overall effect size of $\bar{\bar{d}} = 0.5$ indicates that meditation reliably produces beneficial effects also in the clinical context.

Mindfulness-Based Interventions

Yet another even more recent meta-synthesis (Goldberg et al., 2021) made more differentiations but did not calculate average effect sizes for the respective categories over meta-analyses. Instead, for every category in question, the authors report mean effects and confidence intervals only for the meta-analysis that included the most studies on the respective category (e.g., for children or for cancer patients, see below). The meta-synthesis only considered meta-analyses that examined the effects of MBIs, with randomized controlled trials (RCTs) that differentiated between effects for conventional and active controls. Altogether 44 meta-analyses met their criteria. Unfortunately, Goldberg et al. (2021) did not distinguish between clinical and nonclinical populations, although from skimming through titles and outlets of the respective meta-analyses, it seems that most if not all of them summarized clinical studies. The authors did, however, distinguish between other aspects concerning different populations, as well as the type of problem targeted with meditation, the specific type of MBI, and different kinds of outcome measures. In the following, the results for conventional and active controls are juxtaposed. All figures below, composed from data in their Tables 1 to 4, show "representative" effects – that is, those for the respective meta-analysis with the most studies for a given category (not so rarely, the same meta-analysis was used as showing the "representative effect" for several categories), as well as the range of mean effect sizes found across all meta-analyses that reported effect sizes for that category.

The authors considered six clinical subpopulations: older adults, adults, students, employees, health care (workers), and children (including adolescents). The representative effect size for older adults was rather high ($\bar{d} = 0.74$), but not reliable (95% confidence interval covers the null effect) for conventional controls, and there was no study with active controls. Therefore, it is omitted in Figure 7.2, which shows the other comparisons according to type of controls. The arrows in Figure 7.2 are not error bars but show the range of mean effects obtained in the meta-analyses that fell into a given category. For instance, the "representative" meta-analysis for the category "adults" and conventional controls yielded a mean effect of $\bar{d} = 0.55$ (height of white bar). The meta-analyses with the smallest and largest effects yielded $\bar{d} = 0.21$ and $\bar{d} = 1.27$, respectively (end of downward and upward arrows, leftmost result in Figure 7.2).

It is evident that the effect sizes are considerably smaller for children (adolescents are subsumed under this category), than for adults, at least for the much more frequent comparisons with conventional controls. This is so even when taking into account the huge variability of the average effects found across meta-analyses, as indicated by the arrows, in both categories. For instance, as already mentioned, the average effects found across meta-

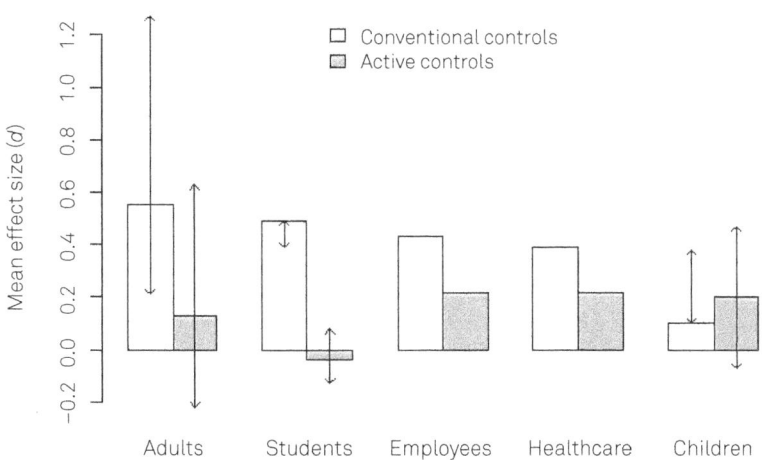

Figure 7.2. Effect sizes ($\bar{d}$) for the "representative" meta-analyses, as well as highest and lowest mean effect sizes from the meta-analyses that examined the respective population, shown by the arrowheads. If there is no arrow, there was only one meta-analysis reporting an effect for that population. Based on Tables 1 and 3 in Goldberg et al. (2021).

analyses (conventional controls) ranged from $\bar{d}=0.21$ to $\bar{d}=1.27$ for adults and from $\bar{d}=0.1$ (in this case the "representative" value) to $\bar{d}=0.38$ for children. Except for the categories "employees" and "health care," for which there was only one meta-analysis each (and therefore no variation in average effect sizes), comparisons with active controls did not exhibit reliable effects. For the "students" category, mindfulness meditation even did worse than the active treatments. The comparison of the different populations is somewhat restricted because obviously, there is some logical overlap in all the categories that include adults (such as students, employees, and health care workers).

Next, we have a look at the problem categories identified in the meta-synthesis. For eight of the problem categories, there was at least one meta-analysis that reported results for comparisons with conventional as well as active control groups (Figure 7.3). The arrows, spanning the range of summary effects across all meta-analyses, show again that results were quite heterogeneous. They also indicate that the "representative" effects as indicated by the bars in Figure 7.3 might not be so representative after all. For instance, the "representative" effect for depression with active controls was the largest across all meta-analyses that reported on this category, and that for substance use (also vs. active controls) was the smallest.

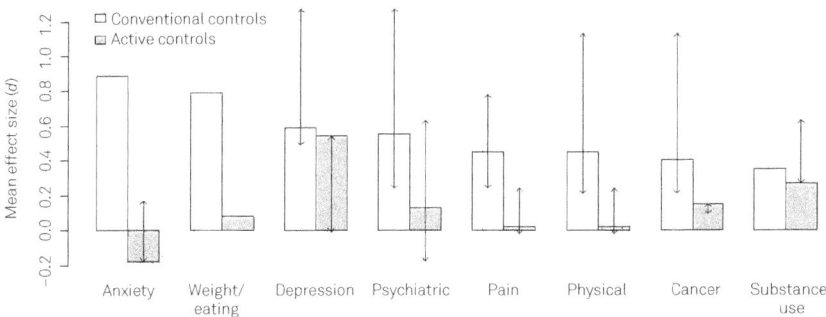

Figure 7.3. Effect sizes (d) for the "representative" meta-analyses, as well as highest and lowest mean effect sizes from the meta-analyses that examined the respective problem targeted by the mindfulness intervention, shown by the arrowheads. If there is no arrow, there was only one meta-analysis reporting an effect for that population. Based on Tables 1 and 3 in Goldberg et al. (2021).

Again, comparisons with active control groups showed unreliable effects for the majority of categories: The smallest effects reported across meta-analyses were negative, which means that active controls did better than meditators (in the categories anxiety, depression, psychiatric, pain, and physical). Only the effect for substance use (and maybe that for cancer) could be considered stable.

Was there a difference across the different kinds of mindfulness interventions? This comparison is limited because the categories identified in the meta-synthesis were not fully distinct: (1) mindfulness-based stress reduction (MBSR) and/or mindfulness-based cognitive therapy (MBCT; i.e., either MBSR, MBCT, or a combination of these), (2) MBCT, (3) various MBIs, (4) mobile health MBIs (mHealth), and (5) MBSR. Figure 7.4 shows that for comparisons with conventional control groups, the differences were not substantial, even though the "representative" results for MBCT and mHealth may be on the upper end of possible effects (see arrows). There is also a large heterogeneity in meta-analytic outcomes for MBSR/MBCT, various MBIs, and MBSR. And again, comparisons with active control groups showed little or no (MBSR/MBCT, various MBIs, MBSR) effects, indicating that MBIs might not do substantially better (and sometimes do worse) than the interventions subsumed under "active controls."

Finally, the meta-synthesis differentiated across types of outcomes, summarized into quite global categories: *psychiatric* (symptoms), *mindfulness, objective* (outcomes), *physiology, physical* (symptoms), *stress,* and *sleep* (Figure 7.5). For the comparisons with conventional controls, "representative"

Different interventions

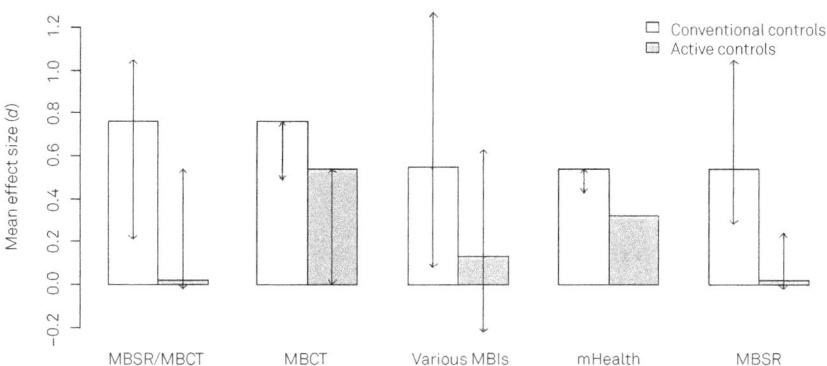

Figure 7.4. Effect sizes (*d̄*) for the "representative" meta-analyses, as well as highest and lowest mean effect sizes from the meta-analyses that examined the respective problem targeted by the mindfulness intervention, shown by the arrowheads. If there is no arrow, there was only one meta-analysis reporting an effect for that population. MBCT = mindfulness-based cognitive therapy; MBI = mindfulness-based intervention; MBSR = mindfulness-based stress reduction. Based on Tables 1 and 3 in Goldberg et al. (2021).

Different outcomes

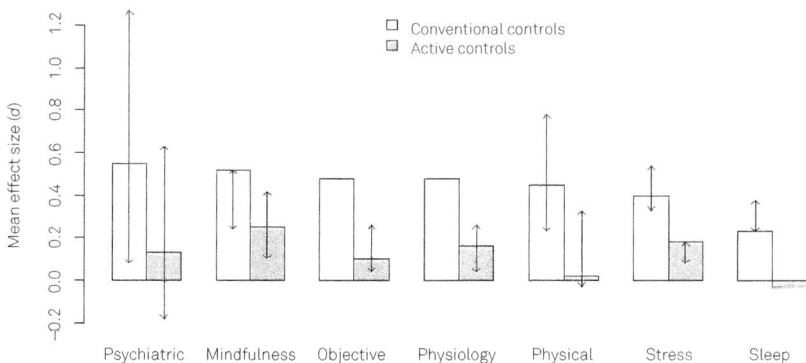

Figure 7.5. Effect sizes (*d̄*) for the "representative" meta-analyses, as well as highest and lowest mean effect sizes from the meta-analyses that examined the respective outcomes of mindfulness interventions, shown by the arrowheads. If there is no arrow, there was only one meta-analysis reporting an effect for that population. Based on Tables 1 and 3 in Goldberg et al. (2021).

effects do not differ very strongly across outcome types, and there is a considerable heterogeneity of effects across meta-analyses for psychiatric and physical symptoms. For both of them (which also accounted for most effect sizes), meditation does not yield reliably better effects than active control interventions. And for sleep, meditation did not seem to have helped at all, as compared with some other (active) intervention.

Goldberg et al. (2021) also summarized the results of follow-up measurements (on average after 7.2 months) and found generally somewhat decreased but still persistent effects.

What Can We Learn From the Meta-Syntheses?

All three meta-syntheses discussed above agree that meditation does on average have substantial beneficial effects in the clinical context. However, the Goldberg et al. (2021) analysis indicates that this effect is only obtained if meditators are compared with conventional controls and almost vanishes in comparisons with active control groups, with a few exceptions. Because of the generally high heterogeneity of meta-analytic (summary) effects, it would be interesting to know whether the active treatments were comparable across conditions. A potential drawback of this very detailed meta-synthesis is that it is not really a meta-synthesis in the usual sense, but rather a selective summary of meta-analyses. The "representative" effects taken to be typical of the respective categories sometimes definitely were not because for typical results, one would expect results of other meta-analyses to be more or less evenly spread on both sides. Figure 7.2, Figure 7.3, Figure 7.4, and Figure 7.5 show a number of categories where this is definitely not the case. And, as in the meta-synthesis of Rose et al. (2020), effect sizes for a given category are summarized across all other potentially relevant dimensions, which might have obscured specific effects and differences between effects. Just an arbitrary example: The effects for children might differ according to whether psychiatric or physical symptoms are measured, whether their problem is more a physical or a psychological one, and whether they receive MBSR or some special MBI variant as treatment. Thus, the most salient impression from the figures that depict the results of these meta-syntheses is that of a high degree of heterogeneity. This speaks strongly against the idea of a uniform meditation effect. However, if there are different effects for different combinations of meditation types, populations, problems targeted, and outcomes, the information we can get from meta-syntheses may be limited because averaging across different categories and populations may "wash out" the differential effects. Moreover, additional factors that could not be targeted by the meta-syntheses might also play a role.

Some of the differences one might expect could become more visible when we step down one level of abstraction, to more specific meta-analyses. But in some cases, even if summary studies concentrated on rather narrow foci, such as on the effect of meditative movement on sleep quality (Wang et al., 2016) or on the effects of mantra meditation on mental health (Lynch et al., 2018), it turned out that the heterogeneity was (as of yet) still too great to meaningfully conduct meta-analyses. However, in many areas, meaningful summaries were possible. In the next sections, we will summarize a representative selection of these works, beginning with an early, very influential meta-analysis, and then giving an overview first of meta-analyses that examined the effects of meditation on what can be considered predominantly mental health problems and then on works that targeted predominantly physical health problems.

An Influential Early Meta-Analysis

The most renowned meta-analysis on the effects of meditation in the clinical context (adults only) seems still to be the one conducted by Goyal et al. (2014). This analysis was commissioned by the US government and used very strict criteria for selecting and analyzing studies. For instance, it included only studies with control groups that matched the time and attention of the meditation groups (waitlist or usual care controls were excluded), and all studies had to have randomized controlled trials. Moreover, the authors differentiated between active controls and specific active controls, the latter also matching expectations of benefit (e.g., exercise or progressive muscle relaxation). For analysis, Goyal et al. (2014) divided their final sample of 47 studies into specific and nonspecific control groups, as well as into mindfulness-based programs (MBSR, MBCT, Vipassana, Zen, and other mindfulness meditation), and mantra-based programs (TM and other mantra meditation). The top part of Figure 7.6 shows the mean effects for the comparisons with nonspecific controls. The largest mean effect size was found for anxiety ($\bar{d}$ = 0.38, and the smallest for sleep ($\bar{d}$ = 0.14). Reliable effects were only found for anxiety, negative effect, alleviation of pain, and (barely – the lower end of the 95% confidence interval is exactly 0) for depression. Only one (nonreliable) effect is shown for mantra meditation because many studies using mantra meditation did not meet the methodological inclusion criteria.

When meditation was compared with specific controls, meditation and alternative interventions were basically indistinguishable (Figure 7.6, bottom). Mindfulness-based programs were somewhat less effective for alleviating anxiety and pain, as well as increasing well-being and somewhat more effective in reducing stress, quality of life, and depression. But as the substantial overlap of the 95% confidence intervals with the null effect indicates, none of these effects are reliable. Comparing these effects with those

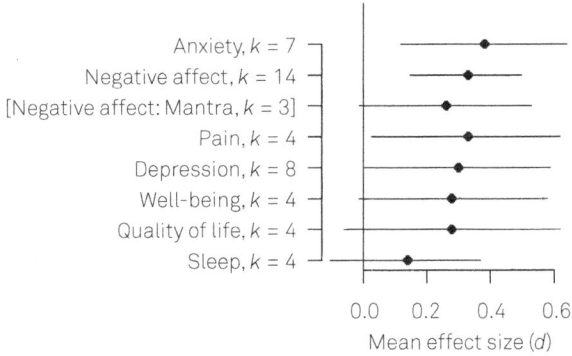

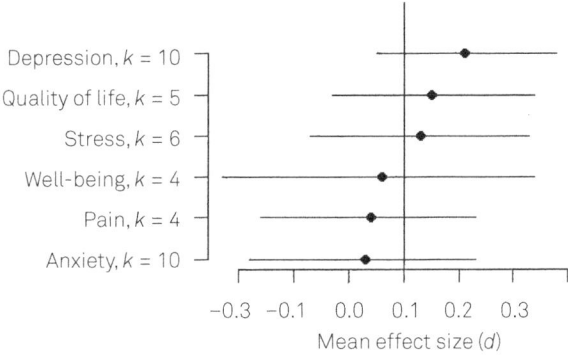

Figure 7.6. Effect sizes (d) averaged over k studies with nonspecific (top) and specific control groups (bottom) for different categories of dependent variables (multiple comparisons possible). Error bars show 95% confidence intervals. With the exception of negative affect, for which also results from mantra meditation could be used, data are summarized from mindfulness-based programs. Only average effects for categories with $n \geq 3$ studies are shown. For some dependent measures, study results in the source (online supplement) were divided into two time intervals for time of measurement after intervention. In that case, the shorter one was always used. Based on Goyal et al. (2014).

obtained for healthy practitioners with active control groups (see Figure 6.3 and Figure 6.4 in Chapter 6) indicates that the effects for patients might be generally smaller than those for practitioners from a nonclinical population, given that "active control group" has a comparable meaning in both kinds of studies. This seems to be the case because some sort of relaxation technique was the most prevalent kind of active intervention in research, both with healthy and with clinical populations. One reason for the effect size differences, which were already discussed in Chapter 6, might be that if one is continually anxious, depressed, or very stressed, it is probably much harder to learn to meditate, especially if meditating means turning your attention to adverse thoughts and feelings, as is the case in many MBIs.

As already mentioned above, in recent years, an avalanche of meditation studies with clinical populations have been conducted, which were summarized in numerous meta-analyses. In the following, we will concentrate on recent summaries (works published after 2015) that examined the effects of meditation on specific clinical conditions and did not exclusively focus on very brief trainings. The results of very brief trainings (in the extreme, only one short session) are hard to disentangle from expectancy or placebo effects. One such summary found no effect at all when publication bias was accounted for (Schumer et al., 2018). Moreover, only summaries of control group comparisons are considered (not with pre-post comparisons or results mixed over both types of studies). Quite a number of meta-analyses did not differentiate between the effects for the two kinds of design (for an arbitrarily chosen example, see Chimiklis et al., 2018), although the internal validity for pre-post comparisons may have been very low, and in any case not comparable to those for control group studies.

Both the early Goyal et al. (2014) meta-analysis as well as the meta-synthesis by Goldberg et al. (2021) strongly indicate that it does not make sense to average effects across designs with different types of control groups. Therefore, only meta-analyses that differentiated between conventional and active control groups (and reported effects for at least one of them) were included. Examples of meta-analyses that only reported studies for mixed groups (and therefore were not included) are Auty et al., (2017), DiRenzo et al. (2018), Grant et al. (2017), Maglione et al. (2017), Paudyal et al. (2018), and Rogers et al. (2017). And finally, only meta-analyses that explicitly reported effects for clinical populations will be discussed. Meta-analyses that only reported effects for a mix of studies with healthy and clinical samples (e.g., Chen et al., 2020; Lv et al., 2020) were not considered.

Predominantly Mental Health Problems

The following paragraphs give an overview of the results of meta-analyses for some predominantly mental health problems, in alphabetical order. It seems that the areas listed there are those with the highest activities of meditation research. There are, of course, many more studies, targeting many other mental health problems.

ADHD in Adults

Are MBIs helpful for adults with attention-deficit/hyperactivity disorder (ADHD)? Poissant et al. (2020) found nine studies with control groups (conventional ones, it seems, albeit no further information was given) that had explored this question. The answer was a tentative "yes." For different forms of MBIs, the average improvements in lessening ADHD symptoms amounted to $\bar{g} = 0.61$ ($k=9$), and there were also benefits in lowering depression ($\bar{d} = .36$, $k=5$) and improving executive functioning ($\bar{g} = .26$, $k=9$).

Anxiety

Singh and Gorey (2018) synthesized the effects from nine randomized controlled trials (RCTs) with anxiety patients that compared different forms of MBIs to cognitive behavioral interventions. They found no difference between the two groups on the alleviation of anxiety ($\bar{d} = -0.02$). The results in a meta-analysis by de Abreu Costa et al. (2019) that only considered RCTs for patients with anxiety disorder were similar. There was no difference in fear symptoms if MBIs (MBSR and MBCT) were compared with several control conditions ($\bar{d} = 0.03$, $k=2$), and behavioral therapy did even better than MBIs ($\bar{d} = -0.28$, $k=3$). The authors report that more experienced MBI therapists did better than less experienced ones and having more than one anxiety disorder diagnosis also covaried with larger effects. Moreover, women seemed to have profited more from the MBIs than men.

In another meta-analysis with RCTs, Montero-Marin et al. (2019) report the results of comparing meditation interventions against relaxation therapies for anxiety patients and found an overall small positive effect of $\bar{g} = 0.23$ ($k=16$). They divided the meditation interventions into focused attention (focus, e.g., on mantra; different focal stimuli; breath; but also open monitoring) and "constructive" meditation practices (Dahl et al., 2015, see also Chapter 10 in this present work) with a values orientation added to the attentional practice. For the latter the effect was larger ($\bar{g} = 0.36$, $k=5$) than for the former ($\bar{g} = 0.13$, $k=11$, nonreliable).

Taken together, these results indicate that "pure" mindfulness meditation might not be a strong alternative to cognitive behavior therapy for anxiety disorders, whereas for meditation practices combined with a values orientation, the results look more promising. There might also be some potential in meditative movement [Zou et al., 2018; they report an average effect of mindful movements on the reduction of anxiety of $\bar{g} = 0.46$ ($k=6$), but to calculate this effect, they mixed active and conventional controls (about evenly)].

Depression

Considering the sheer number of meta-analyses that include it, the topic of *depression* seems to have received the most attention, so far, in meditation research. However, not all of the surveys fulfilled the requirements mentioned above. Table 7.1 summarizes the results of seven recent meta-analyses on the topic that did. It is evident that all interventions showed substantial effects when compared with conventional controls. The effects decreased markedly if MBIs were compared with other interventions (active controls). It seems that the remarkable heterogeneity of effect sizes in the latter comparisons can partially be explained by what kind of active control group the MBIs were compared with. For instance, Lenz et al. (2016) found effects between $\bar{g}=0.75$, for a comparison with psychoeducation and $\bar{g}=0.27$ for one with cognitive behavior therapy.

Two of the meta-analyses report amazingly high effects for studies conducted with Asian participants. Wang et al. (2018) found an effect of $\bar{d}=1.5$ ($k=2$) for Chinese and a much smaller effect of $\bar{d}=0.38$ for non-Chinese samples (including results for conventional controls). A similar discrepancy can be seen in a study by Reangsing et al. (2021) – Asian samples ($k=5$): $\bar{g}=1.28$, North American samples ($k=9$): $\bar{g}=0.32$, and European samples ($k=6$): $\bar{g}=0.59$. However, these differences might be partly due to a missing differentiation between studies with conventional and active controls, for these comparisons.

Most of the MBIs in Table 7.1 included psychotherapy parts, and the intervention most often applied, either in its standard form or in a variant, was MBCT (see Chapter 2). There was only one summary of stand-alone interventions. Zou et al. (2018) found the effects of meditative movements to be quite effective, especially when exercises were practiced both in a group and individually ($\bar{g}=0.84, k=3$) as compared with group practice only ($\bar{g}=0.55, k=15$). With the exception of the meta-analysis by Lenz et al. (2016) in which follow-up measurements showed even increased effects, all other summary studies that reported such measurements found a (sometimes strong) decline in long-time effects.

In an additional meta-analysis, Kuyken et al. (2019) looked at a different kind of effect. They summarized studies that had examined the likelihoods of depressive relapse. For the nine studies that compared MBCT with conventional controls, they found a mean hazard ratio of 0.69. (A hazard ratio of 1 would indicate that the treatment does not have an impact on relapse, a hazard ratio of 2 would suggest that the treatment doubles the likelihood of relapse, and a hazard ration of 0.5 suggests that it halves it.) The ratio increased to 0.79 if MBCT was compared with active controls ($k=5$). This is consistent with the results in Table 7.1. In sum, these results indicate that it might be very useful to include mindfulness procedures as part of the therapeutic interventions for depression.

Table 7.1. Results of seven recent meta-analyses (published after 2015, listed here in chronological order) on the effects of mindfulness-based interventions on depressive symptoms

Study	Problem	Intervention	Measure	ES (k), Conventional controls	ES (k), Active controls
Lenz et al. (2016)	Acute depression	Standard MBCTs	Depressive symptoms	0.76 (16)	0.54 (16)
Perestelo-Perez et al. (2017)	Depressive rumination	MBCTs, different variants	Depressive rumination	0.59 (8)	0.02 (3)
Chu et al. (2018)	Bipolar disorder	Adjunct mindfulness interventions	Depressive symptoms	0.46 (3)	none
Wang et al. (2018)	Major depressive disorder	MBIs, different kinds	Depressive symptoms	(not given separately)	0.24 (8)
Zou et al. (2018)	Major depressive disorder	Meditative movements	Depressive symptoms	0.79 (6)	0.45 (13)
Goldberg et al. (2019)	Current depressive symptoms	MBCT	Depressive symptoms	0.71 (10)	0.0002 (6)
Reangsing et al. (2021)	Depression in older adults (≥ 65 years)	MBIs, different kinds	Depressive symptoms	0.80 (13)	0.39 (7)

Note. Only meta-analyses published after 2015 with clearly specified control groups are included. Effect sizes (ES) are standardized mean differences ($\bar{g}$ or $\bar{d}$), and k is the respective number of studies. MBCT = mindfulness-based cognitive therapy; MBI = mindfulness-based intervention.

Schizophrenia

Sabe et al. (2019) summarized effects of meditation in 15 RCTs that examined changes in negative (e.g., apathy) and positive symptoms (e.g., hallucinations) for stabilized patients with schizophrenia or schizoaffective disorder. All comparisons used nonspecific control groups. The overall effect for reductions in negative symptoms was $\bar{d}=0.36$. This effect was largest for MBIs ($\bar{d}=0.45$, $k=3$), followed by yoga interventions ($\bar{d}=0.39$, $k=10$), and tai chi ($\bar{d}=0.16$, $k=2$, not reliable). The respective results for decreases in positive symptoms were smaller and barely reliable only for yoga interventions ($\bar{d}=0.27$, $k=10$).

In another recent meta-analysis, Jansen et al. (2020) concentrated on the effects of acceptance- and mindfulness-based approaches on several symptoms of persons with a psychotic or schizophrenia disorder. Control groups received treatment as usual (TAU). Overall, the authors found comparable effects for negative and positive symptoms, $\bar{d}=0.24$, $k=7$, and $\bar{d}=0.27$, $k=9$, respectively, both barely reliable. However, MBIs showed larger effects than acceptance-based interventions: $\bar{d}=0.41$, $k=3$ versus $\bar{d}=0.03$, $k=4$ for negative symptoms, and $\bar{d}=0.29$, $k=5$ versus $\bar{d}=0.27$, $k=4$ (not reliable) for positive symptoms. In sum, it seems that MBIs have some potential in treating patients with psychosis, although in this area, as we will see in the next chapter, several restrictions apply for intervention procedures.

Stress-Related Disorders

Gallegos et al. (2017) summarized meditation interventions for posttraumatic stress disorder (PTSD). They found an effect of $\bar{d}=0.70$ ($k=3$) for conventional and $\bar{d}=0.34$ ($k=16$) for active control groups on self-report PTSD measures and clinician-administered diagnostic interviews. Overall effects were highest for yoga-based approaches ($\bar{d}=0.71$, $k=4$) and lowest for mindfulness-based approaches ($\bar{d}=0.33$, $k=10$). A third category containing other meditation approaches (TM and other mantra meditation, kriya yoga, and loving kindness meditation) yielded $\bar{d}=0.37$ ($k=6$). Similar results were found for military veterans who also can be considered a clinical population (see Goldberg et al., 2020). These authors summarized reports on the effects of MBIs [excluding approaches that include a higher amount of psychotherapy, such as acceptance and commitment therapy (ACT)] and found decreased PTSD symptoms for comparisons with nonspecific controls ($\bar{g}=0.64$, $k=7$) and specific controls ($\bar{g}=0.25$, $k=4$).

De Abreu Costa et al. (2019) synthesizing the effects of MBSR and MBCT on stress-related disorders found smaller effects for measures of distress: $\bar{d}=0.45$ ($k=5$) for comparisons with mixed control groups, and $\bar{d}=0.002$ ($k=3$) with group cognitive behavioral therapy.

Koncz et al. (2021) summarized the effect of meditation (different types) on stress across studies that compared samples with a risk for elevated cortisol levels to no-risk samples. They looked at changes in cortisol levels and found a relatively strong effect on blood cortisol that, astonishingly, was stronger for comparisons with active (wide variety of interventions) than with passive controls: $\bar{g}=0.85$ ($k=4$) versus $\bar{g}=0.40$ ($k=3$). Corresponding measurements of salivary cortisol yielded consistent but smaller (and non-reliable) effects: $\bar{g}=0.33$ ($k=8$) versus $\bar{g}=0.13$ ($k=11$). The authors argue that the difference might in part be due to stronger effects for at-risk samples with somatic illnesses, which were more prevalent in the blood sample studies.

The number of studies covered in these meta-analyses is relatively small, but considering the convergence of psychological and hormonal measures, meditation appears to be useful as an adjunct treatment for chronic stress. The relatively strong effects with yoga-based treatments hint at the possibility that meditative movements might be a useful alternative meditational ingredient in treating stress-related disorders.

Effects of Meditation on Predominantly Mental Health Problems: A Recapitulation

The meta-analyses summarized above cover only a small part of all studies on the general topic, but chances are that the studies included herein are among the methodologically sounder ones. Moreover, the topics targeted are probably the ones most researched, possibly because they also are the ones considered most promising for meditative interventions. Indeed, the results indicate that different types of meditation may be quite helpful for treating depression and stress-related disorders, especially if embedded in a broader psychotherapy context. However, it seems unclear whether mindfulness meditation can add substantially to conventional therapeutic approaches, an issue which needs further clarification for potential effects of meditation for adult patients with ADHD. Especially for patients with anxiety disorders, it might be worthwhile to explore alternative meditative practices such as meditative movements or mantra meditation as possible adjunctive treatments. As far as patients with schizophrenia are concerned, the usefulness of the relatively small effects of meditation should be judged in comparison with the available alternatives. Consistent with the results of Goldberg et al. (2021), a view of specific meta-analyses makes clear that both the categories of meditative interventions as well as the type of control groups need to be specified more precisely so as to be able to come to stronger conclusions.

Predominantly Physical Health Problems

Cardiovascular Disease and/or Hypertension
In Chapter 6, we have already seen that meditation has some potential to lower blood pressure in healthy populations. Does it also have beneficial effects for patients with cardiac problems? Yang et al. (2017) summarized the effects of different kinds of meditation on blood pressure for hypertensive patients. They reported results separately for qigong, tai chi, and yoga, as well as for different kinds of controls. Here, only results that include three or more studies are presented, first for systolic blood pressure (SBP). The mean reductions for comparisons with no-intervention controls were qigong: 18.32 mm HG ($k=3$), and yoga: 8.10 mm HG ($k=3$, not reliable). The authors present effects for both fixed and random-effects models. All effects reported here refer to the random-effects models. The effects of yoga versus care were somewhat smaller but reliable: 7.55 mm HG mean reduction ($k=6$), whereas the comparison of yoga with exercise yielded even smaller and nonreliable results (2.89 mm HG, $k=3$). The results for diastolic blood pressure (DBP) resembled those for SBP. Qigong versus no intervention: 13.03 mm HG ($k=3$), and yoga versus care: 5.43 mm HG ($k=6$). Again, the comparisons of yoga with no-intervention and exercise groups were not reliable. The authors contend that qigong may be the optimal exercise to lower blood pressure, but their conclusion is partly based on only one study for the respective comparisons.

Gathright et al. (2019) concentrated on the effect of TM for patients with hypertension and/or cardiovascular diseases. In the six studies that allowed for calculation of changes in blood pressure, all control groups received health education. In this summary, the effects for SBP and DBP were calculated as standard mean deviations and amounted to small effects of $\bar{d}=0.26$ and $\bar{d}=0.28$, respectively. This seems also to be true for MBIs. For comparisons with a mix of control groups, Scott-Sheldon et al. (2020) found basically no effect for DBP, although a rather high average effect for SBP ($\bar{d}=0.88$, $k=7$), which might, however, be invalidated by some pronouncedly outlying effects, e.g., one huge effect of $\bar{d}=3.38$.

Given the different kinds of effect sizes in these studies, the results cannot be compared directly. However, it appears to be that, overall, effects were quite modest. Meditative movements seem to hold some promise but should be compared with physical exercise.

Diabetes
Xia et al. (2020) reviewed studies that examined the effects of meditative movements (qigong, tai chi, and yoga) for patients with type 2 diabetes. For

the most-often-reported measure, fasting blood glucose (FBG), they found effects of $\bar{d}=1.42$ ($k=12$) for comparisons with nonexercise controls but still $\bar{d}=0.27$ ($k=6$) for comparisons with groups that practiced some form of physical exercise (e.g., seated calisthenics, stretching, aerobics). Other glycemic and lipid profile measures apparently did not allow for differentiating between conventional and active controls, but meditative movements showed stable overall results throughout these measures as well. Only in the case of body mass index (BMI) was no effect found.

Eating Disorders and Obesity

Summary research about the impact of meditation on eating disorders and obesity seems to be plagued by the problems that (a) many studies did not employ control groups and (b) meta-analyses did not differentiate between comparisons with conventional and active controls (Rogers et al., 2017; Turgon et al., 2019). Astonishingly, Carrière et al. (2018) found that the effects of mindfulness meditation, when compared with active controls (e.g., resistance training and stress eating intervention) was higher ($\bar{g}=0.59$, $k=5$) than that for all studies with control groups ($\bar{g}=0.35$, $k=13$). (Six of the studies summarized in this meta-analysis did not employ a control group, and the report focuses mainly on pre-post analyses that may be hard to interpret.) Thus, it seems difficult to draw any strong conclusions until the quality of studies in this field has improved.

Fatigue

Many patients with neurological injuries or illnesses such as traumatic brain injury or multiple sclerosis experience fatigue as a lasting symptom, which seems hard to treat. Ulrichsen et al. (2016) found four studies that compared the effects of MBIs (MBSR and MBCT) with conventional controls. Meditation interventions showed a mean effect of $\bar{d}=0.37$. This effect is rather modest but if other effective treatment is lacking (as seems to be the case), MBIs can be considered a useful option.

Multiple Sclerosis

Can physical symptoms of multiple sclerosis be alleviated by MBIs? Summarizing seven studies that targeted this question and fulfilled their inclusion criteria, Simpson et al. (2020) realized that only two physical symptoms could be summarized for three or more studies: fatigue and pain. The effects were small. Comparisons with active control groups could only be made separately for fatigue: $\bar{d}=0.1$ ($k=3$, not reliable). The overall effect of fatigue (active and nonactive controls) was not much larger: $\bar{d}=0.24$ ($k=7$, not reliable). Also, the effect on pain (two TAU controls, one psychoeducation) was about the same size: $\bar{d}=0.16$ ($k=3$, not reliable). Moreover, two of the seven studies reported on adverse events associated with MBSR (increased spasticity during mindful body awareness, increased anxiety following MBSR retreat, and increased pain symptoms following the raisin exercise). Thus, it seems that at least MBSR might not be very helpful in the treatment of multiple sclerosis.

Pain
Does meditation reduce chronic pain? Veehof et al. (2016) assessed the effects of several meditation interventions. They found mean effects of $\bar{d}=0.31$ ($k=14$) for comparisons with conventional control groups and $\bar{d}=0.13$ ($k=8$, not reliable) when comparing meditators with active controls. It seems, however, that the type of intervention made a noticeable difference. ACT (see Chapter 2) yielded higher effects ($\bar{d}=0.38$, $k=9$) than other MBIs (mostly MBSR, $\bar{d}=0.15$, $k=13$, not reliable).

Hilton et al., (2017) restricted their meta-analysis to mindfulness meditation only (e.g., ACT was explicitly excluded), used either as monotherapy or adjunctive therapy. The 30 studies included in the analysis used treatment as usual, passive controls, and education and/or support groups that is, basically conventional controls as comparators. Overall, the effect size describing change in pain symptoms was only $\bar{d}=0.32$ ($k=30$). This effect was barely reliable overall, but not for the two most prevalent subgroups (MBCT: $\bar{d}=0.26$, $k=4$; MBSR: $\bar{d}=0.41$, $k=16$) because of the high heterogeneity in effects across the studies included.

A third meta-analysis, also examining the effects of different kinds of mindfulness meditation, concentrated on a special type of chronic pain: migraine and tension-type headache (Gu et al., 2018). The authors calculated mean effects of headache intensity, frequency, and duration. All but one of the 11 comparisons (a relaxation group) involved conventional controls. Seven studies reported decreases in pain intensity with a $\bar{d}=0.89$. However, this large effect seems to have been mostly due to one pronounced outlier ($d=2.92$). The same study (Kiran et al., 2014), which was the only one that used a concentration meditation as opposed to a mindfulness-based intervention, also inflated the effect for headache frequency ($\bar{d}=0.89$, $k=5$, effect for outlying study: $d=1.78$). The effect for pain duration ($\bar{d}=0.54$, $k=5$) was not reliable, even though also here the outlying study contributed a large effect ($d=1.2$).

In sum, meditation seems to have a small pain-reducing effect, but it also seems that "pure" MBIs are not the method of choice for treating chronic pain. It might be worthwhile to shift the emphasis to exploring approaches with large psychotherapy components (e.g., ACT), or concentrative meditative procedures.

Sleep Disturbance

Does mindfulness meditation improve sleep quality? Rusch et al. (2019) come to the conclusion that it (different forms) may be effective for some aspects of sleep disturbance, although effects are not very strong for the population in question: People with clinically significant sleep disturbance. It had no effect on sleep quality when mindfulness groups were compared with specific active controls – that is, evidence-based sleep treatments ($\bar{g}=-0.03$, $k=7$); but when compared with nonspecific active controls – that is, time- and attention-matched interventions, there was a small effect ($\bar{g}=0.33$, $k=11$). However, effects deteriorated somewhat in the first, and increased a little in the second, case at measurements for 5- to 12-month follow-ups.

Effects of Meditation on Predominantly Physical Health Problems: A Recapitulation

Comparing the effect sizes for predominantly physical with those for predominantly mental problems, there is a clear tendency: Meditation is observed to be generally less effective when applied to remedy issues that manifest physically versus mentally. And these effects do not generally surpass those of the usual therapeutic approaches. This is not to say that practicing meditation as an adjunct treatment is not worthwhile in these cases, with the possible exception of multiple sclerosis, for which there might be a heightened probability for meditation-induced adverse effects (at least for MBI interventions). Especially for the treatment of fatigue, meditation might prove to be a very useful supplement to conventional treatments. And as far as pain is concerned, there is some indication that different types of mindfulness meditation might work differentially. There is a possibility that other forms of meditation might yield additional benefits (such as including meditational movements in treatment regimens for type 2 diabetes). Moreover, it seems that the quality of studies that examined predominantly physical effects might be even lower than that of studies that looked at predominantly mental health problems. This is exemplified by the large number of studies without control groups in the research on the effects of meditation on eating disorders and obesity.

Conclusion

The most important conclusion from this review of the effects of meditation in clinical populations is the same as that for healthy practitioners: Meditation works! Although it is hard to compare the size of the effects, one can probably say with some certainty that effects on aspects of physical health are generally smaller than those on mental aspects. Whether patients profit more from meditation than healthy practitioners do is a question that, upon reflection, might not make much sense: Effects for patients may be based on different underlying mechanisms and may be a composite of generally smaller effects mixed with the effects of spontaneous remission, which might seemingly increase effects (see Chapter 6). However, several other conclusions can be drawn from the present results.

Meditation Works Better in Combination With Psychotherapy

For clinical populations, I could not find a single summary in which "pure" meditation worked better than if meditative interventions were embedded in a larger therapeutic context, such as, for instance, with MBCT or ACT. Also MBSR is often used in clinical settings and might be considered a category in between pure mindfulness meditation and explicitly therapeutic approaches. In any case, it seems fair to say that a given meditation technique may rarely be suited as a stand-alone intervention for treating mental and physical health problems.

Meditation Probably Needs Continuity

If meta-analyses reported the effects of follow-up measurements, these were usually lower and sometimes much lower than measurements at post-test. This could be due to systematic attrition (predominantly participants who still struggle very much are still in the sample). But the most plausible explanation for this pattern of results seems to be that the effects of meditation do not last when participants end their practice. I have not yet come across a study that randomized continuation of meditation after post-test and followed up patients for an extended amount of time. But the issue could easily be resolved empirically by running studies of this kind.

The Kind of Meditation Intervention Can Make a Difference

As might be expected by the huge variety of meditation approaches summarized in Chapters 1 to 4, the kind of meditation also makes a difference in clinical settings. Several of the meta-analyses discussed in this present chapter found strong variations in effects for different approaches. And some of those differences may have been overlooked by using the term "mindfulness-based meditation" as the sole summary term. Sometimes, especially if the total number of studies that could be included in a given meta-analysis was small, that might have been the best term to use, but the more studies that are available, the more important it becomes to clearly specify what authors mean by "mindfulness meditation" (see Chapters 2 and 10).

The Kind of Control Group Can Make a Difference
A theme that pervades this whole chapter is that the type of control group has a strong impact on the size of the meditation effect. This chapter has sometimes stuck to the expression used by the authors when describing the type of comparator, but sometimes it has also just used the distinction between conventional and active controls. This distinction is clearly insufficient. For instance, some authors classify "attentional training" as conventional or as "specific conventional," while others classify it as "active." As evidenced by the multitude of very specific meta-analytic summaries, research specializes more and more, which is a good thing. It should become easier and easier to also specify the type of controls and systematically compare different types of specific interventions administered in these control groups.

Quality of Basic Studies and Meta-Analyses Has to Be Improved
Meta-analyses can only be as good as the studies they summarize. Most of the meta-analyses cited in this chapter mention many studies that had to be excluded for methodological reasons. This state of affairs might be transient though because meditation studies are increasingly published in mainstream journals with high methodological standards. But also the quality of meta-analyses varies considerably. Future meta-analyses should be as specific as possible, not only in their description of single studies, but also in their summaries. There can be no harm in being as specific as possible, for instance with respect to meditation techniques and control groups used.

Meditative Movements Are Gaining Ground
Which meditation practices receive most attention by researchers at a given period of time seems in part to be dependent on current trends and the cultural background of researchers. Whereas in the late 1970s and into the 1980s, TM and Western researchers dominated meditation research, nowadays clearly "mindfulness meditation" is the market leader (still mostly guided by Western teachers and examined by Western researchers), although the ambiguity of the term might eventually yield to a branching of terms. However, in recent times, it seems that more and more meditative movement practices (yoga, tai chi, and qigong) come into meditation researchers' focus. This research is increasingly done in the Asian context (mainly China) and summarized by Asian authors who have access to re-

search literature published in languages other than English, the current lingua franca in meditation research.

In sum, given the unbroken increase in the number of studies on the clinical effects of meditation it should become easier and easier to make sound recommendations for the use of meditation in the therapeutic context, as long as the quality of studies improves as well. It would help tremendously if we had good theories to navigate this research process (see Chapters 10 and 11). But even if we only had a good evidence-based foundations for choosing the best meditation approach in assisting a given therapeutic aim, this would be extremely beneficial.

Chapter 8
Hot Topics in Meditation Research

Most current studies seem to pursue this question: "Does mindfulness meditation (in its different varieties) have an effect on [insert basically anything, but most commonly some kind of problematic mental or somatic condition]?" However, some of the recent research also concentrates on theoretical underpinnings (see the next two chapters) and on other interesting but so far underresearched topics. This chapter will focus on the results for four such topics: (1) the use of digital forms of meditation instruction, (2) the negative effects of meditation, (3) comparisons of effects of different kinds of meditation or different components within a given approach, and (4) the impact of spiritual and ethical contexts, which are always included in traditional meditation approaches, but (almost) never in Western ones.

Is the Future of Meditation Training Digital?

The use of apps and online-based interventions to teach how to meditate has been going on for some time now, and Mrazek et al. (2019) suggest in the title of their paper that "The Future of Mindfulness Training Is Digital, and the Future Is Now." What does the evidence say?

An early meta-analysis (Spijkerman et al., 2016) summarized the effects of 17 digital mindfulness-based interventions (MBIs) – mostly mindfulness-based stress reduction (MBSR), mindfulness-based cognitive therapy (MBCT), and acceptance and commitment therapy (ACT), partly in modified versions – intended to improve mental health. Most interventions (14 out of 17) were delivered via a website, while one was delivered via a smartphone app, and two via a virtual online classroom. In nine comparisons, therapist guidance was also offered digitally. Effects (calculated for from 9 to 12 studies for each measure) were reliable (95 % confidence intervals did not cross 0) but somewhat smaller than those found in conventional studies (cf. results in Chapter 7): depression ($\bar{g}=0.29$), anxiety ($\bar{g}=0.22$), well-being ($\bar{g}=0.23$) and mindfulness, ($\bar{g}=0.32$), with the exception of stress ($\bar{g}=0.51$). For stress and mindfulness, guided meditations showed larger effects than unguided ones.

A more recent meta-analysis (Gál et al., 2021), including 34 randomized controlled trials (RCTs), examined the effects of mindfulness apps and found similar results (comparison of post-test results): depression ($\bar{g}=0.33$), anxiety ($\bar{g}=0.28$), psychological well-being ($\bar{g}=0.29$), and stress ($\bar{g}=0.46$). Other reliable effects were found for life satisfaction ($\bar{g}=0.41$), positive and negative affect ($\bar{g}=0.26$ and 0.21, respectively), and burnout ($\bar{g}=0.54$). For general well-being and distress, no reliable effects could be identified.

Attrition and adherence were not examined separately in these two meta-analyses. However, another one looked exactly at these two topics in 70 RCTs with smartphone apps that targeted mental health symptoms or disorders, or the improvement of general well-being. The authors' conclusion was that "study attrition and low adherence are common, problematic, and may undermine the validity of findings in RCTs of smartphone delivered interventions for mental health problems" (Linardon & Fuller-Tyszkiewicz, 2020, p. 1). This meta-analysis also included some studies with meditation apps.

In sum, these results indicate that at least the near future of meditation should not be fully digital. Effects (it seems that conventional control groups were used throughout) were generally smaller than in comparable studies summarized in Chapters 6 and 7. There are indications that additional guidance yields stronger effects (see also Linardon et al., 2019) and might help prevent participants from leaving a program prematurely. Moreover, meditation apps might not be so suitable for vulnerable practitioners who are especially prone to adverse effects of meditation if they do not practice it with a teacher (see section How Severe Are the Problems and How Can They Be Dealt With?). Nonetheless, meditation training will probably become more and more digital but human teachers and co-meditators might still be essential. Further clarification on this issue can be obtained if digital training is directly compared with conventional training that includes the same components. It would also be interesting to explore potential differential effects of apps with teachers and co-meditators absent vs. available online.

Undesirable Outcomes

Although most studies on the effects of meditation only report positive outcomes, there is also a darker side, increasingly targeted in recent years. As already mentioned several times, traditional meditative approaches, including Abrahamic ones, explicitly talk about very difficult periods that may appear on the path. To describe the highly negative experiences that might go along with giving up one's (false) ego, metaphors such as "death" and "dying" or "dark night" are used (e.g., Fisher, 2019; Greenwell, 1990; Mahasi, 1973; Trungpa, 2002; Tsong-Kha-pa, 2000; see also references in Kornfield, 1979). Traditional meditation teachers' knowledge about such difficult periods might also have been one reason they were so selective when choosing their students (see Chapter 6). As became clear in Chapter 5, many meditators in the West may come with some vulnerabilities, and therefore, chances of negative experiences when practicing meditation might be more prevalent these days than they were in the past. On the other hand, most practitioners probably practice at less deep levels (levels 3 and 4 in Goleman and Davidson's, 2017, nomenclature), and therefore, negative experiences, often brought about by a demanding practice, might not be so prevalent after all. Let us have a look at the evidence. First, we will focus on difficulties that come up in "normal" practice, followed by a brief summary of the evidence for very adverse effects usually to be found for vulnerable practitioners; and finally, the issue of problematic student-teacher relationships will be dealt with.

Problems in "Normal" Practice

Traditional Approaches and Experienced Meditators

An early study by Kornfield (1979) examined the range and patterns of experiences during intensive Vipassana meditation retreats. Meditation students' ($n=163$) experiences were collected by recording what students told their teachers at the end of interviews held every 2 days and by collecting questionnaires that had been filled out by students every 2 or 3 days. Students reported a wide variety of unusual experiences, some of which consisted of strong negative emotions such as heavy sadness, huge release of anger, incredibly strong hate or acute anxiety, and depression. On the other hand, almost all long-term meditators and also 40% of beginners reported some experience of bliss or rapture. Kornfield concludes that in their entirety, meditators' experiences conform to what should be expected in the progress of meditation according to traditional sources.

In another early study targeting transcendental meditation (TM) meditators, Otis (1984) found adverse effects of about 20% for dropouts from the TM program ($n=121$), 35% for mediators with a practice of 3 to 6 months ($n=156$), and 49% for more experienced meditators ($n=78$). A similar picture emerged in a study with 27 experienced Vipassana meditators by Deane Shapiro (1992b). He found that 63% had had at least one negative meditation-related experience (ranging from 40% for meditators with an average meditation experience of 17 months, to 75% with an average of 105 months), with 2 out of the 27 reporting very adverse experiences.

In a later study by Lomas et al. (2015b), all of the 30 mostly experienced male meditators (37% of whom had had some previous engagement with psychiatric of psychological therapy) described meditation as challenging, and six (20%) even reported psychotic episodes. These episodes generally arose under two conditions: (1) less experienced meditators who practiced advanced meditation techniques, and (2) meditating alone without a teacher. However, all respondents saw meditation as valuable and conducive to well-being. An online survey was used by Cebolla, Demarzo et al. (2017) who contacted a variety of meditation centers. Participants were asked whether they had experienced any type of unwanted or adverse reactions resulting from the practice of meditation. The 342 meditators in the sample practiced quite different techniques, and 25 % of them reported unwanted effects. These effects were more frequent if meditators practiced individually, with some kind of focused attention meditation, and for more than 20 min. However, approximately 50 % of respondents did not provide complete details about the respective episodes.

Lindahl et al. (2017) interviewed practitioners and experts (longtime meditation teachers, therapists who applied Buddhist meditation in clinical settings, or both) in three Buddhist traditions (Theravada, Zen, and Tibetan) who had had challenging meditation experiences. Because of the selectivity of the sample, all of the respondents recounted such experiences, which, however, were not necessarily negative. Of the 60 practitioners (60 % of whom were meditation teachers themselves), 32 % reported a psychiatric history, and 43 % a trauma history. The main aim of the study was not to estimate the incidence of adverse effects (which would not have been possible because of the selective sample) but to construct a taxonomy of 59 challenging meditation-related experiences. Even where the phenomenology of experiences was similar across participants, the associated valence ranged from very positive to very negative, and the associated level of distress from minimal to severe.

More recently, Schlosser et al. (2019) sent a survey link to Buddhist communities, meditation centers, and mindfulness associations. Potential participants were informed that the study aimed to advance the scientific understanding of meditation practices. Of the 2,599 individuals who started the survey, 1,706 completed it. After excluding yoga-only practitioners, respondents with less than 2 months of meditation experience, as well as a few who had not answered the question about particularly unpleasant meditation-related experiences, there remained 1,232 participants, with a median meditation experience of 6 years. Of these, 26 % reported having had particularly unpleasant meditation-related experiences. There were some qualifications: very unpleasant experiences occurred less for female and religious participants and more for participants with higher levels of repetitive negative thinking, as well as for those who practiced Vipassana/insight meditation, and for those who had attended a meditation retreat at any point in their life.

The two studies with the largest samples (Cebolla, Demarzo et al., 2017; Schlosser et al., 2019) found about one fourth of their respondents reported having had unpleasant meditation-related experiences. In both samples, the percentage of nonresponders was quite high, so we cannot be sure whether one fourth was upwardly or downwardly biased. One could think of potential reasons for either, so just starting with this figure might be a good preliminary estimate of the incidence of negative experiences in long-term meditators with a rather intensive practice.

Different Kinds of Approaches and Meditators
Do incidence rates change if not only experienced meditators with a demanding practice are asked? Farias et al. (2020) searched the meditation literature (1974 to 2019) for papers that explicitly reported adverse events. They found 83 studies. The average incidence rate calculated from 57 reports (case studies not included) was 8.3%. However, when they made separate analyses for observational studies (such as the ones with experienced meditators described in the last paragraph) and experimental studies (such as probably most studies that examined the impact of Western mindfulness interventions on beginners), a strong difference emerged: Whereas the mean prevalence was 33.2% in the observational studies, it was only 3.7% in the experimental studies. Because of the highly selective search procedure, these figures should be regarded as an upper limit – actual numbers might be considerably smaller. Of course, adverse events might go unnoticed and thus not be reported in studies. But chances are that, if they do occur, they are mentioned in the research reports. If then many studies with no adverse events are excluded from a survey that intends to estimate the incidence of such experiences, the overall estimate will probably be strongly inflated.

Western Mindfulness Interventions
Wong et al. (2018) only looked at reports of MBIs (any kind of population, publications up to 2017) that included any mention of adverse events (could also have been that there were none). The authors identified 36 RCTs, of which 25 examined the effects of MBSR and 11 those of MBCT (see Chapter 2). Altogether, the incidence rate of adverse events was 1% in the mindfulness intervention groups, but also 0.9% in the control groups. The figures for MBSR and MBCT were 0.49% and 1.5%, respectively, and none of the studies reported any serious event.

In sum, the available evidence indicates that the incidence of adverse events strongly depends on how demanding the meditation practice is. In contemporary Western style mindfulness meditation, it might be more or less negligible. Contrary to the expectation that long-term meditators might be those practitioners who experienced fewer problems than others (who then might have ended their practice), the available evidence indicates that long-term meditators retrospectively have dealt with more problems. But upon second thought, this finding is plausible because they spent much more time meditating (giving problems a much higher chance to occur). The incidence of problems might also depend on how vulnerable practitioners are (e.g., Lomas et al., 2015b), although the summaries do not give enough information to arrive at a clear picture. There is, however, also some literature that deals with the effects of meditation on especially vulnerable practitioners.

Case Reports of Very Adverse Meditation-Induced Effects

There are a number of case reports that illustrate very adverse effects of meditation. For instance, Kuijpers et al. (2007, p. 462) describe a young male artist who had the sensation of being mentally split during a special (Hindustan-type) kind of meditation. A psychiatric examination uncovered hallucinations and the idea that he had caused the end of the world. He also experienced very bright colors as well as general anxiety and feelings of guilt. Apparently, there were some pre-existing problems. He mentioned one hypomanic and some mild depressive problems (never treated) but no drug abuse or epilepsy. Common personality tests revealed vulnerability combined with some lack of insight in emotional functioning as well as a depressive, anxious disposition. He had recently lost 7 kg of weight because of extensive marathon training and, in addition, experienced work-related stress and relationship problems. Treatment with psychiatric drugs (haloperidol, administered in high doses for 1 week and gradually tapered over 3 months) led to a complete recovery from psychotic symptoms and a gradual normalization of mood that persisted at follow-up after 6 months.

Kuijpers et al. (2007) list 19 additional case studies of presumably meditation-induced psychosis and conclude that meditation may act as a stressor in vulnerable persons. The resulting psychotic syndrome may, however, be rather specific and transient, and not always require antipsychotic treatment. Another list of case studies (with partly overlapping references) was compiled by Lustyk et al. (2009; see Miller, 1993, for three especially interesting cases). These authors emphasize the crucial role of meditation retreats, where factors such as sensory deprivation, loss of sleep, and fasting may serve as precipitants of a psychotic episode.

Problematic Student–Teacher Relationships

Learning to meditate is not possible without a teacher. At the minimum, the teacher might "speak" through some text in a booklet or book, or via audio instructions. However, for a longer and intensive practice, a live teacher who is open to the student's potential problems is indispensable. Traditionally and ideally, a teacher guides the students in their spiritual progress without pursuing special interests of their own, and the student does not expect otherwise from the teacher. However, there is some evidence, most of it anecdotal, that this is not always so. And in such cases, negative effects might arise for both teachers and, more so, students.

Spiritual Bypassing

Sometimes, people expect to solve their psychological problems by striving for spiritual goals, such as awakening or liberation. Thereby, spiritual ideas and practices are used to sidestep or avoid facing unresolved emotional issues, psychological wounds, and unfinished developmental tasks. This was termed "spiritual bypassing" by John Welwood some 40 years ago (Fossella, 2011; see also Masters, 2010). Spiritual bypassing may be difficult to notice by the person practicing it and tackling the problem head-on might be hard. Both aspects of the problem are illustrated by the following extended quote by Jack Kornfield (1993, pp. 6–7):[19]

> My first ten years of systematic spiritual practice were primarily conducted through my mind. I studied, read, and then meditated and lived as a monk, always using the power of my mind to gain understanding. I developed concentration and samadhi (deep levels of mental absorption), and many kinds of insights came. I had visions, revelations, and a variety of deep awakenings. The whole way I understood myself in the world was turned upside down as my practice developed and I saw things in a new and wiser way. I thought that this insight was the point of practice and felt satisfied with my new understandings.

And then he adds:

> But alas, when I returned to the U. S. as a monk, all of that fell apart. ... Although I had arrived back from the monastery clear, spacious, and high, in short order I discovered ... that my meditation had helped me very little with my human relationships. I was still emotionally immature, acting out the same painful patterns of blame and fear, acceptance and rejection that I had before my Buddhist train-

---

19   Jack Kornfield is one of the most well-known contemporary Western insight meditation (Vipassana) teachers. He underwent a long period of psychotherapy and also used other means to successfully overcome his problems. Stating the whole of that process publicly can be seen as an indicator of a really mature meditation teacher.

ing; only the horror now was that I was beginning to see these patterns more clearly. I could do loving-kindness meditations for a thousand beings elsewhere but had terrible trouble relating intimately to one person here and now. I had used the strength of my mind in meditation to suppress painful feelings, and all too often I didn't even recognize that I was angry, sad, grieving, or frustrated until a long time later. ... I began a long and difficult process of reclaiming my emotions, of bringing awareness and understanding to my patterns of relationship, of learning how to feel my feelings, and what to do with the powerful forms of human connection. (Reprinted with permission from The Random House Group Ltd.)

The problem of spiritual bypassing may be aggravated when meditation teachers have been raised in a different culture from that of their students. Then they may not be able to easily recognize emotional problems of students coming from a different culture and may not even be aware that a problem does exist.

Abusive Teachers

An even more severe problem arises if influential and presumably enlightened teachers consciously abuse their students physically, sexually, or financially. This may be a rather small problem overall, but there are quite a few cases from all spiritual and religious backgrounds that have been made public over the years (e.g., Broad, 2012; CNN Staff, 2015; Coleman, 2002; Falk, 2009; Ford, 2006; Halser, 2020; Harris, 1994; Johnson, 2012; Lucia, 2018; Malhotra, 2017; Rodarmor, n.d.; Williamson, 2010; Wirth, 2006). The danger for such abusive behavior may be much higher in communities where the guru has a very authoritative (and sometimes even godlike) position, such as in many Hindu ashrams and partly in Zen circles, than in communities where the teacher is more seen as a good friend, as in most Theravada communities.

The potential problem might lessen with age: Wink et al. (2005) found no relation between spirituality and overt or covert narcissism for practitioners of spiritual paths who were at that time in their late adulthood (late 60s/mid 70s). Note that not all kinds of narcissism are necessarily detrimental – "healthy" or "normal" narcissism relates to creativity and wisdom, and expresses robust and autonomous self-investment (Kohut, 1977; Stone, 2000). Pathological or unhealthy narcissism comes in two forms which both include exaggerated self-entitlement, exploitativeness, and grandiosity. Overt (or "willful") narcissists show external grandiosity and exhibitionism, whereas covert (or "hypersensitive") narcissists also have a sense of entitlement and grandeur. The latter do not express it but may realize it in a symbiotic relationship with overt narcissists (Cooper, 2000; Wink, 1991).

Walach (2008) argues that the combination of overt and covert narcissists may be found in symbiotic relationships of charismatic leaders with worshipping followers. Teachers with a fragile and demanding ego who have had a strong spiritual experience may use it to compensate for their own shortcomings and thus stagnate on the path. However, they may find students who are very willing to join in as their narcissistic counterparts. Staying in such a relationship may be very attractive and fulfilling, at least for some time, for people with the respective complementary personality structures. However, eventually, it is detrimental for both, working against the true spiritual task of transcending one's false ego and finding one's "true" Self.

How Severe Are the Problems and How Can They Be Dealt With?

As evidenced in the case studies that connect meditation with psychosis, there have been some severe cases of meditation-induced problems. It seems that most of these cases had several issues in common: history of psychiatric illness, intensive meditation practice, and meditation outside a clinical framework setting (Shonin et al., 2014a). Chances are that the respective practitioners conceived of meditation as a therapy. Can meditation possibly serve as therapy in such severe cases? Shonin et al. (2014a) reviewed 11 studies that examined the effects of MBIs for the treatment of psychosis with generally positive outcomes (e.g., Lukoff et al., 1986). Studies mostly used small samples, poorly defined or inactive control conditions, and heterogeneous treatment regimens. Nonetheless, the evidence was sufficient for the authors to conclude that mindfulness meditation, delivered within a clinical framework, can play a beneficial role in the treatment of psychosis (see also the section Schizophrenia in Chapter 7). To mitigate the risk of mindfulness meditation inducing psychotic episodes, they recommend short sessions (≤ 15 min), omission of prolonged periods of silence, additional instruction in basic anchoring techniques (e.g., counting the breath, body scanning, etc.), and avoidance of explicitly analytical or insight-based methods (e.g., Vipassana). All treatments should be administered in small groups with occasions for one-to-one discussions with experienced facilitators or clinicians with at least 3 years of supervised mindfulness practice and teaching experience (see Shonin et al., 2014b, for an example of such a treatment).

However, meditators may view meditation-induced experiences not necessarily just as unwanted problems but also as "results of meditative practices and as signposts of their mystical path" (Grof & Grof, 1989, p. x.; see also Miller, 1993). As mentioned above, somewhat severe problems have been described in all spiritual traditions, also for not so vulnerable practitioners. This was acknowledged already in the fourth edition of the *Diagnostic and Statistical Manual of Mental Disorders*, (DSM-IV; published by the American Psychiatric Association) as a "religious or spiritual problem" (Lukoff et al., 1998). For the traditional paths, there usually was (and is) a competent teacher who can deal with problems of this sort. Many meditation teachers might, however, not be able to respond properly if a problem induced by intensive meditation practice (e.g., in a demanding retreat) is augmented by preexisting psychological or mental problems. This is why screening procedures have been suggested (e.g., Lustyk et al., 2009), which nowadays seem to be in some form or other applied in many mediation centers that conduct retreats. A personalized discussion of how to meet the program's likely challenges may be helpful in this respect (e.g., Williams et al., 2014).

Summarizing the research on the adverse effects of MBIs, Baer et al. (2019a) concluded that adverse events are not more common in participants of the mindfulness programs than in control group participants (and less common than in conventional psychotherapy). Moreover, as already mentioned above, the risk of adverse events with standardized mindfulness programs such as MBSR and MBCT might be almost negligible (Goldberg et al., 2021; Wong et al., 2018). Nonetheless, meditation teachers should be aware of potential problems and know how to deal with them (see Treleaven, 2018).

Especially if experienced meditators report a negative meditation-induced effect, a central question is whether it is a religious or mystical experience, or one that indicates psychopathology. Lindahl et al. (2019) argue that the answer to that question may depend on interpretations, causal explanations, and recommended responses. All of these are not obvious but need to be negotiated between practitioners and people they interact with. Because a consensus about the right interpretation might not be reached, they suggest that a more useful question may be "What type of support does this particular experience require?" That question might sometimes be easy to answer, but sometimes it may require a deeper understanding of the social and cultural contexts of meditation as well as the interaction of meditators and the social context they live in: Further research is definitely needed on the negative effects of meditation. As mentioned above, there are already some indications that concentrative meditation might have a higher probability of eliciting negative side effects, but other differences depending on the kind of meditation might also play a role. Research on such differences is another hot topic in meditation research.

How to approach the problem of spiritual bypassing? Prospective students might not be aware of the problem, but teachers, once they know about this special motivation for meditating, might be more prone to alert their students in that respect. Generally, it might be a good idea to mention this potential problem in introductory courses to meditation.

It is unclear how widespread the problem of unhealthy teacher-student relationships is, but it may be rather small. Nonetheless, such relationships can have severe and long-lasting negative effects on teachers and even more so on students. Problems of this sort are possibly absent in most Western forms of MBIs but might play some role in traditional approaches to meditation involving long-term stays in spiritual groups. However, these days, because of widespread globalization, problems due to misunderstanding of cultural issues (or due to mistaking patriarchy for "cultural differences") might be in the decline. However, as the mostly anecdotal evidence above indicates, the general problem of abusive relationships persists also if both teachers and students come with a Western socialization. Making all such cases public might be a good means to increasing both teachers' and potential students' sensitivity to the issue.

Comparisons of Meditation Techniques

In Chapters 2 and 3, we have seen that if practitioners and researchers talk about different kinds of meditation, they usually talk about bundles of techniques and not single ones. One could of course do research on the whole bundle (which is what has mostly been done so far), but even bundles carrying the same name may differ widely – "mindfulness meditation" being the best example (see Chapters 2 and 10). So, if we know that mindfulness meditation works, what do we really know? For a practitioner, it may be fully enough if the whole bundle works, but to really increase our understanding of how and why meditation works, it seems necessary to dissect the bundle and look at the components, which we will call here "basic meditation techniques." These basic meditation techniques can be components in different bundles.

Focused Attention Versus Open Monitoring

We have seen in Chapter 3 that the traditional meditation limbs in early Buddhism are right mindfulness (*samma sati*) and right concentration (*samma samadhi*). In the West, meditation techniques falling under these two rubrics are often termed *open monitoring* (OM) and *focused attention* (FA) and are expected to elicit different effects (e.g., Lutz et al., 2008). Also traditionally, these two types of meditation are generally used for different purposes (see Chapter 9). A few studies have addressed the difference in direct comparisons.

In an early study, Valentine and Sweet (1999) classified 19 meditators from a Buddhist center (not described in more detail) into concentrative and mindfulness meditators on the basis of a brief recruitment questionnaire. A second cross-categorization was that between short-term (< 24 months of meditation experience) and long-term (≥ 25 months) meditators. As expected, they found that long-term meditators demonstrated superior performance on a measure of sustained attention compared with short-term meditators, but the more interesting result was that OM showed superior performance as compared with FA meditators when the stimulus was unexpected. When the stimulus was expected, there was no difference between the two groups. According to the authors, the two different types of meditation might have different attentional effects, and OM meditators might be better able to quickly overcome expectancy effects than FA meditators.

Perlman et al. (2010) examined nine long-term meditators' behavioral reactions to pain induced by a thermal stimulator. Meditators had at least 10,000 (up to 40,000) hrs of formal meditation practice in a Tibetan Buddhist tradition. In this tradition, both OM and FA techniques are used. All meditators underwent several trials in both kinds of practice and gave ratings on intensity and unpleasantness of the pain. The authors calculated interaction effects for type of meditators (experts vs. novice meditators – the latter a matched group of 10 individuals) and type of meditation. In the OM condition, experienced meditators felt the pain to be somewhat less intense and markedly less unpleasant than in the FA condition.[20]

In a third study, differential effects of FA and OM meditation on creativity were explored (Colzato et al., 2012). Participants were 19 experienced meditators (average meditation practice of 2.2 years) with a practice in both FA and OM. In a counterbalanced design, they performed both an FA and an OM meditation session, and afterwards completed two tasks on creative thinking. In one of the tasks (remote association task), they were presented with three unrelated words (such as time, hair, and stretch), and asked to find a common associate (e.g., long). And in the other task (divergent thinking), they were asked to list as many uses as possible for six common household items (brick, shoe, newspaper, pen, towel, bottle), which were then rated for originality, fluency, flexibility, and elaboration. There was no difference between the two conditions for the remote association task, but the OM practice had a stronger effect on divergent thinking than the FA practice.

---

20 The interaction is, of course, not the best way to test the difference between OM and FA (although results for the controls could be used as a good baseline because they did not differ much across the two meditation conditions), and the statistical power for a direct test might have been pretty low due to the small sample size.

Whereas the preceding studies dealt with experienced meditators, Ainsworth et al. (2013) compared two groups of meditators after a relatively short (mean of 21.5 days of meditation practice) training in either OM or FA meditation. They found no marked differences between the two meditation groups and a relaxation control group, for anxiety, attention control, and trait mindfulness, as well as two components of the attention network test (orienting and alerting). Only the executive attention component improved (equally) for both meditation groups in comparison with the control group. Comparing this result with the findings in the previous three studies might indicate that it takes time for any kind of meditation to have a strong impact on aspects of attention, which might be necessary to detect specific differences between the effects of OM and FA meditation.

However, it seems that for some dependent variables, OM and FA meditation might show distinctive effects early on. Sedlmeier et al. (2020) summarized studies on how meditation practice influenced time perception. Overall, they found that subjectively, time passed more quickly during meditation for practitioners who predominantly practiced concentrative techniques compared with those whose main practice was open awareness. In a study of their own, they could find the same difference in time perception even for student participants who had had only a single guided session in one of the two techniques.

Two very interesting studies that bring us back to experienced meditators were conducted by Amihai and Kozhevnikov (2014). In their Study 1, they compared OM and FA meditators from two different Buddhist traditions, 10 Theravada practitioners (average of 8 years of meditation experience) from a temple in Thailand, and 9 Vajrayana (Tibetan Buddhist) practitioners (average of 7.4 years of meditation experience) from a temple in Nepal. Both groups first performed the respective FA and then the OM practice. The authors measured both neurophysiological [electroencephalography (EEG) and electrocardiography] and cognitive correlates thought to utilize either FA or OM. Contrary to what one might expect, the greatest differences were not found for the comparison between FA and OM practice but between the two kinds of meditation approaches. Whereas Theravada practitioners produced enhanced parasympathetic activation (a relaxation response), the Vajrayana practitioners exhibited sympathetic activation (arousal). In their Study 2, conducted with four separate groups (two Vipassana and two Vajrayana) from different monasteries who only practiced either the FA or the OM type of meditation in their respective traditions, the authors again found much stronger differences between the traditions than between OM and FA practice. Following Vajrayana practice (both FA and OM), performance on cognitive tasks increased markedly, but not following Theravada practice, indicating enhanced phasic alertness due to arousal only for Vajrayana practitioners (for a similar heterogeneity in heart rate measures for other kinds of meditation see Peng et al., 1999, 2004). Consistent qualitative differences between the two Buddhist schools were also found in EEG results. Amihai and Kozhevnikov (2015) argue that this difference is to be expected according to the respective scriptural descriptions (heightened arousal during Vajrayana, and a calm and alert state of mind during Theravada meditation). They also point out that their previous findings demonstrate the importance of the context (cultural and philosophical) out of which the practices developed.

Conclusions from the few studies summarized above are limited, but whereas the results in several studies indicate differential effects for OM and FA practices (see also Manna et al., 2010, who found neural correlates that might covary with the psychological distinctions), the results of Amihai and Kozhevnikov (2014) make clear that the general distinction between focused attention and open awareness needs to be rethought, in that one might take into account the historical background and probably also differences in techniques across traditions.

Components of MBIs (Western Style)

In Chapter 2, we have seen that Western kinds of mindfulness meditation include not only OM and FA practices but also loving kindness meditation and body-oriented techniques such as the body scan or yoga postures. Although the term "mindfulness meditation" is still widely used in an indiscriminate way, research in recent years has begun to investigate potential differences between the components of MBI packages.

Sauer-Zavala et al. (2013) compared three components commonly included in MBIs: mindful yoga, sitting meditation (presumably awareness of the breath – that is, an FA practice), and body scan, which lasted for 3 weeks each. Their undergraduate participants ($n=141$) completed pre and post measurements on the *Five Facet Mindfulness Questionnaire* (FFMQ; see Chapter 2), as well as measures of psychological symptoms, rumination, emotion regulation, self compassion, and psychological well-being. Comparisons between the effects for the three components revealed only a few, inconsistent differences: superior effects for mindful yoga in psychological well-being, smaller effects for the body scan than in the two other practices in emotion regulation, and smaller effects for the body scan in the nonjudging facet of the FFMQ.

The effects of concentration (awareness of the breath) and loving kindness meditation ($n=15$ and $n=16$, respectively, both cohorts were undergraduate participants) were contrasted by May et al. (2014). They used a multiple baseline design with baselines ranging from 1 to 4 weeks and treatment lasting 5 weeks. Before practicing concentration or loving kindness, both groups started their practice sessions with a body scan exercise. Measurements were taken on 19 days. A multilevel model (with measurement points on level 1, and meditation group on level 2) did not reveal any marked differences, which, however, could have been partly due to the small statistical power of the study. There might also have been some confounding effects due to the initial body scan exercise that preceded the two components to be compared.

Fredrickson et al. (2017) randomized their 339 participants (pooled across two studies) into mindfulness meditation (close to the traditional satipatthana approach – see Chapter 2) and loving kindness meditation. Both groups received a 6-week training and rated their positive and negative emotions daily for a total of 9 weeks. For both groups, no change was found for negative emotions, but a gain was found in positive emotions. However, no difference was identified between the two conditions. Only practice intensity (frequency and duration) was more tightly coupled to same-day reports of positive emotions in the loving kindness than in the mindfulness condition.

The relationships between frequency and duration with which experienced meditators (> 1 year) practiced four different kinds of meditation – FA, OM, compassion meditation, and informal practice (mindfulness in daily life) – and the five facets of the FFMQ were explored by Cebolla, Campos et al. (2017). In a structural model analysis, they found several (rather small) differential relationships between the four kinds of meditation and the five mindfulness facets. However, their results have to be interpreted with caution because it seems that the frequency variables did not possess a prerequisite for structural modeling: an interval scale (an interval scale requires that equal differences in numerical values refer to equal differences in empirical values. Here the empirical values for frequency were every day, 3 or 4 times a week, once a week or less, 2 or 3 times per month, sporadically, or never).

Hunt et al. (2018) compared the effects of a multicomponent mindfulness training (mindful breathing, body scan, mindful listening, mindful eating, loving kindness, meditations on stress and anxiety, $n=22$), with yoga (pranayama and asanas, $n=24$), and a combined condition ($n=22$). After a 4-week training, they found that their undergraduate participants did not differ significantly in measures of anxiety, negative affect, and heart rate variability, although there was a trend toward superior results for the combined condition in all three measures. When heart rate variability was compared at rest, with after a challenging event (an IQ test), the mindfulness condition fared best.

In one of our own studies (Kropp & Sedlmeier, 2019), 56 university students followed meditation instructions either in a breathing awareness

(n=18), body scan (n=14), or loving kindness (n=24) condition for 6 weeks. For most of the dependent variables measured (trait mindfulness, self-rated attention, self-compassion, emotion regulation, and life satisfaction), the effects of body scan were substantially higher than those for breathing awareness, and for trait mindfulness and life satisfaction, they were also higher than those for loving kindness meditation. Astonishingly, loving kindness meditation did better than breathing awareness in the subjective attention scale.

A recent study (Roca et al., 2021) did not compare single components but two composite mindfulness programs, MBSR and *compassion cultivation training* (CCT; Goldin & Jazaieri, 2017). Although some of the effect founds for the two training programs were comparable, they differed in other aspects. MBSR did better in present-moment awareness (decentering and body awareness), whereas the effects of CCT were larger for socioemotional changes (common humanity and empathetic concern).

In sum, no clear picture emerges from the studies that have compared different components of MBIs or different MBI packages. The most plausible explanation for this state of affairs seems to be that the studies compared different things, both on the side of independent variables (different kinds of meditation) and on the side of dependent measures. Nonetheless, the amount of variation found probably cannot be explained by sampling error alone. Specific effects of a given component might take some time to arise, which could be another reason for the heterogeneous results because Western MBIs usually only last for some weeks, and all studies only covered a relatively short period of time.

The ReSource Project

By far the most laborious and extensive comparison of different kinds of meditation has been conducted in the ReSource project led by Tania Singer (overview in Singer & Engert, 2019). In this project, three consecutive 3-month meditative training modules were compared along a multitude of dependent measures, with a total of 332 healthy participants. Although the modules contained components from the usual MBIs, two of them also included dyadic techniques not usually subsumed under the umbrella term of "meditation." The *Presence* module consisted of breathing meditation (FA) and body scan, the *Affect* module included loving kindness meditation and an *affect dyad*, and the *Perspective* module was composed of observing thoughts meditation (OM) and a *perspective dyad*. In the dyads, realized with different weekly partners, a speaker and a listener took part, with the listener just listening. In the affect dyad, the speaker was to describe feelings and bodily sensations experienced during a difficult situation, as well as during a gratitude-eliciting situation from the last day; and in the perspective dyad, the speaker was to describe a recent situation from the perspective of a randomly selected so-called inner part, such as "the judge" or "the loving mother," which are expected to describe distinct patterns of thoughts, feelings, and behaviors (see Kok & Singer, 2017a).

Figure 8.1 shows the design of the study that in its entirety lasted for about 2 years. This design is not without problems. First, the training cohorts 1 and 2 (upper two rows in Figure 8.1) both begin with the Presence module. Thus, the effects to be found in the later modules are likely to be influenced by the effects of breathing meditation and body scan practiced in this first module. Moreover, in the first cohort, the effects of the last module (Perspective) are likely to be also influenced by the second (Affect), whereas in the second cohort, the reverse holds true, or in other words, effects in later treatments may in part be due to carry-over effects. After all, each module was practiced for 3 months (and not only the usual 3 to 6 weeks to be found in most studies described in the last paragraph). One might argue that the only comparison that fully makes sense is the one between the two Presence modules combined (in the first two cohorts) and the Affect module in the third cohort (lowest line in Figure 8.1) because these modules are not preceded by another. But also here, there is a possible confounding: Modules were not concurrent. A sound comparison would assume that the context – here used as a summary term for all potential variables that might have an additional effect on the dependent measures – can be assumed not to have changed over time.

Despite these potential shortcomings due to its suboptimal design, the project has yielded an impressively large number of publications. Three of

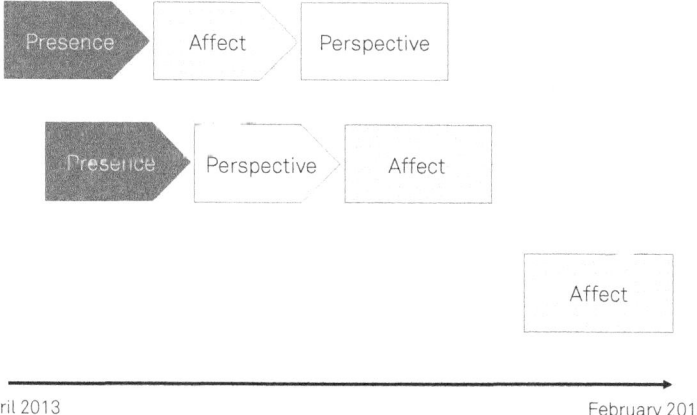

Figure 8.1. Design and timeline of the ReSource project. Based on Singer and Engert (2019).

them will be briefly summarized here. An especially interesting result, referring to data from the first two cohorts, is described in Lumma et al. (2015). These authors examined heart rate (HR), high-frequency heart-rate variability (HF-HRV), both measured during the weekly meditation session, experienced effort ("How demanding was the exercise for you?"), and likeability ("How enjoyable was the exercise for you?"). Measurements took place after the completion of the respective meditation exercise (breathing meditation, loving kindness meditation, and observing thoughts meditation). No significant difference among the three kinds of meditation was found for HF-HRV, although it decreased substantially over time. But note that differences between the three kinds of meditation could have been obscured by combining data irrespective of the order of the modules. Especially the Presence module – that is, the effects of breathing meditation, which always came first – might have been underestimated due to the design (see Figure 8.1).

HR increased over time and was highest for loving kindness meditation and lowest for breathing meditation, and the results for experienced effort followed the same pattern. Breathing meditation was liked most (because it was always practiced first?), followed by observing thoughts and loving kindness meditation. The authors also looked at the changes in HR (which went up) and HF-HRV (which went down) and found that they were greater for the later modules. Moreover, there was a lack of correlation between changes in HR and changes in effort during loving kindness and observing thoughts meditation (in the two later modules). The authors interpret this noncorrelation as potential evidence for increased cognitive processes (based on the heart measures) that were not experienced as effortful. This might be taken as another piece of evidence for the conclusion previously advanced by Amihai and Kozhevnikov (2014) that meditation is not always relaxing.[21]

Kok and Singer (2017b) investigated the short-term effects (measurements were taken before meditation sessions began and immediately afterwards) for variables that measured affect, mind wandering, meta-cognition, and interoception. Using a multilevel analysis with measurements at level 1, and kind of meditation (breathing meditation, body scan, loving kindness, and observing thoughts) at level 2, they found that after the body scan, interoceptive awareness had increased most, and thought content had decreased most. Loving kindness meditation led to most feelings of warmth and positive thoughts about others and observing thoughts meditation yielded the highest increase in meta-cognitive awareness. These are

---

21 An even more convincing test of this issue would be to see whether this pattern also holds for the participants in the third cohort, in which the Affect module was not preceded by one or two other modules.

plausible results, but again, it is unclear whether the results might have changed if the kinds of meditation had been administered in a different order.

A more recent publication (Trautwein et al., 2020) concentrated on attention, compassion, and theory of mind as dependent variables. The authors argue that the Presence module focuses on cultivating present-moment attention and interoceptive awareness; the Affect module on cultivating affective qualities of care, gratitude, and loving kindness; and the Perspective module on metacognitive awareness and theory of mind (perspective taking on self and others). In contrast to the other two publications described above, the dyads in the Affect and Perspective modules were explicitly mentioned in deriving the predictions. The measurements for attentional performance (a cued flanker task), compassion, and theory of mind (both measured with a video task) were taken on the same day during functional magnetic resonance imaging (data not reported). There were four points of measurement for the first two cohorts (before training and toward the end of each of the three modules) and two for the third cohort (because there was only the Affect module in this condition, see Figure 8.1). The authors conclude that attention most consistently improved after attention training. But an inspection of results indicates that attention consistently improved most in the initial module (also in the Affect module in cohort 3 there is a strong increase – see their Figure 2c). Compassion increased most after the Affect module in cohort 1, in which it was placed second, followed by increases in the Affect module in cohort 2, in which it was placed third. However, in the condition that should have shown the least contaminated effect of compassion – that is, in the Affect module of cohort 3 (Affect module only) – the increase in compassion was negligible (Trautwein et al., 2020, p. 8). This might indicate that the Perspective module (an FA task plus body scan) is necessary for loving kindness meditation to unfold its effect on increasing compassion. Finally, a second look at the data reveals that also the theory of mind measures increased most consistently in the first module, irrespective of whether it was the Presence module (cohorts 1 and 2) or the Affect module (cohort 3, see their Figure 2e). Thus, also in this study it seems hard to disentangle the effects of specific modules and the effects of the order of modules.

In sum, although the ReSource project was immensely laborious, and employed excellent methods, measurements, and statistical analyses, all of that unfortunately could not make up for the deficiencies in design. Many of the authors' conclusions are open to alternative explanations (see above) and many of the effects (measured during or immediately after meditation sessions) might be short-lived. But still, overall, the results indicate that different meditational practices yield different results.

How Do the Effects of Different Kinds of Meditation Differ?

Chapter 6 has already briefly described the results of a meta-analysis with functional magnetic resonance imaging (fMRI) data for experienced meditators indicating pronounced differences for four (mainly practiced) kinds of meditation: FA, OM, loving kindness, and mantra (Fox et al., 2016). At first glance, the results of the ReSource project also show that different kinds of meditation might differ along the lines one would expect: more attentional abilities after FA, more compassion after loving kindness meditation. However, as detailed above, while this may be so, alternative explanations still linger. Attempts to examine the relative effects of components in mindfulness-based approaches did not detect unanimous effects. A very interesting finding is that not all kinds of meditation are relaxing and, maybe most important, that the long-held central distinction between FA and OM meditation needs further clarification. In sum, the most plausible conclusion based on the present body of research is that different kinds of meditation indeed yield (at least partly) different effects. It should only be a matter of time before we arrive at a clearer picture. When the effects of basic meditation techniques are understood better, combinations of these techniques could be explored more advantageously (see Chapter 11). We have already seen, both for potential negative effects of meditation and with respect to comparing different kinds of meditation (OM versus FA), that the tradition context may make a huge difference. Two context aspects in particular have recently come into focus in research: ethics and spirituality.

The Impact of Ethical and Spiritual Context

As already detailed in Chapter 3, traditionally, meditation has always come with a spiritual and, maybe even more importantly – because it has even direct consequences on daily living – an ethical context (for background accounts from different traditions, see Condon, 2019; Feuerstein, 1989; Hilert & Gutierrez, 2020; Karunamuni & Weerasekera, 2019; Oman et al., 2020; Thupten, 2019; Whitaker & Smith, 2018). For years now, there has been a debate about whether MBIs need to be at least partially practiced within the original Buddhist ethical and spiritual context, or whether the Buddhist context can be disposed of without losing much or anything at all (e.g., Greenberg & Mitra, 2015; Monteiro et al., 2015; see also Chapter 2). A variant of the latter position has recently been dubbed *McMindfulness* (Purser, 2019). Van Gordon and Shonin (2020) summarize why that position is potentially detrimental to the original Buddhist intention:

The essence of the McMindfulness assertion appears to be that some modern renderings of mindfulness have contributed to the creation of a "mindfulness-ego," that enables cliques of mindfulness teachers and stakeholders to profit from the integration of (what they claim to constitute) mindfulness into a range of life and work contexts. (van Gordon & Shonin, 2020, p. 1)

As a countermeasure, they propose *second-generation mindfulness-based interventions* that prominently include issues of spirituality and ethics. They are also concerned about meditation teachers' expertise and suggest that instructor-training programs should require several years of supervised mindfulness practice (as is the case in all traditional approaches). Although there has been considerable debate about this issue, research directly examining whether meditation with or without ethics and spirituality makes a difference, and what this difference might be, is still scarce.

Ethics

One could argue that if meditation interventions are complemented by an ethics component (like in the traditional approaches), effects on variables that measure ethical aspects should be stronger as compared with meditation interventions without that complement. Unfortunately, so far, most of the evidence is only indirect and concentrates on self-ratings of prosociality and prosocial behavior. As discussed in Chapter 6, the effects of mindfulness-only interventions seem to be comparable to those of compassion-based interventions. However, the respective meta-analyses do not really allow for disentangling the effects of different kinds or different components of meditation interventions. It would be best to compare meditation interventions with or without an ethics component, for the same population.

This is what Chen and Jordan (2020) did. With a large sample ($n=621$), they found that, compared with a control group, there were similar effects for both groups for stress reduction, life satisfaction, self-awareness, and most measures of psychological well-being. However, whereas the mindfulness-only group did not differ from the control group with respect to personal growth, the group with the ethics component did. This group donated significantly more money to a charity than the mindfulness-only group. The latter effect was moderated by trait empathy. Interestingly, low trait empathy participants in the mindfulness-only group gave even less money than the participants in the control group.

In another recent study, Bayot et al. (2020) compared an *ethics-oriented mindfulness training* (EMT) with a *standard mindfulness training* (SMT), both lasting for 8 weeks ($n=78$). Both groups improved compared with a control group, in trait mindfulness, empathy, self-compassion, and well-being. A trend for the long-term (follow-up measurement after 3 months) superiority of the EMT condition was only found for self-compassion. The authors suggest that participants' personality traits might be important moderators for whether the ethics component in meditation courses turns out beneficial for meditators or not. Matko et al. (2021b) used a single-case experimental design (see Chapter 11) to explore the incremental effects of ethical education and physical yoga on mantra meditation. Adding ethical education substantially increased the effect of mantra meditation on well-being but not on stress, the two dependent variables reported in the study.

Spirituality

There are quite a large number of studies that have compared meditation techniques including spiritual components (i.e., basically all studies that used traditional approaches) with control groups. But to find out about the specific effects of spirituality, one ideally has to compare interventions that only differ in whether there is a spiritual component added or not. Only a few studies, comparing the effects of traditional mantras with "placebo mantras" seem to have explored this issue to date.[22]

Wolf and Abell (2003) compared the effects of the *maha mantra* as used in the Hare Krishna movement ("hare krishna hare krishna krishna krishna hare hare/hare rama hare rama rama rama hare hare"; See also Chapter 1) with that of a (meaningless) pseudo mantra, made up from Sanskrit syllables ("sarva dasa sarva dasa dasa dasa sarva sarva/sarva jana sarva jana jana jana sarva sarva") and found stronger effects for the former, for stress, depression, and the *sattva guna*, a personality measure derived from early Yoga theory. (Only F-tests that compared all three conditions – maha mantra, pseudo mantra, and a control group – were calculated but the maha mantra fared best in all comparisons.)

Wachholtz and Pargament (2005) had their participants ($n=84$ college students) either practice a spiritual mantra (choice of "God is peace," "God is joy," "God is good," or "God is love.") or a secular mantra (choice of "I am content," "I am joyful," "I am good," "I am happy") for 2 weeks. The spiritual meditation group's anxiety decreased more than that of the secular meditation group and a control group, and had higher increases in positive mood, spiritual health, and spiritual experiences. Moreover, the spir-

---

22 Other studies compared only spiritually based mantra meditations with control groups and found positive effects (e.g., Bormann & Carrico, 2009; Bormann et al., 2008; Oman et al., 2006, 2008).

itual mantra group tolerated pain (cold pressure task) twice as long as the other two groups.

Similar results were found in a later study targeting 83 participants who suffered from migraine (Wachholtz & Pargament, 2008). This time, spiritual meditation (again a choice of "God is peace," "God is joy," "God is good," or "God is love"; but this time "God" could be replaced by another term such as "Mother Earth") was compared with two versions of secular meditation: internal secular meditation (choice of "I am content," "I am joyful," "I am good," "I am happy") and external secular meditation (choice of "Grass is green," "Sand is soft," "Cotton is fluffy," "Cloth is smooth"). The three meditation groups and a relaxation group (progressive muscle relaxation) were asked to practice 20 min daily for 30 days. Compared with the other groups, the spiritual meditation group experienced greater decreases in the frequency of migraine headaches, anxiety, and negative affect, as well as greater increases in pain tolerance, headache-related self-efficacy, daily spiritual experiences, and existential well-being, but not headache severity, positive affect, depression, spiritual well-being, and religious well-being. This result was more or less replicated in a more recent study (Wachholtz et al., 2017). Employing the same procedure (spiritual meditation, internal and external secular meditation, and relaxation practiced for 30 days), it was found that spiritual meditation did not reduce pain sensitivity as compared with the other groups but did improve pain tolerance, accompanied by reduced headache-related analgesic medication usage.

Are Spirituality and Ethics Necessary?

The term "spirituality" is notoriously difficult to define (Kristeller & Jordan, 2018; Oman, 2013; Speck, 2005; Waaijman, 2007; Walach, 2011), but in meditation research it is often used as a shorthand for traditional context except ethics. For meditators, this means, for instance, to have assumptions about the real nature of the world (e.g., purusha, Brahman, nirvana, but not necessarily the existence of a god; see also Chapter 9). Such assumptions are part of all traditional mediation practices and manifest themselves, among other things, in recitations, chanting, rituals (such as prostrations), or in the meditation techniques themselves (e.g., visualizing a goddess). Also, the unexpected findings by Amihai and Kozhevnikov (2014, see above: the section Focused Attention Versus Open Monitoring) might be regarded as due to differences in aspects of spirituality connected with Tibetan Buddhism versus Theravada.

Is spirituality absolutely necessary? It seems not because otherwise the results for secular meditation interventions would be considerably lower than those for traditional kinds of meditation, which is not the case (see Chapter 6). But is it beneficial? The few results summarized in the preceding paragraph point to a tentative "yes," although only a specific aspect of spirituality was examined there: spiritual versus nonspiritual mantras. It might also depend on which dependent measures one looks at, whether or not an effect of spirituality can be detected. In any case, spirituality seems to have a stabilizing function: Basically, all long-term meditators who have participated in empirical research have been members of some traditional lineage. If, as in the traditional approaches, the aim of meditation is liberation or enlightenment (and not well-being as in Western-style secular meditation), spirituality, in the sense that practitioners assume that some kind of altered consciousness can be reached, is inevitable. Shared spirituality might also be very helpful to stay motivated, find mutual support and solace if needed, and overcome dry spells in the practice (e.g., Ahn, 2020). However, some aspects of spirituality might be difficult to measure using questionnaires. For that purpose, qualitative approaches seem to be more suitable (see Chapter 11).

Are ethics components necessary? Here also the best answer given the currently available evidence seems to be that *it depends.* We have seen that on average, prosociality increases also when practicing mindfulness-only meditation (Chapter 6). But one could say that in all traditional approaches, a central aim of meditation is to deflate one's inflated ego and eventually totally get rid of it (the "false" ego, that is – see also Chapter 9). Recent studies indicate that very brief mindfulness interventions may indeed tend to *inflate* the ego (Gebauer et al., 2018; Vonk & Visser, 2020). Whether this happens or not may depend, among other things, on meditators' personalities. Especially practitioners low on empathy and high on narcissism might be prone to show unintended effects (Ridderinkhof et al., 2017; Winning & Boag, 2015). The latter results have to be regarded with caution, however, due to the extremely short interventions in these studies, and the issue certainly needs more research. If additional studies happen to confirm this specific influence of empathy and narcissism, it will be a challenge for meditation teachers. Whereas empathetic and nonnarcissist meditators probably can do well without additional ethical instructions, nonempathetic and narcissist meditators who would need an additional ethics component most, might be especially hard to motivate to follow ethical principles. That meditation without an ethical component can lead to very destructive results even in experienced meditators can also be seen in the history of Zen meditation in Japan (Victoria, 2020). For instance, Japanese Zen masters emphasized the effectiveness of meditation-induced samadhi power in battle: to more effectively kill the enemy. But this is by no means a problem of a specific country. Recent events in Myanmar and Sri Lanka also indicate that ethics is not automatically a strong component even in largely Buddhist societies, including at least some monastics.

In sum, the safest answer to whether meditation would profit from an ethics component seems to be "yes": The inclusion of ethics in meditation instruction does not hurt and may be especially beneficial for some practitioners.

The Effects of Meditation: A Short Résumé

After looking at all the evidence presented in the last three chapters (including the present one), one cannot but conclude that meditation works. However, it also has become clear that it does not work uniformly: Different meditation techniques have different effects on different people. The highly complex interactions between kind of meditation, dependent measures looked at, personality characteristics, and traditional context (especially spirituality and ethics) have also become evident in three of the topics discussed in this chapter.

What can be done about this problematic state of affairs? The best global answer for meditation research is probably: Include all important aspects and make them more precise! (see also Lutz et al., 2008, p. 169). First of all, this means theory work. The next two chapters will summarize first, theoretical approaches extracted from selected meditation traditions (Chapter 9), and second, theoretical frameworks developed in the West (Chapter 10). Sound theories allow for asking more precise questions and for narrowing down the focus of research. In that way, measurements should be theoretically derived in a more consistent way. In addition, one might also want to use research designs that will take into account the huge heterogeneity often seen in meditation research. In Chapter 11, we will come back to the issue of how meditation research can be improved in these respects.

Part 3
Theories

Chapter 9
Traditional Theories of Meditation

Traditional theories of meditation are not theories in the sense we usually have in mind. Instead, they have to be extracted from ancient texts in which religion, philosophy, and psychology are all rolled into one to provide pathways to salvation. The author of this present work was fortunate to have K. Srinivas, a philosophy professor from Pondicherry University, India – who sadly deceased so young – to help me through the initially seemingly impenetrable jungle of often drastically different translations and interpretation of those ancient texts. Our aim was to extract the psychology part and do justice, as much as possible, to the other parts of the texts (see Sedlmeier & Srinivas, 2016, 2019). Some (short) parts in the paragraphs referring to Samkhya-Yoga and early Buddhism below are slight reformulations of portions of texts in these two sources. What I present below will, in all likelihood, not find unanimous agreement. This will not be surprising, however, given the vast diversity of opinion to be found among both ancient and contemporary scholars in the two traditions, Hindu and Buddhist, with which this chapter will be mainly concerned. And what will be presented here will not be one more of the innumerable exegeses of those texts, but rather an attempt to formulate testable psychological theories that can provide a basis for understanding the effects of meditation. Such a fundamental building block may eventually allow for arriving at one or more comprehensive theories of meditation, in combination with the Western approaches (see Chapter 10).

As I understand them, from the perspective of psychological research, traditional theories can be characterized foremost as theories about cognitive change. So, for each of the four theories to be discussed in this chapter, we will begin with an outline of the basic theory of cognition (cognition understood in a wide sense) and then go on to describe the respective model of cognitive change, presumably brought about by meditation practice (also understood in a wide sense). In this, the chapter will concentrate on two approaches each from Hinduism and Buddhism: Samkhya-Yoga, Advaita Vedanta, early Buddhism, and Zen. Actually, some experts might object to grouping Samkhya-Yoga and also Advaita Vedanta under "Hinduism," because when these thought systems originated, the term "Hindu" did not yet exist. Moreover, Hinduism is an external name, initially mainly used for political reasons (Singh, 2008). Nonetheless, to not complicate things more than necessary, this chapter will follow common usage.

In Chapter 3, we have already met meditation techniques connected to these four approaches. Ideally, the corresponding theories dealt with in this chapter should explain why and how these meditation techniques work. There are, of course, many other Hindu and Buddhist approaches to meditation, notwithstanding those from other religious backgrounds (for treatments of some other Hindu and Buddhist approaches, see Feuerstein, 1998; Grabovac et al., 2011; Lutz et al., 2007). However, the four approaches selected here should give a good impression regarding what kinds of theories stand behind traditional systems of meditation. The ancient texts referred to in the following have been written in (different forms of) Sanskrit and in the Pali language. These languages are quite contextual and rich, and therefore, translations into Western languages are sometimes ambiguous and can differ considerably. That is why the central Sanskrit or Pali (for early Buddhism) terms are usually included in the translations below. However, because these languages use a different script (Devanagiri) there is no one-to-one correspondence to the Latin script used in nearly all Western languages. Therefore, the translations often employ so-called diacritical marks. In the following, I will abstain from using diacritical marks because they are hard to read, and their omission usually does not create any problems in identifying the original terms.

The Context of Traditional Theories

In a way, all traditional Indian theories of meditation can be connected to the ancient Indian scriptures called *Vedas* (there are four with four parts each), with the earliest one (Rigveda Samhita) dated between 3500 and 1200 BCE (e.g., Frawley, 2001; Hiriyanna, 2000; Klostermaier, 2006; Sharma, 2003). *Veda* means "knowledge". The *Vedas*, composed in archaic Sanskrit, were initially transmitted orally, and probably first written down only after 300 BCE (B.A. West, 2009, p. 282). The huge discrepancy in dating the first Vedic scriptures may be seen as an indicator of (a) how little historical recording of events was done in the prehistoric Vedic civilizations and (b) how discrepant experts' opinions may be not only about their contents but also about the context of this ancient source of meditation theories. Nonetheless, the question is how can the four selected explanatory systems be connected to them?

Relationship to the Vedas

Meditation techniques are already mentioned in the *Vedas* (see Chapter 4 in Feuerstein, 1998), but they (and their context) were elaborated only in later schools of interpretations of the Vedas. Samkhya and Yoga are two such schools, which are usually treated in combination. Another school that draws on the last (most recent) part of the Vedas is called *Vedanta*. And Advaita (meaning "nondual") *Vedanta* is a subschool of Vedanta. These (and some more) Indian schools of thought are usually referred to as *orthodox schools*, because they are assumed to be fully in line with the Vedic teachings. There are six schools, usually seen as consisting of pairs: *Samkhya* and *Yoga*, *Nyaya* and *Vaisheshika*, and *Mimamsa* and *Vedanta*. Other schools of thought also referred to the Vedas but (in part) were critical and were also not accepted into the fold for various reasons. These are termed the *heterodox schools* (for details, see Dasgupta, 1930; Hiriyanna, 2000; Sedlmeier, 2014). Two examples of the latter are Buddhism and Jainism (not dealt with here). Thus, all four theories of meditation treated below can be said to be outcomes from encounters with the Vedas: Samkhya-Yoga and Advaita Vedanta as elaborate interpretations of (parts of) the Vedas, and early Buddhism and Zen as critical confrontations with them. As so often in this area of research, there are also dissenting voices. For instance, Nicholson (2010) argues that the difference between orthodox and heterodox systems has been exaggerated, and that Buddhism and Jainism have also belonged to the former class at some time. But all four theories dealt with here can be said to be derivative of philosophical encounters with the regional philosophies of their time, with varying degrees of entrenchment within or outside the broad range of ideas encompassed in the Vedas.

What Is the Source of These Theories?

If the Vedas are so important as the basis for traditional theories of meditation, one might be compelled to ask how did they originate? The conventional answer is *shruti* ("that which is heard"), or in other words, they are considered the product of divine revelation, heard and transmitted by earthly sages. Later texts, including the basic texts for Samkhya-Yoga and Advaita Vedanta are not shruti but *smriti:* "that which is remembered" by ordinary human beings. This distinction plays an important role in religious and spiritual contexts, but it is not relevant for psychological theories of meditation. The working hypothesis followed here is that psychological insights about the practice of meditation contained in ancient Indian texts are likely based on personal experiences of very curious meditators. Such an empirical and investigative view seems also to be held by some contemporary Hindu scholars (e.g., Burley, 2007; Phillips, 2009), as well as leading Hindu teachers of the recent past. Swami Vivekananda held the opinion that "if a religion is destroyed by such investigations, it was then all the time useless, unworthy superstition; and the sooner it goes the better" (Jitatmananda, 2004, p. 171). And according to Sri Aurobindo, the applied part of Hindu theory "is nothing but practical psychology" (Aurobindo, 1996, p. 39). The latter poet-sage also kept an elaborate diary on the effects of his yoga practice over many years (Aurobindo, 2001).

This empirical approach is even more evident in Buddhism. There, the primary source of the theories of meditation is the Buddha. Indeed, the Buddha stressed his empirical approach, most prominently in the *Kalama Sutta* (e.g., Soma, 1994). There, he admonished the Kalamas (inhabitants of a village situated in what is nowadays the Indian state of Bihar) not to believe in something just because they might have heard of it, because it is spoken and rumored by many, because it is written in religious books, or just because of the authority of teachers and elders. He also admonished them not to believe in traditions just because they have been handed down for many centuries.

In sum, it is assumed here that the source of the four theories of meditation described below (and similar ones) is empirical evidence, acquired and elaborated by what in contemporary psychology would be termed qualitative research.

Samkhya-Yoga

Despite occasional objections to such a view (e.g., Ranganathan, 2008), the schools of Samkhya and Yoga are usually treated together. Somewhat simplified, the older Samkhya is the theory part, and Yoga fully accepts the theory part but is more concerned with practice. It is, however, still a philosophical system and not a description of the (mostly physical) practices commonly known as yoga in the West. These were described in detail only in (much) later texts (for overview, see Feuerstein, 1998; Phillips, 2009; Simpson, 2021).

The first version of the Samkhya school seems to have originated around the 5th century BCE (Burley, 2007). However, early texts have been lost, and Ishvarakrishna's *Samkhya Karika* (about 200 CE, Dasgupta, 1997, p. 212) is considered the most authentic text (Raju, 1985, p. 305). The basic text for the school of Yoga are the four books of the *Yogasutras* (e.g., Bryant, 2015; Whiteman, 1993; Woods, 1998). These are usually attributed to one *Pantanjali* but were most likely to have been composed by several authors between the 2nd century BCE and the 5th century CE (Dasgupta, 1997;

Flood, 1996). Here we will first summarize the *theory of cognition* contained in Samkhya-Yoga and then the *theory of change* – that is, changes to be expected in the practice of yoga (see Chapter 3) with meditation as its central part (see for the following, Bryant, 2015; Chatterjee & Datta, 1984; Dasgupta, 1930; Jah, 2008; Puligandla, 1997; Rao & Paranjpe, 2008; Sedlmeier & Srinivas, 2016).

Cognition in Samkhya-Yoga

A basic distinction in the Samkhya-Yoga theory is that between *prakriti* (usually translated as "nature") and *purusha* (sometimes translated as "true person" or "true self" but, especially in translations by Indian scholars, mostly rendered as "pure consciousness"). Each person consists of both parts, and both are involved in cognition (Figure 9.1). Prakriti is everything material and is regarded as composed of three qualities (or *gunas*): *sattva* (purity), *rajas* (energy), and *tamas* (inertia). Each person consists of a given mixture of the three gunas, which is the basis for their personalities, and their minds (see Puta, 2016; Puta & Sedlmeier, 2014). Samkhya-Yoga assumes a tripar-

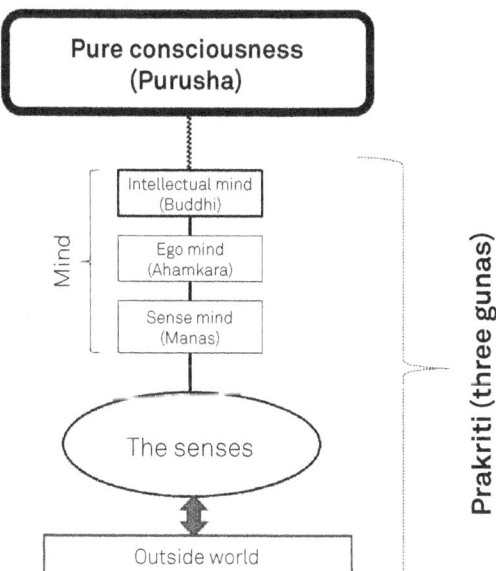

Figure 9.1. Cognition in Samkhya-Yoga. Reprinted with permission from "Psychological theories of meditation in early Buddhism and Sāmkhya/Yoga" by P. Sedlmeier & K. Srinivas (2019), in M. Farias, D. Brazier, & L. Mansur (Eds.), *The Oxford handbook of meditation*, Oxford Handbooks Online, p. 11. https://doi.org/10.1093/oxfordhb/9780198808640.013.27

tite mind, which is fully material, but the three compartments differ in their "coarseness."

The coarsest part, the sense mind (*manas*), reacts to all kinds of information provided from the inside and outside. For instance, if the senses are presented a banana, the sense mind receives information about shape, color, smell, taste, etc., combines these pieces of information, and concludes: "this is a banana." This perception of the banana is appropriated by the less coarse ego mind (*ahamkara*), which might think: "I see a banana." And finally, the intellectual mind (*buddhi*), the subtlest but still material part of the mind that also includes autobiographic memory, reacts to the information of the ego mind and might deliberate: "Should I eat this banana?" However, all this would not work if prakriti were on its own because it is fully material. Thinking (and consciousness) only works in combination with purusha, the nonmaterial part of a person. Only this pure consciousness – that is, consciousness that, in contrast to all Western concepts of consciousness, does not have any objects – makes cognition possible. According to Samkhya-Yoga, the mind must "mirror" pure consciousness to become conscious itself. However, ordinary people are not aware of the existence of pure consciousness – and this is the main problem of life: Suffering in life arises because people are not aware of pure consciousness, which makes life exclusively driven by sensory inputs and ego cravings. Only if one realizes pure consciousness, is one liberated from the burdens of life, or sees one's true nature. This liberation, called *kaivalya* ("aloofness"), is the ultimate aim of Samkhya-Yoga. How can it be achieved? By practicing the classical eightfold path (see Chapter 3). There are many varieties of yoga that use partly different techniques and formulate their ultimate aim of liberating practitioners from their limited experience of the world somewhat differently (for an overview, see Feuerstein, 1998; Phillips, 2009). However, they all relate in some way to the *Yogasutras*.

Change in Samkhya-Yoga

What happens when the eightfold path with meditation as its central ingredient is practiced? The basic answer is given in the second sutra of Book I: "Yoga is the stilling of the changing states of the mind" (Bryant, 2015, Section 10.19). Only if the fluctuations of the mind are brought to a standstill, can the intellectual mind gain access to pure consciousness and the meditator achieve liberation. Practice of the eightfold path goes along with changing the mixture of the three gunas, making *sattva* (purity) more and more dominant, which means that meditators become calmer, more disciplined, relaxed, and have a more well-meaning attitude toward others, as well as a more positive view of the world (see right part of Figure 9.2). This process of *sattvification* of the personality is strongly helped by practicing the first four limbs of the eightfold path (ethics, inner spiritual discipline, body postures, and breath control; see Chapter 3; see also Frawley & Summerfield Kozak, 2001). A high level of sattva facilitates meditation, and in turn, meditation increases the level of sattva (and decreases the levels of rajas and tamas). The other four limbs of the eightfold path can be regarded as successively calming the mind by "cutting off" or shutting down the connections to the three parts of the mind shown in Figure 9.1. First, the control of the senses (*pratyahara*) weakens or cuts the connections of the senses to the outside world. Then by practicing the limb of concentration (*dharana*), the meditator cuts off the senses. And then, the sense mind and the ego mind are cut off by practicing meditation (*dhyana*) and meditative absorption (*samadhi*), respectively.

Gaining access to pure consciousness is not easy: There are five hindrances (*kleshas*) that have to be overcome by the practice of the eightfold path, possibly augmented by other techniques mentioned in the *Yogasutras* (see Chapter 3). The most prominent one is ignorance (*avidya*), not being able to discriminate between good and evil, true and false, permanent and impermanent, and so forth. Then there are greed and craving for enjoyment (*raga*), aversion to anything unpleasant (*dvesha*), the belief that the experience of the self (the mind) is the true self (*asmita*), and the fear of death and clinging to life (*abhinivesha*). The practice of the eightfold path diminishes these hindrances, and only if they are gone, can pure consciousness be accessed and liberation obtained (Figure 9.2, left).

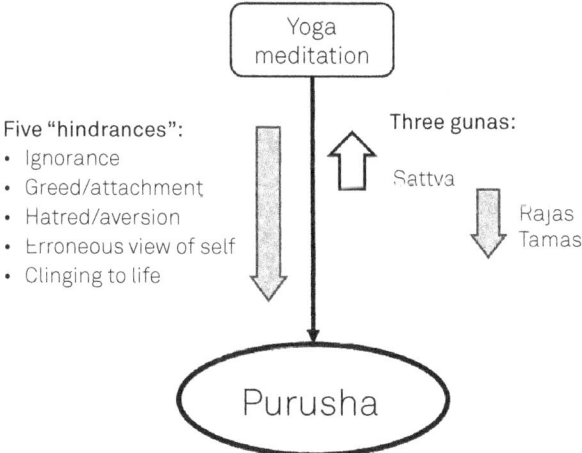

Figure 9.2. Effects of meditation in Samkhya-Yoga.

Advaita Vedanta

Some scholars regard Advaita Vedanta as currently the most famous Indian school of thought and its greatest authority, *Adi Shankara*, the most famous Indian philosopher-sage ever to have lived (Flood, 1996, p. 239). Apart from the *Upanishads* (Vedanta), Advaita Vedanta also draws heavily from two later sources: the *Bhagavadgita* (2nd century BCE, considered the primary holy scripture for Hinduism, and the best known and most famous of Hindu texts) and the *Brahmasutras*, which systematize and summarize the philosophical and spiritual ideas in the *Upanishads* (completed in the 5th century CE). And since Shankara's *Brahmasutra Bhashya* (around the 8th century CE), there have been many different newly added sources, interpretations, and modifications of the school (see Deutsch & Dalvi, 2004; Lucas, 2013). In the following, only the basic parts of the theories of cognition and change are summarized.

Cognition in Advaita Vedanta

Similar to in the Samkhya-Yoga approach, cognition in Advaita Vedanta cannot really be separated from the Advaitins' conception of a person. We begin with a look at that conception, before going on to describe how perception and cognition work according to the Advaita Vedanta view (see Deutsch & Dalvi, 2004; Paranjpe & Rao, 2008; Potter, 1998; Raju, 1985). Figure 9.3, left, shows that according to the Advaitin view, the person (*jiva*) consists of five layers or sheaths (*koshas*) that are nested one inside another, similar to the concentric sheaths of an onion. The outermost sheath is "sustained by food" (*annamaya kosha*) and designates the (gross) body. Then comes the "sheath of the vital breath" (*pranamaya kosha*), which involves breathing and other bodily processes that activate the organs and keep them functioning. The third layer is the "mental sheath" (*manomaya kosha*), containing the sense mind (*manas*), which processes sense information, and the memory (*citta*), which contains concepts or constructs that one uses to get to know the world.[23] This sheath and the fourth one are also the seat of a sense of ego, of "me," and "mine." The fourth inner layer is the intellect/wisdom/knowledge or, in short, "cognitive sheath" (*vijnanamaya kosha*), which refers to the psyche/reason part or the intellect (*buddhi*) that is the basis for making decisions. Finally comes the innermost layer, the "sheath of bliss"

---

23 Please note that some terms that are used in several systems do not have completely identical meanings, as is the case for *citta* in Yoga and Advaita Vedanta.

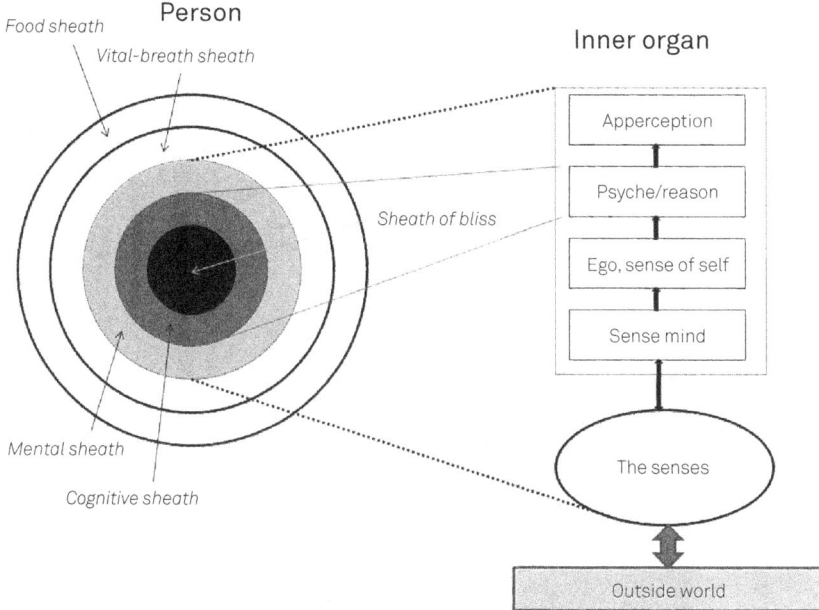

Figure 9.3.   Cognition in Advaita Vedanta.

(*anandamaya kosha*), which is considered the seat of consciousness or the true *Self* (often written with a capital "S").

Figure 9.3 shows that especially the third and fourth layers of the person (mental and cognitive sheaths) contain the totality of the mind or "inner organ" (*antahkarana*) that perceives and thinks. How does this work? Like in Samkhya-Yoga, the sense mind (*manas*) analyses and synthesizes what is perceived by the senses. Again, if, for instance, the senses are presented with a banana, the sense mind gets all the impressions of color, shape, taste, and so forth, combines them, and separates the total unified object built in this way from other objects. Then the ego function (*ahamkara*) appropriates the objects as its own as in "I see a banana." At this stage of perception, the object in question (e.g., a banana) is an object of one's experience but is not seen as an object of the objective world. Intellect or reason (the *buddhi*) makes it such an object through an assertion or a decision yielding something like "This banana is food!" as the result of that process. Then the inner organ (*antahkarana*) finally invokes the apperception part (*citta*), which collects different aspects of the banana, such as the banana tree, my eating it, its price, its nutrients, and so forth, and relates them to the perceived banana. However, the whole process only works with the help of consciousness, situated in the sheath of bliss (*anandamaya kosha*), whose light is (similar to purusha in Samkhya-Yoga) reflected in the mind and senses. Hereupon, the sense mind (*manas*), acting through the senses, takes on the form of the object. This experience is also saved in the apperception part (*citta*) of the inner organ as a memory.

Advaita Vedanta assumes that in addition to experiences received from the outside world, there is an element of imagination (*kalpana*) that is added by the mind. Shankara, the founder of Advaita Vedanta, for instance, compared people to moths that spin around themselves a self-constructed cocoon and live within it (Paranjpe & Rao, 2008, p. 270). In a way, humans are thus considered constructivists who perform cognitive constructions of the world that need not be correct (and indeed are often not).

So, how does cognition in Advaita Vedanta differ from that in Samkhya-Yoga? There are some minor differences in the conception of the mind (compare the inner organ in Figure 9.3 with the mind in Figure 9.1), but these probably could be reconciled, at least as far as the psychological theory is concerned. The real difference lies in the conception of a person. Whereas in Samkhya-Yoga, a person consists of two fundamentally different parts (*prakriti* and *purusha*), one material and one not, in Advaita Vedanta, there is no such difference. There is only one reality, alternatively called "Atman" (or the true Self) or "Brahman" (Ultimate Reality), and one of the most famous sentences attributed to Shankara is "Brahman is real, the world is false, the soul is only Brahman, nothing else" (Brooks, 1969, p. 385). Atman, the true Self, is not something distinct from Brahman – to realize Atman is to realize Brahman because they are really the same thing – but the two terms emphasize different aspects of the Absolute: the ultimate reality (Brahman) and the true nature or Self of an individual (Atman). Advaitins explain the phenomenal world as an illusion, created by the cosmic force of *maya* (illusion), reflected in the ignorance about the real nature of the self, which is not the empirical ego but in fact identical with Brahman. According to Advaita Vedanta, reality must be (1) experienceable, (2) nonillusory or nonimaginary, and (3) stable, lasting, or permanent. In a strict sense, only Brahman fulfills these criteria, but in a loose sense, there are degrees of reality, an assumption that seems to be indispensable for Advaita metaphysics (Brooks, 1969, p. 398).

Brahman is also central for enlightenment, liberation, or *moksha*, as it is called in Advaita Vedanta:

> For Shankara, moksha, liberation, is the realization that I am, and always have been, Brahman; my individual ego-consciousness is destroyed, but not the pure, non-dual consciousness which it was always just a reflection of. It must be emphasized that one does not attain or merge with this Brahman; one merely realizes that one has always been Brahman. (Loy, 1982, p. 68)

So, as in Samkhya-Yoga, the basic problem is ignorance (*avidya*). What are the methods to overcome that ignorance?

Change in Advaita Vedanta

The Advaitins assume that there are four states of consciousness: the states of wakefulness, dream, deep sleep, and a fourth state (*turiya*) that lets one realize one's true nature. The difference between that fourth state and the "normal" state of wakefulness is sometimes described as being similar to that between the state of wakefulness and that of dreaming. Once one awakes, one realizes that the dream was not real. Similarly, if one obtains knowledge associated with the fourth state, one realizes that the normal life was but an illusion. This true nature is not to be found outside oneself – it is the innermost sheath of a person (Figure 9.3), which usually people are not aware of. At the same time, according to the Advaitins, one realizes that one's true Self is ultimately the same as Brahman, the ultimate reality. The method to arrive at this insight is not so clearly connected with the theory of cognition as it is in Samkhya-Yoga. It is called the "knowledge path" (*jnana marga*) and consists of four preparation aids and three further basic steps (Dasgupta, 1997, pp. 489–490; Paranjpe & Rao, 2008, pp. 275–276; see also Raju, 1985, p. 407). The first preparation aid is to make a wise discrimination between the permanent and the impermanent (*nitya-anitya-viveka*) with regard to the self – that is, to decide against the ego self in the mental and cognitive sheaths and for the true Self because only the latter is permanent, and the former will be lost at death. A second preparatory aid is to attain detachment with regard to gains in this or the next life. Then in the third preparatory step, one should acquire the following six virtues:

1. Controlling the mind by resting it on a single objective
2. Withdrawing the senses from the objects of pleasure
3. Preventing the mind from being controlled from outside objects
4. Enduring hardships without lamenting or becoming anxious
5. Having faith in the scriptures and a capable teacher and
6. Firmly resting the mind (concentrating) on the formless Brahman

Finally, the fourth preparatory aid is to develop an intense desire for liberating oneself from egoism and the perceptual chain of action and its consequences. If these four preliminary demands are fulfilled, one may approach the three basic steps to self-realization. First, one has to carefully "listen" to the nondualist teachings of Vedanta (*shravana*). Then, one should repeatedly and deeply reflect upon or contemplate what is learned from those teachings (*manana*). And finally, one should become so completely absorbed in contemplation (*nididhyasana*) of Brahman that no other thoughts enter the mind.

As in the eightfold Yoga path, the last and most important parts can be seen as a kind of (more and more concentrative) meditation practice. An important part of this practice consists of contemplating on the so-called *mahavakyas* (great sayings – we met them already in Chapter 1), which are four in number, and which express the insight that the individual self is in essence nothing but Brahman. The mahavakyas (stemming from different *Upanishads*) are:

"Insight is Brahman" or "Brahman is insight" (*prajnanam brahma*),
"The Atman is Brahman" (*ayam atma brahma*),
"Thou art that" (*tat tvam asi*), and
"I am Brahman" (*aham brahmasmi*).

Comparing the knowledge path (*jnana marga*) with the eightfold yoga path, there are commonalities and differences. Both paths emphasize the use of concentration, although in Advaita Vedanta, concentration is totally focused on Brahman, whereas the yoga path allows for all kinds of concentration objects. The knowledge path has many more contemplative (one might also say "intellectual") components than the yoga path, but the final insight (Brahman) is not considered intellectual at all.

Early Buddhism

The origin of Buddhism can be traced back to the 6th or 5th century BCE. As already mentioned, it arose as a reaction to then-prevalent teachings and in turn largely influenced later Hindu thinking (Frauwallner, 2010, p. 1; Raju, 1985, p. 304; Upadhaya, 1968). The Buddha never saw a written line of his teachings, and even when around 543 BCE, the main Buddhist canon was compiled (at the first council held in Rajagriha), the whole canon was memorized by the monks. Only in the 1st century BCE, was it written down in the Pali language (de Silva, 1990). Therefore, it is known as the *Pali Canon*. It consists of three portions, called baskets (*pitaka*). All original terms in this paragraph are given in the Pali language. The first of the three baskets (*tipitaka*) is the basket of discipline (*vinaya pitaka*) and contains mainly the numerous rules for monks (227 rules) and nuns (311 rules). The second basket, the basket of aphorisms (*sutta pitaka*) consists of the sermons of the Buddha. And the third basket of higher teaching (*abhidhamma pitaka*), which was added to the other two about 200 years afterwards, summarizes early interpretations of the Buddha's teachings. The Pali Canon is the main basis for what is referred to as "early Buddhism" in this text. But as the main aim here is to extract theories of cognition and change (and not to do full justice to some specific scriptures), we will occasionally also freely refer to later sources such as the famous *Visuddhimagga*, a commentary on the Pali Canon by the monk Buddhaghosa who lived in the 5th century CE in Sri Lanka. Buddhism includes many different schools that rely on many different authoritative texts, but there is some general agreement on most of the teachings in the Pali Canon (some differences will be pointed out in the paragraph on Zen).

Cognition in Early Buddhism

The theory of cognition in early Buddhism is quite different from what we have seen in Samkhya-Yoga and Advaita Vedanta (for the following, see Bodhi, 2013; de Silva, 2005; Frauwallner, 2010; Gombrich, 2013; Hamilton, 2000; Kalupahana, 1992; Olendzki, 2003; 2010; Rahula, 1959; Sedlmeier & Srinivas, 2019). The most salient difference is that in early Buddhism, there is no permanent Self (Atman) - *anatta*. This is clearly different from the two Hindu schools. The other two of the *three hallmarks* or characteristics of life (*tilakkhana*; e.g., Anālayo, 2003, pp. 102–106; Premasiri, 2008, p. 97) may be seen as having some correspondences to Samkhya-Yoga and Advaita Vedanta. The second characteristic of life is the transient nature or impermanence of all phenomena, material and mental: *anicca*. Transient objects and phenomena tend to produce a feeling of unsatisfaction or suffering: *dukkha*. Dukkha, the third characteristic of life is upheld by the three "fires" of greed/passion, hatred/aversion, and ignorance/delusion – somewhat simplified these refer to the fact that we do not have what we want, do not want what we have, and don't understand why.[24]

But if there is no self and nothing permanent, how does cognition work according to early Buddhism? As especially well described in the abhidhamma pitaka, the third part of the Pali Canon (e.g., Bodhi 2013), cognition is nothing but a continuous stream of consciousness consisting of very rapidly succeeding and extremely short moments of "consciousnesses," one at a time and each specific for one sense organ. Figure 9.4 (right) shows that apart from the traditional five senses (eye – seeing, ear – hearing, nose – smelling, tongue – tasting, and body – feeling), there is also a sixth sense, the mind. Thus, in early Buddhism, thinking is nothing but the perception of mental objects or thoughts. So, cognition is a rapid succession of, say, seeing something that is yellow and bent, thinking "banana," feeling the smooth surface of the banana in the hand, tasting the sweetness of the banana, thinking "good!" hearing "are you eating my banana?" and so on. Actually, moments of consciousness are assumed to be much shorter than the ones described here and a bit more complicated, consisting of several submoments each (e.g., Bodhi, 2013, p. 155), but this somewhat simplified description should

---

24 It seems that the Buddha took the idea of the three fires (as expressed in the "Fire Sermon" contained in the *Vinaya Pitaka*) from the Vedas (Gombrich, 2013, p. 112).

be adequate for our purpose. How does content enter cognition, as obviously is the case in the banana example? The answer is contained in the so-called five *khandas*, usually translated as "aggregates." Consciousness is itself one of the khandas, and each moment of consciousness is accompanied by other bodily and mental activities that are summarized in one of the other four khandas. The khanda of form (*rupa*) includes both the external physical world and, internally, the material body and the physical sense organs (see lower right part of Figure 9.4). Then there is the khanda of feeling (*vedana*): Every moment of consciousness is accompanied by either a pleasant, neutral, or unpleasant feeling. The next khanda, the khanda of apperception (*sanna*) can provide memories of sense impression, images, ideas, or concepts to the current moment of consciousness. The khandas of consciousness, feeling, and apperception (together with the khanda of form) work together to answer the question, "What is going on here?" And the last khanda, the khanda of mental formations or inclinations (*samkhara*), with volition as the central ingredient (Gombrich, 2013, p. 135) can provide the basis for an answer to the question: "How do I respond to this?" The last khanda also contains mental constituents.[25] For each moment of consciousness, the combination of activities in the khandas is dependent on prior combinations: According to the *law of dependent arising* (*paticca samuppada*), postulated by the Buddha, all physical and mental phenomena arise and pass away dependent upon multiple causes and conditions.

So, there is this ongoing stream of consciousness, but what drives it? It is the three "fires" of greed, hatred, and ignorance. And what keeps these fires burning? Our *kamma* (Sanskrit: *karma*) – that is, our action, work, or deed serves as fuel. How do we acquire and accumulate it? Partly, it is the product of our volitions (in the khanda of formations), and partly it comes from previous lifetimes.[26] Buddhists claim that the stream of consciousness does not completely end at death but continues to a new birth. There is a stream of so-called *bhavangas* ("ground of becoming" or "condition for existence"), an ongoing default process that is always active if no conscious cognition takes place, and it does not stop at the end of an individual life (Bodhi, 2013). Anyway, as long as there is fuel for the fires of greed, hatred, and ignorance, the unsatisfaction of our lives, present and future, does not come to an end.

---

25 The distinction between the khandas of apperception vs. mental formations is reminiscent of that between knowing *that* vs. knowing *how* (Ryle, 2009).
26 Note that unfavorable kamma can only arise if we are responsible for our volitions. However, the concept of "free will," and also the relationship between free will and volitions, seem to be underspecified in early Buddhism. It seems that nowhere in the process of dependent origination (from which volitions arise), is there space for one's own decisions. But if we do not have the opportunity to decide, we cannot be made responsible for our actions.

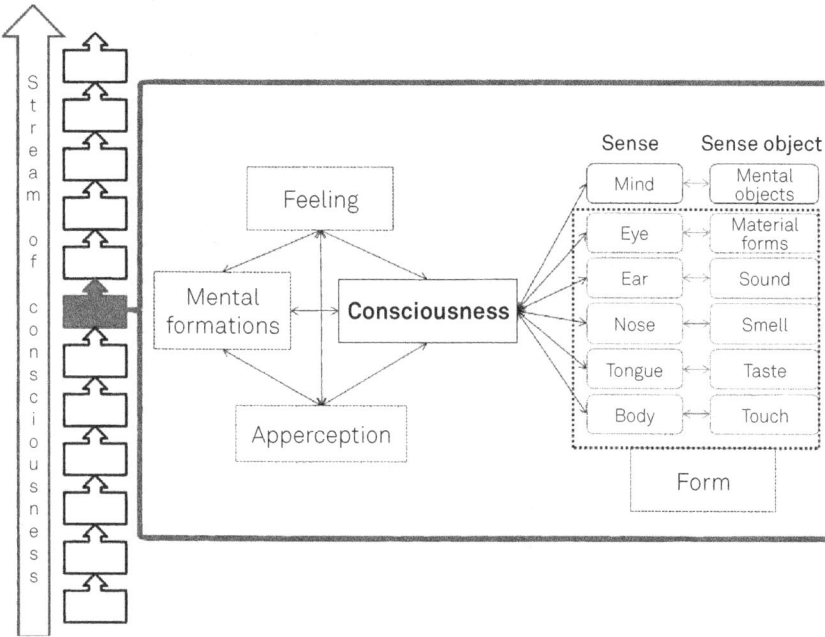

Figure 9.4. Cognition in early Buddhism. Reprinted with permission from "Psychological theories of meditation in early Buddhism and Sāṃkhya/Yoga" by P. Sedlmeier & K. Srinivas (2019), in M. Farias, D. Brazier, & L. Mansur (Eds.), *The Oxford handbook of meditation*, Oxford Handbooks Online, p. 11. https://doi.org/10.1093/oxfordhb/9780198808640.013.27

Obviously, a theory of change needs to specify how the fires may eventually be extinguished, and unsatisfaction may end.

Change in Early Buddhism

Here, meditation and the rest of the Noble Eightfold Path become relevant. Meditation is supposed to yield a deep insight into the working of the five khandas, thereby reducing and finally extinguishing the fires of greed, hatred, and ignorance that sustain our "thirst" (*tanha*) described in the second noble truth as the basis for the unsatisfaction we encounter in our lives (Frauwallner, 2010, p. 14). In the Buddha's own words: "It is the thirst leading to rebirth, which, accompanied by delight and passion, finds enjoyment here and there, namely, thirst for desire, thirst for becoming, thirst for annihilation" (cited after Frauwallner, 2010, p. 14). In later sermons, the thirst for annihilation seems to have lost its importance. Instead, the concept of ignorance has gained much importance as a step in the chain of dependent arising (Frauwallner, 2003, 2010; Gombrich, 2013).

If the three fires are extinguished and replaced by their positive counterparts – that is, by contentment, kindness, and wisdom – then no more unfavorable kamma is produced, and the cycle of rebirths ends, or in other words, *nibbana* (literally "blown out"; Sanskrit: *nirvana*) is attained (e.g., S. Batchelor, 2015, p. 145; Kalupahana, 2009, p. 139). This goes along with fully understanding the three characteristics of life: impermanence, non-self, and unsatisfaction (e.g., Anālayo, 2003, pp. 102ff; Premasiri, 2008, p. 97; Thanissaro, 2004). Such a view of reality might, after all, not sound so tempting to achieve, but although the Buddha mostly used the negative term of *nibbana* to refer to this state, he mentioned several times in the Pali Canon that the extinguishing of the fires also yields experiences of bliss (*nibbuti*; see Gombrich, 2013, p. 113).

Walpola Rahula, a Theravada Buddhist monk and scholar, has compiled a description of an enlightened person from the suttas (Rahula, 1959, p. 43), which is closely mirrored by the following more contemporary account:

> People who have been through it tend to be described by others as simple, natural, genuine and straightforward; serene and peaceful yet alert and full of life and vitality; wise in their words and economical and effective in their actions; kind, friendly, gentle and considerate in their dealings with people; perceptive and intelligent; at ease in their bodies and at home in the world. They seem to have shed the neurotic baggage that the rest of us reluctantly carry about: anxiety, irritation, resentment, regret, guilt, meanness, greed, jealousy, possessiveness, worry, confusion and the rest of the familiar catalogue. (Claxton, 1986, p. 9)

We have already treated the Noble Eightfold Path to some extent in Chapter 3. Here we will concentrate on the last two "meditation limbs", mindfulness and concentration (Figure 9.5). Mindfulness (*sati*) coupled with clearly knowing (sampajanna; see Anālayo, 2020) may be seen as the fundamental new contribution of the Buddha to the then already existing (mostly concentrative) approaches to meditation (e.g., Hart, 1987). As described in Chapter 2, practicing mindfulness means being continuously aware of one or more of the "four foundations of mindfulness": bodily processes, feeling tones, the working of the mind, and the objects of mind (Anālayo, 2003). This practice is assumed to decrease and finally extinguish the three fires. But it also, in conjunction with the limb of right effort (see Chapter 3), should allow the four *brahmaviharas* or immeasurables (loving kindness, compassion, sympathetic joy, and equanimity) to shine through.[27] These four states

---

[27] The meta-analytic results summarized in Chapter 6 indicate that the effects of Western versions of mindfulness meditation on the immeasurables might be as strong as training on the immeasurables themselves (usually as loving kindness meditation or compassion meditation).

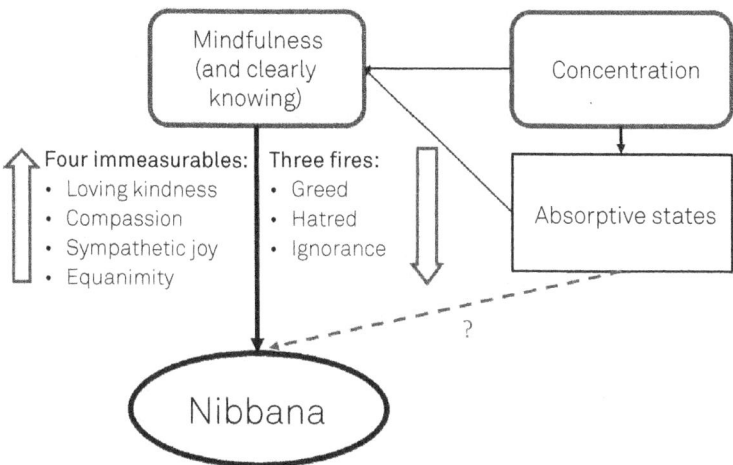

Figure 9.5. Effects of meditation in early Buddhism.

should become more and more spontaneous with increasing meditation practice, and the mind will get less resentful, and experience less tension and irritability (Nyanaponika, 1999, p. 11). Indeed, some authors identify *nibbana* with the four immeasurables being in full bloom (e.g., Gombrich, 2013, p. 85; Hart, 1987, pp. 124 and 126; Maithrimurthi, 1999, p. 34; Olendzki, 2010, p. 24).

One might be tempted to ask, "if mindfulness does the whole job, what do we need concentration or calm abiding (*samadhi*) for?" (right part in Figure 9.5). Indeed, some Buddhist teachers argue that meditation can dispense with special concentration techniques (e.g., Mahasi, 1973). Most scholars and teachers see concentration, often termed *samatha* meditation, as a good preparation for mindfulness practice, often referred to as vipassana (e.g., M. Batchelor, 2016; Gombrich, 2006; Gunaratana, 2015; Pa-Auk, 2000). But there are also some who argue that concentrative meditation might be a direct way to nibbana (see Griffiths, 1981; and indicated in Figure 9.5 here by the "?"). According to Buddhist theory, continued and extensive concentration (*shamata*) practice leads to absorptive states called *jhanas*, which are eight in number. Similar to the five hindrances that obstruct advancement on the yoga path, there are also five hindrances in early Buddhism that hinder progress toward attaining the absorptive states. These are sensory desire (seeking happiness through sight, sound, smell, taste, and physical feeling), ill-will (feelings of hostility, resentment, hatred, and bitterness), sloth and torpor (heaviness of body and dullness of mind), restlessness and worry (inability to calm the mind), and doubt (lack of conviction or trust).

The first four jhanas are called "form jhanas" (*rupa jhana*) because concentration focuses on some material object, and the last four are called "formless jhanas" (*arupa jhana*) and have nonmaterial things such as infinite space, infinite consciousness, or nothingness as concentration objects. To attain these absorptive states, many different concentration objects can be used, such as body parts, the brahmaviharas, or the so-called kasinas, which are typically employed as colored discs that either represent something else (e.g., earth or water) or just stand for a given color (Bomhard, 2010; Buddhaghosa, 2010; Pa-Auk, 2000). The *Visuddhimagga* gives some recommendations for which concentration objects are suited to which kinds of monks. For instance, monks with a greedy temperament should concentrate on foulness, and ones with a hating temperament on the brahmaviharas (e.g., Buddhaghosa, 2010, p. 109). However, some of these concentration objects can only be used to attain the first or the first three or four jhanas (Shankman, 2008, pp. 62–63). The classic object of concentration, which can be used to attain all jhanas, is the breath as described in the Anapanasati Sutta (e.g., Pa-Auk 2000). [As already mentioned, this sutta (*ana*=inbreath, *apana*=outbreath) is referred to for both mindfulness (*sati*) and concentration practice. For translation see, for instance, Thanissaro (2006).] All concentration objects are eventually replaced by more subtle (inner) "signs" (*nimittas*) that arise by themselves in the course of concentrative meditation (Brahm, 2014; Moneyya, 2006; Wallace, 2006).

The Buddha, before he actually became a Buddha (= "awakened one"), successively learned from two yogic teachers, Alara Kalama and Udaka Ramaputta, and attained the "base of nothingness" and the "base of neither-perception-nor-nonperception," which is usually interpreted as his having achieved the last two (formless) jhanas. However, the Buddha rejected his attainments for not leading to nibbana (S. Batchelor, 2015, p. 160). In contrast to that view, Ajahn Brahm (2014, p. 129) argues that these terms may have been used for some other kinds of experiences, and he indeed claims that the attainment of the "base of nothingness" *does* lead to nibbana. But apart from that, the attainment of jhanas means that "the meditator's mind is stilled of all thought, secluded from all five-sense activity, and is radiant with otherworldly bliss" (Brahm, 2014, p. 127). There is some dispute about what exactly happens in the different jhanas (and also how exactly the jhanas are achieved), but the currently most prevalent view shown in Table 9.1 is usually taken to be the one proposed in the *Visuddhimagga* (see Shankman, 2008): With increasing deeper states of absorption, less and less happens (see "Characteristics" in Table 9.1). The only characteristic retained in the four formless jhanas is the one-pointedness of the mind. Therefore, they are omitted from Table 9.1. The absorptive states are expected to carry with them very pleasant experiences (amply described in Brahm, 2014), and the strong experiences elicited by an extended practice of concentrative meditation might also elicit the illusion of enlightenment (e.g., Jayasaro, 1989; Sumedho, 1995, p. 90).

Table 9.1. Summary of what happens in the first four jhanas.

Level of absorption	Characteristics
First jhana	• Applied thinking (*vitakka*) [thinking about some object of meditation] • Sustained thinking (*vicara*) [sustained thinking on the meditation object] • Rapture (*piti*) [different forms of manifestation to various meditators, from minor rapture to suffusing joy or all-pervading rapture, depending on personality] • Bliss (*sukkha*) [far superior to all forms of worldly happiness] • One-pointedness of the mind (*ekaggata*)
Second jhana	• Rapture • Bliss • One-pointedness of mind
Third jhana	• Bliss • One-pointedness of mind
Fourth jhana	• One-pointedness of mind • Equanimity (*upekkha*)

So, in early Buddhism, we are left with two meditation paths, mindfulness (vipassana) and concentration (samatha), and its theory of change says that they lead to different effects: to attention opened to everything or concentrated on one point or, in other words, to insight (mindfulness) and tranquility (concentration). One need not, however, see these two paths as exclusive, or one as the minor and the other as the major one. Anālayo (2018b) argues that, originally, they were not even set apart as separate practices but rather should be understood as complementary qualities of meditative cultivation. Nonetheless, a theory of meditation has to account for different effects, depending on these two kinds of meditation, at least as far as the intermediary stages of the path are concerned.

Zen

The history of Zen, with its blend of Indian and Chinese traditional backgrounds, has already been briefly summarized in Chapter 3.[28] The Chinese

---

28 Apart from Chan, there were three other (earlier) Chinese schools of Buddhism (for details, see Hershock, 2005): *Tiantai* (largely based on the *Lotus Sutra*), *Huayan* (largely based on the *Flower Ornament Sutra*), and *Qingtu* (aka *Pure Land*, largely based on the *Sukhavati-vyuha Sutra*).

contribution consisted of Confucian elements but especially of the tradition of the *Dao* (or *Tao*; often translated as "Way"). Confucianism (Confucius lived from 551 to 479 BCE) contributed the high importance of social connectedness, prominently expressed in Zen as the centrality of lineage, and the doctrine of direct transmission from teacher to student: "Chan awakening is no private affair, but an irreducibly social process. Whether we are standing, sitting, walking, or lying down, Chan means realizing horizonless and responsive presence with and for one another" (Hershock, 2005, p. 2).[29] In contrast to the three other theoretical approaches discussed above, for which there exist acknowledged canons of authoritative sources, many of the teachings used in Zen are stories, poems, and commentaries on these. This is, for instance, expressed in the "Bodhidharma legend," attributed to Bodhidharma, the legendary founder of Zen, but actually composed much later:

> A special transmission outside the sutras,
> Not founded on words and letters;
> By pointing directly to (one's) mind;
> It lets one see into (one's own true) nature and (thus) attain Buddhahood.
> (Dumoulin, 2005, p. 85. Reprinted with permission from World Wisdom.)

This idea of direct transmission is also exemplified in a famous koan, the second from the Denkoroku (Record of Transmitting the Light), compiled by the Japanese Soto Zen master Keizan (1268-1325). It features Mahakashyapa, the first successor of the Buddha according to the Zen lineages. In Cook's (2003) translation it reads:[30]

> The first patriarch was Mahakashyapa. Once, the World-honored One [the Buddha] held up a flower and blinked. Kashyapa smiled. The World-honored One said, "I have the Treasury of the Eye of the True Dharma and Wondrous Mind of Nirvana, and I transmit it to Mahakashyapa." (Cook, 2003, p. 30. © 2003 Wisdom Publications. Reprinted by arrangement with Wisdom Publications, Inc. wisdompubs.org)

Another strong influence from Confucianism seems to have been the idea (introduced by MengZi, 3rd century BCE) of the inherent goodness of human nature and the innate capacity of personal self-cultivation, which

---

29 The Buddha seems not to have been interested in a personal succession but instead relied on the community (the *sangha*) and his teachings (e.g., S. Batchelor, 2015; Ford, 2006).
30 Somewhat ironically, "the articulation of Zen has been so inseparable from written communication that imagining Zen without writing is like imagining a hand without bones" (Hershock, 2014, Section 3.3).

contributed to the Zen teaching that all beings have *buddha nature* (e.g., Hershock, 2005, p. 49).

Daoism, the other main Chinese influence on Zen, originated around the 5th century BCE and does not have, according to Komjathy (2013), a founder or authoritative figure. From the beginning, Daoists performed meditation to realize the Dao, which for them has four primary characteristics: source of everything, unnamable mystery, all-pervading sacred presence, and universe as transformative process (Komjathy, 2019, p. 2). This conception of the Dao fits well with the concept of *prajnaparamita* (*prajna:* "wisdom/understanding/insight," *paramita:* "perfection"), central in Mahayana Buddhism. Similar to the characteristics of the Dao, prajnaparamita also refers to both the outcome (full perfection of insight) as well as the process of arriving at such perfection (e.g., Brunnhölzl, 2016, p. 23). The *Prajnaparamita Sutras* are among the oldest of the Mahayana sutras and considered to be one of the foundations of Zen, the first of which were put in writing in the 1st century BCE (Mäll, 2005, p. 96). In contrast to early Buddhism, in the context of which Pali expressions are used, Zen Buddhism usually expresses traditional Indian terms in Sanskrit (e.g., *sutra* instead of *sutta*). There is one special text from the *Prajnaparamita Sutras*, which is daily recited in most Zen centers: the *heart sutra*. Its is the most frequently used and recited text in the entire Mahayana Buddhist tradition (Brunnhölzl, 2016, p. 7), although it originally seems in part to have been taken from a much longer prajnaparamita sutra, the *Great Perfection of Wisdom Sutra* and received its name only after a Chinese monk's translation of that portion of the text in 649 CE (Red Pine, 2004, p. 8). Some scholars regard it as a basically Chinese text (McRae, 1988; Nattier, 1992). This sutra can be used to outline large parts of the Zen theory of cognition.

Cognition in Zen

In the paragraph on early Buddhism, we have seen a quite elaborate theory of cognition. Going now through the heart sutra part by part, we will see that one principal aim of this sutra is to completely refute the theory of cognition postulated by early Buddhism. There are many translations of the heart sutra. The present version stems from the Bodhi sangha Web page (http://www.bodhisangha.net/index.php/en/zen/recitation). There are also numerous commentaries on the heart sutra. In the following, I have tried a (selective) synthesis between some of them (Brunnhölzl, 2016; Conze, 2001; Nath Hanh, 2012; Lopez, 1988; Red Pine, 2004; Tanahashi, 2014), concentrating on issues that might be relevant for a theory of cognition in Zen.

> Avalokiteshvara Bodhisattva,
> practicing deep Prajna Paramita
> clearly saw that all five skandhas are empty,
> transforming all suffering and distress.

In Mahayana Buddhism, a bodhisattva is somebody who strives to attain buddhahood not primarily for themselves but out of compassion to help all sentient beings attain liberation. In the heart sutra, the bodhisattva Avalokiteshvara is the primary teacher (in contrast to the other *Prajnaparamita Sutras* in which the Buddha himself teaches). Avalokiteshvara is a special bodhisattva in that she embodies the compassion of all Buddhas. The appearance of Avalokiteshvara is usually taken as an indication that the teachings of compassion – central in Mahayana Buddhism – are included in the heart sutra. Avalokiteshvara now sees that all five *skandhas* (*khandas* in Pali) are empty – that is, contrary to the theory of cognition in early Buddhism (see Figure 9.4), they have no real substance. This statement is sometimes interpreted as their being empty of a separate independent existence – that is, each skandha (and each part contained in the skandhas) depends so much on others and is so much interconnected with them that it is nothing by or in itself (e.g., Conze, 2001, p. 86; Tanahashi, 2014, p. 56). And realizing this emptiness is the key to liberation.

> Shariputra, form is no other than emptiness,
> emptiness no other than form;
> form is emptiness, emptiness is form;
> feeling, perception, mental reaction, consciousness
> are also like this.
> Shariputra, all dharmas are essentially empty:
> not born, not destroyed;
> not stained, not pure, without loss, without gain.
> Therefore in emptiness there is no form, no feeling,
> no perception, mental reaction, consciousness;
> no eye, ear, nose, tongue, body, mind;
> no color , sound, smell, taste, touch, objects of mind;
> no seeing and so on to no thinking

Interestingly, the addressee of this tutorial is none other than one of the Buddha's two chief disciples, who is especially known for his wisdom. So, one would expect Shariputra to teach, and not to obtain teachings. Lopez (1988, p. 51) sees this as an intentional irony: Even the wisest of the Buddha's early disciples must have the (superior) Mahayana teachings explained to him. He is instructed that form, one of the five skandhas is but an expression of emptiness (*sunyata*), but also emptiness does not exist apart from the phenomena it qualifies. Also, the other four skandhas are included in the argument, as well as the six sense organs and their objects (see Figure 9.4). But then there is a heavy blow to the theory of cognition in early Buddhism. There, all things (*dharmas*) except nirvana are conditioned – that is, they are born (often translated as "arising"), stained, and incomplete. Only nirvana is unconditioned – that is, a state where all conditioned events have stopped (are destroyed). Moreover, it is pure and complete (without gain). In contrast, the heart sutra says that things are *not* born, there is no opposition between conditioned and unconditioned dharmas, or, in other words no difference between the cycle of rebirth and death (*samsara*) and nirvana (no more rebirth). Especially interesting for a theory of cognition is the idea that in emptiness, there is no thinking (and no not-thinking)!

> no ignorance and also no ending of ignorance
> and so on to no old age and death,
> and also no ending of old age and death;
> no suffering, cause of suffering, cessation, path

Now, two basic building blocks of early Buddhism, the chain of dependent arising (from ignorance to old age and death) and the Four Noble Truths (suffering, cause of suffering, cessation, and the Noble Eightfold Path as the means) are negated. The chain (or law) of dependent arising (or dependent origination) usually (there are some variations) consists of 12 links, two of which are ignorance, and old age and death. According to that teaching, all physical and mental phenomena arise and pass away in dependence upon multiple causes and conditions.

> no wisdom and no attainment.
> Since there is nothing to attain,
> the Bodhisattva lives by Prajna Paramita
> with no hindrance in the mind; no hindrance, thus no fear:
> far beyond delusive thinking right here is Nirvana.
> All Buddhas past, present, and future
> live by Prajna Paramita,
> attaining Anuttara Samyak Sambodhi [the highest, most perfect enlightenment].

Even the "heart of the heart sutra" – that is, wisdom (sometimes translated as "knowledge") does not exist, and there is also nothing to attain (such as the four stages of enlightenment postulated in Theravada Buddhism). Being freed from everything (as is the case for a bodhisattva who lives by prajna paramita) leads to nirvana right here and now. And this is not only true for the bodhisattvas but for all of the Buddhas who have lived and will live.

The rest of the sutra will be left aside because it does not contribute additional ingredients to the Zen theory of cognition. So, what is the Zen theory of cognition? One could say that the emptiness or groundlessness of our experience is the basic theme of the heart sutra. At a first glance, the theory of cognition seems to be "no, no, no!" This is exemplified in some koans, as for instance, in the following Case 20 from the *Book of Equanimity* [Japanese: *Shoyoroku*, Chinese: *Cong-Ron-Lu*], compiled by the Chinese Chan master Wanson Xingxiu (1166-1246). In Wick's (2005) translation:[31]

> Master Jiso asked Hogen, "Where have you come from?" "I pilgrimage aimlessly," replied Hogen. "What is the matter of your pilgrimage?" asked Jizo. "I don't know," replied Hogen. "Not knowing is the most intimate," remarked Jozo. At that, Hogen experienced great enlightenment. (Wick, 2005, p. 63. © 2005 Wisdom Publications. Reprinted by arrangement with Wisdom Publications, Inc. wisdompubs.org)

But this is not the whole story. Consistent with the Daoist tradition, Zen texts also offer a positive conception of the groundless ground:

> Zen, using the traditional, common terminology of Buddhism that has developed in China, often calls it the "Buddha nature," or simply "Mind," "No-mind," the "Master," the "True-man-without-any-rank", "your-original-Face-which-you-possessed-prior-to-the-birth-of-your-father-and-mother," or more simply, "This Thing," "That" or still more simply "It." (Izutsu, 1982, p. 72)

This assumption of an eternal, imperishable self was, according to some scholars (e.g., Zimmermann, 2002, p. 82), already expressed in the Mahayana *Tathagatagarbha Sutra* (*Tathagatagarbha* means "Buddha Essence," lit. "the womb of the thus-come-one"). But unlike in the Advaita theory, where only Brahman is real, this does not hold for Buddha nature (occasionally shortened to "Buddha") as, for instance, expressed in Cases 18 and 21 in the famous *Mumonkan* (Chinese: *Wu-men kuan*), a koan collection compiled by the Chinese Chan master Wu-men (1183-1260). In Aitken's translation:

> A monk asked Tung-shan, "What is Buddha?"
> Tung-shan said, "Three pounds of flax." (Aitken, 2015b, 27.5)

and

> A monk asked Yün-men, "What is Buddha?"
> Yün-men said, "Dried shitstick." (Aitken, 2015b, 30.2)

---

31 Please note that Koan collections differ in how they render the names of the persons described in the koans – mostly Zen masters and their students. In this example, Japanese names are used, but in some examples to follow, transcriptions – either Pinyin or Wade-Giles – of Chinese names are used. As these names are not essential in the current context, I just leave the ones used by the respective translators.

In Zen, form or thinking (or cognition) is as real as emptiness, but there is a qualification as expressed in a famous Zen saying:

> Before enlightenment, mountains are mountains, trees are trees. During the process of enlightenment, mountains are not mountains, trees are not trees. After enlightenment, mountains are mountains, trees are trees! (cited after Samy, 2013, p. 17)

So, an insight into emptiness or Buddha nature, in Japanese Zen termed *kensho* (seeing one's true nature) or *satori* (comprehension/understanding), leads to a transformation in how the world is seen. In contrast to the impression one can get reading popular descriptions of "enlightenment experiences" (e.g., Kapleau, 2000, pp. 228ff), some authors argue that kensho is not so much an experience or a "state of mind" but rather a form of knowledge and mode of activity (Samy, 2013; Sharf, 1995).

Now, after this somewhat lengthy exposition you might still wonder what Zen's theory of cognition is. Many Zen experts (if they have thought about it at all) would, for pragmatic purposes, probably not object to the theory of cognition in early Buddhism, as summarized in Figure 9.4. This can, for instance, be evidenced in the commentaries in well-known koan collections that not so rarely mention bits and pieces of this theory (e.g., the five skandhas or the six senses). However, whereas early Buddhism stops there, Zen postulates that the bits and pieces contained in the early Buddhist theory have no existence by themselves, and there is something variously called "emptiness," "Buddha nature," "Dao," or just "It" that can be directly seen after extensive cognitive training. Seeing this (*kensho*) then has a transformative effect on cognition.

Change in Zen

What does bring about such a change in cognition? Certainly not discriminative or dualistic thinking, as made clear in many koans. A famous example koan is Case 19 in the Mumonkan (e.g., Aitken, 2015b, Section 28.8; Sekida, 2005, p. 73). There, the monk Chao-chou (Japanese: *Joshu*) asks the master Nan-ch'üan (Japanese: *Nansen*) what the Tao (or "Way") is. As we have seen, Tao (Dao) or Way could also have been termed "emptiness" or "Buddha nature." How can it be realized? As Nan-ch'üan replies in this koan, not "at the level of affirmation and negation." Interestingly, saying this, triggers Chao-chou's kensho. There are many different kinds of triggers mentioned in the koan collections. Often seemingly innocuous phrases, as in the above example, serve as triggers, but also sounds (of birds, bells, or pebbles), sights (of a hill, a flower), being hit or beaten up, or just the touch of water when taking a bath.

However, practitioners, of course, have to prepare themselves. What does this preparation consist of? As already briefly described in Chapter 3, monastic Rinzai Zen practitioners may use an extended koan practice to try to push themselves into a state of mind beyond the dualism of ordinary consciousness. But this "pressure cooker" tactic might not necessarily lead to kensho (Samy, 2013, p. 107).

Yamada (2015, Chapter 14) argues that the three necessary conditions for enlightenment are *great faith, great doubt,* and *great determination.* Great faith means that it is necessary to believe that all beings are intrinsically awake (have Buddha nature). Great doubt, in his description, means unconditional concentration (on a koan), and great determination is to continue the practice fullheartedly: "To meet the true Buddha within us, we must be ready give up our lives" (Yamada, 2015, Section 24.21). So, somewhat simplified, single-pointed concentration is one way of preparation.

The other way of preparation is to watch your own thinking (everything your self does), as expressed by Dogen, the famous founder of the Soto sect:[32]

> To study the Buddha Way is to study the self.
> To study the self is to forget the self.
> To forget the self is to be actualized by myriad things.
> When actualized by myriad things, your body and mind as well as the bodies and minds of others drop away.
> No trace of enlightenment remains,
> and this no-trace continues endlessly. (Samy, 2013, pp. 15-16)

These two kinds of preparation are often connected to the ways of sudden awakening (single-pointed concentration) and silent illumination (concentration on everything that happens in the self). [Originally, the distinction between sudden and gradual enlightenment that accompanied the distinction between the northern and southern Ch'an schools, might have mainly served political purposes – that is, for the northern school to gain predominance (McRae, 1987).] However, even in the Rinzai school, nobody seems to claim that realizing kensho is the final aim of Zen. In fact, the koan collections mention many cases of repeated insights, with the very influential Japanese Zen master Hakuin Ekaku (1686-1769) probably being the champion: He reported 18 great awakenings and little insights too numerous to

---

32 Please note that Dogen described his enlightenment as "I came to realize clearly that [my] mind is nothing other than mountains and rivers and the great wide earth, the sun and the moon and the stars" (Loy, 1982, p. 70).

count (Ford, 2006, p. 50). All Zen texts discourage staying with kensho (no trace of enlightenment remains). This goal of transcending even enlightenment and coming back to everyday life is most prominently described in the *Ten Oxherding Pictures*, a series of short poems and accompanying drawings (e.g., Kapleau, 2000, pp. 332ff). These pictures describe the levels of realization one can expect in Zen practice using the picture of the ox who stands for Buddha nature or emptiness. First, practitioners have to seek the ox, then they find tracks, have a first glimpse, catch it, tame it, ride it, forget it, forget both the ox and the self, return to the source (mountains are again mountains, and trees are again trees), and finally enter the marketplace with helping hands. So, after having one or several profound insights, the empirical ego or self is gone and finally, the practitioner comes back to a wise and compassionate everyday life: "The Zen way is to abide in Emptiness while walking on the roads of the marketplace, to walk on the roads of the marketplace while abiding in Emptiness" (Samy, 2013, p. 139).

This final goal of the change process postulated in Zen is clearly different from that postulated in the other three approaches discussed above. However, one could argue that the theory of change, seen at an abstract level is not so much different from that in early Buddhism, although the final state is.

The Four Traditional Approaches Compared

All of the traditional approaches to meditation have as their main and often single goal a dramatic change in cognition and consciousness, variously termed enlightenment, liberation, awakening, etc. This is also true for the four approaches discussed above. Samkhya-Yoga, Advaita Vedanta, early Buddhism, and Zen all postulate some kind of "special" cognition that ordinary people are not aware of but that can be obtained by specific training. One aspect that goes along with that change is the deflation and eventually dissolution of the conventional ego or self. So, one could say that changes in cognition go along with changes in personality. Apart from these general commonalities, there are also partly profound differences among the four approaches.

Theories of cognition in the four approaches differ widely with respect to how detailed the descriptions are and their ontological assumptions. Early Buddhism gives a very detailed picture of all kinds of cognitive processes and is very pragmatic in dealing with the material-immaterial dichotomy (it does not). Samkhya-Yoga also describes cognitive processes in some detail and makes a clear distinction between the material (*prakriti*) and immaterial (*purusha*). The two later approaches, especially Zen, are less specific in describing cognitive processes. But as both strongly relate to the respective earlier systems, one can assume that Advaita Vedanta largely agrees with the Samkhya-Yoga theory of cognition, and Zen with that of early Buddhism. This holds for descriptions of mundane activities but, at least in the case of Advaita Vedanta, not for the ultimate reality. In Advaita Vedanta, only the immaterial Brahman is considered real, whereas in Zen, there is a kind of coexistence or, more aptly, an intimate intertwining between the material and the immaterial.

The ontological differences do not, however, seem to be too important for the respective theories of change. One could argue that all four theories involve concentration tasks as their main means of change. However, the exact nature of the concentration tasks differs across approaches. In both Samkhya-Yoga and Advaita Vedanta, the main meditation technique can be described as single-pointed concentration, although in the latter, there is only one dominating object of concentration: Brahman. In the Buddhist approaches, single-pointed concentration also plays a role, although less so in early Buddhism (with some exceptions) and more so in Zen. At least at an abstract level, koan work in Zen and the use of the mahavakyas (or Ramana Maharishi's "Who am I"?) do not seem to be so much different (see the section The Final Goal, below). Open concentration or awareness of everything is peculiar to the Buddhist approaches. In early Buddhism, it plays a central role in the practice of the four satipatthanas, and in Zen, shikantaza practice dominates the Soto school and is increasingly practiced in all Zen communities (Ford, 2006).

It seems that all approaches deal very flexibly with assigning specific meditation techniques to practitioners.[33] This flexibility is, for instance, explicitly stated in the already mentioned *Visuddhimagga* (Buddhaghosa, 2010), which advises monks to select objects of concentration according to their personality tendencies. Zen teachers may recommend different kinds of practice depending on students' goals (Kapleau, 2000, pp. 48ff) and give individual advice in regular meetings (*dokusan*). In the Hindu approaches, the relationship between teacher and student is often especially close, and one can expect a large amount of custom-tailored advice (Raina, 2002).

---

33 Transcendental meditation, which claims to belong to the Advaita Vedanta tradition, might be regarded as an exception to this assumption. However, mantra meditation might also be seen as just a small and not so central part of the practice traditionally advocated in Advaita Vedanta.

The Final Goal

Are the final goals that can be reached according to the four theories the same or different, or, in other words, are there different kinds of enlightenment? At a first glimpse, these goals are indeed quite different. Fully understanding the three characteristics of life and thereby realizing nibbana, the goal stated by early Buddhism, clearly differs from getting access to pure consciousness (*purusha*). Different goal states might be expected from the differences in the main meditation practices (narrowing down consciousness maximally in yoga meditation vs. enlarging it maximally in mindfulness meditation). However, getting access to pure consciousness does not seem to differ so much from realizing Brahman; and this in turn may be interpreted as being astonishingly close to realizing one's (and others') Buddha nature. After pondering about commonalities and differences in Hindu and Buddhist conceptions of enlightenment, Loy concludes:

> that the difference between the Buddhist nirvana and the Vedantic moksha is one of perspective. The Vedantic explanation – that of merging into the One – is a more objective philosophical view. The Buddhist interpretation is more accurately a phenomenological description. But in each case the actual experience is the same. (Loy, 1982, p. 73)

What does empirical research say? There are several case studies of both Hindu and Buddhist meditators who are regarded as enlightened. For instance, Rao and Paranjpe (2016) report three such studies, of which we shall look at the one involving Ramana Maharishi, a famous modern Advaitin.[34] Ramana was self-taught (no known guru) but practiced the three steps of jnana yoga mentioned above: listening, reflection, and contemplation, probably mixed with ingredients from yoga. Apart from the realization of noself, Rao and Paranjpe (2016, p. 297) mention two marks of enlightenment or self-realization: his genuine and unlimited compassion and that people visiting him felt deep peace in his presence.

In a more systematic study, Gisela Full interviewed 18 advanced Theravada meditators in Myanmar who were considered to have reached the stage of sotapanna, the first of the four stages of enlightenment assumed in early Buddhism (Anālayo, 2021). The four stages of enlightenment in Theravada Buddhism are: *sotopanna* (stream enterer), *sakadagami* (once-returner), *anagami* (nonreturner), and *arahant* who has reached the highest level of en-

---

34 Actually, he is generally regarded a neo-Vedantin because his focus was less on philosophical speculation and more on self-inquiry (Davis, 2010, p. 48). The two other cases, which were examined by Rao and Paranjpe, those of B. G. Tilak and Tukarama, are not dealt with here because the two respective theoretical backgrounds to karma yoga and bhakti yoga have not been explicated in this chapter.

lightenment. Remember that enlightenment (*nibbana*) means to leave the cycle of rebirths. So, the stream enterer is on the safe path to nibbana but will be born again several times (at most seven times), and the sakadagami will be born again only once. This classification does not contribute to a psychological theory of meditation and is therefore not considered further in the discussion here. The 18 meditators, with an average meditation practice of nearly 40 years, reported a profoundly improved clarity in perception, a deep comprehension of interdependencies in perception processing, and a deconstruction of the notion of I, self, or me (Full et al., 2013). Also, another very experienced meditator interviewed by Ataria et al. (2015) reported a total lack of the sense of self, time, internal versus external, and of the sense of a first-person-egocentric bodily perspective.

Boyle (2015) interviewed 11 purportedly enlightened Western Buddhist teachers, with Theravada, Vajrayana, and Zen (and also mixed) backgrounds to find out about the paths they had followed and where those had led them. First, he concludes that, in contrast to the conception of a sudden and total enlightenment experience, the interviews "show more a pattern of small or medium-size insight experiences that occur along the path, sometimes almost unnoticed" (Boyle, 2015, p. 203). From his interviews, Boyle extracts three major properties of awakened consciousness that differ from ordinary awareness. First, there is a *lack of separation from the environment:*

> We experience ourselves as part of what is going on around us – not as the director or principal actor in that system, and not separate from it. As a consequence, we feel more intimately involved in our environment, freer, more connected with what is going on and more sensitive to the existence and feelings of those around us. (Boyle, 2015, p. 211)

The second property of awakening according to Boyle is the *elimination of emotional attachments to the self:*

> We can observe what is going on in the world and act appropriately, but emotional connections with the scripts that normally govern this activity have come unplugged and the flow of awareness that was organized around the self, playing the central role in the drama, "stops." Because we no longer feel any responsibility for managing events or for protecting or advancing the interests of the self, we feel a sense of freedom and lightness, peace and equanimity. (Boyle, 2015, p. 214)

And the third property he terms "not knowing": *awareness co-arises with action, freely, at each moment:*

> What we become aware of and what we find ourselves doing in each moment emerge together, as unconscious processing in our brains and bodies interacts with our environment. This way of living feels deliciously fluid and dynamic. (Boyle, 2015, p. 216)

You might have noted that compassion is missing. It seems that Boyle was also surprised, but after also considering other cases from the literature, he concludes (Boyle, 2015, pp. 232ff) that awakening is possible without compassion, and that this kind of "awakening without compassion" might be found more frequently in the Zen world than in the Theravada world: "Compassion, it appears, must be cultivated for its own sake" (Boyle, 2015, p. 292).

The qualitative approach used by the abovementioned authors is probably the best empirical way to find out about properties of enlightenment. However, at the current level of theoretical development, it seems impossible to decide unerringly whether somebody is enlightened or not. In Zen, for instance, there is a clear criterion: The Zen masters decide whether a student is enlightened or not. In the Hindu world, it seems that mostly the devotees "know" that their teacher is enlightened. And in the Theravada world, there are detailed lists of criteria (e.g., Thanissaro, 2011; see also the contemporary description above in the section Change in Early Buddhism), but the process of authentication often appears to be a compromise between a practitioner's own judgment and that of others, such as those of fellow monks and nuns.[35]

There are also critical voices doubting the enlightenment of some Buddhist (e.g., Coleman, 2002; Samy, 2005; Yamada, 2002, pp. 241 and 392) as well as Hindu teachers (e.g., Conway, 2006; Shaw, 2003). It might be much easier to find out if somebody is *not* enlightened. The realization of no-self (or emptiness) seems to be the dominant property visible in the qualitative studies summarized above: Clearly, narcissism – that is, a highly inflated self – and enlightenment do not go together. Indeed, the experience of no-self seems to be quite rare even among experienced meditators. For instance, Pagis (2010) could only find one in 60 experienced Vipassana practitioners who reported it. In contrast, persons with inflated egos are clearly *not* enlightened according to any of the four traditional approaches. Especially if teachers exploit their students sexually or financially, or if their behavior is strongly driven by greed, hatred, or anger, claims of enlightenment can be seriously doubted. There is, of course, still the possibility that there is nothing like enlightenment at all (e.g., everything made up by practitioners with weird personality structures). But the numerous reports from different independent sources (many of them not dealt with in this book,

---

35 There is also a Western attempt to measure enlightenment, relying on writings from different cultural backgrounds. Boyd-Wilson and Walkey (2015) constructed the *Enlightenment Scale*, which contains two factors: "At Peace" and "Open-Hearted." Here are two sample items: "In the 'core' of me, I'm content no matter what" (At Peace), and "I don't belittle people" (Open-Hearted).

for want of space) point to the veracity of such unusual experiences and insights.

To come back to the initial question: Are there different kinds of enlightenment experiences and insights? At the moment, there seems to be no strong empirical basis to answer this question (but see Chapter 11).

The Role of God(s)

Overall, gods do not play a central role in the four traditional approaches. There is no god in Samkhya or Buddhism, although in some later Buddhist developments, the Buddha acquired godlike status. In Yoga and Advaita Vedanta, gods have some kind of auxiliary status. The Yogasutras mention a personal but essentially inactive deity, *Isvara*, who serves as a "transformative catalyst or guide for aiding the yogin on the path to spiritual emancipation" (Whicher, 1998, p. 86). And Advaita Vedanta differentiates between *nirguna* (higher) Brahman and *saguna* (lower) Brahman. Only nirguna Brahman is free from all name and form; saguna Brahman (or God) is Brahman viewed from the aspect of ignorance (Potter, 1998, p. 74). So, somewhat simplified, one could argue that practitioners of (the eightfold path of) yoga and Advaita Vedanta who need some more support may resort to the idea of a god for that. Note, however, that this conclusion would not hold for other traditional soteriological paths such as Bhakti-Yoga, or meditation in the Christian or Muslim context, in which god(s) play(s) an indispensable role.

Reincarnation and Supernatural Cognition

The idea of reincarnation or rebirth plays a central role in all four soteriological systems (remember that liberation means liberation from the cycle of births). It is, however, hard to see how the concept could be incorporated into a psychological theory of meditation. There is some empirical research headed by the late Ian Stevenson (for a summary, see Stevenson, 2006), but it is probably fair to say that, as yet, no definitive conclusions can be drawn. Psychologically more interesting because in principle testable, is the claim that extended meditation practice might yield supernatural powers (*siddhis*). Indeed, the *Yogasutras* devote their entire third book to this topic, although many commentators agree with the 38th sutra in this third book, saying that "the emergence of these accomplishments are an obstacle to samadhi" (Ranganathan, 2008, p. 246). However, several scholars see the accomplishment of siddhis as a sign of true progress (e.g., Braud, 2010; Phillips, 2009; Sarbacker, 2012).

In contrast to Samkhya-Yoga, there is no special emphasis on the attainment of supernormal cognition (*siddhis*) in Advaita Vedanta, but as siddhis are mentioned in the parts of the Vedas that Advaitins refer to (e.g., in the *Upanishads*) and as Advaitins accept the teachings of Yoga (Raju, 1985), they are not excluded, either. Actually, some Advaitins such as Paramahamsa Yogananda explicitly mention the attainment of special powers (Yogananda, 1950), and detailed descriptions of the attainment of supernormal powers can be found in the autobiographical writings of Sri Aurobindo (2001), who is often considered to be a "neo-Advaitin" (see Raju, 1985).

In early Buddhism, supernatural cognition is expected as a by-product of extended concentrative practice. Mastering the fourth jhana (see Table 9.1) is generally seen as the basis for experiencing such *higher knowledges*, such as clairaudience, clairvoyance, or mind reading (Buddhaghosa, 2010; in the West, such postulated effects are known as *psi* effects, e.g., Radin, 2013). However, the attainment of such higher knowledges is mostly seen as an impediment – in the Buddha's words: "Seeing the danger of such miracles, I dislike, reject, and despise them" (cited in S. Batchelor, 2015, p. 166). In the Zen literature, mentions of supernatural cognition are not absent but seem to decline as the context of the Zen stories moves from India to China. In the Japanese Zen literature, special experiences are usually regarded as illusions (*makyo*).

In sum, the idea that (concentrative) meditation may lead to supernatural cognition is part of all four approaches but more prominent in the earlier ones. Clinging to these special experiences is generally regarded as hindering progress on the soteriological path. However, supernatural cognition might be important in empirically testing the traditional theories. There is some indication that some kind of supernatural cognition may exist, but the evidence is far from conclusive (for a summary, see Sedlmeier, 2018).

Other Aspects

So far, we have almost exclusively focused on cognition (viewed in a very comprehensive way), but all four theories also contain other parts, such as a stronger or less strong teacher-student relationship and most prominently rituals and ethics.

Rituals can be found in all ashrams and monasteries and also among many lay communities. They can be quite different across different schools, but all schools have texts to recite or chant, and all have gestures of respect and forms of worship such as pujas, prayers, the lighting of candles, performing of prostrations, greeting of teachers and fellow meditators, and so on. Usually, these rituals give a good structure to days, weeks, or the year, and they mark the separation from routine and more formal practice.

Also, rules of conduct and other ethical rules are part of all four approaches. In the earlier two approaches, they are prominently included in the respective eightfold paths; and the later systems seem to largely agree with these rules. In Zen, they are formulated in several (similar) versions of precepts including the so-called 10 grave or cardinal precepts (e.g., Kapleau, 2000, p. 415). These exhort the practitioner to avoid (1) the taking of life, (2) theft, (3) misuse of sexuality, (4) lying, (5) causing others to abuse drugs or alcohol or doing so oneself, (6) speaking of the shortcomings of others, (7) praising oneself and reviling others, (8) withholding spiritual or material aid, (9) indulging in anger, and (10) disparaging the Three Treasures [i.e., the Buddha, the Dharma (teaching of the Buddha), and the Sangha (the Buddhist community)].

In yoga, breathing exercises and bodily postures play an important role as well. This explicitly bodily aspect is less pronounced in the Buddhist approaches, which, however all include walking meditation to varying extents. The practice of Advaita Vedanta seems to be possible without recourse to any body work, although, as already mentioned, Advaita Vedanta accepts the teachings of Yoga and therefore nothing speaks against Advaitins including pranayama and asanas in their path of salvation.

What Is Necessary in a Comprehensive Theory of Meditation?

Scholars of Hinduism and Buddhism may not be totally happy with how I have dealt with the four traditional approaches. However, to make this clear again: The main aim here is not to be as true as possible to the respective traditions, although I have done my best. Rather, I was interested in extracting pieces of a psychological theory of meditation that could be used for improving meditation research. Let us assume, for the moment, that it is possible to develop a comprehensive theory of meditation: what would be needed in such a theory? At the moment, we are, of course, talking about a theory that covers everything all the way to the one and central aim of all traditional approaches to meditation: enlightenment or liberation (but see next chapter).

A Theory of Cognition and Change

First, we obviously need a theory of cognition and, in this context even more important, a theory of how cognition can be changed to achieve the goal.

All four theories above would qualify in providing this, but it is hard to see how they could be combined into a single one. We could then try to find out which one is the best. Because the main issue in all theories is change, we could argue that the most important criterion in that respect is effectiveness: Which theory yields the highest rate of "success" if the respective path is practiced? Obviously, this question cannot be answered at the moment because as we have seen above, "success" is still ill-defined, and data are very sparse. So, a pragmatic way to proceed might be to begin with the most elaborate or detailed theory and try to build on that. Here we have a clear winner: the early Buddhist theory of meditation.

In all the four approaches dealt with here, concentrative techniques play a central role as the means for cognitive change. One apparent dichotomy has come up repeatedly: that between concentration and mindfulness. However, as already emphasized in Chapter 8, on a closer look, there is no clear separation between these two categories – at least not at the practical level. Beginners and even experienced meditators, when trying to put their full concentration on an object – say, the breath – often or occasionally find their minds wandering. So, the task is not only concentration but also recognizing that attention has been drawn away, letting go other contents of cognition, and trying to come back and stay on the object of concentration again. Even more difficult for most meditators is to stay fully open to everything that appears in one's awareness. Therefore, mindfulness practices are often connected to some object or process of concentration such as the body scan. For instance, in the Goenka and Mahasi Vipassana practices (see Chapter 3), mindfulness practice is strongly connected to (different) forms of body scan. Scanning the body in a prespecified order is a concentration task, and, in these two cases, mindfulness is largely reduced to being mindful of bodily processes. For mindfulness practice, using the breath as an anchor is also often recommended. The point to be illustrated here is that, although theoretically the endpoints are clearly defined, there is no strict dichotomy between concentration and mindfulness. At first sight, there are seemingly clear predictions for the effects of mindfulness and concentration in early Buddhism (Figure 9.5), but a good theory of change should be able to make more precise predictions based on clearly specified meditation techniques (see also Chapter 11).

Flexibility in Taking Meditators' Personalities and Circumstances Into Account

Some meditation teachers react very flexibly to the needs of their students. In Buddhism, this sort of flexibility is expressed by the term *skillful means* (*upaya*). So, a good theory of meditation should include as many contingencies of that sort as possible. An important question could be, "Which meditation technique or instruction is appropriate for a person with that personality under these circumstances?" The *Visuddhimagga* guidelines for choosing objects of meditation according to meditators' temperaments or the consideration of the relative proportions of the three gunas in Samkhya-Yoga might be good starting points for developing evidence-based selection criteria for parts of meditation practice.

Should Practitioners Believe in Something?

Judging from the role personal god(s) play in the four approaches, it does not seem necessary to include them in a theory of meditation. However, if – and this might be added to the previous paragraph – practitioners find it helpful to have such a belief (or they hold such a belief anyway) it might be very beneficial for them. Or, stated differently, it is not necessary, to *not* believe in god(s). A different case is great faith – that is, the belief that enlightenment is possible, that purusha, Brahman, or Buddha nature really exist. (Faith is also different in the Indian traditions: Unlike the Abrahamic ones where it may be belief in something, there faith can indicate trust in the process and in acceptance of cause and effect, more than anything else.) Such a belief is part of all four (and probably all traditional) systems. This consistency among the approaches might signal that great faith is absolutely necessary. To some extent, this is a trivial assumption because who would take on an arduous path of salvation if salvation did not exist? So, practitioners following these paths need at least to be open to the possibility of such a final state. But does it make a difference how firmly they believe in it? At the moment, I am not aware of a good answer to that question, but it seems to be open to empirical scrutiny.

Are Bodily Exercises, Rituals, and Ethics Necessary?

Bodily exercises, including breath control, are not necessary, according to the standard of whether all four approaches include them. However – and this also might be an important contribution to the issue of skillful means – they may turn out to be very helpful for at least some practitioners. In contrast, all four approaches dealt with here and probably all traditional salvation paths contain rituals and ethical rules of conduct. Thus, both should be included in a theory of meditation. There are several plausible reasons they might be important. Rituals may give structure to the day – that is, make the practice easier. They may also maintain a sense of connectedness among meditation groups, which also should help staying with the practice. As far as rules of ethics are concerned: If practitioners do not heed them, their minds should be much more distracted than if they do. And distracted minds are a severe impediment to all kinds of concentrative tasks. Be that as it may, a comprehensive theory of meditation should include both rituals and ethics and try to derive and test precise predictions about what happens when they are missing.

Could Such a Theory Be Connected to Western Theories of Cognition?

The issue of whether and how traditional theories of meditation can be connected to Western cognitive theories would need a book on its own. However, it would not be a good sign if a contemporary theory of meditation, using building blocks derived from traditional theories, could not connect to the state of the art in cognitive science. Since I have argued that the cognitive theory of early Buddhism might be a good starting point for a contemporary theory of meditation, I will briefly discuss how connections can be made between current Western theorizing and even seemingly unusual parts of the traditional theory of cognition. There are several assumptions in the cognitive theory of early Buddhism that one might, at first glance, not expect in Western psychological theories: a continuous stream of consciousness, not governed by a central instance or self, but only interactions of "cognitive parts," with future cognitions (moments of consciousness) in principle dependent in the interplay of all previous parts. Thus, thinking is only a kind of perception, and every perception is accompanied by a very rudimentary form of feeling: pleasant, neutral, or unpleasant. Can we find counterparts to these assumptions in current theorizing? Yes, we can. The stream of consciousness can, of course, already be found in the writings of William James (Natsoulas, 1992). A model of how the idea of a self could emerge without it existing as an entity of its own is, for instance, nicely shown in a computational model by Nowak et al. (2000). Cognitions that arise just by the interplay of many parts of the brain are the bread and butter of neural network models (e.g., O'Reilly et al., 2020), and there is the theory of biased competition or integrated competition that describes attention as a form of competition among different cognitive inputs (see Smith & Kosslyn, 2007, pp. 139–143). A specific dynamic model that describes cognition as trajectories through the state space of the human brain seems to be quite consistent with early Buddhist theory, using, of course, totally different language (Spivey, 2007). A hard-to-swallow contention for Western psychologists might be that cognition is nothing but perception. However, a growing number of scholars assert just that (e.g., Firestone & Scholl, 2016; Michel 2020). Mercier and Sperber (2017) argue that goal-directed rational thinking, requiring a central planning instance, is largely a myth. And something akin to the Buddhist vedanas (pleasant, neutral, unpleasant) can be found as an essential building block in Damasio's (2012) theory of consciousness.

This short list does not, of course, provide for a strong argument, but it shows that early Buddhist theory may be in principle connectable to current theorizing about cognition. So far, traditional theories of meditation have played only a very minor role in meditation research. If they did have an impact on Western theoretical approaches to meditation, it was usually early Buddhism that was (mostly only loosely) connected. We will have a look at these Western models of meditation in the next chapter.

Chapter 10
Western Explanations

Why and how does meditation work? In the last chapter, we looked at the answers given by four traditional Eastern theories. This chapter deals with explanations that have been advanced in the West since the 1960s. Early explanations tended to be quite idiosyncratic and did not really differentiate between different forms of meditation, whereas some later ones almost exclusively focus on "mindfulness meditation." However, recently, the scope of meditation techniques referred to in models of meditation has been opened up to include other meditation practices as well.

Most of the later explanations are secular – that is, free of spiritual and religious content, and also largely free of ethics and rituals. And the main aim of meditation as seen in the majority of these explanatory models is well-being. The issue of enlightenment, central to the traditional theories (and early Western accounts), is almost never mentioned there. Readers will recognize some of the approaches discussed in this chapter from the exposition of the classifications contained in them, as detailed in Chapter 4.

Early Explanations

Three early explanations have gained some prominence. Two of them center on mystical experiences, and the other on the "relaxation response."

Deautomatization

It seems that the first systematic Western attempt to explain the mechanisms of meditation stems from the psychiatrist Arthur Deikman who himself practiced Zen and Sufi meditation. In contrast to later explanations, he did not see well-being as the main goal of meditation but the "mystic experience," the description of which resembles a selection of elements used for the descriptions of enlightenment in several traditional schools (see Chapter 9). In fact, he does not differentiate between the effects of different schools of meditation – he mentions, for instance, Christian mysticism, Buddhism, and Yoga. Deikman summarizes meditative practices as *contemplation* and argues that the mechanism by which the mystic experience, this "unusual state of consciousness" is brought about is *deautomatization*

(Deikman, 1963, 1966a). He argues that the mechanism of deautomatization follows from the emphasis on focused attention and "not thinking" found in traditional meditation instructions, which leads to the phenomenon of "fresh vision." In contrast, he describes automatization as a basic process that leads to the disappearance from consciousness of the intermediate steps of an action or perception. As we grow up, automated cognitive and emotional processes are very helpful, both biologically and evolutionarily because they enable us to quickly turn our limited attention to the important things of life. Infants already recognize other people, animals, and objects without being deliberately aware of having to construct these summary perceptions from a mixture of sensory perceptions of colors, structures, smells, sounds, and tactile sensations. We do not even think of such a construction process as "normal," because we never do it consciously. In adults, the connection between thoughts and emotions is largely automatic: If, for instance, our partner criticizes us, we get angry without deliberating where the anger might come from. In fact, we might hear a sequence of speech sounds, which we automatically translate into language. These "language stimuli," we interpret (e.g., as criticism), and this interpretation in turn activates emotions (e.g., anger). Deikman argues that automatization can be at least partly suspended if (1) our attention is directly directed to a sensory perception, (2) no controlled analytical thinking takes place, and (3) the person has an open attitude toward all sensory perceptions. This is exactly what, according to Deikman, happens in meditation.

Relaxation Response

Herbert Benson, a cardiologist at the Harvard Medical School proposed a different mechanism for why meditation works: the *relaxation response*. At first, Benson related his explanation to mantra meditation. He was initially urged by members of the transcendental meditation (TM) movement to conduct studies on the effects of TM (see Chapter 4), but later, he also included a large part of the techniques described here in Chapter 1 under the term "meditation" (Benson & Klipper, 1974; Benson et al., 1974; R. K. Wallace et al., 1971). Members of the TM movement do not agree with Benson's explanation. In particular, his explanation is that meditation is nothing but a relaxation technique. According to Benson, meditation reduces metabolism, pulse, blood pressure, and breathing rate, and improves brain functions of attention and decision making. Indeed, in his own studies, Benson always found the relaxation response, and many meditation techniques do have relaxing effects. However, the evidence presented in Chapter 6 for studies that compared meditation groups with groups that practiced a relaxation technique, clearly speaks against this assumption: There must be more to meditation than relaxation. Moreover, some meditation techniques not only do not relax but even have activating effects (see Chapter 8).

Why God Won't Go Away

The psychiatrist Eugene d'Aquili and his colleague Andrew Newberg were significantly involved in developing a field variously termed *neuroscience of religion, neurotheology,* or *spiritual neuroscience*. This approach tries to explain religious or spiritual experiences by the working of specific brain processes. D'Aquili and Newberg (1993, 1998, 2000; with more details in Newberg et al., 2002) were especially interested in explaining how mystical experiences of unity come about. They argue that meditation, possibly combined with extended fasting and long isolation, increasingly blocks the access of neural stimuli to specific parts of the brain (parts of the parietal lobe and adjacent areas). These brain parts are, according to them, responsible for separating self and other, and for experiencing space and time. If this part of the brain is shut off, the experience of being united with the whole world emerges. This experience of mystical unity might also be interpreted as meeting god – so god cannot go away because he or she "is" in the brain.

D'Aquili and Newberg connect their neurological argument with an evolutionary one, relying on group selection. Why is such a mystical experience of unity adaptive? If the spiritual leader of a group who faced a difficult situation withdrew into solitude, fasted, and meditated, they produced such an experience of unity or, in other words, saw god. This experience was so strong that it enabled the leader to convey to their group a strong sense of religiosity, which in turn considerably strengthened the group's cohesion. And this gave the group an evolutionary advantage as compared with groups with less charismatic leaders. However, the ability to experience unity is not an adaptation per se but a by-product ("spandrel") of evolution, the real adaptive mechanism being orgasm. Orgasm is regarded as central for mate selection and sexual activities. Like orgasm, mystical experiences of unity are often accompanied by bliss, rapture, ecstasy, and elation (see the characteristics of the jhanas, Chapter 9, Table 9.1). The experience of unity or god, so to speak, "uses" the already present adaptive mechanism of orgasm. There is some evidence for this explanation from studies with Tibetan Buddhists and French nuns (e.g., Newberg et al., 1997, 2001, 2003), but there are also contradictory results, at least concerning French nuns (Beauregard & Paquette, 2006).

Buddhism-Inspired Explanations

As already mentioned, contemporary Western explanations can rarely be explicitly related to Buddhist theory, although Buddhist sources are still cited now and then. However, a closer look usually reveals that there are such connections and that they are much stronger than any connections to any other spiritual or religious backgrounds. Not explicitly mentioning a spiritual background may have made these explanations more acceptable for Western researchers and for the public.

FA-OM Framework

In their influential theoretical framework, Lutz et al. (2008) group meditation techniques into two broad categories, thereby relating to common Buddhist practices (see also Chapters 3 and 9): *focused attention* (FA) and *open monitoring* (OM) meditation. They conceive of meditation techniques as emotional and attentional regulatory training regimes for the cultivation of well-being and emotional balance. FA meditation is conceptualized as focusing attention on a chosen object in a sustained fashion, and OM meditation is defined as nonreactively monitoring the content of experience from moment to moment. The authors first ask which skills are required for performing these two kinds of meditation and then make predictions about the neural systems connected with these skills. They argue (see Table 1 in Lutz et al., 2008) that FA meditation needs (1) directing and sustaining attention on a selected object (e.g., breath sensation), (2) detection of mind wandering and distractors (e.g., thoughts), (3) disengagement of attention from distractors and the shifting of attention back to the selected object, and (4) cognitive reappraisal of distractors (e.g., "just a thought"). In contrast, OM meditation is described as (1) having no explicit focus on objects, (2) performing nonreactive metacognitive monitoring (e.g., for novices, labeling of experience), and (3) being nonreactively aware of automatic cognitive and emotional interpretations of sensory, perceptual, and endogenous stimuli.

Based on this analysis, the authors, for instance, predict that during (or as a consequence of) FA meditation, increased activities should be observed in brain areas connected with conflict monitoring, selective attention, and sustaining attention. OM meditation should activate brain regions implicated in monitoring, vigilance, and disengaging attention from stimuli that distract attention from the ongoing stream of experience. Neurophysiological changes in the respective areas should then be correlated with improvements in behavioral measures. Lutz et al. (2008) cite a number of studies that corroborate their framework but also concede that the classical neuroanatomical top-down influences might be insufficient to describe what happens in the brain as a consequence of meditation. Instead, they suggest that a better description may be that of a succession of large-scale brain states, with each state becoming the source of top-down influences for the subsequent state (Lutz et al., 2008, p. 167). The FA-OM framework is not a full-fledged theory of meditation but finding out more about the connection of neural and behavioral responses to meditation is certainly an important area of meditation research.

How Does Mindfulness Meditation Work?

Hölzel et al. (2011) propose a framework that specifies several components through which mindfulness meditation supposedly exerts its effects. The aim of mindfulness meditation is specified as increasing well-being and ameliorating psychiatric and stress-related symptoms. Although the authors first define mindfulness meditation as "nonjudgmental awareness of experiences in the present moment" (Hölzel et al., 2011, p. 537), they later also include attention regulation in their definition, referring, for example, to *samatha* practice (p. 539). And when they present empirical evidence, they also refer to a wide variety of other meditation techniques. It seems that they have tried to subsume in their model the mindfulness literature (see Chapter 2), which, however, is quite inconsistent in itself. But mainly, their framework seems to cover the two broad categories of meditation suggested by Lutz et al. (2008) without explicitly differentiating among the effects for either category. Based on previous mindfulness research, their framework consolidates existing findings and addresses several components that have received empirical support. The components proposed to describe the working of mindfulness meditation are depicted in Figure 10.1.

Attention regulation is seen as the prerequisite for the other mechanisms to take place, and there is some dependency among the components, as indicated in Figure 10.1 by the arrows. They express this as follows:

> Focused attention on internal events is necessary in order for practitioners to gain an increased awareness of bodily sensations with the resultant ability to recognize the emergence of emotions. The ability to keep attention focused on conditioned stimuli is also a prerequisite for the successful extinction of conditioned responses. Enhanced body awareness might be very closely related to the changes in the perspective on the self and might replace a narrative form of self-reference. The change in perspective on the self may result in reappraisal of situations in specific ways, which might provide motivation for further development of attention regulation and body awareness. (Hölzel et al., 2011, p. 549)

The component of emotion regulation consists of two subcomponents: (a) reappraisal and (b) exposure, extinction, and reconsolidation. Reappraisal

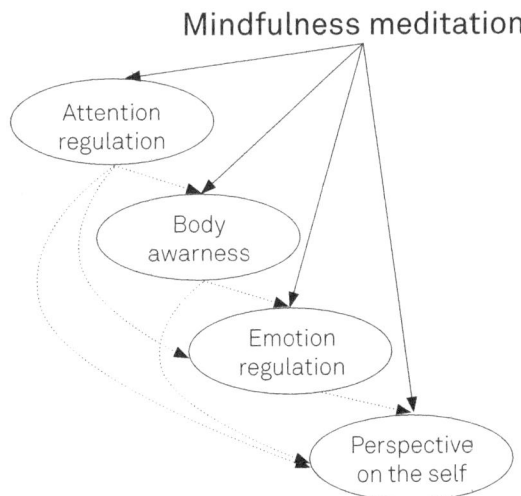

Figure 10.1. Components of mindfulness meditation. Based on Hölzel et al. (2011).

could consist of changing one's emotional response to a stimulus by reinterpreting its meaning. And nonreactively keeping one's attention on an emotional reaction – that is, prolonged exposure to an emotional stimulus – leads to its extinction and eventually to a reconsolidation.

It is not totally clear how the four components of mindfulness meditation are theoretically derived, but it seems that at least the first two are closely tied to what people do when they practice varieties of mindfulness meditation. They cultivate attention (attention regulation), and often the focus of attention is on internal sensory experiences (body awareness). Adding emotion regulation is justified because of a growing body of empirical results indicating improvements in emotion regulation, but also with reference to the *Satipatthana Sutta* (see Chapter 2). Only the final part, change in perspective on the self, is strongly connected to Buddhist theory.

Hölzel et al. (2011) cite ample evidence from behavioral and neurological studies corroborating their framework. The predictions of the model have already been supported in a study by Cebolla et al. (2018) that compared meditators and nonmeditators according to the components proposed (Figure 10.1). However, Hölzel et al. (2011) conclude that "knowledge of the underlying mechanisms of mindfulness is still in its infancy" (p. 551; see also Tang et al., 2015) and propose taking into account differences between various types of mindfulness practice and different personality types.

In a recent study, Verdonk et al. (2020) discuss the components suggested by Hölzel et al. (2011) on the basis of the results in 29 articles that examined *event-related potentials* (ERP, see Chapter 6). They found that neural features of mindfulness are consistently associated with the self-regulation of attention and often with reduced reactivity to emotional stimuli, as well as with improved cognitive control. The authors advance the hypothesis that mindfulness meditation facilitates the conscious processing of information from within (body awareness and self-awareness) and without the body (world awareness) or, stated more generally, decreases the threshold of conscious access to the inside and outside world.

The S-ART Framework

Vago and Silbersweig (2012) argue that, in addition to FA and OM meditation, *ethical enhancement* (EE) – that is, loving kindness and compassion practice – is also part of mindfulness meditation. They propose that mindfulness practice develops *self-awareness, self-regulation, and self-transcendence* (S-ART). Self-transcendence means to cultivate a positive relationship between self and other that transcends self-focused needs and increases prosocial characteristics (Vago & Silbersweig, 2012, p. 1). Relevant processes that help building up S-ART are attention regulation, emotion regulation, extinction and reconsolidation, prosociality, nonattachment, and decentering, as also suggested by Hölzel et al. (2011). Developing the S-ART skills is expected to reduce suffering and create a sustainable healthy mind. In particular, S-ART is proposed to reduce maladaptive emotions and cognitions common to most ordinary experience (e.g., lustful desire, greed, anger, hatred, and worry) and to increase prosocial dispositions (e.g., compassion, empathy, and forgiveness) toward self and others. Moreover, attachments to thoughts and feelings should weaken. Vago and Silbersweig (2012) refer to neurocognitive networks – for example the *experiential enactive self* (EES) and the *experiential phenomenological self* (EPS) – allegedly supporting the S-ART framework and offer very detailed process models of all three kinds of mindfulness practices: concentrative, open monitoring, and ethical enhancement. However, it appears that these process models and the neurobiological model are not very strongly connected, so far.

The PROMISE Model

In contrast to most other contemporary models, the *process of mindfulness meditation leading to insight and equanimity* (PROMISE) model explicitly refers to Buddhist teachings. However, also in contrast to other models, it is mainly a "subjective theory" model, based on the qualitative analysis of 11 interviews with practitioners of Zen, Vipassana, and Tibetan Buddhism, with different levels of experience, supplemented by results from Western research and teachings of Buddhist scriptures (Eberth et al., 2019).

The model (see Figure 10.2) highlights equanimity (reduction in emotional reactivity) and insight (alteration of cognitions) as the two key effects of mindfulness meditation. Mindfulness meditation is largely seen as practicing FA and/or OM meditation, as suggested by Lutz et al. (2008). However, participants also reported having used other meditation practices, such as *constructive* and *deconstructive* techniques (see next paragraph), as well as having heeded ethical rules. In addition to effects that are mostly attributable to FA (improvement of attention) and OM (improvement of metacognitive awareness) meditation, practitioners also used more explicit ways to alter affective experiences (see "Mental actions" and "Training effects" in Figure 10.2). Moreover, meditators postulated that equanimity and insight gave rise to positive behavior changes and altered the view of oneself.

Parts of the model were put to the test. Meditators in Buddhist traditions ($n=102$) with a mean meditation experience of 12 years were compared with a matched control group of nonmeditators to find out whether the former differed from the latter in the mental actions and effects postulated in the model. Consistent with the PROMISE model, Eberth et al. (2019) found strong differences in measures of observation mode and concept deactivation (two mental action variables) and in measures of equanimity, insight, and life satisfaction. An additional path model provided evidence for some processes postulated in the model.

Beyond (Solely) Buddhism-Inspired Explanations

The two models described in this section still draw on Buddhist theory. However, the first also incorporates meditation techniques from other traditional backgrounds, and the second attempts to identify a common mechanism across different forms of meditation.

Three Families of Meditation Practices

In Chapter 4 (in the section Classifications According to Types of Meditation), we have already met the *family model* of Dahl et al. (2015). There, the description of the meditation techniques focused on grouping them into attentional, constructive, and deconstructive families. Here, the focus is on postulated mechanisms and effects (Figure 10.3). The *attentional family* more or less conforms to the FA-OM framework discussed above but is augmented by clinical mindfulness approaches such as *mindfulness-based stress*

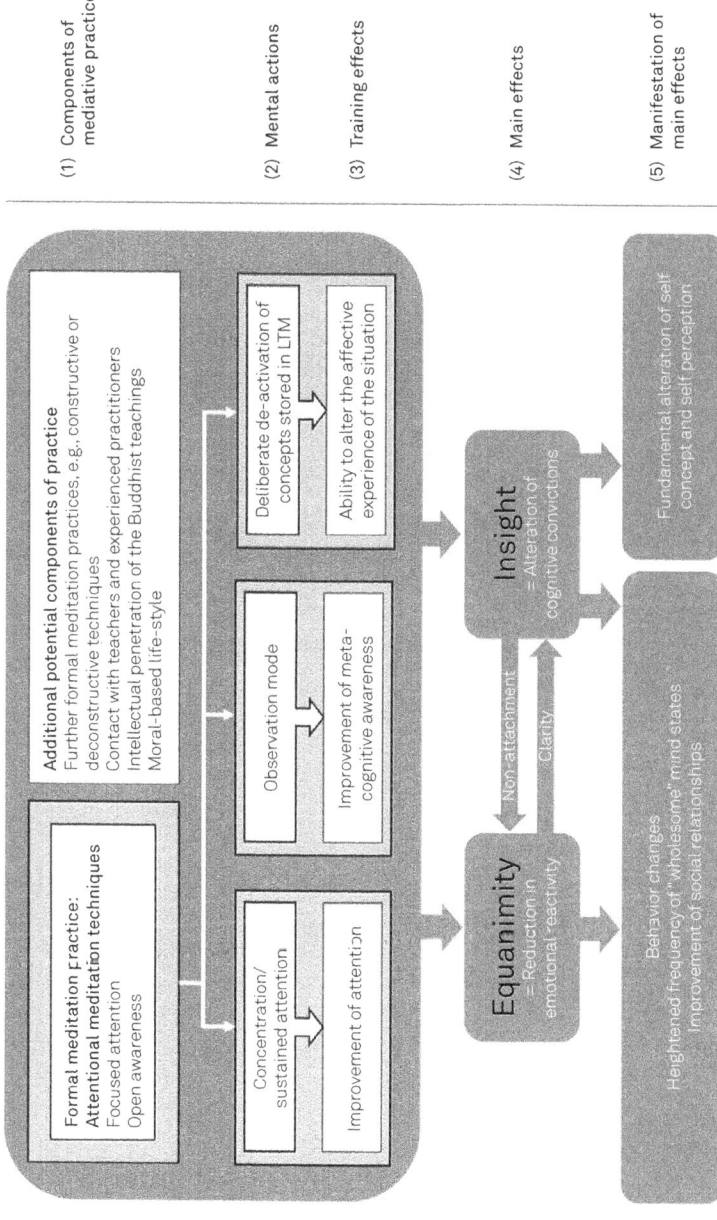

Figure 10.2. The PROMISE model. LTM = long term memory. Reprinted with permission from "PROMISE: A Model of Insight and Equanimity as the Key Effects of Mindfulness Meditation," by J. Eberth, P. Sedlmeier, & T. Schäfer, 2019, *Frontiers in Psychology, 10,* Figure 1. © 2019 The Authors is licensed under CC BY.

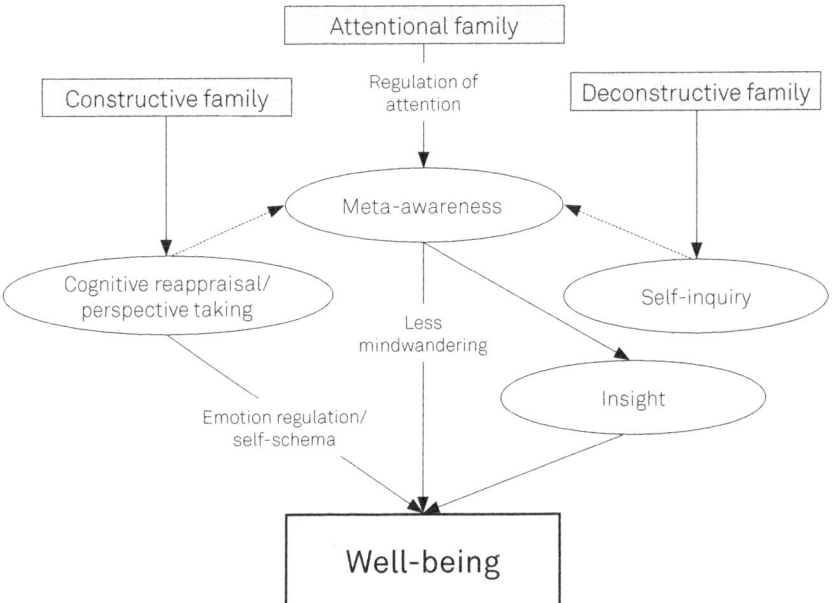

Figure 10.3. Three families of meditation practices. Based on Dahl et al. (2015).

reduction (MBSR), *mindfulness-based cognitive therapy* (MBCT), and *acceptance and commitment therapy* (ACT; see Chapter 2), as well as the cultivation of attention as described in Greco-Roman philosophy. The *constructive family* comprises techniques that intend to systematically alter (*construct*) thoughts and emotions. Some of these methods are expected to cultivate protective qualities such as patience and equanimity. Others are practiced for restructuring values and priorities toward conducting a more meaningful life. And still others are meant to nurture prosocial qualities such as kindness and compassion. Examples of techniques that fall into the latter subcategory of the constructive family are loving kindness and compassion meditation, the Jesus prayer, contemplation of mortality, meditation on foulness (see Chapters 1 and 2), and many Western psychotherapeutic approaches. Finally, the *deconstructive family* consists of techniques that explore (deconstruct) the dynamics of perception, emotion, and cognition. Techniques that fall into this category are, for instance, the first and second foundations of mindfulness (body and feeling tones, see Chapter 2), koan practice, shikantaza, or the self-inquiry in Advaita Vedanta.

Dahl et al. (2015) argue that although the final effect of the techniques in all three families is to reduce suffering and increase well-being, they do so in different ways. The attentional-family methods are meant to improve several aspects of attention and thereby become more aware of the processes of thinking, feeling, and perceiving – that is, they strengthen meta-awareness. The authors illustrate the difference between the presence and absence of meta-awareness with an example: If you are sitting in a movie theater and watching an enthralling movie, you might be so attentive to the movie that you are experientially fused with it and no longer consciously aware that you are sitting in a movie theater. This is, so to speak, the opposite of meta-awareness, during which you are aware of the movie but also of your surroundings and the fact that you are viewing images on a screen. Higher meta-awareness leads to less mind wandering, and less mind wandering in turn increases well-being.

How do techniques of the constructive family work? All of these techniques train one to view the world and oneself from a new perspective. The authors again use an example for illustration. When you are on an airplane and hear a baby crying, that might at first elicit a feeling of distress followed by aversion. But when you take the perspective of the baby's mother, that might trigger a sense of warmth and compassion, and you might view the experience as an opportunity to cultivate kindness and concern. The practices in this family necessitate meta-awareness and also serve to strengthen and sustain it. Eventually, they should improve emotion regulation and replace maladaptive self-schemas with more adaptive conceptions of self, which again increases well-being.

And the deconstructive-family techniques? The central activity when performing them is "self-inquiry," the process of investigating the nature and dynamics of conscious experience. Self-inquiry works better with a stronger meta-awareness, which is also itself strengthened by the practice of self-inquiry. In combination, meta-awareness and self-inquiry can be expected to lead to insights about the world and oneself. The stronger the meta-awareness, the more likely such insights will come. And if one understands oneself and the world better, well-being increases.

Meditation and the Wandering Mind

Brandmeyer and Delorme (2021) first argue that the aim of meditation (short, in their view, for "meditation practices and mindfulness-based interventions") is to increase dispositional mindfulness. Then they go on to say that most meditation practices aim to generate mindfulness by (a) cultivating attentional clarity and stability, (b) regulating emotional responses to the content of our thoughts and experiences, and (c) cultivating compassion for oneself and others (Brandmeyer & Delorme, 2021, p. 39). However, their own model seems to center on FA meditation and the role of meta-awareness, which again has a strong impact on mind wandering which is seen as the opposite of mindfulness. Their core model might be summarized as shown in Figure 10.4 (solid lines indicate main processes).

Although an increase in the allocation of attentional resources (improved sustained attention) is used several times in the text as a potential mediator variable, Brandmeyer and Delorme (2021) favor the hypothesis that meditation foremost increases metacognitive awareness and accuracy:

> It is our perspective that it is most likely the case that meditative experience enhances metacognitive skills from the onset, increasing an individual's propensity to detect spontaneous thought. This would occur through the initial and repetitious "flexing" of the cognitive activity associated with the meditative cycle, with an emphasis placed on detecting when attention has drifted away from the meditative focus and bringing it back to the object. (Brandmeyer & Delorme, 2021, pp. 54–55)

Increased metacognitive awareness might, with growing practice, lead to an increased sensitivity to the occurrence of mind wandering and the ability to detect its occurrence earlier and thus facilitate the capacity for longer periods of sustained attention (see arrow from metacognitive awareness to sustained attention in Figure 10.3). According to the authors, metacognitive awareness plays a key role in enhancing cognitive regulation, which, in turn, "may serve to potentially buffer individuals against a wide array of cognitive deficiencies that arise from the inability to regulate self-generated thought content (i.e., rumination, habitual thinking)" (Brandmeyer & Delorme, 2021, p. 56). They concede that there are many open research

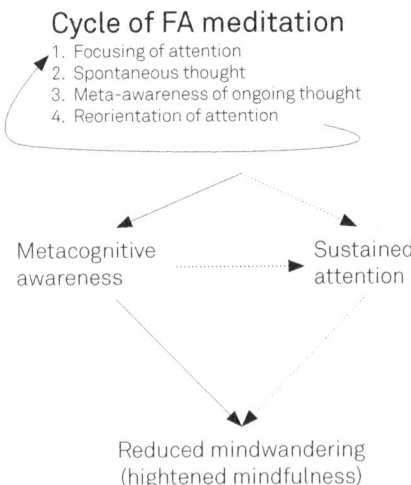

Figure 10.4. Meditation and the wandering mind. FA = focused attention. Based on Brandmeyer and Delorme (2021).

questions, such as about differential effects of different types of meditation on the wandering mind, and they deplore incompatible definitions and conceptions of mindfulness and meditation, as well as the very concept of mind wandering.

Other Models

Some of the other models of meditation have only little or no explicit connection to Buddhism and propose to build explanations on assumptions about attentional processes and Western theories of consciousness. Some authors pursue an integration of mindfulness meditation and consciousness within a neuroscientific perspective. Manuello et al. (2016) advance the hypothesis that consciousness and mindfulness meditation can be integrated into one model by identifying brain areas that play an essential role in both types (e.g., anterior cingulate cortex, insula, posterior cingulate cortex, some regions in the prefrontal cortex, and the thalamus). They expect that by looking at the impact of meditation on the activation of these brain areas, one might learn more about the neural counterparts of subjective experience connected to meditation. Raffone and Srinivasan (2017) also suggest that it should be worthwhile to work toward a unifying framework for mindfulness and cognitive functions. Two such models have been described in more detail, the *contemplative cognition framework* and the *consciousness state space model*.

Contemplative Cognition Framework

In their contemplative cognition framework, Grossenbacher and Quaglia (2017) refer to Western Buddhism-inspired models and other Buddhist sources but intend to go one step further and identify the components that are necessary for a parsimonious account of meditative cognition. To be able to describe what happens in the meditative mind, they rely on three foundational psychological constructs: attention, intention, and awareness. Relying on these three fundamentals, they define three new cognitive constructs to describe meditative cognition: *intended attention* (IA), *attention to intention* (A→I), and *awareness of transient information* (ATI). Here is an example of how the authors think these three constructs may be used:

> During focused attention practices such as shamatha, practitioners intend to attend to the meditation object (e.g., sensations of breathing), thereby increasing the likelihood of so attending (IA). Because respiratory sensations dynamically update, they provide a renewing source of transient sensory information. Practi-

tioners can thereby recurrently utilize ATI (e.g., maintained or diminishing awareness of respiratory sensations) as input that can inform the intentional tuning of attention so as to better ensure that sensations of breathing are foregrounded in consciousness. Along with IA to breathing, a practitioner may also (perhaps unconsciously) select and monitor the intention to attend to the breath (A→I), promoting ongoing focus on sensations of breathing, e.g., by inhibiting meditation-irrelevant intentions. (Grossenbacher & Quaglia, 2017, p. 1527)

Inter alia, Grossenbacher and Quaglia (2017) recommend the use of their model to come to terms better with the notoriously difficult construct of mindfulness, which "is compromised by polysemy, vagueness, and definitional confusion" (p. 1590). The authors even make suggestions about how the three new constructs can be measured (e.g., IA by the d2 test, A→I by Go/No-Go tasks, and ATI by an attentional blink task), but they do not detail theoretical connections between constructs and tests, and they suggest several tests per construct. Although the model allows for descriptions of what happens in the mind during meditation, it is not evident how precise meditation-related predictions can be derived from it, in its current version.

Consciousness State Space Model

Berkovich-Ohana and Glicksohn (2014, 2017) argue that their *consciousness state space* (CSS) model can be used to explain certain aspects of meditation. Their model assumes that every experience takes place in a three-dimensional phenomenological space – the dimensions being time, awareness, and emotion. Another core assumption is that all phenomenological states fall into two categories of consciousness, core (CC) and extended (EC). CC supports only a "minimal self" and has no temporal extension – that is, its scope is the here and now. EC in contrast involves personal identity, continuity across time, memory imagination, and conceptual thought, thereby supporting a "narrative self." CSS is concentrically organized, with the body as the central point, surrounded by CC, which in turn is surrounded by EC. The authors make ample connections between this phenomenological model and empirical findings in the neuroscientific literature.

They postulate that if the sense of the "narrative self" is changed, as, for example, by practicing meditation, an altered state of consciousness can occur. And if this happens repeatedly, *altered states* may change into *altered traits*. Berkovich-Ohana and Glicksohn (2017) argue that the central prediction of CSS is that any (!) long-term meditation practice leads to a phenomenological transition toward the center of the CSS. This general prediction can be specified in four more specific ones: Meditation leads (1) to a reduced sense of the (narrative) self, (2) to a reduced sense of the timeline, (3) to heightened implicit and direct awareness of experience (prior to any reflection on the experience), and (4) to a reduction in valence of the experiences, both positive and negative (heightened equanimity).

Berkovich-Ohana and Glicksohn (2017) compared meditators (mindfulness meditation practitioners and TM practitioners) with a control group to test three of the above predictions. Compared with nonmeditators, the meditators were found to have higher trait absorption (heightened-awareness prediction), higher scores on a *mysticism scale* (reduced-sense-of-narrative-self prediction), and partly reduced scores on the Positive and Negative Affect Schedule (PANAS) (heightened-equanimity prediction). There were no substantial differences between practitioners from the two traditions, and the level of expertise also seems not to have mattered. Berkovich-Ohana and Wittmann (2017) summarized results for the fourth hypothesis (the time hypothesis), which were somewhat inconsistent. It seems that, contrary to their original assumption (any meditation practice), the kind of meditation practice does make a difference in whether meditation leads to a reduced sense of the timeline or not (see Sedlmeier et al., 2020).

It is certainly interesting to connect theories of consciousness to meditation. However, the processes specified in the CSS model could probably still gain from being specified more precisely and from giving some more attention to the possibly different effects of different meditation techniques. Moreover, the connection between constructs and measurement instruments could possibly be strengthened.

Western Models Put Into Perspective

Early models proposed by Western scientists were quite diverse, but it seems that more recent explanations converge on common characteristics that generally seem to be loosely connected to Buddhist theory, even the ones specified above under the category "other models." In recent times, meditation techniques stemming from Hindu and other spiritual backgrounds are also increasingly dealt with, as for instance in the three-family model (Dahl et al., 2015). In the following, we will concentrate on the commonalities of the more recent explanations.

What Is the Aim of Meditation?

Early Western models are quite close to traditional theories of meditation in that they postulate that the aim of meditation is a mystical experience meant to transform one's life (d'Aquili & Newberg, 1993; Deikman, 1963). Herbert Benson was more modest in equating the aim of meditation in different spiritual and religious contexts, with the relaxation response (Benson, 1983). The models summarized above as "other models" do not deal much with what the aim of meditation should be. Rather, their aim seems mostly to be to describe changes in cognition and consciousness in a general way. The aim of meditation as described in more recent models that have at least some connection to Buddhism is still quite removed from enlightenment and probably best summarized as *well-being*.

Centrality of Meta-Awareness

In Western explanations of the effects of meditation, one construct seems to be central: meta-awareness (see also Dunne et al., 2019). As yet, there seems not to be full agreement about what exactly that is, but all of the more recent models include it as a central part. One might argue that already Deikman (1963) had it in mind when he spoke about deautomatization, and the contemplative cognition framework of Grossenbacher and Quaglia (2017) as well as the CSS of Berkovich-Ohana and Glicksohn (2017) also may allow for connections to the same construct. Meta-awareness could also be well connected with classical mindfulness practice (Chapter 2). Several models connect meta-awareness to mind wandering or to mindfulness, with these often seen as opposite constructs. A reduction of mind wandering (or an increase of mindfulness) is equated with greater well-being. However, this suggested causal connection seems not to be fully justified and at least needs some qualification (e.g., Miś & Kowalczyk, 2021; Poerio et al., 2013; Smallwood & Andrews-Hanna, 2013).

Bernstein et al. (2015, 2019) see meta-awareness as one part of a higher-order construct they call *decentering*, the other two parts being *disidentification from internal experience* and *reduced reactivity to thought content*. One could argue that the latter two components are already included in other uses of the term "meta-awareness" discussed above, and sometimes the concepts of meta-awareness and decentering are regarded as being on the same level (e.g., Garland et al., 2019). The inconsistency in defining the construct can also be seen in the variety of measurement instruments listed in the respective papers. The problem of operationalizing meta-awareness might be similar to that of doing justice to "mindfulness" (see Chapter 2).

The "Mindfulness Problem"

Dahl and Davidson (2019) write that there are important gaps in our understanding of how specific forms of meditation may contribute to well-being but propose that mindfulness practices, falling most clearly into the attentional family (Dahl et al., 2015), play an important role as the foundation for other contemplative practices related to prosocial qualities, cognitive insight, and meaning and purpose. However, they also concede that there are many different "mindfulness practices" influenced by cultural, religious, and philosophical contexts, which may affect individuals in different ways.

In Chapter 2, we have already seen that "mindfulness" is far from a unitary concept, even if one differentiates between mindfulness as a state or trait and mindfulness as a practice. Moreover, mindfulness in mindfulness meditation is not the same as mindfulness in classical Buddhism (see also Giles, 2019; Jinpa, 2019; Waldron, 2019). When one reads Buddhism-inspired explanations, such as the ones discussed above, one can get the impression that the authors feel obliged to cite all or most "mindfulness experts." The problem is that the experts' views are not consistent (Chapter 2). So, there is the difficulty that a theory of mindfulness meditation has no firm fundament. In principle, there is no problem if recent definitions of mindfulness do not coincide with ancient ones, but there is a problem when it is unclear what "mindfulness" should stand for. So, it seems that theories of mindfulness meditation are still waiting for a clear definition of what mindfulness (or mindfulnesses, possibly using different terms) should be.

One basic difficulty seems to be that sometimes the same explanations are expected to hold for different kinds of meditation practices, such as mindfulness and concentration or calming practices in the original sense (sati and samatha, see Chapter 4), and sometimes also for loving kindness and compassion meditation. It could be that in the end, all techniques lead to the same result. Although then questions arise such as is one technique enough, or do I need more of them? If more of them, does it make a difference which one I begin with? Does a given technique have the same effects as an ensemble of techniques? However, as we have seen, the final aim according to the traditional approaches (Chapter 9) – that is, enlightenment – is not the same as that to be expected in most Western explanations, which might best be termed well-being. But even if eventually the effects of different kinds of meditation converged toward a common end, be that enlightenment or well-being, there are strong indications that different mindfulness techniques yield different effects in the short and medium term (Vago et al., 2019; see also Chapter 8), and also in the long term (e.g., Fox et al., 2016).

Testing Predictions Versus Looking for Suitable Data

All of the recent Western explanations cite ample evidence in support of the theoretical frameworks they postulate. However, it seems that, so far, their predictions have only rarely been tested, usually by comparing meditators and nonmeditators, using scales that are not always very closely connected to the constructs in question.

Of course, good theories should be consistent with already existing empirical results. But relying solely on already published results, stemming from different theoretical backgrounds (or little or no theoretical background), to support a theoretical model encourages cherry picking – that is, selecting results that fit the model, and discarding others. Good theories need to include precise predictions that can easily be falsified. One might even think of computer models to make predictions in meditation research more precise (van Vugt et al., 2019). The potential is there and should be used. In the next and last chapter, I will suggest some ways in which meditation research might be improved by putting more emphasis on good theories, suitable measurement devices, and apt methodology.

Part 4
Perspectives

Chapter 11
Perspectives on Meditation Research

Before we have a look at future prospects of meditation research, let me quickly recapitulate. In Chapter 1, we have seen that there are hundreds of different ways to practice meditation. It is hard to see how all of these techniques can be subsumed under one single term. But indeed, they are, and there might even be some justification to it. If meditation has a common aim, if the choice of practice does not make a difference, and if all practices lead to the same or similar results, one might as well give them the same term. However, none of these "ifs" really holds.

Practitioners of meditation differ widely in the aims they pursue by practicing meditation, as we have seen in Chapter 5. And comparing Eastern and Western theoretical approaches (in Chapters 9 and 10), one might conclude that the two central aims propagated there, enlightenment and well-being, cannot be reduced to a single aim. It also seems to make a difference which practices are chosen. As we have seen in Chapters 3 and 4, both traditional and secular approaches usually suggest not a single practice but a bundle of practices. But even these bundles differ widely across approaches (Matko et al., 2021a). Moreover, meditators' personal predilections seem to differ considerably (e.g., Anderson & Farb, 2018; Burke, 2012). Unfortunately, the fit between meditators' personalities and motivations, on the one hand, and the choice of practice, on the other, seems not to have received much attention in research, so far. Finally, there is growing evidence (briefly summarized in Chapter 8) that different meditation techniques may yield different effects. In sum, we have no generally agreed-upon conclusion of what meditation is, how it should be practiced, what effects can be expected from different techniques, and no general agreement about what its aim should be. Many practitioners might not be particularly bothered by that state of affairs, and content with their practice. They may even say "my teacher reacts flexibly to my needs and those of my co-meditators - what else do I need?" This is, of course, a fully acceptable point of view, but curious meditation researchers might want to know why the teacher reacts in which way to which diagnostic signs of the student under which circumstances, to better understand what is going on.

Then there is the issue of mindfulness. Chapter 2 sets apart the different meanings of the term - as a state, a trait, and a process - and finds no clear definition (see also Davidson & Kaszniak, 2015). Even if mindfulness is solely regarded as a process – that is, a meditation technique – views of what exactly it is differ widely. This is also evidenced in Western theoretical explanations (Chapter 10). In contrast to these theoretical weaknesses, we have an abundance of empirical studies that, in their vast majority, demonstrate the beneficial effects of basically all kinds of meditation practices. However, increasingly, qualifications can be made. For instance, it seems that conventional mindfulness regimes have lower effects on adolescents than adults (Chapter 6), and less effect on anxiety than depression (Chapter 7). Both results are interesting but lack a good explanation. And this, it seems, exemplifies the currently most pressing problem in meditation research: the absence of a solid theoretical basis for meditation research. This chapter addresses the question of how this problem and two other connected ones, suboptimal measurement and research methods, might be overcome (see also Sedlmeier et al., 2016).

Obviously, the first suggestion is to improve on the theoretical foundation for meditation research. A real improvement would already consist of more studies examining the existing predictions of both traditional and Western theoretical approaches discussed in Chapters 9 and 10, instead of just asking, "Does meditation/mindfulness help with *xyz*?" To prevent misunderstanding: I would like to clarify that there is, in fact, nothing wrong with conducting evaluation studies. If one wants to know whether, say, mantra meditation helps with anxiety, one should of course examine empirically whether this is the case or not. At first glance, no specific theory is required for examining such a research question. But when several studies of this kind have been conducted, one will in all likelihood find differences, for different kinds of practitioners, different teachers, different kinds of mantra meditation, different lengths and intensities of intervention, different kinds of anxiety measurements, and for other factors one might not even be aware of in the beginning. And the variation in the effects found will very likely markedly surpass the variation expected by sampling error alone. So, how could the differences in findings be explained? One could think of conducting many more, hundreds or even thousands of studies on the same topic and hope to eventually detect a pattern that helps to explain the variation. But still, one might overlook some of the determining factors. So, even when conducting evaluation studies, it pays to have (and test) a good theory, even if this would "only" spare the need for a lot of studies. However, if we really want to understand why, for whom, and under which conditions meditation works, a good theory is indispensable. Good theories then enable better measurements and give hints for improving the way research can be done, resulting in better research designs and methods. Moreover, one has to be aware that meditation research is faced with some special obstacles that need to be, and can be, overcome.

Toward Better Theories

Both traditional and Western explanations of why and how meditation works vary considerably. However, the variation within traditional and Western explanations is much less than the variation between them (disregarding the early Western attempts). So, is it worthwhile to work toward a single unified theory of meditation?

One or Several Theories?

Whereas traditional theories focus on enlightenment, contemporary Western theoretical approaches concentrate on well-being as the main aim of meditation practice. In the traditional theories, meditation is embedded within a path to salvation (*sadhana*) that ideally is pursued for one's whole life, whereas Western approaches regard meditation as a more or less isolated practice that may be used as a relatively short intervention. Usually (with some exceptions, e.g., Ott, 2021; Kristeller & Jordan, 2018), Western-style interventions come without ethics, moral rules, and spirituality, in contrast to the traditional practices, where these issues play a central role. Moreover, traditionally, the meditative path is meant for especially suitable and determined practitioners, whereas meditation practice in the West targets, if the number of published studies is an indicator, especially people with mental or somatic problems. Can such differences be reconciled?

A spontaneous answer to that question might be "no." But when we look at what people really do when they say they meditate, the picture is different. Although the arsenal of meditative practices used in the Western secular approaches is smaller, most of these techniques arise out of traditional approaches. So, one might conceive of the common meditation practice in the West as a first step in the meditation practice described in traditional approaches. A comprehensive theory of meditation could include Western-style meditative practice as a special addition. However, to date, such a theory, if feasible at all, seems to be far off. Therefore, it might be better to first concentrate separately on how both traditional and recent Western theorizing can be improved.

Working With Traditional Approaches

The traditional approaches dealt with in Chapter 9 are not just theories of meditation but in principle full-fledged psychological theories. One way to proceed would be to try to make these theories testable in their entirety. For instance, all of these theories postulate (or at least do not exclude) some sort of supernatural cognition. However, attaining supernatural cognition is not seen as necessary on the path to salvation, rather the Buddha and also parts of the Yogasutras see it as obstacles (see Chapter 9). Thus, for a theory of meditation, the respective parts are not necessary and might safely be omitted, at least initially. The same argument holds for the issue of rebirth or reincarnation.[36] Recall that the exposition in Chapter 9 was not meant as an exegesis of the original teachings but as identifying building blocks for a theory of meditation.

Examining Existing Predictions

From the original versions of the traditional theories of meditation, several predictions can already be derived. For illustration, only some of them will be repeated here, taken from the two early theoretical approaches: Samkhya-Yoga and early Buddhism (for more predictions, also from other approaches, see Grabovac et al., 2011; Lutz et al., 2007; Sedlmeier & Srinivas, 2016, 2019).

Two testable predictions of Samkhya-Yoga are illustrated in Figure 9.2 (Chapter 9). Recall that Samkhya assumes that the whole physical world (including cognition) consists of a mixture of three qualities or *gunas* (Chapter 9). One prediction of what changes when practicing yoga (with meditation as its central ingredient) is this: The proportion of the sattva part in practitioners' personalities should eventually increase (see Puta, 2016). With that, increases of positive and decreases of negative aspects of personality, as well as less fluctuation of the mind or less mind wandering can be expected (for some evidence for the latter, see Hasenkamp et al., 2012). Another prediction to be derived from the Samkhya-Yoga theory concerns the five hindrances (ignorance, greed/attachment, hatred/aversion, erroneous view of self, and clinging to live). These hindrances should weaken in the course of practice. Note, however, that these predictions can, without restrictions, only be derived for the practice of the complete eightfold yoga path. But tentatively, one might expect the same effects, possibly in a weakened form, from the meditation part alone.

The early Buddhist theory of meditation differentiates between the effects of mindfulness meditation (*sati*; see Chapter 2) and concentrative meditation (*samatha*) (see Figure 9.5). The practice of mindfulness produces insight, which can be expected to dampen the *three fires* – that is, reduce the

---

36 Buddhists prefer the term "rebirth" instead of "reincarnation," because, in contrast to Hindu belief systems, there is, in their view, no soul that could be reincarnated in another body. Nonetheless, there is a transmission of some kind of consciousness involved in both cases.

affective states of greed and hatred, as well as the ignorance about the impermanent, interdependent self (see also M. Batchelor, 2016; Hamilton, 2000). Moreover, the *brahmaviharas* (loving kindness, compassion, sympathetic joy, and equanimity) should become more natural with increasing meditation practice. In turn, concentrative meditation, if done as a high-intensity practice should lead to successive absorptive states that are initially characterized by experiences of bliss and rapture and eventually should lead to a ceasing of the fluctuations of the mind (see Table 9.1).

As illustrated here with the two theoretical approaches of Samkhya-Yoga and early Buddhism, several specific predictions can be derived concerning constructs (e.g., the three gunas or the brahmaviharas) contained in these approaches. Although not explicitly stated in the respective scriptures, the changes according to the two concentrative approaches (Samkhya-Yoga and the samatha part of early Buddhism) can be expected to go along with improved attentional and concentrative abilities after an extended practice of concentrative meditation. And reducing the three fires and letting the brahmaviharas flourish by sati practice should lead to improved abilities of emotion regulation, less negative and more positive emotions, increasingly clear thinking, and wiser decisions. In sum, both traditional approaches might be taken to predict positive effects on a wide variety of aspects of life, which, similarly formulated, can also be found in the Western theoretical approaches. However, plausibility predictions such as these should not be the last word.

Refining Traditional Approaches

The traditional theories described in Chapter 9 are quite old, and therefore one cannot expect them to include scientific findings that need special technological equipment. In more recent times, science has accumulated instruments (such as brain scanners) and new scientific insights (such as knowledge about genetics) that the founders of the traditional theories did not have available. This naturally leaves the theories incomplete from the perspective of science. For a good scientific theory of meditation, it is irrelevant whether it adheres to or deviates from a traditional belief system, or whether a well-known authority endorses it or not. What is relevant is how close to reality it is. And how close to reality a theory is can be examined better, the more precise its predictions are. Making the predictions of the traditional theories more precise (and measureable!) necessarily involves connecting them with current theories of cognition and cognitive change. The difficulty in doing this varies across the four theories discussed; it seems easiest to accomplish for the early Buddhist theory of meditation. In Chapter 9, I have already hinted at some potential connections to current psychological theorizing. However, the main aim of this endeavor, as I understand it, is not to "justify" the traditional theories but to improve the description, explanation, and prediction of the effects of meditation. This might in the end even lead to giving up a traditional theory altogether.

Working With Western Approaches

So far, the overwhelming majority of studies that have examined the effects of meditation (mostly in the clinical context) have not relied much on any theoretical basis, although a number of theoretical frameworks have been proposed also in the West (see Chapter 10).

Examining Existing Predictions

Again, we will only have a look at some selected predictions (see the literature cited in Chapter 10 for more). The framework proposed by Hölzel et al. (2011) makes clear predictions (see Figure 10.1): Mindfulness meditation has positive effects on attention regulation, body awareness, emotion regulation, and the perspective on one's self. Moreover, there is an order in the above list of effects: the ones before have an impact on the ones listed later. This is a quite strong prediction, the only problem being that the causal agent – that is, mindfulness meditation – is not well defined (see Chapter 10).

This is different for the *three-families model* (Dahl et al., 2015). There, different predictions are made for the three families of meditation practices (see Figure 10.3). However, on a second look, predictions are less clear. For instance, meditation techniques belonging to the attentional family are expected to improve attention regulation and thereby increase meta-awareness. But meta-awareness is also "strengthened indirectly in the constructive and deconstructive families" (Dahl et al., 2015, p. 515). Can meta-awareness be increased equally by techniques from any of the three families? If not, what would be the best way to strengthen meta-awareness? Apart from unclear relationships between families and effects, the techniques grouped in the three families are quite heterogeneous, and practitioners of the respective techniques might not always agree with the authors' classifications. Can, for instance, *koan* practice and *shikantaza* (both members of the deconstructive family) be expected to yield the same or similar effects? Some Zen experts might object. Or can one expect similar effects by loving kindness meditation, centering prayer, and meditation on foulness (constructive family) or mantra meditation and *mindfulness-based stress reduction* (MBSR; attentional family)? A closer look at the techniques (or collections of techniques, such as MBSR – no clear difference is made) contained in the three families may yield the impression that the categorizations might have been performed partly ad hoc. Instead of relying on predefined categories, one could rely on the judgments of experienced meditators about which meditation techniques are similar. This has been done in several studies (Matko & Sedlmeier, 2019; Matko et al., 2021a) whose results might be a useful starting point for developing and testing alternative classification systems.

Refining Western Approaches
Although most of the Western approaches are only loosely connected to traditional theories, traditional approaches often "shine through" the texts. It might not hurt if such connections were made more explicit. Some of the processes postulated in Western theoretical approaches to meditation are much more detailed than those claimed in the traditional approaches. But on a closer look, it is still far from clear how these processes relate to specific meditation techniques, to one another, and to brain processes. All of the Western frameworks discussed in Chapter 10 readily acknowledge this deficiency. There are at least two ways out of this unsatisfactory state of affairs. First, theories have to be made more precise, so that predictions can undergo strong tests. And a second way out might be to have a closer look at the effects of the basic meditation techniques themselves.

Bottom-Up Approach

The usual way of testing the effects of meditation is to use bundles of techniques, referred to, for instance, as MBSR, Vipassana, transcendental meditation (TM), or mindfulness meditation. If that bundle works in a specific way, it could be that only the ensemble works, but it could also be that one of the techniques is mainly or even solely responsible for the effect found. The only way of finding out is to compare the effects of basic meditation techniques. Empirical evidence discussed in Chapter 8 indicates that different techniques indeed may yield different effects. Because of the abundance of basic meditation techniques, a pragmatic approach is to restrict comparisons initially to typical representatives of categories of meditation techniques. For that, any theoretically or empirically founded categorization of meditation techniques may be used. Thereby it is crucial to use theoretically derived dependent measures that cover a wide range of possible effects (see below).

Once there is some clarity about the effects of basic meditation techniques, one can add other components to search for incremental effects. In principle, such incremental procedures are also practiced in some traditional approaches. For instance, in Goenka-style Vipassana, the practice of concentration on the breath, practiced during the first 3 days of the common 10-day retreat is followed by a body scan practice. This indicates that there is some sense in that order.

However, it could well be that some practitioners do as well without the preceding concentration task, which brings us to another question that probably can be dealt with more easily using the bottom-up rather than the top-down approach: the impact of personality. It seems that, so far, none of the Western approaches holds any firm assumption about the effects of personality characteristics. (The traditional approaches do – see Chapter 3 for some examples in the Buddhist world. Also Yoga theory recommends different body postures for practitioners with different mixtures of the three *gunas*, and the related three *doshas* of *vata*, *pitta*, and *kapha* used in Ayurveda; Frawley & Kozak, 2001.) So, personal experiences, especially of researchers who meditate (or meditators who do research) and those of their colleagues and fellow meditators, might be a good basis for examining potential sequence effects and the impact of personality characteristics. Also, other potential components of meditation such as bodily exercises and ethical education or breathing techniques could easily be examined the bottom-up way. Incorporating rich information about such characteristics in research might, in addition to leading to new theoretical insights, eventually yield a custom-tailored recommendation for a given person who wants to practice meditation. Note that in traditional schools of meditation, custom tailoring meditation practices is not a one-time issue but usually a long, ongoing, and interactive process between teacher and student. However, also such a sequential process would be open to empirical scrutiny.

Still, the bottom-up approach to doing meditation research might seem to be a bit reductionist. But there is also another way that may complement this way of doing meditation research: the use of qualitative methods.

The Qualitative Exploratory Approach

At the beginning of Chapter 9, we speculated about the origin of the traditional theories, and the conclusion was that they stemmed from the experiences of ancient master practitioners: single-case qualitative studies, so to speak. If that is true, then why not engage more current long-term meditators in meditation research? Prominent ancient meditators, such as the Buddha, tried out different ways for themselves and for their students. For their students, they developed *skillful means (upaya)* to best advance their practice. Skillful means encompass both good diagnostics and apt interventions. Ideally, the results of such studies might coincide with results obtained with a bottom-up approach, with the additional benefit that meditation experts might already have sound assumptions about why different interventions work for specific practitioners. But also the subjective theories novices develop when practicing meditation or the experiences of long-term meditators may generate precious contributions to theory development (e.g., Bringmann et al., 2021a; Lindahl et al., 2017; Panda et al., 2020). Such subjective theories of both novice and expert meditators may have the potential to contribute greatly to theory refinement.

A special exploratory approach is to take oneself as the participant. Probably the most famous example for that was the Hindu mystic and saint Ramakrishna who practiced different paths (including Sufism and Christian contemplation) and found that all of these paths lead to the same goal – in his case, to an experience of God or the Divine (Prabhavananda, 2019). A more recent example of exploratory research including herself as a participant comes from Divya Parasher, a young woman who grew up in the Aurobindo Ashram in Pondicherry (southern India) and wanted to study the *guru-sishya* (teacher-student) relationship in different spiritual traditions (Parasher, 2015, and personal communication). She interviewed 19 long-term members in four of the most famous Indian ashrams: the Aurobindo ashram and the three other ashrams of Ramakrishna (and Vivekananda, his best-known student), Ramana Maharshi, and Sivananda. Before conducting the interviews, she prepared herself for several months for each ashram, reading the respective spiritual texts, listening to audio tapes, and watching films about the communities. She spent considerable time in each of the three other ashrams and lived the ordinary ashram life as the long-term members did. Parasher found pronounced differences but also strong commonalities. However, her most interesting finding was this: In the beginning she was of the opinion that her own (the Aurobindo) ashram was superior in all respects. But in the end, she came to the conclusion that in fact, the main focus in all ashrams was the same: to give up the (false) ego, to quiet the mind, and to learn to feel the presence of something greater.

For some issues regarding effects of long-term meditation, there may even be no other than the qualitative exploratory way because there are no preexisting suitable measurement devices. However, to be able to meaningfully interpret what expert meditators say (and to be able to ask good questions), it is necessary that interviewers also have sufficient expertise, both in meditation practice and background knowledge. Divya Parasher's study is a good case in point, as is the study done by Boyle (2015) with 11 purportedly awakened Western Buddhist teachers, briefly described in Chapter 9. Boyle is himself a very experienced meditator, and he claims that in the course of his exploratory study, he himself gained awakening, catalyzed by his interviewees (Boyle, 2015, pp. 12–13).

Recapitulation

Good theories of meditation should contain what all good theories should contain. They should allow for apt descriptions of what happens when people meditate. They should also be able to make precise predictions about the effects of specific meditation practices. And they should contain good how and why explanations for that. The first and the second postulates depend on the third. The "how" in the third postulate refers to the changes over time expected by meditation practice, and the "why" should yield a good cause-and-effect model for these changes. If we know why and how meditation works, it is easy to make precise predictions and describe what happens. Unfortunately, overall, the how and why of meditation is also the least specified in meditation theories. To be sure, though, if that part were easy to specify, it would already have happened. Above, I have argued that there are four ways to come closer to the goal of one or more good theories of meditation: working with traditional as well as with already existing western theories, trying to understand the effects of meditation with a bottom-up approach, and learning more by using the qualitative exploratory approach.

Doing that, one should not forget that meditation is always embedded in a context. All meditators (and researchers) come with their personality characteristics, their experiences, their beliefs, and their predilections. Also, meditators differ widely in the intensity of their practice. So far, meditation research has largely omitted context variables, but they might play a very influential role. As long as we do not know, we should try to include them as comprehensively as possible into our research. Other important issues to be included in a comprehensive theory of meditation have already been identified in Chapter 9:, the role of the community, rituals, and ethic or moral rules. Moreover, the role of spirituality, as part of the context of practicing meditation, is still largely unclear (for first results on these issues, see Chapter 8).

Toward Better Measurements

When we conducted our first meta-analysis on the effects of meditation (Sedlmeier et al., 2012) we were surprised by the sheer number of dependent variables used in those studies. In hindsight, the huge number of tests and measures made sense: If there is no precise theory, one might be tempted to try out all sorts of things. Meanwhile, that state of affairs has changed, especially in clinical studies. This is, however, not mainly due to better theories but to more focused questions about specific groups of clients. For instance, if studies are conducted with people suffering from anxiety, measures of anxiety (and not measures for some other variables) immediately suggest themselves.

Western Constructs

By far the most often used measure in meditation research is "mindfulness," usually conceived of as a trait. I have already tried to show in Chapter 2 that, as the term is currently used, it may not be very helpful for the advancement of our understanding of the effects of meditation because the meanings of this concept are so diverse (see also Grossenbacher & Quaglia, 2017; Schmidt, 2011; van Dam et al., 2018). This is not to say that the concept is not at all useful, but it definitely needs to be made more precise, possibly resulting in a number of clearly defined terms (e.g., Hadash & Bernstein, 2019). It is also quite illustrative to note that most Western explanatory models discussed in Chapter 10 do not include the concept of mindfulness as a central effect of meditation, and in the Brandmeyer and Delorme (2021) model, it is just treated as the opposite of mind wandering.

In contrast, another concept, meta-awareness (or metacognitive awareness), is a central part of many if not most Western models. But this concept also seems, as yet, not to be really well-defined (see Chapter 10). Also here, it may be better to diversify the construct instead of trying to reconcile quite diverse conceptions. The latter unavoidably would lead to vaguer theories or weak theory testing.

How about attention regulation, body awareness, emotion regulation, and the perspective on the self, the main effects of mindfulness meditation postulated by Hölzel et al. (2011)? The study of attention has a long history in psychology, and although it is generally acknowledged that it is not a uniform concept, there is also disagreement about its purported components. Some scholars even go as far as saying that "no one knows what attention is" (Hommel et al., 2019, p. 2288). Similar arguments can be made for body awareness (e.g., Mehling et al., 2009), and mood and emotion measures (e.g., Hoge et al., 2019; Mauss & Robinson, 2009). And the perspective on the self, as understood in the model, might be especially difficult to operationalize in a questionnaire.

The vagueness of measures that purport to measure psychological constructs is not specific to meditation research, and it is often due to the vagueness of the constructs themselves (e.g., Meier, 1994). Again, it would help to have a good theory that allows for defining precise constructs. If such a theory could make good connections between the type of meditation practice and, say, the type of attention (to name just a few: tonic and phasic alertness, vigilance, divided attention, and selective attention) that would largely restrict the choice of tests. Other (less good) possibilities to deal with the problem could be to systematically compare the effects of different measurement tools that purport to measure the same construct. If the results are comparable, any of the measures could be used, and if not, some selection criteria would need to be found to rank order the measures.

Constructs From Traditional Theories

As already mentioned several times, traditional theories contain constructs that are directly connected to the theories of meditation. One case in point is the three gunas as postulated by the Samkhya theory (see Chapter 9). A number of guna questionnaires has been developed, but apart from measuring slightly different things, there is the additional problem of some questionnaires using concepts from the Indian culture that may not easily be understood by Western practitioners (for an overview, see Puta & Sedlmeier, 2014). After surveying the theoretical basis of the guna model, and considering the available guna instruments, Maika Puta (2016) developed a comprehensive guna questionnaire that is also suitable for participants who have grown up in a Western culture (in the original work, items are given in German, but English items are available at: http://selfleadershipexperts.com/wp-content/uploads/2021/04/TriGunaScales_English.pdf).

In early Buddhism, the brahmaviharas play an important role (Chapter 9). To measure practitioners' degrees of loving kindness, compassion, sympathetic joy, and equanimity, Kraus and Sears (2009) developed a short scale for these. Other questionnaires concentrate on parts of the brahmaviharas, such as equanimity (Chan et al., 2014; Rogers et al., 2021) or the self-component of compassion (Neff, 2003). Also, for the three fires (greed, hatred, and ignorance), another central concept in early Buddhism, there already exists a questionnaire (van Dam et al., 2015).

The above questionnaires (and similar ones hopefully to be developed soon) have the big advantage that they are directly connected to traditional theories of meditation. Such theories are usually underspecified, and it might be hard to operationalize the respective constructs in the form of questionnaire items. Nonetheless, measurements should be as strongly connected to theory as possible. If such questionnaires turn out not to work, the respective failures might at least give some hints regarding how the underling theory could be improved. Without this process of constructing theory-guided measurements and continuously refining them, theories cannot really be tested.

Physiological and Brain Measurements

It seems that many researchers in psychology hold the view that physiological and brain measures are more precise than behavioral or verbal measures. However, physiological and brain measures do not speak for themselves but always need psychological interpretation. Once theories of meditation make exact predictions about physiological and brain processes, such measurements will be indispensable for meditation research. Of course, such measures are already now an important complement to psychological measures. Exploratory studies that, for instance, compare brain patterns of very experienced meditators with those of controls may yield exciting results (e.g., Lutz et al., 2004; Luders & Kurth, 2019). However, brain measures are also subject to similar restrictions, as discussed in Chapter 6, section Effects on the Brain. Obviously, traditional theories do not contain any specific hypotheses about what to expect in terms of physiological and brain processes. But it seems that even Western theoretical approaches, although usually citing ample evidence from physiological and especially brain studies (see Chapters 6 and 10), are not yet in a state to make precise agreed-upon predictions about the effects of meditation on physiological and brain measures. There seems to be some promise though in applying individualized functional magnetic resonance imaging (fMRI) analyses (Weng et al., 2020).

Temporal Aspects of Measurements

The timing of measurements in meditation research is important in several respects. If the effects of meditation are measured immediately after meditation practice, chances are that at least some of these effects will be quite short-lived. There may be interesting research questions about immediate effects of meditation, but for research interested in the stable long-term effects of meditation, a potential mixture of short- and long-term effects of meditation is unfortunate and can lead to distorted conclusions. In addition, the time of the day may make a difference. If, in a conventional group study, premeasurements are taken, say, early in the morning, and post measurements at noon, some effects of meditation may go unnoticed or may be exaggerated due to changes due to the circadian rhythm (e.g., Hasler et al., 2008; Takano & Tanno, 2011). This problem of different measurement times is especially prominent in studies with many repeated measurements, such as single-case studies (see section Single-Case Experimental Designs). But also if there is only a pretest and a posttest as in many group comparisons, it would be recommended to perform them at the same time of the day.

Toward Better Research Designs and Methods

The typical meditation study is one in which a group of meditators is compared with a group of nonmeditators. Increasingly though, nonmeditators do not just not meditate but receive a treatment that is as comparable to meditation as possible – active control groups. If, in such a design, participants are randomized into the two groups, and measurements are taken before and after the intervention, one could be quite content, could one not? Compared with many studies that have been conducted in the field not so long back, such studies could indeed make one quite content, but there is still room for improvement. Why? At least for three reasons. First, participants in meditation studies are often quite heterogeneous, in many respects. If measurements are averaged over all group members, actual effects might go unnoticed because of the large variation within groups. Second, if we only have two measurements per person (and sometimes only one), we cannot deduce anything about the process by which meditation may work overtime. And third, to derive sound conclusions under these circumstances, we need very large groups, which, especially as the experience of meditators increases, are hard to collect. I will suggest one possible way out of these three restrictions, that could enrich meditation research: single-case (experimental) designs.

Single-case designs are especially amenable to including all kinds of context variables. As we have seen throughout this book, there are many potential influences on the effects of meditation. Therefore, a rich description of the respective variables is necessary. Let us have a look at this issue before discussing single-case experimental designs.

Rich Description

To find out about potential moderating (or even mediating) effects of context variables, understood in a wide sense, we first need to get hold of them. This need for a rich description of the components of meditation research has already been emphasized several times in the literature, such as, for instance, by Davidson and Kaszniak (2015), and there are quite a number of proposals for classification systems for meditation techniques and also other aspects of meditation research (see Chapter 4). For instance, van Dam et al. (2018) provide extensive (and still nonexhaustive) lists of defining features for the characterization of a given meditation practice (their Table 2), and for study designs for a mindfulness-based intervention (their Table 3). The features for characterizing meditation techniques include primary features such as *arousal* (low, medium, high), *orientation of attention* (inward, outward, no orientation), *spatial dynamic of attention* (fixed vs. moving), *tem-*

poral dynamic of attention (constant/stable vs. rhythmic/sporadic), *object of attention* (specific, aspecific, none), *aperture of attention* (narrow, intermediate, diffuse), and *effort* (low, medium, high). As secondary features of a given meditation practice, they list *complementary activity* (e.g., walking, mantra recitation, dancing), *affective valence* (positive, neutral, negative), *emotional intention* (e.g., loving kindness, compassion, forgiveness, generosity), *motivation* or *goal* (wellness, mitigation of illness, self-improvement, enlightenment), *proficiency required* (low, medium, high), and *posture* (lying, sitting, standing).

Pilla et al. (2020) performed a content analysis of 118 systematic reviews of meditation-based intervention studies and applied altogether 2,048 codes. From these, they derived a *meditation-based intervention design* framework that included five features: (1) program aim, (2) program time frame, (3) meditation-based practices, (4) complementary activities, and (5) philosophy, with 11 subfeatures. Just an example: For Feature 3 (meditation-based practices) there were four subfeatures: (a) practice aims, (b) practice time frame, (c) delivery, and (d) directive action(s). These subfeatures in turn were characterized by 35 "themes" – for example, (i) frequency and (ii) duration for the subfeature practice time frame. The authors propose their framework as a reporting guideline to improve the quality of research in the field and to promote more valid comparisons and generalizations. The basis for that study was existing research, which, however, might not be optimal.

These are certainly valuable lists of features: However, because of the partly quite abstract nature of the description, they might, in their entirety, be more useful for summaries of meditation research than for describing the particularities of studies. For a rich description of a given meditation study, it might suffice to describe exactly the kind of meditation practice in question and use parts of the above list that allow for describing the intervention procedure, compliance with the intervention, the participants (preferentially also some important personality characteristics, as well as reasons for and aims of meditating), the teachers, the procedure, and the measurements. In sum, a rich description of meditation research is very important, and it can most effectively be applied if all study participants are looked at separately, as in single-case designs.

Single-Case Experimental Designs

We have already touched on some advantages of single-case designs: no averaging-out of measurements (thus doing justice to the heterogeneity of practitioners), being able to examine the trajectories of change over time, and not being dependent on large samples. However, not just any kind of single-case design will do, if causal conclusions need to be drawn, which is the main aim of any kind of research. Causal conclusions can be drawn when using single-case *experimental* designs (e.g., Barlow et al., 2009; Sedlmeier & Renkewitz, 2018, Chapter 30). The defining feature of single-case experimental designs is some sort of randomization, and the most common type of single-case experimental design is the so-called multiple baseline design with the length of the baseline (period without intervention or with some other treatment) randomly assigned to participants. This kind of design has already been applied several times in meditation research (e.g., May et al., 2014). Figure 11.1 shows an example. Singh et al. (2011) had their three juvenile participants with Asperger's syndrome learn a technique they termed "meditation on the soles of the feet" – that is, their participants learned to concentrate on the soles of the feet when they sensed tantrums coming up. Figure 11.1 shows that irrespective of the length of the baseline (3, 4, and 5 weeks), the intervention had the desired effect of reducing the number of aggressive incidents per week. Moreover, meditating on the soles of the feet yielded a stable long-term effect (see follow-ups in Figure 11.1).

There is even a meta-analysis of the effects of mindfulness-based interventions on disruptive behavior in children and adolescents, covering 10 multiple-baseline design studies (Klingbeil et al., 2017). The authors found substantial effects of the mindfulness-based interventions. The effects in single-case studies are not fully comparable to the conventional effect sizes used in between designs (d, g, and r) because measurements are obviously dependent. This is, however, not a problem, as several alternative effect sizes for single-case designs have been developed, among others *TauU*, a nonoverlap measure that can be interpreted similarly to r (Brossart et al., 2018; Parker et al., 2011). *TauU* has also been used in the Klingbeil et al. (2017) meta-analysis. In contrast to conventional meta-analyses that summarize effects over groups, a meta-analysis for single-case designs summarizes effects over measurement units – that is, children and adolescent meditators in this case.

Although, because of the randomization procedures involved, internal validity can be considered high in single-case experimental designs, researchers might worry about the issue of external validity – that is, the degree to which results in single-case experimental studies can be generalized. However, one might argue that the usual argument for external validity, that a sample must be representative of its population (ideally operationalized by a random sample taken from this population), does not hold so strongly in intervention research anyway (see Barlow et al., 2009, Chapter 2). If, say, somebody wants to find the best treatment (e.g., the most suitable meditation technique) for themselves, one might use the average results found in a study as the best prediction for administering a treatment. This can be a rather imprecise procedure. It would be much better to rely on several single-case studies and use that (or those) case(s) that is (are)

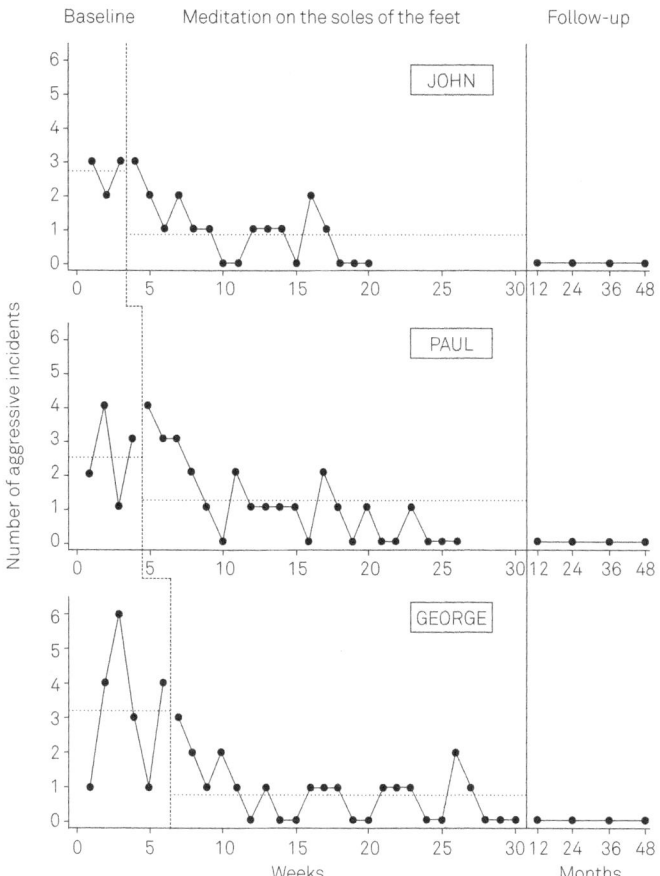

Figure 11.1. Example of a multiple-baseline design to study the effects of mindfulness meditation in a patient population. Based on Singh et al. (2011).

most similar to the new client to make a recommendation. This would be *logical generalization*, another perfectly legitimate way of generalizing research results. Nothing speaks against collecting a representative sample of single-case studies and using their results in the same way as group results are used. But the definitive advantage of such a large sample of single-case results would be that logical generalizations are also possible, which would be impossible with group-study results.

Single-case experimental studies allow for examining very elegantly the effects of combinations of interventions (e.g., combining two different meditation techniques) by a procedure termed *interaction design* (Barlow et al., 2009, Chapter 6). Moreover, single-case designs are very flexible. There is, of course, an additional effort involved with the necessity of making many repeated measurements, which also has an impact on the suitability of dependent measures. If the values of a given measurement tool change systematically by simply repeatedly applying it, one has to find either an alternative, or control for this change induced by practice. One way of doing the latter is to apply alternative single-case experimental designs such as the alternating-treatment design (Barlow et al., 2009, Chapter 8).

Traditionally, results of single-case design studies are subjected to visual analysis, but increasingly also effect sizes are calculated. If there are many results and therefore many effect sizes, these can be used in meta-analyses, as exemplified in the work by Klingbeil et al. (2017), and also be subjected to a multilevel analysis (e.g., Hox et al., 2018; Raudenbush & Bryk, 2002). Such multilevel analyses do not require exorbitantly large numbers of cases (e.g., Maas & Hox, 2005). Meanwhile, there exist very comfortable statistical tools to conduct all kinds of analyses for single-case experimental designs (e.g., McGill, 2017; Wilbert, 2021).

Single-case experimental designs seem very promising for examining the effects of meditation practice for beginners (the bulk of studies to date), and maybe also for intermediate practitioners. This kind of design also seems to be very suitable for examining experienced meditators, especially when targeting physiological and brain measures. Also, when examining differential effects of different meditation practices, such single-case experimental designs may be the method of choice. However, when the use of standardized measurement devices is not feasible, or when one wants to find out more about subjective experiences of long-term meditators, qualitative methods are better suited.

Qualitative Research

Above, I have already described two qualitative studies (Boyle, 2015; Parasher, 2015) that could not have been conducted using conventional methods (see section The Qualitative Exploratory Approach). For examining experiences as postulated by traditional theories of meditation for experienced meditators, talking to these practitioners may often be the only way to gain knowledge. This concerns issues such as awakening or enlightenment, or experiences in absorptive states (e.g., Ataria et al., 2015; Full et al., 2013). Issues of special experiences or meditative insights are also part of some Western approaches and have already been investigated using qualitative procedures (e.g., Eberth et al., 2019). But also the subjective experiences of beginners or intermediate meditators can make important contributions to understanding the effects of meditation. Qualitative studies can, for instance, shed light on the meditation experiences of special groups (e.g., Miller & Nozawa, 2002), examine relational effects (Gillespie et al., 2015), clarify potential detrimental effects of meditation (e.g., Lomas et al., 2015b), and give insights into therapeutic processes (e.g., Bringmann et al., 2021b; Köhle et al., 2017).

Especially for qualitative studies with experienced meditators, it seems necessary that interviewers also have some meditation experience to better understand what their interview partners say – the so-called *second-person method* (Olivares et al., 2015; Varela & Shear, 1999). (In the *first-person method*, the observer is identical with the observed, and in the *third-person method*, the ideal in natural science, in principle any third person, fully outside the physical process or phenomenon, could do the observations after some training.)

In addition, special interview techniques can be very helpful here (Petitmengin, 2006, 2011). Doing qualitative research well is by no means easier than pursuing the conventional quantitative approach. On the contrary, it is very time-consuming and demanding. There is a smooth transition between "just so stories" and high-level qualitative research. The measurement instruments in qualitative research are the researchers themselves, but there is always the danger that the personalities, personal experiences, belief systems, and cultural backgrounds of researchers could have a systematic impact on interpretations. All major approaches to qualitative analysis deal with that problem by keeping the researcher detached and aware of this potential pitfall. The main method of doing so is to use coding rules of different sorts (e.g., Miles & Huberman, 1994; Miles et al., 2018). There are many varieties of qualitative methods, and specific ways of doing qualitative research are connected to quite different epistemological backgrounds (e.g., Smith, 2003). The methods range from very elaborate, closed approaches such as *grounded theory* (Glaser & Strauss, 1967) to very open and flexible frameworks such as *thematic analysis* (Braun & Clarke, 2012).

Participants as Collaborators

In qualitative studies with experienced meditators (e.g., Boyle, 2015; Eberth et al., 2019), the role of the meditators is clearly not comparable to the role of participants in a typical psychology study. Instead, meditators are collaborators. This idea of meditators as collaborators could and should be employed fruitfully in all kinds of meditation studies. Blinded studies are rarely possible in meditation research anyway: If participants receive instructions to meditate, they can be assumed to be aware of the fact that they are members of the meditation group. And if there are several different meditation groups, they will also soon know which group they are in.

But even more important, it is safe to assume that participants in meditation studies are probably interested in meditation (given that nobody is forced to participate, which would not be in accordance to any ethics guidelines anyway). So, it is plausible to expect that participants in a meditation study are curious regarding what will come out of it. They might come with certain beliefs and expectations. Therefore, rather than attempting to blind out these beliefs and expectations, it would be better to disclose everything about the study beforehand. If researchers work with responsible collaborators instead of potentially distrustful participants, results are better interpretable, and chances are that these collaborators are also interested in finding out more about a given research question. Neither would it be such a good idea to offer financial compensation for participants for the time they spend meditating. That might undermine their motivation and lead to quite different results from when participants take part out of their own interest. However, if extensive measurements are required, the time spent on those would warrant some financial (or other) compensation.

Special Obstacles in Meditation Research

Meditation research is exciting but also faces some potential difficulties, which are either never, or at least not so extensively, encountered in other areas of psychological research.

Compliance in Meditation Studies

Meditation takes time, and if stable effects are the aim of research, it takes at least several weeks of practice. We have all optimized our daily life, and this makes it potentially hard to insert an additional slot of 20 to 30 min per day and keep at it for several weeks. This time issue may be the biggest obstacle to full compliance in meditation studies. Therefore, it is necessary that prospective participants are fully aware of the potential problem in time management. It might also be helpful to include weekly meetings with participants to discuss problems with sitting postures, distractions, upcoming new experiences, etc. Just giving meditation instructions and leaving participants alone until the end of the study may often not be enough to guarantee a smooth running of the study. At the very least, there should always be a contact person who is constantly available to address participants' questions and problems.

Hard-to-Get Experienced Meditators

In their exciting book, Goleman and Davidson (2017, pp. 209–211) describe an attempt by a group of meditation researchers to perform brain measurements on very experienced Tibetan Buddhist meditators. In the spring of 1992, the group, among them Davidson himself, came to a village (now a suburb of Dharamsala) in the north of India, where these meditators lived, carrying with them electroencephalography (EEG) equipment weighing several hundred pounds. They brought with them a letter of recommendation written by the Dalai Lama urging the meditators to cooperate. In addition, the Dalai Lama had sent with them a monk from his private office as a personal emissary. When they asked the meditators whether they could monitor their brains while they meditated, the unanimous answer was "no." Only a very experienced monk of French origin, Matthieu Ricard, with a PhD in molecular genetics, whom we have already met in Chapter 1, himself trained in science, was later able to open the door because he is very well connected in the Tibetan meditative world.

This anecdote illustrates the fact that finding participants for studies that aim to examine long-term effects of meditation may not be easy, especially if participants are to be recruited from non-Western cultures. However, this difficulty may lessen with time because, for one, very experienced meditators from non-Western cultures are increasingly exposed to science and may find better access to the Western way of thinking about meditation. Moreover, more and more very experienced meditators have now grown up in the West, and these meditators, like Ricard, may feel the necessity to put meditation research on a good theoretical foundation with strong empirical evidence.

Closed Circles

Many meditation researchers (including myself) are affiliated with some meditation community. Belonging to communities can easily trigger "Us/Them-ing" (Sapolsky, 2017, Chapter 11). Meditators are not exempt and may even be especially susceptible to negative associations about "outsiders." In his foreword to Goleman's 1977 book which advances a balanced view about different approaches to meditation, Ram Dass wrote, "Those who consider their path the only way will be especially upset" (Goleman, 1977, pp. xvi–xvii). And in that, he did not only refer to fundamentalist groups but also to

> the subtle snobbery that permeates almost all traditions. Apparently, each of us, in our insecurity, must feel that his or her way is the best way. A more mature perception is that one method is the best way for me, but other paths suit other people. (Goleman, 1977, pp. xvi–xvii)

Starting with such (possibly implicit) preconceptions (e.g., "my teacher is the only really awakened one" or "my approach is the only true and authentic one") can be very detrimental to research. For some schools of meditation, it might be easy to acknowledge that another school has deficiencies, but when some empirical results indicate that one's own teacher is wrong, this might quickly become an insurmountable barrier for accepting these results. Also, if research questions may threaten basic beliefs of a meditation community, members might show little willingness to participate at all. At least researchers who meditate might be able to cultivate the idea that in the end open research is beneficial for all: Who would want to spend their life in suboptimal practice (and recommend it to others), if it could be substantially improved?

"Teacher Theories"

Meditation teachers come with their own experiences, belief systems, cultural backgrounds, and teaching methods. Some of them might hold subjective theories of meditation that are strongly connected to their own culture, as well as to their experiences and spiritual backgrounds, and they might implicitly generalize their experiences to all of their students: "This worked for me (and my teacher) so it must work for everybody." Also, it seems hard sometimes for meditation teachers with a cultural background different from that of their students to fully empathize with them (and vice versa; e.g., Coleman, 2002; Ford, 2006; Williamson, 2010). Therefore, when doing research that involves teachers from cultures different from that of the researchers, the latter should keep in mind that their and the teachers' subjective theories might not fully coincide. However, meditation research should always be conducted in a trusting atmosphere, and therefore, it should not be a problem to talk to each other when in doubt.

Meditation as a Research Method

A special feature of meditation is that it can serve not only as an object of research but also as a means of research. In a way, all meditators conduct single-case studies on themselves, with the aim of finding out more about themselves. (Some meditators may be very conscious of this research process, and others less so, but even if practitioners "only" want to alleviate some kind of suffering, they will monitor themselves at least in that respect.) Especially some forms of mindfulness meditation (such as *shikantaza* or the mindfulness techniques described in the *Satipatthana Sutta;* see Chapter 3) involve learning to observe one's own mind, which can be regarded as similar to what early *introspectionists* in psychology did (e.g., Wundt, Külpe, Müller, Stumpf, James, and Titchener; see Boring, 1953). There, the professors served as participants because they were regarded to be more experienced in watching themselves; and their assistants were the "experimenters."

There are indeed some indications that experienced meditators may be especially suited to be research "instruments" in the study of mind and consciousness. For instance, Slagter et al. (2011) argue that the focus of meditation practices on enhancing core cognitive processes may specifically foster process-specific learning. This, in conjunction with neuroimaging methods, may be very useful for studying brain and cognitive plasticity.

Furthermore, and maybe even more interestingly, meditation may also considerably increase introspective accuracy. Baird et al. (2014) found greater awareness in meditators, of their own cognitive and affective states, both in a short review of previous studies (e.g., Brown et al., 1984; Fox et al., 2012; Kerr et al., 2008; Khalsa et al., 2008; MacLean et al., 2010) and in a study of their own. Jo et al. (2015) interpreted meditators' reactions in performing Libet-type tasks, as even showing higher sensitivity to brain processes (the emergence of negative deflections of slow cortical potentials) than nonmeditators' reactions, which could have fundamental effects on initiating a voluntary bodily movement with awareness. Moreover, meditation practice seems to have small but consistently positive effects on body awareness (Treves et al., 2019). And a recent summary of respective research (Upton & Brent, 2019) concludes that "meditation provides a useful model for understanding and categorizing a variety of types of mental actions" (p. 14).

In sum, this aspect of meditation research, meditation as a research tool, definitely deserves much more attention than has been given to it, so far. It may be especially promising in exploring hard-to-measure cognitive processes and aspects of consciousness (e.g., Petitmengin et al., 2017).

Why It Is Worthwhile to Put a Lot of Effort Into Better Meditation Research

Looking at the massive body of evidence collected on the effects of meditation (see especially Chapters 6 and 7) there can be no doubt that meditation works and yields a multitude of beneficial effects. Researchers could now lean back and just practice it. Budding practitioners could shop the "meditation market" and find out for themselves what suits them best. This is in any case what many meditators have always done. However, such a trial-and-error strategy, even if guided by personal predilections and motivations (subjective theories), may take a long time and lead to suboptimal decisions. Systematic evaluation studies can help customtailor the assignments of practices and practitioners. This, as we have, for instance, seen in Chapter 7, can be done with little or no theoretical background. But it can be done much better, and eventually with much less effort, by relying on good theories. So, also with this practical aspect of meditation research in mind, it is worthwhile to put more effort into theory-guided research.

The same holds for another practical aspect of meditation research. As we have just seen, the practice of meditation is unique in that the skills acquired can also be used as a means to do research on our "mental worlds," with potential that reaches far beyond common consciousness research. This is also true for meditators working as researchers, who can be seen as "research tools" for a better understanding of the processes involved, which should eventually yield more precise results.

However, if we really want to understand the why and how of the effects of meditation, we are lost without good theories. As detailed in Chapters 9 and 10, there is already a sizable stock of both traditional and more recent Western theories that can serve as the basis for refining and testing our understanding of what meditation is, how and why it works, and which effects can be expected under what circumstances. Some of these expected effects are comparable to effects to be expected from psychotherapy, and this alone should be motivation enough to devote much time and energy on theory development and testing. However, traditional theories of meditation in particular make promises about the attainability of mental states that are far away from everyday cognition. Doing research on these hypothesized higher mental states or different varieties of consciousness has the potential to increase our understanding of human cognition dramatically. If it also helps us to become better humans, this prospect really makes it worthwhile to put as much effort into meditation research as possible. At the moment, it does not seem to be so important whether we strive for a unified theory of meditation or several distinct ones. But it is important to strive for as good and precise theories as we possibly can and test them with as good measurements and methods as we have at our disposal. Looking at the vast empirical evidence, one can conclude that meditation is a success story, but real success will lie in finding out why it is so successful: There are exciting times ahead for the psychology of meditation.

References

Ahn, J. Y. (2020). Meditation sickness. In M. Farias, D. Brazier, & L. Mansur (Eds.). *The Oxford handbook of meditation*. Oxford Handbooks Online. https://doi.org/10.1093/oxfordhb/9780198808640.013.45

Ainsworth, B., Eddershaw, R., Meron, D., Baldwin, D. S., & Garner, M. (2013). The effect of focused attention and open monitoring meditation on attention network function in healthy volunteers. *Psychiatry Research, 210*, 1226–1231. https://doi.org/10.1016/j.psychres.2013.09.002

Aitken, R. (1987). The Future of Zen Buddhism in the West. *Mind Moon Circle (Winter 1987)*, 1–3.

Aitken, R. (1993). *Encouraging words: Zen Buddhist teachings for western students* [eBook]. Pantheon Books.

Aitken, R. (2015a). *Taking the path of Zen* [eBook]. North Point Press.

Aitken, R. (2015b). *The gateless barrier: The Wu-Men Kuan (Mumonkan)* [eBook]. North Point Press.

Alda, M., Puebla-Guedea, M., Rodero, B., Demarzo, M., Montero-Marin, J., Roca, M., & Garcia-Campayo, J. (2016). Zen meditation, length of telomeres, and the role of experiential avoidance and compassion. *Mindfulness, 7*, 651–659. https://doi.org/10.1007/s12671-016-0500-5

Alexander, C. N., Rainforth, M. V., & Gelderloos, P. (1991). Transcendental meditation, self-actualization, and psychological heath: A conceptual overview and statistical meta-analysis. *Journal of Social Behavior and Personality, 6*, 189–247.

Amaro, A. (2015). A holistic mindfulness. *Mindfulness, 6*, 63–73. https://doi.org/10.1007/s12671-014-0382-3

Amihai, I., & Kozhevnikov, M. (2014). Arousal vs. relaxation: A comparison of the neurophysiological and cognitive correlates of Vajrayana and Theravada meditative practices. *PLoS One, 9*(7): e102990. https://doi.org/10.1371/journal.pone.0102990

Amihai, I., & Kozhevnikov, M. (2015). The influence of Buddhist meditation traditions on the autonomic system and attention. *BioMed Research International*. https://doi.org/10.1155/2015/731579

Anālayo, Bh. (2003). *Satipaṭṭhāna: The direct path to realization*. Silkworm Books.

Anālayo, Bh. (2012). The dynamics of Theravāda insight meditation. In K.-P. Chuang (Ed.), *Buddhist meditation traditions: An international symposium* (pp. 23–56). Dharma Drum Publishing.

Anālayo, Bh. (2013). *Perspectives on Satipaṭṭhāna*. Windhorse Publications.

Anālayo, Bh. (2018a). Mindfulness constructs in early Buddhism and Theravāda: Another contribution to the memory debate. *Mindfulness, 9*, 1047–1051. https://doi.org/10.1007/s12671-018-0967-3

Anālayo, Bh. (2018b). *Satipaṭṭhāna meditation: A practice guide.* Windhorse Publications.
Anālayo, Bh. (2019a). Immeasurable meditations and mindfulness. *Mindfulness, 10,* 2620–2628. https://doi.org/10.1007/s12671-019-01237-0
Anālayo, Bh. (2019b). The emphasis on the present moment in the cultivation of mindfulness. *Mindfulness, 10,* 571–581. https://doi.org/10.1007/s12671-018-1074-1
Anālayo, Bh. (2019c). Mindfulness-based interventions and the four satipaṭṭhānas. *Mindfulness, 10,* 611–615. https://doi.org/10.1007/s12671-019-1097-2
Anālayo, Bh. (2020). Clear knowing and mindfulness. *Mindfulness, 11,* 862–871. https://doi.org/10.1007/s12671-019-01283-8
Anālayo, Bh. (2021). The four levels of awakening. *Mindfulness, 12,* 831–840. https://doi.org/10.1007/s12671-020-01530-3
Anderson, T., & Farb, N. A. (2018). Personalising practice using preferences for meditation anchor modality. *Frontiers in Psychology, 9.* https://doi.org/10.3389/fpsyg.2018.02521
Antonova, E., Chadwick, P., & Kumari, V. (2015). More meditation, less habituation? The effect of intensive mindfulness practice on the acoustic startle reflex. *PLoS One, 10,* e0123512. http://dx.doi.org/10.1371/journal.pone.012351
Arbel, K. (2015). The liberative role of jhānic joy (pīti) and pleasure (sukha) in the early Buddhist path to awakening. *Buddhist Studies Review, 32,* 179–205. https://doi.org/10.1558/bsrv.v32i2.28328
Ataria, Y., Dor-Ziderman, Y., & Berkovich-Ohana, A. (2015). How does it feel to lack a sense of boundaries? A case study of a long-term mindfulness meditation. *Consciousness and Cognition, 37,* 133–147. https://doi.org/10.1016/j.concog.2015.09.002
Atchley, R., Klee, D., Memmott, T., Goodrich, E., Wahbeh, H., & Oken, B. (2016). Event-related potential correlates of mindfulness meditation competence. *Neuroscience, 320,* 83–92. https://doi.org/10.1016/j.neuroscience.2016.01.051
Aurobindo, S. (1995). *Savitri: A legend and a symbol.* Sri Aurobindo Ashram Press.
Aurobindo, S. (1996). *The synthesis of yoga.* Lotus Light Publications.
Aurobindo, S. (2001). *Record of yoga.* Sri Aurobindo Ashram Press.
Auty, K. M., Cope, A., & Liebling, A. (2017). A systematic review and meta-analysis of yoga and mindfulness meditation in prison: Effects on psychological well-being and behavioural functioning. *International Journal of Offender Therapy and Comparative Criminology, 61,* 689–710.
Azeemi, K. S. (2005). *Muraqaba: The art and science of Sufi meditation.* Plato.
Baer, R., Crane, C., Miller, E., & Kuyken, W. (2019a). Doing no harm in mindfulness-based programs: Conceptual issues and empirical findings. *Clinical Psychology Review, 71,* 101–114. https://doi.org/10.1016/j.cpr.2019.01.001
Baer, R., Gu, J., Cavanagh, K., & Strauss, C. (2019b). Differential sensitivity of mindfulness questionnaires to change with treatment: A systematic review and meta-analysis. *Psychological Assessment, 31,* 1247–1253. https://doi.org/10.1037/pas0000744
Baer, R. A., Smith, G. T., Hopkins, J., Krietemeyer, J., & Toney, L. (2006). Using self-report assessment methods to explore facets of mindfulness. *Assessment, 13,* 27–45. https://doi.org/10.1177/1073191105283504
Baird, B., Mrazek, M. D., Phillips, D. T., & Schooler, J. W. (2014). Domain-specific enhancement of metacognitive ability following meditation training. *Journal of Experimental Psychology: General, 143,* 1972–1979. https://doi.org/10.1037/a0036882

Bamber, M. D., & Morpeth, E. (2019). Effects of mindfulness meditation on college student anxiety: A meta-analysis. *Mindfulness, 10,* 203–214. https://doi.org/10.1007/s12671-018-0965-5

Barlow, D. H., Nock, M. K., & Hersen, M. (2009). *Single case experimental designs: Strategies for studying behavior change.* Pearson.

Bartlett, L., Martin, A., Neil, A. L., Memish, K., Otahal, P., Kilpatrick, M., & Sanderson, K. (2019). A systematic review and meta-analysis of workplace mindfulness training randomized controlled trials. *Journal of Occupational Health Psychology, 24,* 108–126. https://doi.org/10.1037/ocp0000146

Batchelor, M. (2016). Meditation: Practice and experience. In M. West, (Ed.), *The psychology of meditation: Research & practice* (pp. 27–47). Oxford University Press.

Batchelor, S. (2015). *After Buddhism: Rethinking the dharma for a secular age.* New Haven: Yale University Press.

Bayot, M., Vermeulen, N., Kever, A., & Mikolajczak, M. (2020). Mindfulness and empathy: Differential effects of explicit and implicit Buddhist teachings. *Mindfulness, 11,* 5–17. https://doi.org/10.1007/s12671-018-0966-4

Beauregard, M., & Paquette, V. (2006). Neural correlates of a mystical experience in Carmelite nuns. *Neuroscience Letters, 405,* 186–190. https://doi.org/10.1016/j.neulet.2006.06.060

Becker, B. (1988). Synthesizing standardized mean-change measures. *British Journal of Mathematics and Statistical Psychology, 41,* 257–278. https://doi.org/10.1111/j.2044-8317.1988.tb00901.x

Belzer, F. Schmidt, S., Lucius-Hoene, G., Schneider, J. F., Orellana-Rios, C. L., & Sauer, S. (2013). Challenging the construct validity of mindfulness assessment – A cognitive interview study of the Freiburg Mindfulness Inventory. *Mindfulness, 4,* 33–44. https://doi.org/10.1007/s12671-012-0165-7

Bennett, C. M., Baird, A., Miller, M., & Wolford, G. (2011). Neural correlates of interspecies perspective taking in the post-mortem Atlantic salmon: An argument for multiple comparisons correction. *Journal of Serendipitous and Unexpected Results, 1,* 1–5.

Benson, H. (1983). The relaxation response: Its subjective and objective historical precedents and physiology. *Trends in Neurosciences, 6,* 281–284.

Bennett, C. M., Miller, M. B., & Wolford, G. L. (2009). Neural correlates of interspecies perspective taking in the post-mortem Atlantic Salmon: An argument for multiple comparisons correction. *Neuroimage, 47*(Suppl 1), s125. https://doi.org/10.1016/S1053-8119(09)71202-9

Benson, H. (1993). The relaxation response. In D. Goleman & J. Furin (Eds.), *Mind-body medicine: How to use your mind for better health.* Consumers Reports Book.

Benson, H., Beary, J. F., & Carol, M. P. (1974). The relaxation response. *Psychiatry, 37,* 37–46. https://doi.org/10.1080/00332747.1974.11023785

Benson, H., & Klipper, M. Z. (1974). *The relaxation response.* Wings Books. https://doi.org/10.1080/00332747.1974.11023785

Bergomi, C., Tschacher, W., & Kupper, Z. (2013). The assessment of mindfulness with self-report measure: existing scales and open issues. *Mindfulness, 4,* 191–202. https://doi.org/10.1007/s12671-012-0110-9

Berkovich-Ohana, A., & Glicksohn, J. (2014). The consciousness state space – a unifying model for consciousness and self. *Frontiers in Psychology, 5.* https://doi.org/10.3389/fpsyg.2014.00341

Berkovich-Ohana, A., & Glicksohn, J. (2017). Meditation, absorption, transcendent experience, and affect: Tying it all together via the Consciousness State Space (CSS) model. *Mindfulness, 8,* 68–77. https://doi.org/10.1007/s12671-015-0481-9

Berkovich-Ohana, A., & Wittmann, M. (2017). A typology of altered states according to the consciousness state space (CSS) model: A special reference to subjective time. *Journal of Consciousness Studies, 24,* 37–61.

Bernstein, A., Hadash, Y., & Fresco, D. M. (2019). Metacognitive processes model of decentering: Emerging methods and insights. *Current Opinion in Psychology, 28,* 245–251. https://doi.org/10.1016/j.copsyc.2019.01.019

Bernstein, A., Hadash, Y., Lichtash, Y., Tanay, G., Shepherd, K., & Fresco, D. M. (2015). Decentering and related constructs: A critical review and metacognitive processes model. *Perspectives on Psychological Science, 10,* 599–617. https://doi.org/10.1177/1745691615594577

Berry, D. R., Hoerr, J. P., Cesko, S., Alayoubi, A., Carpio, K., Zirzow, H., Walters, W., Scram, G., Rodiguez, K., & Beaver, V. (2020). Does mindfulness training without explicit ethics-based instruction promote prosocial behaviors? A Meta-analysis. *Personality and Social Psychology Bulletin, 46,* 1247–1269. https://doi.org/10.1177/0146167219900418

Biedermann, B., De Lissa, P., Mahajan, Y., Polito, V., Badcock, N., Connors, M. H., Quinto, L., Larsen, L., & McArthur, G. (2016). Meditation and auditory attention: An ERP study of meditators and non-meditators. *International Journal of Psychophysiology, 109,* 63–70. https://doi.org/10.7287/peerj.preprints.2318v1

Bielefeldt, C. (1986). Ch'ang-lu Tsung-tse and the "secret" of Zen meditation. In P. N. Gregory (Ed.), *Traditions of meditation in Chinese Buddhism* (pp. 129–161). University of Hawaii, Press. https://doi.org/10.1515/9780824842932-006

Bishop, S., Lau, M., Shapiro, S., Carlson, L., Anderson, N., Carmody, J., Segal, Z. v., Abbey, S., Speca, M., Velting, D., & Devins, G. (2004). Mindfulness: A proposed operational definition. *Clinical Psychology: Science and Practice, 11,* 230–241. https://doi.org/10.1093/clipsy.bph077

Boccia, M., Piccardi, L., & Guariglia, P. (2015). The meditative mind: A comprehensive meta-analysis of MRI studies. *BioMed Research International.* https://doi.org/10.1155/2015/419808

Bodhi, Bh. (2013). *A comprehensive manual of Abhidhamma: The Abhidhammattha Sangaha of Ācariya Anuruddha.* BPS Pariyatti Editions.

Bomhard, A. R. (2010). *Buddhist meditation in theory and practice: A general exposition according to the Pāḷi Canon of the Theravādin school.* Charleston Buddhist Fellowship. [Original author: Paravahera Vajirañāṇa Mahāthera]

Bomhard, A. R. (2013). *An outline of the Pāḷi Canon.* Charleston Buddhist Fellowship.

Bond, F. W. (2016). Personal meditation journey. In M. A. West (Ed.), *The psychology of meditation: Research & practice* (pp. 255–256). Oxford University Press.

Bond, K., Ospina, M. B., Hooton, N., Bialy, L., Dryden, D. M., Buscemi, N., Shannahoff-Khalsa, D., Dusek, J., & Carlson, L. E. (2009). Defining a complex intervention: The development of demarcation criteria for "meditation". *Psychology of Religion and Spirituality, 1,* 129–137. https://doi.org/10.1037/a0015736

Boring, E. G. (1953). A history of introspection. *Psychological Bulletin, 50,* 169–189. https://doi.org/10.1037/h0090793

Bormann, J. E., & Carrico, A. W. (2009). Increases in positive reappraisal coping during a group-based mantram intervention mediate sustained reductions in anger in HIV-positive persons. *International Journal of Behavioral Medicine, 16*, 74–80. https://doi.org/10.1007/s12529-008-9007-3

Bormann, J. E., Thorp, S., Wetherell, J. L., & Golshan, S. (2008). A spiritually based group intervention for combat veterans with posttraumatic stress disorder: Feasibility study. *Journal of Holistic Nursing, 26*, 109–116. https://doi.org/10.1177/0898010107311276

Bowen, S., Witkiewitz, K., Dillworth, T. M., Chawla, N., Simpson, T. L., Ostafin, B. D., Larimer, M. E., Blume, A. W., Parks, G. A., & Marlatt, G. A. (2006). Mindfulness meditation and substance use in an incarcerated population. *Psychology of Addictive Behaviors, 20*, 343–347. https://doi.org/10.1037/0893-164X.20.3.343

Boyd-Wilson, B. M., & Walkey, F. H. (2015). The enlightenment scale: A measure of being at peace and open-hearted. *Pastoral Psychology, 64*, 311–325. https://doi.org/10.1007/s11089-013-0586-9

Boyle, R. P. (2015). *Realizing awakened consciousness: Interviews with Buddhist Teachers and a new perspective on the mind*. Columbia University Press. https://doi.org/10.7312/boyl17074

Braboszcz, C., Cahn, B. R., Levy, J., Fernandez, M., & Delorme, A. (2017). Increased gamma brainwave amplitude compared to control in three different meditation traditions. *PLoS One, 12*(1), e0170647. https://doi.org/10.1371/journal.pone.0170647

Brahm, A. (2014). *Mindfulness, bliss, and beyond: A meditator's handbook* (2nd ed.). Wisdom Publications.

Brandmeyer, T., & Delorme, A. (2021). Meditation and the wandering mind: A theoretical framework of underlying neurocognitive mechanisms. *Perspectives on Psychological Science, 16*, 39–66. https://doi.org/10.1177/1745691620917340

Brandmeyer, T., Delorme, A., & Wahbeh, H. (2019). The neuroscience of meditation: Classification, phenomenology, correlates, and mechanisms. In N. Srinivasan (Ed.), *Progress in brain research* (Vol. 244, pp. 1–29). Academic Press. https://doi.org/10.1016/bs.pbr.2018.10.020

Brasington, L. (2015). *Right concentration: A practical guide to the jhānas*. Shambala.

Braud, W. G. (2010). Patanjali Yoga Sutras and parapsychological research: Exploring matches and mismatches. In K. R. Rao (Ed.), *Yoga and parapsychology: Empirical research and theoretical studies* (pp. 241–260). Motilal Barnarsidass.

Braun, V., & Clarke, V. (2012). Thematic analysis. In H. E. Cooper, P. M. Camic, D. L. Long, A. T. Panter, D. E. Rindskopf, & K. J. Sher (Eds.), *APA handbook of research methods in psychology: Vol 2. Research designs: Quantitative, qualitative, neuropsychological, and biological* (pp. 57–71). American Psychological Association.

Bravo, A. J., Pearson, M. R., Wilson, A. D., & Witkiewitz, K. (2018). When traits match states: Examining the associations between self-report trait and state mindfulness following a state mindfulness induction. *Mindfulness, 9*, 199–211. https://doi.org/10.1007/s12671-017-0763-5

Breedvelt, J. J., Amanvermez, Y., Harrer, M., Karyotaki, E., Gilbody, S., Bockting, C. L., Cuijpers, P., & Ebert, D. D. (2019). The effects of meditation, yoga, and mindfulness on depression, anxiety, and stress in tertiary education students: A meta-analysis. *Frontiers in Psychiatry, 10*, 193. https://doi.org/10.3389/fpsyt.2019.00193

Bringmann, H. C., Bringmann, N., Jeitler, M., Brunnhuber, S., Michalsen, A., & Sedlmeier, P. (2020). Meditation-based lifestyle modification: Development of an integrative mind-body program for mental health and human flourishing. *Complementary Medicine Research*. https://doi.org/10.1159/000512333

Bringmann, H.C., Bringmann, N., Jeitler, M., Brunnhuber, S., Michalsen, A., & Sedlmeier, P. (2021a). Meditation based lifestyle modification (MBLM) in outpatients with mild to moderate depression: A mixed-methods feasibility study. *Complementary Therapies in Medicine, 56,* 102598. https://doi.org/10.1016/j.ctim.2020.102598

Bringmann, H.C., Vennemann, J., Gross, J., Matko, K., & Sedlmeier, P. (2021b). "To be finally at peace with myself": A qualitative study reflecting experiences of the Meditation Based Lifestyle Modification Program in mild to moderate depression. *Journal of Alternative and Complementary Medicine.* https://doi.org/10.1089/acm.2021.0038

Broad, W. (2012, February 27). Yoga and sex scandals: No surprise here. *New York Times.*

Bronkhorst, J. (1993). *The two traditions of meditation in ancient India.* Motilal Banarsidass.

Brooks, R. (1969). The meaning of 'real' in Advaita Vedānta. *Philosophy East and West, 19,* 385-398. https://doi.org/10.2307/1397631

Brossart, D.F., Laird, V.C., & Armstrong, T.W. (2018). Interpreting Kendall's Tau and Tau-U for single-case experimental designs. *Cogent Psychology, 5,* 1518687. https://doi.org/10.1080/23311908.2018.1518687

Brown, D., Forte, M., & Dysart, M. (1984). Visual sensitivity and mindfulness meditation. *Perceptual and Motor Skills, 58,* 775-784. https://doi.org/10.2466/pms.1984.58.3.775

Brown, K.W., & Ryan, R.M. (2003). The benefits of being present: Mindfulness and its role in psychological well-being. *Journal of Personality and Social Psychology, 84,* 822-848.

Brunnhölzl, K. (2016). *The heart attack sutra: A new commentary on the heart sutra.* Shambhala.

Bryan, D.B. (1991). *A Western way of meditation: The rosary revisited.* Loyola University Press.

Bryant, E.F. (2015). *The yoga sūtras of Patañjali: A new edition, translation, and commentary* [eBook]. North Point Press.

Buchheld, N., Grossman, P., & Walach, H. (2001). Measuring mindfulness in insight meditation (Vipassana) and meditation-based psychotherapy: The development of the Freiburg Mindfulness Inventory (FMI). *Journal for Meditation and Meditation Research, 1,* 11-34.

Buddhaghosa, B. (2010). *The Path of purification (Visuddhimagga).* (B. Ñāóamoli, Trans.; from the Pali language). Kandy, Sri Lanka: Buddhist Publication Society.

Buksbazen, J.D. (2002). *Zen meditation in plain English.* Wisdom Publications.

Burke, A. (2012). Comparing individual preferences for four meditation techniques: Zen, Vipassana (Mindfulness), Qigong, and Mantra. *Explore, 8,* 237-242. https://doi.org/10.1016/j.explore.2012.04.003

Burley, M. (2007). *Classical Sāṃkhya and Yoga: An Indian metaphysics of experience.* Routledge. https://doi.org/10.4324/9780203966747

Burton, A., Burgess, C., Dean, S., Koutsopoulou, G.Z., & Hugh-Jones, S. (2017). How effective are mindfulness-based interventions for reducing stress among healthcare professionals? A systematic review and meta-analysis. *Stress and Health, 33,* 3-13. https://doi.org/10.1002/smi.2673

Buswell, R.E. (2006). The "short-cut" approach of K'an-hua meditation. In J.D. Loori (Ed.), *Sitting with koans: Essential writings on the practice of zen koan introspection* (pp. 75-90). Wisdom Publications.

Cahn, B. R., & Polich, J. (2006). Meditation states and traits: EEG, ERP, and neuroimaging studies. *Psychological Bulletin, 132,* 180-211. https://doi.org/10.1037/0033-2909.132.2.180

Cahn, B. R., & Polich, J. (2009). Meditation (Vipassana) and the P3a event-related brain potential. *International Journal of Psychophysiology, 72,* 51-60. https://doi.org/10.1016/j.ijpsycho.2008.03.013

Cardaciotto, L., Herbert, J. D., Forman, E. M., Moitra, E., & Farrow, V. (2008). The assessment of present-moment awareness and acceptance: The Philadelphia Mindfulness Scale. *Assessment, 15,* 204-223. https://doi.org/10.1177/1073191107311467

Carmody, J., Baer, R. A., Lykins, E., & Olendzki, N. (2009). An empirical study of the mechanisms of mindfulness in a mindfulness-based stress reduction program. *Journal of Clinical Psychology, 65,* 613-626. https://doi.org/10.1002/jclp.20579

Carpenter, J. K., Conroy, K., Gomez, A. F., Curren, L. C., & Hofmann, S. G. (2019). The relationship between trait mindfulness and affective symptoms: A meta-analysis of the Five Facet Mindfulness Questionnaire (FFMQ). *Clinical Psychology Review, 74.* https://doi.org/10.1016/j.cpr.2019.101785

Carrière, K., Khoury, B., Günak, M. M., & Knäuper, B. (2018). Mindfulness-based interventions for weight loss: A systematic review and meta-analysis. *Obesity Reviews, 19,* 164-177.

Carsley, D., Khoury, B., & Heath, N. L. (2018). Effectiveness of mindfulness interventions for mental health in schools: A comprehensive meta-analysis. *Mindfulness, 9,* 693-707. https://doi.org/10.1007/s12671-017-0839-2

Carson, J., Carson, K., Gil, K., & Baucom, D. (2004). Mindfulness-based relationship enhancement. *Behavior Therapy, 35,* 471-494. https://doi.org/10.1016/S0005-7894(04)80028-5

Catherine, S. (2011). *Wisdom wide and deep: A practical handbook for mastering jhāna and vipassanā.* Wisdom Publications.

Cebolla, A., Campos, D., Galiana, L., Oliver, A., Tomás, J. M., Feliu-Soler, A., Soler, J., García-Campayo, J., Demarzo, M., & Baños, R. M. (2017). Exploring relations among mindfulness facets and various meditation practices: Do they work in different ways? *Consciousness and Cognition, 49,* 172-180.

Cebolla, A., Demarzo, M., Martins, P., Soler, J., & Garcia-Campayo, J. (2017). Unwanted effects: Is there a negative side of meditation? A multicentre survey. *PLoS One, 12*(9), e0183137. https://doi.org/10.1371/journal.pone.0183137

Cebolla, A., Galiana, L., Campos, D., Oliver, A., Soler, J., Demarzo, M., Baños, R. M., Feliu-Soler, A., & García-Campayo, J. (2018). How does mindfulness work? Exploring a theoretical model using samples of meditators and non-meditators. *Mindfulness, 9,* 860-870.

Chan, C. H., Chan, T. H., Leung, P. P., Brenner, M. J., Wong, V. P., Leung, E. K., Wang, X., Lee, M. Y., Chan, J. S. M., & Chan, C. L. (2014). Rethinking well-being in terms of affliction and equanimity: development of a Holistic Well-Being Scale. *Journal of Ethnic and Cultural Diversity in Social Work, 23,* 289-308. https://doi.org/10.1080/15313204.2014.932550

Chan, J. S., Deng, K., Wu, J., & Yan, J. H. (2019). Effects of meditation and mind–body exercises on older adults' cognitive performance: A meta-analysis. *The Gerontologist, 59,* e782-e790. https://doi.org/10.1093/geront/gnz022

Chapple, C. (1990). The unseen seer and the filed: Consciousness in Samkhya and Yoga. In R. K. C. Forman (Ed.), *The problem of pure consciousness: Mysticism and philosophy.* (pp. 53-70). Oxford University Press.

Chapple, C. K. (2008). *Yoga and the luminous: Patañjali's spiritual path to freedom.* SUNY Press.

Chappell, D. W. (1987). Is Tendai Buddhism relevant to the modern world? *Japanese Journal of Religious Studies, 14,* 247-266. https://doi.org/10.18874/jjrs.14.2-3.1987.247-266

Chatterjee, S., & Datta, D. (1984). *An Introduction to Indian philosophy.* Calcutta University Press.

Chen, K. W., Berger, C. C., Manheimer, E., Forde, D., Magidson, J., Dachman, L., & Lejuez, C. W. (2012). Meditative therapies for reducing anxiety: A systematic review and meta-analysis of randomized controlled trials. *Depression and Anxiety, 29,* 545-562. https://doi.org/10.1002/da.21964

Chen, K. W., Comerford, A., Shinnick, P., & Ziedonis, D. M. (2010). Introducing qigong meditation into residential addiction treatment: a pilot study where gender makes a difference. *The Journal of Alternative and Complementary Medicine, 16,* 875-882. https://doi.org/10.1089/acm.2009.0443

Chen, S., & Jordan, C. H. (2020). Incorporating ethics into brief mindfulness practice: Effects on well-being and prosocial behavior. *Mindfulness, 11,* 18-29. https://doi.org/10.1007/s12671-018-0915-2

Chen, T. L., Chang, S. C., Hsieh, H. F., Huang, C. Y., Chuang, J. H., & Wang, H. H. (2020). Effects of mindfulness-based stress reduction on sleep quality and mental health for insomnia patients: A meta-analysis. *Journal of Psychosomatic Research, 135,* 110144. https://doi.org/10.1016/j.jpsychores.2020.110144

Chiesa, A. (2009). Zen meditation: An integration of current evidence. *Journal of Alternative and Complementary Medicine, 15,* 585-592. https://doi.org/10.1089/acm.2008.0416

Chimiklis, A. L., Dahl, V., Spears, A. P., Goss, K., Fogarty, K., & Chacko, A. (2018). Yoga, mindfulness, and meditation interventions for youth with ADHD: Systematic review and meta-analysis. *Journal of Child and Family Studies, 27,* 3155-3168. https://doi.org/10.1007/s10826-018-1148-7

Chittik, W. C. (2008). *Sufism: A beginner's guide.* Oneworld.

Chowdhury, M. R. (2019). *5 health benefits of daily meditation according to science.* PositivePsychology.com. https://positivepsychology.com/benefits-of-meditation/

Chu, C. S., Stubbs, B., Chen, T. Y., Tang, C. H., Li, D. J., Yang, W. C., Wu, C. K., Carvalho, A. R., Vieta, E., Miklowitz, D. J., Tseng, P. T., & Lin, P. Y. (2018). The effectiveness of adjunct mindfulness-based intervention in treatment of bipolar disorder: A systematic review and meta-analysis. *Journal of Affective Disorders, 225,* 234-245.

Claxton, G. (1986). Editor's introduction. In G. Claxton (Ed.). *Beyond therapy: The impact of Eastern religions on psychological theory and practice.* London: Wisdom Publications.

Cleary, T. (1999). *Transmission of light: Zen in the art of enlightenment by Zen Master Keizan.* North Point Press.

Cleary, T. (2005). *Book of Serenity: One hundred Zen dialogues.* Shambala.

CNN Staff. (2015, August 13). *Guru convicted of abusing followers' children fled justice.* The Hunt with John Walsh. https://www.cnn.com/2015/08/06/us/guru-convicted-of-abusing-followers-children-fled-justice/index.html

Cohen, J. (1988). *Statistical power analysis for the behavioural sciences.* Lawrence Erlbaum.

Coleman, J. W. (2002). *The new Buddhism: The western transformation of an ancient tradition.* Oxford University Press.
Colzato, L. S., Szapora, A., & Hommel, B. (2012). Meditate to create: The impact of focused-attention and open-monitoring training on convergent and divergent thinking. *Frontiers in Psychology, 3.* https://doi.org/10.3389/fpsyg.2012.00116
Condon, P. (2019). Meditation in context: Factors that facilitate prosocial behavior. *Current Opinion in Psychology, 28,* 15-19. https://doi.org/10.1016/j.copsyc.2018.09.011
Conway, T. (2006). *My concerns about Sathya Sai Baba (1926-2011).* http://www.enlightened-spirituality.org/Sathya_Sai_Baba_my_concerns.html
Conze, E. (2001). *Buddhist wisdom: Containing the diamond sutra and the heart sutra.* Vintage.
Cook, F. D. (2003). *The record of transmitting the light: Zen master Keizan's Denkoroku.* Wisdom Publications.
Cooper, A. M. (2000). Further developments in clinical diagnosis of narcissistic personality disorder. In E. F. Ronningstam (Ed.), *Disorders of narcissism* (pp. 53-74). Jason Aronson.
Cousins, L. S. (1996). The origins of insight meditation. *The Buddhist Forum, 4,* 35-58.
Dahl, C. J., & Davidson, R. J. (2019). Mindfulness and the contemplative life: Pathways to connection, insight, and purpose. *Current Opinion in Psychology, 28,* 60-64. https://doi.org/10.1016/j.copsyc.2018.11.007
Dahl, C. J., Lutz, A., & Davidson, R. J. (2015). Reconstructing and deconstructing the self: cognitive mechanisms in meditation practice. *Trends in Cognitive Sciences, 19,* 515-523. https://doi.org/10.1016/j.tics.2015.07.001
Damasio, A. (2012). *Self comes to mind: constructing the conscious brain.* Vintage Books.
d'Aquili, E. G., & Newberg, A. B. (1993). Mystical states and the experience of god: A model of the neuropsychological substrate. *Zygon: Journal of Religion and Science, 28,* 177-200. https://doi.org/10.1111/j.1467-9744.1993.tb01026.x
d'Aquili, E. G., & Newberg, A. B. (1998). The neuropsychological basis of religion: Or why god won't go away. *Zygon: Journal of Religion and Science, 33,* 187-201. https://doi.org/10.1111/0591-2385.00140
d'Aquili, E. G., & Newberg, A. B. (2000). The neuropsychology of aesthetic, spiritual, and mystical states. *Zygon: Journal of Religion and Science, 35,* 39-51. https://doi.org/10.1111/0591-2385.00258
Dasgupta, S. (1930). *Yoga philosophy in relation to other systems of Indian thought.* University of Calcutta.
Dasgupta, S. (1997). *A history of Indian philosophy* (Vol. I). Motilal Banarsidass. (Original work published 1922)
Dass, R. (1977). Foreword. In D. Goleman (1977). *The varieties of the meditative experience.* Irvington.
Davidson, R. J. (2010). Empirical explorations of mindfulness: Conceptual and methodological conundrums. *Emotion, 10,* 8-11. https://doi.org/10.1037/a0018480
Davidson, R. J., & Kaszniak, A. W. (2015). Conceptual and methodological issues in research on mindfulness and meditation. *American Psychologist, 70,* 581-592. https://doi.org/10.1037/a0039512
Davis, L. S. (2010). *Advaita Vedānta and Zen Buddhism: Deconstructive modes of spiritual inquiry.* Continuum.
de Abreu Costa, M., de Oliveira, G. S. D. A., Tatton-Ramos, T., Manfro, G. G., & Salum, G. A. (2019). Anxiety and stress-related disorders and mindfulness-based interventions: A systematic review and multilevel meta-analysis and meta-regression of mul-

tiple outcomes. *Mindfulness, 10,* 996–1005. https://doi.org/10.1007/s12671-018-1058-1

Deatherage, G. (1975). The clinical use of "mindfulness" meditation techniques in short-term psychotherapy. *Journal of Transpersonal Psychology, 7,* 133–143.

Deikman, A. J. (1963). Experimental meditation. *Journal of Nervous and Mental Disease, 136,* 329–343. https://doi.org/10.1097/00005053-196304000-00002

Deikman, A. J. (1966a). Deautomatization and the mystic experience. *Psychiatry, 29,* 324–348. https://doi.org/10.1080/00332747.1966.11023476

Deikman, A. J. (1966b). Implications of experimentally induced contemplative meditation. *Journal of Nervous and Mental Disease, 142,* 101–116. https://doi.org/10.1097/00005053-196602000-00001

de Mello, A. (1984). *Sadhana: A way to god.* Doubleday.

de Silva, P. (1990). Buddhist psychology: A review of theory and practice. *Current Psychology, 9,* 236–254. https://doi.org/10.1007/BF02686862

de Silva, P. (2005). *An introduction to Buddhist psychology* (4th ed.). Palgrave Macmillan.

Deutsch, E., & Dalvi, R. (2004). *The essential Vedānta: A new source book of Advaita Vedānta.* World Wisdom.

de Vibe, M., Solhaug, I., Tyssen, R., Friborg, O., Rosenvinge, J. H., Sørlie, T., Halland, E., & Bjørndal, A. (2015). Does personality moderate the effects of mindfulness training for medical and psychology students? *Mindfulness, 6,* 281–289.

Dharmawardene, M., Givens, J., Wachholtz, A., Makowski, S., & Tjia, J. (2016). A systematic review and meta-analysis of meditative interventions for informal caregivers and health professionals. *BMJ Supportive & Palliative Care, 6,* 160–169. https://doi.org/10.1136/bmjspcare-2014-000819

Dhillon, A., Sparkes, E., & Duarte, R. V. (2017). Mindfulness-based interventions during pregnancy: A systematic review and meta-analysis. *Mindfulness, 8,* 1421–1437. https://doi.org/10.1007/s12671-017-0726-x

Dimitrov, D. (2019). *The top 11 reasons why you should take up meditation right now.* https://iheartintelligence.com/top-reasons-you-should-take-up-meditation/

DiRenzo, D., Crespo-Bosque, M., Gould, N., Finan, P., Nanavati, J., & Bingham, C. O. (2018). Systematic review and meta-analysis: Mindfulness-based interventions for rheumatoid arthritis. *Current Rheumatology Reports, 20*(12), 75. https://doi.org/10.1007/s11926-018-0787-4

Donald, J. N., Sahdra, B. K., Van Zanden, B., Duineveld, J. J., Atkins, P. W., Marshall, S. L., & Ciarrochi, J. (2019). Does your mindfulness benefit others? A systematic review and meta-analysis of the link between mindfulness and prosocial behaviour. *British Journal of Psychology, 110,* 101–125. https://doi.org/10.1111/bjop.12338

Dorjee, D. (2020). Psychophysiology of meditation. In M. Farias, D. Brazier, & L. Mansur (Eds.), *The Oxford handbook of meditation.* Oxford Handbooks Online. https://doi.org/10.1093/oxfordhb/9780198808640.013.24

Dumoulin, H. (2005). *Zen Buddhism: A history: Vol. 1. India and China.* World Wisdom.

Dunne, J. D., Thompson, E., & Schooler, J. (2019). Mindful meta-awareness: sustained and non-propositional. *Current Opinion in Psychology, 28,* 307–311. https://doi.org/10.1016/j.copsyc.2019.07.003

Easwaran, E. (2013). *Meditation: Bringing the deep wisdom of the heart into your daily life.* JAICO.

Eberth, J., & Sedlmeier, P. (2012). The effects of mindfulness meditation: A meta-analysis. *Mindfulness, 3,* 174–189. https://doi.org/10.1007/s12671-012-0101-x

Eberth, J., Sedlmeier, P., & Schäfer, T. (2019). PROMISE: A model of insight and equanimity as the key effects of mindfulness meditation. *Frontiers in Psychology, 10.* https://doi.org/10.3389/fpsyg.2019.02389

Eickhoff, S. B., Laird, A. R., Grefkes, C., Wang, L. E., Zilles, K., & Fox, P. T. (2009). Coordinate-based activation likelihood estimation meta-analysis of neuroimaging data: A random-effects approach based on empirical estimates of spatial uncertainty. *Human Brain Mapping, 30,* 2907–2926. https://doi.org/10.1002/hbm.20718

Eifring, H. (2016). Types of meditation. In H. Eifring (Ed.), *Asian traditions of meditation* (pp. 27–47). University of Hawai'i Press. https://doi.org/10.21313/hawaii/9780824855680.003.0002

Eppley, K. R., Abrams, A. I., & Shear, J. (1989). Differential effects of relaxation techniques on trait anxiety: A meta-analysis. *Journal of Clinical Psychology, 45,* 957–974. https://doi.org/10.1002/1097-4679(198911)45:6<957::AID-JCLP2270450622>3.0.CO;2-Q

Ernst, C. W. (2000). *The Shambhala guide to Sufism.* Shambhala South Asia Editions.

Falcone, G., & Jerram, M. (2018). Brain activity in mindfulness depends on experience: A meta-analysis of fMRI studies. *Mindfulness, 9,* 1319–1329. https://doi.org/10.1007/s12671-018-0884-5

Falk, G. D. (2009). *Stripping the Gurus: Sex, violence, abuse and enlightenment.* Million Monkeys Press.

Farias, M., Maraldi, E., Wallenkampf, K. C., & Lucchetti, G. (2020). Adverse events in meditation practices and meditation-based therapies: A systematic review. *Acta Psychiatrica Scandinavica, 142,* 374–393. https://doi.org/10.1111/acps.13225

Feldman, G., Greeson, J., & Senville, J. (2010). Differential effects of mindful breathing, progressive muscle relaxation, and loving-kindness meditation on decentering and negative reactions to repetitive thoughts. *Behaviour Research and Therapy, 48,* 1002–1011. https://doi.org/10.1016/j.brat.2010.06.006

Feuerstein, G. (1989). *The Yoga-Sutra of Patañjali: A new translation and commentary.* Inner Traditions.

Feuerstein, G. (1998). *The yoga tradition: Its history, literature, philosophy and practice.* Hohm Press.

Feuerstein, G. (2001). *The yoga tradition: Its history, literature, philosophy and practice.* Hohm Press.

Feuerstein, G. (2006). Yogic meditation. In J. Shear (Ed.), *The experience of meditation: Experts introduce major traditions* (pp. 87–117). Paragon House.

Firestone, C., & Scholl, B. J. (2016). Cognition does not affect perception: Evaluating the evidence for "top-down" effects. *Behavioral and Brain Sciences, 39,* 1–72. https://doi.org/10.1017/S0140525X15000965

Fisher, N. (2019). The dark nights of the soul in Abrahamic meditative traditions. In M. Farias, D. Brazier, & L. Mansur (Eds.), *The Oxford handbook of meditation.* Oxford Handbooks Online. https://doi.org/10.1093/oxfordhb/9780198808640.013.43

Flood, G. (1996). *An introduction to Hinduism.* Cambridge University Press.

Ford, J. I. (2006). *Zen master Who? A guide to the people and stories of Zen.* Wisdom Publications.

Fortenbaugh, F. C., DeGutis, J., Germine, L., Wilmer, J. B., Grosso, M., Russo, K., & Esterman, M. (2015). Sustained attention across the life span in a sample of 10,000: Dissociating ability and strategy. *Psychological Science, 26,* 1497-1510. https://doi.org/10.1177/0956797615594896

Fossella, T. (2011, Spring). Human nature, Buddha nature. An interview with John Welwood. *Tricycle.* http://tricycle.org/magazine/human-nature-buddha-nature/

Fox, K.C.R., Dixon, M.L., Nijeboer, S., Girn, M., Floman, J.L., Lifshitz, M., Ellamil, M., Sedlmeier, P., & Christoff, K. (2016). Functional neuroanatomy of meditation: A review and meta-analysis of 78 functional neuroimaging investigations. *Neuroscience and Biobehavioral Reviews, 65,* 208-228. https://doi.org/10.1016/j.neubiorev.2016.03.021

Fox, K.C.R., Nijeboer, S., Dixon, M.L., Floman, J.L., Ellamil, M., Rumak, S.P., Sedlmeier, P., & Christoff, K. (2014). Is meditation associated with altered brain structure? A systematic review and meta-analysis of morphometric neuroimaging in meditation practitioners. *Neuroscience and Biobehavioral Reviews, 43,* 48-73. https://doi.org/10.1016/j.neubiorev.2014.03.016

Fox, K.C.R., Zakarauskas, P., Dixon, M., Ellamil, M., Thompson, E., & Christoff, K. (2012). Meditation experience predicts introspective accuracy. *PLoS One, 7,* e45370. https://doi.org/10.1371/journal.pone.0045370

Franke, K., Ziegler, G., Kloppel, S., & Gaser, C. (2010). Estimating the age of healthy subjects from T1-weighted MRI scans using kernel methods: Exploring the influence of various parameters. *NeuroImage, 50,* 883-892. https://doi.org/10.1016/j.neuroimage.2010.01.005

Frauwallner, E. (2003). *Geschichte der indischen Philosophie, I. Band.* [History of Indian philosophy, Vol. I]. Shaker Verlag.

Frauwallner, E. (2010). *The philosophy of Buddhism.* Delhi: Motilal Banarsidass. (Original work published 1956 in German: Die Philosophie des Buddhismus. Akademie-Verlag.)

Frawley, D. (2001). *The Rig Veda and the history of India.* Aditya Prakashan.

Frawley, D., & Summerfield Kozak, S. (2001). *Yoga for your type.* Lotus Press.

Fredrickson, B.L., Boulton, A.J., Firestine, A.M., Van Cappellen, P., Algoe, S.B., Brantley, M.M., Kim, S.L., Brantley, J., & Salzberg, S. (2017). Positive emotion correlates of meditation practice: A comparison of mindfulness meditation and loving-kindness meditation. *Mindfulness, 8,* 1623-1633. https://doi.org/10.1007/s12671-017-0735-9

Full, G.E., Walach, H., & Trautwein, M. (2013). Meditation-induced changes in perception: An interview study with expert meditators (Sotapannas) in Burma. *Mindfulness, 4,* 55-63. https://doi.org/10.1007/s12671-012-0173-7

Gál, É., Ștefan, S., & Cristea, I.A. (2021). The efficacy of mindfulness meditation apps in enhancing users' well-being and mental health related outcomes: A meta-analysis of randomized controlled trials. *Journal of Affective Disorders, 279,* 131-142. https://doi.org/10.1016/j.jad.2020.09.134

Gallegos, A.M., Crean, H.F., Pigeon, W.R., & Heffner, K.L. (2017). Meditation and yoga for posttraumatic stress disorder: A meta-analytic review of randomized controlled trials. *Clinical Psychology Review, 58,* 115-124. https://doi.org/10.1016/j.cpr.2017.10.004

Ganss, G.E. (S.J.) (1992). *The spiritual exercises of Saint Ignatius: A translation and commentary.* Institute of Jesuit Sources.

Gard, T., Hölzel, B.K., & Lazar, S.W. (2014). The potential effects of meditation on age-related cognitive decline: A systematic review. *Annals of the New York Academy of Sciences, 1307*(1), 89-103.

Garland, E. L., & Fredrickson, B. L. (2019). Positive psychological states in the arc from mindfulness to self-transcendence: Extensions of the Mindfulness-to-Meaning Theory and applications to addiction and chronic pain treatment. *Current Opinion in Psychology, 28,* 184–191. https://doi.org/10.1016/j.copsyc.2019.01.004

Gathright, E. C., Salmoirago-Blotcher, E., DeCosta, J., Balletto, B. L., Donahue, M. L., Feulner, M. M., Cruess, D. G., Wing, R. R., Carey, M. P., & Scott-Sheldon, L. A. (2019). The impact of Transcendental Meditation on depressive symptoms and blood pressure in adults with cardiovascular disease: A systematic review and meta-analysis. *Complementary Therapies in Medicine, 46,* 172–179.

Gawrysiak, M. J., Grassetti, S. N., Greeson, J. M., Shorey, R. C., Pohlig, R., & Baime, M. J. (2017). The many facets of mindfulness and the prediction of change following mindfulness-based stress reduction (MBSR). *Journal of Clinical Psychology, 74,* 523–535. https://doi.org/10.1002/jclp.22521

Gebauer, J. E., Nehrlich, A. D., Stahlberg, D., Sedikides, C., Hackenschmidt, A., Schick, D., Stegmaier, C. A., Windfelder, C. C., Bruk, A., & Mander, J. (2018). Mind-body practices and the self: Yoga and meditation do not quiet the ego but instead boost self-enhancement. *Psychological Science, 29,* 1299–1308. https://doi.org/10.1177/0956797618764621

Geoffroy, E. (2010). *Introduction to Sufism: The inner path of Islam.* World Wisdom.

Gethin, R. (1998). *The foundations of Buddhism.* Oxford University Press.

Gilbert, P., Basran, J., MacArthur, M., & Kirby, J. N. (2019). Differences in the semantics of prosocial words: An exploration of compassion and kindness. *Mindfulness, 10,* 2259–2271. https://doi.org/10.1007/s12671-019-01191-x

Giles, J. (2019). Relevance of the no-self theory in contemporary mindfulness. *Current Opinion in Psychology, 28,* 298–301. https://doi.org/10.1016/j.copsyc.2019.03.016

Gillespie, B., Davey, M. P., & Flemke, K. (2015). Intimate partners' perspectives on the relational effects of mindfulness-based stress reduction training: A qualitative research study. *Contemporary Family Therapy, 37,* 396–407. https://doi.org/10.1007/s10591-015-9350-x

Glaser, B. G., & Strauss, A. L. (1967). *The discovery of grounded theory: Strategies for qualitative research.* Aldine.

Goldberg, S. B., Riordan, K. M., Sun, S., & Davidson, R. J. (2021). The empirical status of mindfulness-based interventions: A systematic review of 44 meta-analyses of randomized controlled trials. *Perspectives on Psychological Science.* Advance online publication. https://doi.org/10.1177/1745691620968771

Goldberg, S. B., Riordan, K. M., Sun, S., Kearney, D. J., & Simpson, T. L. (2020). Efficacy and acceptability of mindfulness-based interventions for military veterans: A systematic review and meta-analysis. *Journal of Psychosomatic Research, 138,* 110232. https://doi.org/10.1016/j.jpsychores.2020.110232

Goldberg, S. B., Tucker, R. P., Greene, P. A., Davidson, R. J., Kearney, D. J., & Simpson, T. L. (2019). Mindfulness-based cognitive therapy for the treatment of current depressive symptoms: A meta-analysis. *Cognitive Behaviour Therapy, 48,* 445. https://doi.org/10.1080/16506073.2018.1556330

Goldin, P. R., & Jazaieri, H. (2017). Scientific investigations of compassion cultivation training. In J. R. Doty & E. Seppälä (Eds.), *Handbook on compassion science.* Oxford University Press. https://doi.org/10.1093/oxfordhb/9780190464684.013.18

Goldin, P. R., & Jazaieri, H. (2020). Investigating moderators of compassion meditation training in a community sample. *Mindfulness, 11,* 75–85. https://doi.org/10.1007/s12671-017-0857-0

Goleman, D. (1977). *The varieties of the meditative experience.* Irvington.

Goleman, D., & Davidson, R. J. (2017). *Altered traits: Science reveals how meditation changes your mind, brain, and body.* Avery.

Gombrich, R. (2006). *How Buddhism began: The conditional genesis of the early teachings* (2nd ed). Routledge.

Gombrich, R. (2013). *What the Buddha thought* (Corrected edition). Equinox.

Gonda, J. (1963). The Indian mantra. *Oriens, 16,* 244–297. https://doi.org/10.1163/18778372-01601016

González-Valero, G., Zurita-Ortega, F., Ubago-Jiménez, J. L., & Puertas-Molero, P. (2019). Use of meditation and cognitive behavioral therapies for the treatment of stress, depression and anxiety in students. A systematic review and meta-analysis. *International Journal of Environmental Research and Public Health, 16,* 4394. https://www.mdpi.com/1660-4601/16/22/4394

Goodall, D. (1996). *Hindu scriptures.* University of California Press.

Goswami, H. D. (2015). *A comprehensive guide to Bhagavad-Gita with literal translation.* Torchlight Publishing.

Gotink, R. A., Chu, P., Busschbach, J. J. V., Benson, H., Fricchione, G. L., & Hunink, M. G. M. (2015). Standardised mindfulness-based interventions in healthcare: An overview of systematic reviews and meta-analyses of RCTs. *PLoS One, 10*(4), e0124344. https://doi.org/10.1371/journal.pone.0124344 [this article is still available on the Internet, but has been retracted: https://journals.plos.org/plosone/article?id=10.1371/journal.pone.0124344]

Goyal, M., Singh, S., Sibinga, E. M., Gould, N. F., Rowland-Seymour, A., Sharma, R., Berger, Z., Sleicher, D., Maron, D. D., Shihab, H. M., Ranasinghe, P. D., Linn, S.,Saha, S., Bass, E. B., & Haythornthwaite, A. (2014). Meditation programs for psychological stress and well-being: a systematic review and meta-analysis. *JAMA Internal Medicine, 174,* 357–368.

Grabovac, A. D., Lau, M. A., & Willett, B. R.(2011). Mechanisms of mindfulness: A Buddhist psychological model. *Mindfulness, 2,* 154–166. https://doi.org/10.1007/s12671-011-0054-5

Grant, S., Colaiaco, B., Motala, A., Shanman, R., Booth, M., Sorbero, M., & Hempel, S. (2017). Mindfulness-based relapse prevention for substance use disorders: A systematic review and meta-analysis. *Journal of Addiction Medicine, 11,* 386–396. https://doi.org/10.1097/ADM.0000000000000338

Greenberg, M., & Mitra, J. (2015). From mindfulness to right mindfulness: The intersection of awareness and ethics. *Mindfulness, 6,* 74–78. https://doi.org/10.1007/s12671-014-0384-1

Greenwell, B. (1990). *Energies of transformation: A guide to the kundalini process.* Shakti River Press.

Gregory, P. N. (1986). Introduction. In P. N. Gregory (Ed.), *Traditions of meditation in Chinese Buddhism* (pp. 1–13). University of Hawai'i Press. https://doi.org/10.1515/9780824842932-002

Griffiths, P. (1981). Concentration or insight: The problematic of Theravāda Buddhist meditation-theory. *Journal of the American Academy of Religion, 49,* 605–624. https://doi.org/10.1093/jaarel/XLIX.4.605

Grof, S., & Grof, C. (Eds.). (1989). *Spiritual emergency: When personal transformation becomes a crisis*. Tarcher.

Grossenbacher, P. G., & Quaglia, J. T. (2017). Contemplative cognition: A more integrative framework for advancing mindfulness and meditation research. *Mindfulness, 8*, 1580–1593. https://doi.org/10.1007/s12671-017-0730-1

Grossman, P., & van Dam, N. T. (2011). Mindfulness, by any other name …: Trials and tribulations of sati in western psychology and science. *Contemporary Buddhism, 12*, 219–239. https://doi.org/10.1080/14639947.2011.564841

Gu, Q., Hou, J. C., & Fang, X. M. (2018). Mindfulness meditation for primary headache pain: A meta-analysis. *Chinese Medical Journal, 131*, 829–838. https://doi.org/10.4103/0366-6999.228242

Gunaratana, B. (2015). *Mindfulness in plain English*. Wisdom Publications.

Gunaratana, H. (1980). *A critical analysis of the jhānas in Theravāda Buddhist meditation* [Doctoral dissertation]. American University [Available online: http://buddhanet.net/pdf_file/printguna.pdf].

Hadash, Y., & Bernstein, A. (2019). Behavioral assessment of mindfulness: Defining features, organizing framework, and review of emerging methods. *Current Opinion in Psychology, 28*, 229–237. https://doi.org/10.1016/j.copsyc.2019.01.008

Haigh, E. A., Moore, M. T., Kashdan, T. B., & Fresco, D. M. (2011). Examination of the factor structure and concurrent validity of the Langer Mindfulness/Mindlessness Scale. *Assessment, 18*(1), 11–26. https://doi.org/10.1177/1073191110386342

Halkias, G. T. (2019). Buddhist meditation in Tibet: Exoteric and esoteric orientations. In M. Farias, D. Brazier, & L. Mansur (Eds.), *The Oxford handbook of meditation*. Oxford Handbooks Online. https://doi.org/10.1093/oxfordhb/9780198808640.013.27

Halladay, J. E., Dawdy, J. L., McNamara, I. F., Chen, A. J., Vitoroulis, I., McInnes, N., & Munn, C. (2019). Mindfulness for the mental health and well-being of post-secondary students: A systematic review and meta-analysis. *Mindfulness, 10*, 397–414. https://doi.org/10.1007/s12671-018-0979-z

Halser, M. (2020). Was ans Licht kam [What came to light]. *Süddeutsche Zeitung Magazin* (Booklet 45). https://sz-magazin.sueddeutsche.de/yoga/missbrauch-yoga-89416?reduced=true

Hamilton, S. (2000). *Early Buddhism: A new approach*. Curzon.

Harada, S. R. (2006). Zazen meditation in Japanese Rinzai zen. In J. Shear (Ed.), *The experience of meditation: Experts introduce the major traditions* (pp. 1–21). Paragon House.

Harari, Y. N. (2019). *21 lessons for the 21st century*. Vintage.

Harris, L. (1994, November 14). O Guru, Guru, Guru. *The New Yorker*, 92. https://www.newyorker.com/magazine/1994/11/14/o-guru-guru-guru

Hart, W. (1987). *The art of living: Vipassana meditation as taught by S. N. Goenka*. HarperOne.

Harvey, P. (2004). *An introduction to Buddhism*. Cambridge University Press.

Hasenkamp, W., Wilson-Mendenhall, C. D., Duncan, E., & Barsalou, L. W. (2012). Mind wandering and attention during focused meditation: A fine-grained temporal analysis of fluctuating cognitive states. *NeuroImage, 59*, 750–760. https://doi.org/10.1016/j.neuroimage.2011.07.008

Hasler, B. P., Mehl, M. R., Bootzin, R. R., & Vazire, S. (2008). Preliminary evidence of diurnal rhythms in everyday behaviors associated with positive affect. *Journal of Research in Personality, 42*, 1537–1546. https://doi.org/10.1016/j.jrp.2008.07.012

Hayes, S. C., Strosahl, K. D., & Wilson, K. G. (1999). *Acceptance and commitment therapy: An experiential approach to behavior change.* Guilford Press.

Hayes, S. C., Strosahl, K. D., & Wilson, K. G. (2012). *Acceptance and Commitment Therapy: The process and practice of mindful change* (2nd ed.). Guilford Press.

Hawley, J. S. (2005). *Three Bhakti voices: Mirabai, Surdas, and Kabir in their time and ours.* Oxford University Press.

Heine, S. (1990). Does the koan have Buddha-nature? The Zen koan as religious symbol. *Journal of the American Academy of Religion, 58,* 357–387. https://doi.org/10.1093/jaarel/LVIII.3.357

Heine, S., & Wright, D. S. (Eds.). (2000). *The kōan: Texts and contexts in Zen Buddhism.* Oxford University Press.

Hershock, P. D. (2005). *Chan Buddhism: Dimensions of Asian spirituality.* University of Hawai'i Press.

Hershock, P. D. (2014). *Public Zen, personal Zen* [eBook]. Rowman & Littlefield.

Higgins, J., Thompson, S. G., Deeks, J. J., & Altman, D. G. (2003). Measuring inconsistency in meta-analyses. *British Medical Journal, 327,* 557–560. https://doi.org/10.1136/bmj.327.7414.557

Hilert, A. J., & Gutierrez, D. (2020). Jewish meditation in counseling. *Counseling and Values, 65*(2), 126–136. https://doi.org/10.1002/cvj.12133

Hilton, L., Hempel, S., Ewing, B. A., Apaydin, E., Xenakis, L., Newberry, S., Colaiaco, B., Maher, A. R., Shanman, R. B., Sorbero, M. E., & Maglione, M. A. (2017). Mindfulness meditation for chronic pain: systematic review and meta-analysis. *Annals of Behavioral Medicine, 51,* 199–213. https://doi.org/10.1007/s12160-016-9844-2

Hiriyanna, M. (2000). *Outlines of Indian philosophy.* Motilal Benarsidass. (Original work published 1932)

Hölzel, B. K., Lazar, S. W., Gard, T., Schuman-Olivier, Z., Vago, D. R., & Ott, U. (2011). How does mindfulness meditation work? Proposing mechanisms of action from a conceptual and neural perspective. *Perspectives on Psychological Science, 6,* 537–559.

Hoge, E. A., Philip, S. R., & Fulwiler, C. (2019). Considerations for mood and emotion measures in mindfulness-based intervention research. *Current Opinion in Psychology, 28,* 279–284. https://doi.org/10.1016/j.copsyc.2019.02.001

Hommel, B., Chapman, C. S., Cisek, P., Neyedli, H. F., Song, J. H., & Welsh, T. N. (2019). No one knows what attention is. *Attention, Perception, & Psychophysics, 81,* 2288–2303. https://doi.org/10.3758/s13414-019-01846-w

Hori, G. V. S. (1994). Teaching and learning in the Rinzai Zen monastery. *Journal of Japanese Studies, 20,* 5–35. https://doi.org/10.2307/132782

Hori, V. S. (2006a). The steps of koan practice. In J. D. Loori (Ed.), *Sitting with koans: Essential writings on the practice of zen koan introspection* (pp. 131–146). Wisdom Publications.

Hori, V. S. (2006b). The nature of the Rinuai (Linji) koan practice. In J. D. Loori (Ed.), *Sitting with koans: Essential writings on the practice of zen koan introspection* (pp. 131–130). Wisdom Publications.

Hovorun, C. (2019). Eastern Christianity and meditation. In M. Farias, D. Brazier, & L. Mansur (Eds.), *The Oxford handbook of meditation.* Oxford Handbooks Online. https://doi.org/10.1093/oxfordhb/9780198808640.013.8

Hox, J. J., Moerbeek, M., & van de Schoot, R. (2018). *Multilevel analysis: Techniques and applications* (3rd ed.). Routledge.

Hunt, M., Al-Braiki, F., Dailey, S., Russell, R., & Simon, K. (2018). Mindfulness training, yoga, or both? Dismantling the active components of a mindfulness-based stress reduction intervention. *Mindfulness, 9,* 512-520. https://doi.org/10.1007/s12671-017-0793-z

Huppes, N. (2001). *Psychic education, a workbook.* Sri Aurobindo Education Society.

Husgafvel, V. (2016). On the Buddhist roots of contemporary non-religious mindfulness practice: Moving beyond sectarian and essentialist approaches. *Temenos, 52,* 87-126. https://doi.org/10.33356/temenos.55371

Isgandarova, N. (2019). Muraqaba as a mindfulness-based therapy in Islamic psychotherapy. *Journal of Religion and Health, 58,* 1146-1160. https://doi.org/10.1007/s10943-018-0695-y

Ivanovski, B., & Malhi, G. S. (2007). The psychological and neurophysiological concomitants of mindfulness forms of meditation. *Acta Neuropsychiatrica, 19,* 76-91. https://doi.org/10.1111/j.1601-5215.2007.00175.x

Izutsu, T. (1982). *Toward a philosophy of Zen Buddhism.* Prajñā Press.

Jah, A. K. (2008). Personality in Indian psychology. In K. Rao, A. Paranjpe, & A. Dalal (Eds.), *Handbook of Indian psychology* (pp. 348-360). Foundation Books.

Jansen, J. E., Gleeson, J., Bendall, S., Rice, S., & Alvarez-Jimenez, M. (2020). Acceptance- and mindfulness-based interventions for persons with psychosis: A systematic review and meta-analysis. *Schizophrenia Research, 215,* 25-37. https://doi.org/10.1016/j.schres.2019.11.016

Jayasaro (1989). Luang Por's way. In Ajahn Chah various desciples (Eds.), *Seeing the way: Buddhist reflections on the spiritual life.* Amaravati Publications.

Jinpa, T. (2019). The question of mindfulness' connection with ethics and compassion. *Current Opinion in Psychology, 28,* 71-75. https://doi.org/10.1016/j.copsyc.2018.10.016

Jitatmananda; S. (2004). Spiritual experiences of Ramakrishna-Vivekananda. In K. Joshi & M. Cornelissen (Eds.), *Consciousness, Indian psychology and Yoga* (pp. 145-176). Centre for Studies in Civilizations.

Jo, H.-G., Hinterberger, T., Wittmann, M., & Schmidt, S. (2015). Do meditators have higher awareness of their intentions to act? *Cortex, 65,* 149-158. https://doi.org/10.1016/j.cortex.2014.12.015

Johansson, R. E. A. (1970). *The psychology of nirvana.* Anchor Books.

Johnson, K. (2012). *Sex, lies, and two Hindu gurus: Telling their secrets and finding my truth.* Rishika Books.

Kabat-Zinn, J. (1982). An outpatient program in behavioral medicine for chronic pain patients based on the practice of mindfulness meditation: Theoretical considerations and preliminary results. *General Hospital Psychiatry, 4,* 33-47. https://doi.org/10.1016/0163-8343(82)90026-3

Kabat-Zinn, J. (1990). *Full catastrophe living: Using the wisdom of your body and mind to face stress, pain, and illness.* Dell Publishing.

Kabat-Zinn, J. (2003). Mindfulness-based interventions in context: Past, present, and future. *Clinical Psychology: Science and Practice, 10*(2), 144-156. https://doi.org/10.1093/clipsy.bpg016

Kabat-Zinn, J. (2009). *Wherever you go, there you are: Mindfulness meditation in everyday life.* Hachette Books.

Kabat-Zinn, J. (2011). Some reflections on the origins of MBSR, skillful means, and the trouble with maps. *Contemporary Buddhism, 12,* 281-306. https://doi.org/10.1080/14639947.2011.564844

Kalson, N. S., Brock, T. M., Mangino, M., Fabiane, S. M., Mann, D. A., Borthwick, L. A., Deehan, D. J., & Williams, F. M. K. (2018). Reduced telomere length is associated with fibrotic joint disease suggesting that impaired telomere repair contributes to joint fibrosis. *PLoS One*, e0190120. https://doi.org/10.1371/journal.pone.0190120

Kalupahana, D. J. (1992). *The principles of Buddhist psychology*. Sri Satguru Publications.

Kalupahana, D. J. (2009). *Karma and rebirth: Foundations of the Buddha's moral philosophy*. Buddhist Cultural Centre.

Kaplan, A. (1982). *Meditation and Kabbalah*. Samuel Weiser.

Kapleau, P. (2000). *The three pillars of Zen* (3rd ed). Anchor Books.

Karunamuni, N., & Weerasekera, R. (2019). Theoretical foundations to guide mindfulness meditation: A path to wisdom. *Current Psychology, 38*, 627–646. https://doi.org/10.1007/s12144-017-9631-7

Kelley, G. A., & Kelley, K. S. (2015). Meditative movement therapies and health-related quality-of-life in adults: A systematic review of meta-analyses. *PLoS One, 10*(6), e0129181. https://doi.org/10.1371/journal.pone.0129181

Kerr, C. E., Shaw, J. R., Wasserman, R. H., Chen, V. W., Kanojia, A., Bayer, T., & Kelley, J. M. (2008). Tactile acuity in experienced Tai Chi practitioners: Evidence for use dependent plasticity as an effect of sensory-attentional training. *Experimental Brain Research, 188*, 317–322. https://doi.org/10.1007/s00221-008-1409-6

Khalsa, S. S., Rudrauf, D., Damasio, A. R., Davidson, R. J., Lutz, A., & Tranel, D. (2008). Interoceptive awareness in experienced meditators. *Psychophysiology, 45*, 671–677. https://doi.org/10.1111/j.1469-8986.2008.00666.x

Khoury, B., Lecomte, T., Fortin, G., Masse, M., Therien, P., Bouchard, V., Chapleau, M.-A., Paquin, K., & Hofmann, S. G. (2013). Mindfulness-based therapy: A comprehensive meta-analysis. *Clinical Psychology Review, 33*, 763–771. https://doi.org/10.1016/j.cpr.2013.05.005

Khoury, B., Sharma, M., Rush, S. E., & Fournier, C. (2015). Mindfulness-based stress reduction for healthy individuals: A meta-analysis. *Journal of Psychosomatic Research, 78*, 519–528. https://doi.org/10.1016/j.jpsychores.2015.03.009

Kim, J. J., Cunnington, R., & Kirby, J. N. (2020). The neurophysiological basis of compassion: An fMRI meta-analysis of compassion and its related neural processes. *Neuroscience & Biobehavioral Reviews, 108*, 112–123. https://doi.org/10.1016/j.neubiorev.2019.10.023

King, W. l. (1980). *Theravāda meditation: The Buddhist transformation of yoga*. Pennsylvania State University Press.

Kiran, Girgla, K. K., Chalana, H., & Singh, H. (2014). Effect of rajyoga meditation on chronic tension headache. *Indian Journal of Physiology and Pharmacology, 58*, 157161.

Kirby, J. N., Tellegen, C. L., & Steindl, S. R. (2017). A meta-analysis of compassion-based interventions: Current state of knowledge and future directions. *Behavior Therapy, 48*, 778–792. https://doi.org/10.1016/j.beth.2017.06.003

Kjolhede, B. (2012). *Working on Koans* (An edited transcription of a teisho given by Roshi Bodhin Kjolhede during the 1992 October sesshin). https://www.rzc.org/wp-content/uploads/2012/01/Working-on-Koans.pdf

Klingbeil, D. A., Fischer, A. J., Renshaw, T. L., Bloomfield, B. S., Polakoff, B., Willenbrink, J. B., Copek, R. A., & Chan, K. T. (2017). Effects of mindfulness-based interventions on disruptive behavior: A meta-analysis of single-case research. *Psychology in the Schools, 54,* 70-87. https://doi.org/10.1002/pits.21982

Klingbeil, D. A., & Renshaw, T. L. (2018). Mindfulness-based interventions for teachers: A meta-analysis of the emerging evidence base. *School Psychology Quarterly, 33,* 501-511. https://doi.org/10.1037/spq0000291

Klostermaier, K. K. (2006). *Hinduism: A short history.* Oneworld.

Köhle, N., Drossaert, C. H., Jaran, J., Schreurs, K. M., Verdonck-de Leeuw, I. M., & Bohlmeijer, E. T. (2017). User-experiences with a web-based self-help intervention for partners of cancer patients based on acceptance and commitment therapy and self-compassion: A qualitative study. *BMC Public Health, 17,* 1-16.

Koerner, K. (2012). *Doing dialectical behavior therapy: A practical guide.* Guilford Press.

Kohut, H. (1977). *The restoration of the self.* International Universities Press.

Kok, B. E., & Singer, T. (2017a). Effects of contemplative dyads on engagement and perceived social connectedness over 9 months of mental training: A randomized clinical trial. *Jama Psychiatry, 74,* 126-134. https://doi.org/10.1001/jamapsychiatry.2016.3360

Kok, B. E., & Singer, T. (2017b). Phenomenological fingerprints of four meditations: Differential state changes in affect, mind-wandering, meta-cognition, and interoception before and after daily practice across 9 months of training. *Mindfulness, 8,* 218-231. https://doi.org/10.1007/s12671-016-0594-9

Ko Lay, U. (1990). *Guide to Tipitaka.* Sri Satguru Publications. http://www.buddhanet.net/pdf_file/tipitaka.pdf

Komjathy, L. (2013). *The Daoist tradition: An introduction.* Bloomsbury Academic.

Komjathy, L. (2019). Daoist meditation: From 100 CE to the present. In M. Farias, D. Brazier, & L. Mansur (Eds.), *The Oxford handbook of meditation.* Oxford Handbooks Online. https://doi.org/10.1093/oxfordhb/9780198808640. 013.13

Koncz, A., Demetrovics, Z., & Takacs, Z. K. (2021). Meditation interventions efficiently reduce cortisol levels of at-risk samples: A meta-analysis. *Health Psychology Review, 15,* 56-84. https://doi.org/10.1080/17437199.2020.1760727

Kornfield, J. (1979). Intensive insight meditation: A phenomenological study. *Journal of Transpersonal Psychology, 11,* 41-58.

Kornfield, J. (1988). *Modern Buddhist masters.* Kandy, Sri Lanka: Buddhist Publication Society.

Kornfield, J. (1993). *A path with heart: A guide through the perils and promises of spiritual life.* Bantam Books.

Kornfield, J. (2008). *The wise heart: A guide to the universal teachings of Buddhist psychology.* Bantam Books.

Kraus, S., & Sears, S. (2009). Measuring the immeasurables: Development and initial validation of the Self-Other Four Immeasurables (SOFI) scale based on Buddhist teachings on loving kindness, compassion, joy, and equanimity. *Social Indicators Research, 92,* 169-181. https://doi.org/10.1007/s11205-008-9300-1

Kreplin, U., Farias, M., & Brazil, I. A. (2018). The limited prosocial effects of meditation: A systematic review and meta-analysis. *Scientific Reports, 8,* 2403. https://doi.org/10.1038/s41598-018-20299-z

Kristeller, J. L., Baer, R. A., & Quillian-Wolever, R. (2006). Mindfulness-based approaches to eating disorders. In R. Baer (Ed.), *Mindfulness and acceptance-based interventions: Conceptualization, application, and empirical support.* Elsevier. https://doi.org/10.1016/B978-012088519-0/50005-8

Kristeller, J. L., & Jordan, K. D. (2018). Spirituality and meditative practice: Research opportunities and challenges. *Psychological Studies, 63,* 130–139. https://doi.org/10.1007/s12646-017-0391-0

Kropp, A., & Sedlmeier, P. (2019). What makes mindfulness-based interventions effective? An examination of common components. *Mindfulness, 10,* 2060–2072. https://doi.org/10.1007/s12671-019-01167-x

Kuijpers, H. J., Van der Heijden, F. M. M. A., Tuinier, S., & Verhoeven, W. M. A. (2007). Meditation-induced psychosis. *Psychopathology, 40,* 461–464. https://doi.org/10.1159/000108125

Kushner, B. (2018). Breathe Deep: The key to meditative concentration is not mental, but physical – and you can find it in your lower abdomen. *Tricycle, 28*(2). https://tricycle.org/magazine/hara-breathing-meditation/

Kuyken, W., Warren, F. C., Taylor, R. S., Whalley, B., Crane, C., Bondolfi, G., Hayes, R., Huijbers, M., Ma, H., Schweizer, S., Segal, Z., Speckens, A., Reasdale, J. D., van Heeringen, K., Williams, M., Byford, S., Byng, R., & Dalgleish, T. (2019). Efficacy of mindfulness-based cognitive therapy in prevention of depressive relapse: An individual patient data meta-analysis from randomized trials. *JAMA Psychiatry, 73,* 565–574.

Laneri, D., Schuster, V., Dietsche, B., Jansen, A., Ott, U., & Sommer, J. (2016). Effects of longterm mindfulness meditation of brain's white matter mocrostructure and its aging. *Frontiers in Aging Neuroscience, 7,* 254. https://doi.org/10.3389/fnagi.2015.00254

Langer, E. J. (1989). *Mindfulness.* De Capo Press.

Lau, M. A., Bishop, S. R., Segal, Z. V., Buis, T., Anderson, N. D., Carlson, L., Shapiro, S., Carmody, J., Abbey, S., & Devins, G. (2006). The Toronto mindfulness scale: Development and validation. *Journal of clinical psychology, 62,* 1445–1467. https://doi.org/10.1002/jclp.20326

Leigh, J., Bowen, S., & Marlatt, G. A. (2005). Spirituality, mindfulness and substance abuse. *Addictive Behaviors, 30,* 1335–1341. https://doi.org/10.1016/j.addbeh.2005.01.010

Lenz, A. S., Hall, J., & Bailey Smith, L. (2016). Meta-analysis of group mindfulness-based cognitive therapy for decreasing symptoms of acute depression. *Journal for Specialists in Group Work, 41,* 44–70. https://doi.org/10.1016/j.addbeh.2005.01.010

Levman, B. (2018). Response to ven. Anālayo's once again on mindfulness and memory in Early Buddhism. *Mindfulness, 9,* 1041–1046. https://doi.org/10.1007/s12671-018-0954-8

Lewis, F. D. (2008). *Rumi past and present, east and west: The life, teaching and poetry of Jalâl al-Din Rumi.* Oneworld Publications.

Liang, S.-Y., & Wu, W.-C. (1997). *Quigong empowerment.* Way of the Dragon Publishing.

Liang, S.-Y., & Wu, W.-C. (2006). Taoist quigong. In J. Shear (Ed.). *The experience of meditation: Experts introduce major traditions* (pp. 49–86). Paragon House.

Liang, S.-Y., Wu, W.-C., & Breiter-Wu, D. (1997). *Qigong empowerment: A guide to medical, Taoist, Buddhist, and Wushu energy cultivation.* Way of the Dragon Publishing.

Linardon, J., Cuijpers, P., Carlbring, P., Messer, M., & Fuller-Tyszkiewicz, M. (2019). The efficacy of app-supported smartphone interventions for mental health problems: A meta-analysis of randomized controlled trials. *World Psychiatry, 18,* 325–336. https://doi.org/10.1002/wps.20673

Linardon, J., & Fuller-Tyszkiewicz, M. (2020). Attrition and adherence in smartphone-delivered interventions for mental health problems: A systematic and meta-analytic review. *Journal of Consulting and Clinical Psychology, 88,* 1-13. https://doi.org/10.1037/ccp0000459

Lindahl, J. R., Britton, W. B., Cooper, D. J., & Kirmayer, L. J. (2019). Challenging and adverse meditation experiences: Toward a person-centered approach. In M. Farias, D. Brazier, & L. Mansur (Eds.), *The Oxford handbook of meditation*. Oxford Handbooks Online. https://doi.org/10.1093/oxfordhb/9780198808640.013.51

Lindahl, J. R., Fisher, N. E., Cooper, D. J., Rosen, R. K., & Britton, W. B. (2017). The varieties of contemplative experience: A mixed-methods study of meditation-related challenges in Western Buddhists. *PLoS One, 12*(5), e0176239. https://doi.org/10.1371/journal.pone.0176239

Linehan, M. M. (1993). *Cognitive-behavioral treatment of borderline personality disorder.* Guilford Press.

Lippelt, D. P., Hommel, B., & Colzato, L. S. (2014). Focused attention, open monitoring and loving kindness meditation: effects on attention, conflict monitoring, and creativity: A review. *Frontiers in Psychology, 5,* 1083. https://doi.org/10.3389/fpsyg.2014.01083

Liu, Z., Chen, Q. L., & Sun, Y. Y. (2017). Mindfulness training for psychological stress in family caregivers of persons with dementia: A systematic review and meta-analysis of randomized controlled trials. *Clinical Interventions in Aging, 12,* 1521-1529. https://doi.org/10.2147/CIA.S146213

Lomas, T., Cartwright, T., Edginton, T., & Ridge, D. (2015b). A qualitative summary of experiential challenges associated with meditation practice. *Mindfulness, 6,* 848-860. https://doi.org/10.1007/s12671-014-0329-8

Lomas, T., Ivtzan, I., & Fu, C. H. (2015a). A systematic review of the neurophysiology of mindfulness on EEG oscillations. *Neuroscience & Biobehavioral Reviews, 57,* 401-410. https://doi.org/10.1016/j.neubiorev.2015.09.018

Loori, J. D. (2013). *The eight gates of Zen: A program of Zen training* [eBook]. Shambala.

Lopez, D. S., Jr. (1988). *The heart sūtra explained.* State University of New York Press.

Lowe, S. (2011). Transcendental Meditation, Vedic science and science. *Nova Religio, 14,* 54-76. https://doi.org/10.1525/nr.2011.14.4.54

Loy, D. (1982). Enlightenment in Buddhism and Advaita Vedānta: Are nirvana and moksha the same? *International Philosophical Quarterly, 22,* 65-74. https://doi.org/10.5840/ipq19822217

Lucas, P. C. (2013). Non-traditional modern Advaita gurus in the West and their traditional modern Advaita critics. *Nova Religio: The Journal of Alternative and Emergent Religions, 17,* 6-37.

Lucas, P. C. (2014). Non-traditional modern Advaita gurus in the west and their traditional modern Advaita critics. *Nova Religio, 17,* 6-37. https://doi.org/10.1525/nr.2014.17.3.6

Luberto, C. M., Shinday, N., Song, R., Philpotts, L. L., Park, E. R., Fricchione, G. L., & Yeh, G. Y. (2018). A systematic review and meta-analysis of the effects of meditation on empathy, compassion, and prosocial behaviors. *Mindfulness, 9,* 708-724. https://doi.org/10.1007/s12671-017-0841-8

Lucia, A. (2018). Guru sex: Charisma, proxemic desire, and the haptic logics of the guru-disciple relationship. *Journal of the American Academy of Religion, 86,* 953-988. https://doi.org/10.1093/jaarel/lfy025

Luders, E., Cherbuin, N., & Gaser, C. (2016). Estimating brain age using high-resolution pattern recognition: Younger brains in long-term meditation practitioners. *NeuroImage, 134*, 508-513. https://doi.org/10.1016/j.neuroimage.2016.04.007

Luders, E., Cherbuin, N., & Kurth, F. (2015). Forever young(er): Potential age-defying effects of long-term meditation on gray matter atrophy. *Frontiers in Psychology, 5*, 1551. https://doi.org/10.3389/fpsyg.2014.01551

Luders, E., Clark, K., Narr, K. L., & Toga, A. W. (2011). Enhanced brain connectivity in long-term meditation practitioners. *Neuroimage, 57*, 1308-1316. https://doi.org/10.1016/j.neuroimage.2011.05.075

Luders, E., & Kurth, F. (2019). The neuroanatomy of long-term meditators. *Current Opinion in Psychology, 28*, 172-178. https://doi.org/10.1016/j.copsyc.2018.12.013

Lukoff, D., Lu, F., & Turner, R. (1998). From spiritual emergency to spiritual problem: The transpersonal roots of the new DSM-IV category. *Journal of Humanistic Psychology, 38*, 21-50. https://doi.org/10.1177/00221678980382003

Lukoff, D., Wallace, C. J., Liberman, R. P., & Burke, K. (1986). A holistic program for chronic schizophrenic patients. *Schizophrenia Bulletin, 12*(2), 274-282. https://doi.org/10.1093/schbul/12.2.274

Lumma, A. L., Kok, B. E., & Singer, T. (2015). Is meditation always relaxing? Investigating heart rate, heart rate variability, experienced effort and likeability during training of three types of meditation. *International Journal of Psychophysiology, 97*, 38-45. https://doi.org/10.1016/j.ijpsycho.2015.04.017

Lustyk, M. K., Chawla, N., Nolan, R. S., & Marlatt, G. A. (2009). Mindfulness meditation research: issues of participant screening, safety procedures, and researcher training. *Advances in Mind-Body Medicine, 24*, 20-30.

Lutz, A., Dunne, J. D., & Davidson, R. J. (2007). Meditation and the neuroscience of consciousness: An introduction. In P. Zelazo, M. Moscovitch, & E. Thompson (Eds.), *Cambridge handbook of consciousness* (pp. 497-549). Cambridge University Press. https://doi.org/10.1017/CBO9780511816789.020

Lutz, A., Greischar, L. L., Rawlings, N. B., Ricard, M., & Davidson, R. J. (2004). Long-term meditators self-induce high-amplitude gamma synchrony during mental practice. *Proceedings of the National Academy of Sciences, 101*, 16369-16373. https://doi.org/10.1073/pnas.0407401101

Lutz, A., Jha, A. P., Dunne, J. D., & Saron, C. D. (2015). Investigating the phenomenological matrix of mindfulness-related practices from a neurocognitive perspective. *American Psychologist, 70*, 632-658. https://doi.org/10.1037/a0039585

Lutz, A., Slagter, H. A., Dunne, J. D., & Davidson, R. J. (2008). Attention regulation and monitoring in meditation. *Trends in Cognitive Science, 12*, 163-169. https://doi.org/10.1016/j.tics.2008.01.005

Lv, J., Liu, Q., Zeng, X., Oei, T. P., Liu, Y., Xu, K., ... Liu, J. (2020). The effect of four Immeasurables meditations on depressive symptoms: A systematic review and meta-analysis. *Clinical Psychology Review, 76*. https://doi.org/10.1016/j.cpr.2020.101814

Lynch, J., Prihodova, L., Dunne, P. J., Carroll, A., Walsh, C., McMahon, G., & White, B. (2018). Mantra meditation for mental health in the general population: A systematic review. *European Journal of Integrative Medicine, 23*, 101-108. https://doi.org/10.1016/j.eujim.2018.09.010

Maas, C. J. M., & Hox, J. J. (2005). Sufficient sample sizes for multilevel modeling. *Methodology, 1*, 86-92. https://doi.org/10.1027/1614-2241.1.3.86

MacLean, K. A., Ferrer, E., Aichele, S. R., Bridwell, D. A., Zanesco, A. P., Jacobs, T. L., King, B. G., Rosenberg, E. L., Sahdra, B. K., Shaver, P. R., Wallace, B. A., Mangun, G. R., & Saron, C. D. (2010). Intensive meditation training improves perceptual discrimination and sustained attention. *Psychological Science, 21,* 829–839.

Mäll, L. (2005). *Studies in the Aṣṭasāhasrikā Prajñāpāramitā and other essays.* Motilal Bandarsidass.

Magee, C., & Biesanz, J. C. (2019). Toward understanding the relationship between personality and well-being states and traits. *Journal of Personality, 87,* 276–294. https://doi.org/10.1111/jopy.12389

Maglione, M. A., Maher, A. R., Ewing, B., Colaiaco, B., Newberry, S., Kandrack, R., Shanman, R. M., Sorbero, M. E., & Hempel, S. (2017). Efficacy of mindfulness meditation for smoking cessation: A systematic review and meta-analysis. *Addictive Behaviors, 69,* 27–34. https://doi.org/10.7249/RR1317

Mahasi, S. (1973). *The progress of insight through the stages of purification* (2nd ed.). Buddhist Publication Society.

Mahasi, S. (1991). *Practical vipassana exercises.* Kandy, Sri Lanka: Buddhist Publication Society. http://www.buddhanet.net/pdf_file/mahasit1.pdf

Maithrimurthi, M. (1999). *Wohlwollen, Mitleid, Freude und Gleichmut: Eine ideengeschichtliche Untersuchung der vier apramāṇas in der buddhistischen Ethik und Spiritualiät von den Anfängen bis hin zum frühen Yogācāra* [Benevolence, compassion, joyousness, and equanimity: An analysis from the point of view of a history of ideas, of the four apramāṇas in Buddhist ethics and spirituality from the beginnings up to early Yogācāra]. (Alt- und Neu-Indische Studien, 50). Franz Steiner Verlag.

Malhotra, R. (2017). *Swami Nithyananda – persecution 2.0: My views on Swami Nithyananda's case.* Infinity Foundation. https://rajivmalhotra.com/library/articles/swami-nithyananda-persecution-2-0-views-swami-nithyanandas-case/

Manna, A., Raffone, A., Perrucci, M. G., Nardo, D., Ferretti, A., Tartaro, A., Londei, A., del Gratta, C., Belardinelli, M. O., & Romani, G. L. (2010). Neural correlates of focused attention and cognitive monitoring in meditation. *Brain Research Bulletin, 82,* 46–56. https://doi.org/10.1016/j.brainresbull.2010.03.001

Manuello, J., Vercelli, U., Nani, A., Costa, T., & Cauda, F. (2016). Mindfulness meditation and consciousness: An integrative neuroscientific perspective. *Consciousness and Cognition, 40,* 67–78. https://doi.org/10.1016/j.concog.2015.12.005

Masters, R. (2010). *Spiritual bypassing: When spirituality disconnects us from what really matters.* North Atlantic Books.

Matko, K., & Sedlmeier, P. (2019). What is meditation? Proposing an empirically derived classification system. *Frontiers in Psychology, 10.* https://doi.org/10.3389/fpsyg.2019.02276

Matko, K., Ott, U., & Sedlmeier, P. (2021a). What do meditators do when they meditate? Proposing a novel basis for future meditation research. *Mindfulness.* https://doi.org/10.1007/s12671-021-01641-5

Matko, K., Sedlmeier, P., & Bringmann, H. C. (2021b). Differential effects of ethical education, physical hatha yoga, and mantra meditation on well-being and stress in healthy participants – an experimental single-case study. *Frontiers in Psychology.* https://doi.org/10.3389/fpsyg.2021.672301

Mauss, I. B., & Robinson, M. D. (2009). Measures of emotion: A review. *Cognition and Emotion, 23,* 209–237.

May, C. J., Weyker, J. R., Spengel, S. K., Finkler, L. J., & Hendrix, S. E. (2014). Tracking longitudinal changes in affect and mindfulness caused by concentration and loving-kindness meditation with hierarchical linear modeling. *Mindfulness, 5,* 249–258. https://doi.org/10.1007/s12671-012-0172-8

McCaffrey, R., & Fowler, N. L. (2003). Qigong practice: A pathway to health and healing. *Holistic Nursing Practice, 17,* 110–116. https://doi.org/10.1097/00004650-200303000-00006

McGill, R. J. (2017). Single-case design and evaluation in R: An introduction and tutorial for school psychologists. *International Journal of School and Educational Psychology, 5,* 39–51. https://doi.org/10.1080/21683603.2016.1173610

McRae, J. R. (1986). *The Northern School and the formation of early Ch'an Buddhism.* University of Hawai'i Press.

McRae, J. R. (1987). Shen-hui and the teaching of sudden enlightenment in early Ch'an Buddhism. In P. N. Gregory (Ed.), *Sudden and gradual: Approaches to enlightenment in Chinese thought* (pp. 227–275). University of Hawai'i Press.

McRae, J. R. (1988). Ch'an commentaries on the Heart Sutra: Preliminary inference on the permutation of Chinese Buddhism. *Journal of the International Association of Buddhist Studies, 11,* 85–114.

McRae, J. R. (2003). *Seeing through Zen.* University of California Press.

Mehling, W., Gopisetty, V., Daubenmier, J., Price, C., Hecht, F., & Stewart, A. (2009). Body awareness: Construct and self-report measures. *PLoS One, 4*(5). https://doi.org/10.1371/journal.pone.0005614

Meier, S. T. (1994). *The chronic crisis in psychological measurement and assessment: A historical survey.* AP Professional.

Melnikova, N. (2014). The law of nature and practices leading to its realization in S. N. Goenka's Vipassana and in the oldest Buddhists texts. *Pandanus, 14,* 65–85.

Mercier, H., & Sperber, D. (2017). *The enigma of reason.* Harvard University Press.

Michel, A. (2020). *Cognition and perception: Is there really a distinction?* APS Observer. https://www.psychologicalscience.org/observer/cognition-and-perception-is-there-really-a-distinction

Miles, M. B., & Huberman, A. M. (1994). *Qualitative data analysis: An expanded sourcebook.* Sage.

Miles, M. B., Huberman, A. M., & Saldaña, J. (2018). *Qualitative data analysis: A methods sourcebook.* Sage.

Miller, A. (2021). *15 meditation benefits that will make you secessful.* https://www.lifehack.org/articles/productivity/15-reasons-why-meditation-will-make-you-successful.html

Miller, J. (1993). The unveiling of traumatic memories and emotions through mindfulness and concentration meditation: Clinical implications and three case report. *Journal of Transpersonal Psychology, 25,* 169–181.

Miller, J. P., & Nozawa, A. (2002). Meditating teachers: A qualitative study. *Journal of In-Service Education, 28,* 179–192. https://doi.org/10.1080/13674580200200201

Miś, M., & Kowalczyk, M. (2021). Mind-wandering during long-distance running and mood change: The role of working memory capacity and temporal orientation of thoughts. *International Journal of Sport and Exercise Psychology, 19*(5), 815–833. https://doi.org/10.1080/1612197X.2020.1766538

Mohr, M. (2000). Emerging from nonduality: Kōan practice in the Rinzai tradition since Hakuin. In S. Heine & D. S. Wright (Eds.), *The Kōan: Texts and contexts in Zen Buddhism* (pp. 255-279). Oxford University Press.

Molleur, J. (2009). A Hindu monk's appreciation of Eastern Orthodoxy's Jesus Prayer'. *Religion East & West, 9*, 67-76.

Moneyya, B. (2006). *Teaching and training.* WAVE Publications.

Monteiro, L. M., Musten, R., & Compson, J. (2015). Traditional and contemporary mindfulness: finding the middle path in the tangle of concerns. *Mindfulness, 6*, 1-13. https://doi.org/10.1007/s12671-014-0301-7

Montero-Marin, J., Garcia-Campayo, J., Pérez-Yus, M. C., Zabaleta-del-Olmo, E., & Cuijpers, P. (2019). Meditation techniques v. relaxation therapies when treating anxiety: A meta-analytic review. *Psychological Medicine, 49*, 2118-2133.

Monti, D. A., Peterson, C., Shakin Kunkel, E. J., Hauck, W. W., Pequignot, E., Rhodes, L., & Brainar, G. C. (2006). A randomised, controlled trial of mindfulness-based art therapy for women with cancer. *Psychooncology, 15*, 363-373. https://doi.org/10.1002/pon.988

Mrazek, A. J., Mrazek, M. D., Cherolini, C. M., Cloughesy, J. N., Cynman, D. J., Gougis, L. J., Landry, A. P., Reese, J. V., & Schooler, J. W. (2019). The future of mindfulness training is digital, and the future is now. *Current Opinion in Psychology, 28*, 81-86. https://doi.org/10.1016/j.copsyc.2018.11.012

Naranjo, C. (1971). Meditation: Its spirit and techniques. In C. Naranjo & R. E. Ornstein (Eds.), *On the psychology of meditation* (pp. 1-132). Viking.

Naranjo, C., & Ornstein, R. E. (1972). *On the psychology of meditation.* Viking.

Nash, J. D., Newberg, A. (2013). Toward a unifying taxonomy and definition for meditation. *Frontiers in Psychology, 4*, 806. https://doi.org/10.3389/fpsyg.2013.00806

Natsoulas, T. (1992). The stream of consciousness: I. William James's pulses. *Imagination, Cognition and Personality, 12*, 3-21. https://doi.org/10.2190/247K-7RDX-NLX8-ME2D

Nattier, J. (1992). The heart sūtra: A Chinese apocryphal text? *Journal of the International Association of Buddhist Studies, 15*, 153-223.

Neff, K. D. (2003). The development and validation of a scale to measure self-compassion. *Self and Identity, 2*, 223-250. https://doi.org/10.1080/15298860309027

Newberg, A. B., Alavi, A., Baime, M., Mozley, P. D., & d'Aquili, E. G. (1997). The measurement of cerebral blood flow during the complex cognitive task of meditation using HMPAS-SPCET Imaging. *Journal of Nuclear Medicine, 38*, 95.

Newberg, A. B., Alavi, A., Baime, M., Pourdehnad, M., Santanna, J., & d'Aquili, E. (2001). The measurement of regional cerebral blood flow during the complex cognitive task of meditation: A preliminary SPECT study. *Psychiatry Research: Neuroimaging, 106*, 113-122.

Newberg, A. B., d'Aquili, E. G., & Rause, V. (2002). *Why God won't go away: Brain science and the biology of belief.* Ballantine Books.

Newberg, A., Pourdehnad, M., Alavi, A., & d'Aquili, E. G. (2003). Cerebral blood flow during meditative prayer: Preliminary findings and methodological issues. *Perceptual and Motor Skills, 97*, 625-630. https://doi.org/10.2466/pms.2003.97.2.625

Nhat Hanh, T. (1985). *A guide to walking meditation.* Eastern Press.

Nhat Hanh, T. N. (1997). *Present moment wonderful moment: Mindfulness verses for daily living.* Full Circle.

Nhat Hanh, T. N. (2011). *The long road turns to joy: A guide to walking meditation* [eBook]. Parallax Press.
Nath Hanh, T. (2012). *Awakening of the heart: Essential Buddhist Sutras and commentaries*. Parallax Press.
Nhat Hanh, T., & Anh-Huong, N. (2016). *Walking meditation*. Baker & Taylor.
Nicholson, A. (2010). *Unifying Hinduism: Philosophy and identity in Indian intellectual history*. Columbia University Press. https://doi.org/10.7312/nich14986
Nonomura, K. (2008). *Eat sleep sit: My year at Japan's most rigorous Zen temple* (J. Winters Carpenter, Trans.). Tokyo, Japan: Kodnahsa International. (Original work published 1996 in Japanese).
Noone, C., & Hogan, M. J. (2018). Improvements in critical thinking performance following mindfulness meditation depend on thinking dispositions. *Mindfulness, 9,* 461–473. https://doi.org/10.1007/s12671-017-0789-8
Nowak, A., Vallacher, R. R., Tesser, A., & Borkowski, W. (2000). Society of self: The emergence of collective properties in self-structure. *Psychological Review, 107,* 39–61. https://doi.org/10.1037/0033-295X.107.1.39
Nyanaponika, T. (1999). *The four sublime states*. Inward Path. (Original work published 1958)
Odgers, K., Dargue, N., Creswell, C., Jones, M. P., & Hudson, J. L. (2020). The limited effect of mindfulness-based interventions on anxiety in children and adolescents: A meta-analysis. *Clinical Child and Family Psychology Review, 23,* 407–426. https://doi.org/10.1007/s10567-020-00319-z
Olendzki, A. (2003). Buddhist psychology. In S. Segall (Ed.), *Encountering Buddhism: Western psychology and Buddhist teachings*. State University of New York Press.
Olendzki, A. (2010). *Unlimiting mind*. Wisdom Publications.
Olivares, F. A., Vargas, E., Fuentes, C., Martínez-Pernía, D., & Canales-Johnson, A. (2015). Neurophenomenology revisited: second-person methods for the study of human consciousness. *Frontiers in Psychology, 6*. https://doi.org/10.3389/fpsyg.2015.00673/
Oman, D. (2013). Defining religion and spirituality. In R. F. Paloutzian & C. L. Park (Eds.), *Handbook of the psychology of religion and spirituality* (pp. 23–47). Guilford Press.
Oman, D. (2021). Studying the effects of meditation: The first fifty years. In M. Farias, D. Brazier, & M. Lalljee (Eds.), *The Oxford handbook of meditation* (pp. 41–75). Oxford University Press. https://doi.org/10.1093/oxfordhb/9780198808640.013.3
Oman, D., Bormann, J. E., & Kane, J. J. (2020). Mantram repetition as a portable mindfulness practice: Applications during the COVID-19 pandemic. *Mindfulness*. https://doi.org/10.1007/s12671-020-01545-w
Oman, D., Hedberg, J., & Thoresen, C. E. (2006). Passage meditation reduces perceived stress in health professionals: A randomized, controlled trial. *Journal of Consulting and Clinical Psychology, 74,* 714. https://doi.org/10.1037/0022-006X.74.4.714
Oman, D., Richards, T. A., Hedberg, J., & Thoresen, C. E. (2008). Passage meditation improves caregiving self-efficacy among health professionals: A randomized trial and qualitative assessment. *Journal of Health Psychology, 13,* 1119–1135. https://doi.org/10.1177/1359105308095966
Omar, S. H. S., Rahimah, E., Fadzli Adam, O., Mohamad, Z., & Suhaibah, O. (2017). Techniques of practicing Muraqaba by Sufis in Malay Archipelago. *International Journal of Academic Research in Business and Social Sciences, 7,* 2222–6990.

Ooi, S. L., Giovino, M., & Pak, S. C. (2017). Transcendental meditation for lowering blood pressure: An overview of systematic reviews and meta-analyses. *Complementary Therapies in Medicine, 34,* 26–34. https://doi.org/10.1016/j.ctim.2017.07.008

O'Reilly, R. C., Munakata, Y., Frank, M. J., Hazy, T. E., & Contributors. (2020). *Computational cognitive neuroscience* (4th ed.). Wiki Book. https://CompCogNeuro.org

Ornstein, R. E. (1971). The techniques of meditation and their implications for modern psychology. In C. Naranjo & R. E. Ornstein (Eds.), *On the psychology of meditation* (pp. 137–234). Viking.

Ortner, C. N., Kilner, S. J., & Zelazo, P. D. (2007). Mindfulness meditation and reduced emotional interference on a cognitive task. *Motivation and Emotion, 31,* 271–283. https://doi.org/10.1007/s11031-007-9076-7

Osho (2004). *Meditation: A first and last freedom.* St. Martin's Griffin.

Ospina, M. B., Bond, K., Karkhaneh, M., Buscemi, N., Dryden, D. M., Barnes, V., Carlson, L. E., Dusek, J. A., & Shannahoff-Khalsa, D. (2008). Clinical trials of meditation practices in health care: characteristics and quality. *Journal of Alternative and Complementary Medicine, 14*(10), 1199–1213. https://doi.org/10.1089/acm.2008.0307

Otis, L. S. (1984). Adverse effects of transcendental meditation. In D. H. Shapiro & R. N. Walsh (Eds.) *Meditation: Classic and contemporary perspectives* (pp. 201–208). Aldine.

Ott, U. (2010). *Meditation für Skeptiker: Ein Neurowissenschaftler erklärt den Weg zum Selbst.* [Meditation for sceptics: A neuroscientist explains the way to the self]. O. W. Barth.

Ott, U. (2021). *Spiritualität für Skeptiker: Wissenschaftlich fundierte Meditationen für mehr Bewusstheit im Alltag* [Spirituality for sceptics: Scientifically grounded meditations towards more awareness in daily life]. O. W. Barth.

Pa-Auk, S. (2000). *Knowing and seeing.* Buddha Dharma Education Association. http://www.buddhanet.net/pdf_file/know-see.pdf

Pagis, M. (2010). From abstract concepts to experiential knowledge: Embodying enlightenment in a meditation center. *Qualitative Sociology, 33,* 469–489. https://doi.org/10.1007/s11133-010-9169-6

Palden Drolma, L. (2019). *Love on every breath: Tonglen meditation for transforming pain into joy.* New World Library.

Panda, S., Whitworth, A., Hersh, D., & Biedermann, B. (2020). "Giving yourself some breathing room ...": An exploration of group meditation for people with aphasia. *Aphasiology.* https://doi.org/10.1080/02687038.2020.1819956

Paranjpe, A., & Rao, K. (2008). Psychology in the Advaita Vedānta. In K. Rao, A. Paranjpe, & A. Dalal (Eds.), *Handbook of Indian psychology* (pp. 253–285). Foundation Books. https://doi.org/10.1017/UPO9788175968448.014

Parasher, D. (2015). Guru-disciple relationship: An exploration into the process of spiritual growth. In K. R. Priya & A. K. Dalal (Eds.), *Qualitative research on illness, wellbeing and self-growth: Contemporary Indian perspectives* (pp. 244–262). Routledge.

Parker, R. I., Vannest, K. J., & Davis, J. L. (2011). Effect size in single-case research: A review of nine nonoverlap techniques. *Behavior Modification, 35,* 303–322. https://doi.org/10.1177/0145445511399147

Paudyal, P., Jones, C., Grindey, C., Dawood, R., & Smith, H. (2018). Meditation for asthma: systematic review and meta-analysis. *Journal of Asthma, 55,* 771–778. https://doi.org/10.1080/02770903.2017.1365887

Paul, G., Elam, B., & Verhulst, S. J. (2007). A longitudinal study of students' perceptions of using deep breathing meditation to reduce testing stresses. *Teaching and Learning in Medicine, 19,* 287–292. https://doi.org/10.1080/10401330701366754

Peng, C. K., Henry, I. C., Mietus, J. E., Hausdorff, J. M., Khalsa, G., Benson, H., & Goldberger, A. L. (2004). Heart rate dynamics during three forms of meditation. *International Journal of Cardiology, 95,* 19-27. https://doi.org/10.1016/j.ijcard.2003.02.006

Peng, C. K., Mietus, J. E., Liu, Y., Khalsa, G., Douglas, P. S., Benson, H., & Goldberger, A. L. (1999). Exaggerated heart rate oscillations during two meditation techniques. *International Journal of Cardiology, 70,* 101-107. https://doi.org/10.1016/S0167-5273(99)00066-2

Pennington, B. (2006). Centering prayer: An ancient Christian way of meditation. In J. Shear (Ed.), *The experience of meditation: Experts introduce major traditions.* (pp. 245-257). Paragon House.

Pepping, C. A., Walters, B., Davis, P. J., & O'Donovan, A. (2016). Why do people practice mindfulness? An investigation into reasons for practicing mindfulness meditation. *Mindfulness, 7,* 542-547.

Perestelo-Perez, L., Barraca, J., Peñate, W., Rivero-Santana, A., & Alvarez-Perez, Y. (2017). Mindfulness-based interventions for the treatment of depressive rumination: Systematic review and meta-analysis. *International Journal of Clinical and Health Psychology, 17,* 282-295.

Perez-De-Albeniz, A., & Holmes, J. (2000). Meditation: Concepts, effects and uses in therapy. *International Journal of Psychotherapy, 5,* 49-58. https://doi.org/10.1080/13569080050020263

Perlman, D. M., Salomons, T. V., Davidson, R. J., & Lutz, A. (2010). Differential effects on pain intensity and unpleasantness of two meditation practices. *Emotion, 10,* 65-71. https://doi.org/10.1037/a0018440

Persico, T. (2019). Judaism and meditation. In M. Farias, D. Brazier, & L. Mansur (Eds.), *The Oxford handbook of meditation.* Oxford Handbooks Online. https://doi.org/10.1093/oxfordhb/9780198808640.013.6

Petitmengin, C. (2006). Describing one's subjective experience in the second person: An interview method for the science of consciousness. *Phenomenology and the Cognitive Sciences, 5*(3), 229-269. https://doi.org/10.1007/s11097-006-9022-2

Petitmengin, C. (2011). Describing the experience of describing? The blindspot of introspection. *Journal of Consciousness Studies, 18*(1), 44-62.

Petitmengin, C., van Beek, M., Bitbol, M., & Nissou, J. M. (2017). What is it like to meditate? Methods and issues for a micro-phenomenological description of meditative experience. *Journal of Consciousness Studies, 24,* 170-198.

Phillips, S. (2009). *Yoga, karma, and rebirth: A brief history and philosophy.* Columbia University Press.

Pilla, D., Qina'au, J., Patel, A., Meddaoui, B., Watson, N., Dugad, S., & Sakin, M. (2020). Toward a framework for reporting and differentiating key features of meditation- and mindfulness-based interventions. *Mindfulness, 11,* 2613-2628.

Pinniger, R., Brown, R. F., Thorsteinsson, E. B., & McKinley, P. (2012). Argentine tango dance compared to mindfulness meditation and a waiting-list control: A randomised trial for treating depression. *Complementary Therapies in Medicine, 20,* 377-384. https://doi.org/10.1016/j.ctim.2012.07.003

Poerio, G. L., Totterdell, P., & Miles, E. (2013). Mind-wandering and negative mood: Does one thing really lead to another? *Consciousness and Cognition, 22,* 1412-1421. https://doi.org/10.1016/j.concog.2013.09.012

Poissant, H., Moreno, A., Potvin, S., & Mendrek, A. (2020). A Meta-analysis of mindfulness-based interventions in adults with attention-deficit hyperactivity disorder: Impact on ADHD symptoms, depression, and executive functioning. *Mindfulness, 11,* 2669-2681. https://doi.org/10.1007/s12671-020-01458-8

Potter, K.H. (Ed.). (1998). *The encyclopedia of Indian philosophies: Vol. 3. Advaita Vedānta up to Samkara and his pupils.* Motilal Banarsidass.

Prabhavananda, S. (2019). *Religion in practice.* Routledge. https://doi.org/10.4324/9780429052903

Premasiri, P.D. (2008). Varieties of cognition in early Buddhism. In K.R. Rao, A.C. Paranjpe, & A.K. Dalal (Eds.), *Handbook of Indian psychology* (pp. 85-104). Cambridge University Press. https://doi.org/10.1017/UPO9788175968448.006

Puligandla, R. (1997). *Fundamentals of Indian philosophy.* D.K. Printworld.

Purser, R. (2019). *McMindfulness: How mindfulness became the new capitalist spirituality.* Repeater Books.

Puta, M. (2016). *Promoting health by Sattva-Guna* [Doctoral dissertation]. Chemnitz University of Technology. http://nbn-resolving.de/urn:nbn:de:bsz:ch1-qucosa-224078 [English items available at http://selfleadershipexperts.com/wp-content/uploads/2021/04/TriGunaScales_English.pdf]

Puta, M., & Sedlmeier, P. (2014). The concept of tri-guna: A working model. In S. Schmidt & H. Walach (Eds.), *Meditation: Neuroscientific approaches and philosophical implications* (pp. 317-364). Springer.

Quaglia, J.T., Braun, S.E., Freeman, S.P., McDaniel, M.A., & Brown, K.W. (2016). Meta-analytic evidence for effects of mindfulness training on dimensions of self-reported dispositional mindfulness. *Psychological Assessment, 28,* 803-818. https://doi.org/10.1037/pas0000268

Radin, D. (2013). *Supernormal: Science, Yoga, and the evidence for extraordinary psychic abilities.* Deepak Chopra Books.

Raffone, A., & Srinivasan, N. (2017). Mindfulness and cognitive functions: Toward a unifying neurocognitive framework. *Mindfulness, 8,* 1-9. https://doi.org/10.1007/s12671-016-0654-1

Rahula, W. (1959). *What the Buddha taught.* Grove Press.

Raina, M.K. (2002). Guru-shishya relationship in Indian culture: The possibility of a creative resilient framework. *Psychology and Developing Societies, 14,* 167-198. https://doi.org/10.1177/097133360201400109

Raju, P.T. (1985). *Structural depths of Indian thought.* South Asian.

Ramkrishna Das, S. (2003). *Nama-japa in the Yoga of Transformation.* Sri Aurobindo Ashram.

Rana, A.S. (2021). *Top 10 benefits of meditation for prosperous life.* https://www.itsarun.com/2021/10/Top-10-Benefits-of-Meditation-for-Prosperous-Life.html

Ranganathan, S. (2008). *Patañjali's Yoga Sutrā.* Penguin Books India.

Rao, K.R., & Paranjpe, A.C. (2008). Yoga psychology: Theory and application. In K.R. Rao, A.C. Paranjpe, & A.K. Dalal (Eds.), *Handbook of Indian psychology* (pp. 186-216). Foundation Books. https://doi.org/10.1017/UPO9788175968448.011

Rao, K.R., & Paranjpe, A.C. (2016). *Psychology in the Indian tradition.* Springer India. https://doi.org/10.1007/978-81-322-2440-2

Rapgay, L. (2019). Mindfulness and memory in early Buddhism: A response to Ven. Anālayo. *Mindfulness, 10,* 590-591. https://doi.org/10.1007/s12671-018-1033-x

Raudenbush, S.W., & Bryk, A.S. (2002). *Hierarchical linear models. Applications and data analysis methods* (2nd ed.). Sage.

Reangsing, C., Rittiwong, T., & Schneider, J. K. (2021). Effects of mindfulness meditation interventions on depression in older adults: A meta-analysis. *Aging & Mental Health, 25*, 1181-1190. https://doi.org/10.1080/13607863.2020.1793901

Red Pine. (2004). *The heart sutra: The womb of buddhas.* Shoemaker & Hoard.

Ricard, M. (2011). *The art of meditation.* Atlantic Books.

Ridderinkhof, A., de Bruin, E. I., Brummelman, E., & Bögels, S. M. (2017). Does mindfulness meditation increase empathy? An experiment. *Self and Identity, 16*, 251-269.

Roca, P., Vazquez, C., Diez, G., Brito-Pons, G., & McNally, R. J. (2021). Not all types of meditation are the same: Mediators of change in mindfulness and compassion meditation interventions. *Journal of Affective Disorders, 283*, 354-362. https://doi.org/10.1016/j.jad.2021.01.070

Rodarmor, W. (n.d.). *The secret life of Swami Muktananda.* http://www.leavingsiddhayoga.net/secret.htm

Rogers, J. M., Ferrari, M., Mosely, K., Lang, C. P., & Brennan, L. (2017). Mindfulness-based interventions for adults who are overweight or obese: A meta-analysis of physical and psychological health outcomes. *Obesity Reviews, 18*, 51-67. https://doi.org/10.1111/obr.12461

Rogers, H. R., Shires, A. G., & Cayoun, B. A. (2021). Development and validation of the equanimity Scale-16. *Mindfulness, 12*, 107-120. https://doi.org/10.1007/s12671-020-01503-6

Rose, S., Zell, E., & Strickhouser, J. E. (2020). The effect of meditation on health: A meta-synthesis of randomized controlled trials. *Mindfulness, 11*, 507-516. https://doi.org/10.1007/s12671-019-01277-6

Roth, H. (2015). Daoist apophatic meditation: Selections from the classical Daoist textual corpus. In L. Komjathy (Ed.), *Contemplative literature* (pp. 89-143). State University of New York Press.

Rusch, H. L., Rosario, M., Levison, L. M., Olivera, A., Livingston, W. S., Wu, T., & Gill, J. M. (2019). The effect of mindfulness meditation on sleep quality: A systematic review and meta-analysis of randomized controlled trials. *Annals of the New York Academy of Sciences, 1445*, 5-16. https://doi.org/10.1111/nyas.13996

Ryle, G. (2009). *The concept of mind.* Routledge. (Original work published 1949 by Hutchinson) https://doi.org/10.4324/9780203875858

Sabe, M., Sentissi, O., & Kaiser, S. (2019). Meditation-based mind-body therapies for negative symptoms of schizophrenia: Systematic review of randomized controlled trials and meta-analysis. *Schizophrenia Research, 212*, 15-25. https://doi.org/10.1016/j.schres.2019.07.030

Salmon, D. (2006). The practice of meditation in the integral yoga of Sri Aurobindo and the Mother. In J. Shear (Ed.), *The experience of meditation: Experts introduce major traditions.* (pp. 171-199). Paragon House.

Samy, A. M. A. (2002). *Zen heart, Zen mind.* Cre-A.

Samy, A. M. A. (2005). *Zen: Awakening to your original face.* Cre-A.

Samy, A. M. A. (2013). *Zen: The wayless way.* Bodhi Zendo.

Santorelli, S. F., Meleo-Meyer, F., Koerbel, L., & Kabat-Zinn, J. (2017). *Mindfulness-based stress reduction (MBSR) authorized curriculum guide.* Center for Mindfulness in Medicine, Health Care, and Society (CFM), University of Massachusetts Medical School.

Sapolsky, R. (2017). *Behave: The biology of humans at our best and worst.* Vintage.

Sarbacker, S. R. (2012). Power and meaning in the Yogasūtra of Pantañjali. In K. A. Jacobsen (Ed.), *Yoga powers: Extraordinary capacities attained through meditation and concentration* (pp. 195–222). Brill.

Sauer, S., Walach, H., Schmidt, S., Hinterberger, T., Lynch, S., Büssing, A., & Kohls, N. (2013). Assessment of mindfulness: Review on state of the art. *Mindfulness, 4,* 3–17.

Sauer-Zavala, S. E., Walsh, E. C., Eisenlohr-Moul, T. A., & Lykins, E. L. (2013). Comparing mindfulness-based intervention strategies: Differential effects of sitting meditation, body scan, and mindful yoga. *Mindfulness, 4,* 383–388. https://doi.org/10.1007/s12671-012-0139-9

Salzberg, S. (1995). *Loving-kindness: The revolutionary art of happiness.* Shambhala.

Schäfer, T., & Schwarz, M. A. (2019). The meaningfulness of effect sizes in psychological research: Differences between sub-disciplines and the impact of potential biases. *Frontiers in Psychology, 10,* 813. https://doi.org/10.3389/fpsyg.2019.00813

Schimmel, A. (2003). *Rumi: Ich bin Wind und du bist Feuer: Leben und Werk des großen Mystikers.* [Rumi: I am wind and you are fire: Life and work of the great mystic]. Hugendubel.

Schimmel, A. (2014). *Sufismus: Eine Einführung in die islamische Mystik* (5th ed.). [Sufism: An introduction into Islamic mysticism]. C. H. Beck.

Schlosser, M., Sparby, T., Voros, S., Jones, R., & Marchant, N. L. (2019). Unpleasant meditation-related experiences in regular meditators: Prevalence, predictors, and conceptual considerations. *PLoS One, 14*(5): e0216643.

Schmidt, S. (2011). Mindfulness in East and West – is it the same? In H. Walach, S. Schmidt, & W. B. Jonas (Eds.), *Neuroscience, consciousness and spirituality* (pp. 23–38). Springer. https://doi.org/10.1007/978-94-007-2079-4_2

Schmidt, S. (2014). Opening up meditation for science: The development of a meditation classification system. In S. Schmidt & H. Walach (Eds.), *Meditation: Neuroscientific approaches and philosophical implications* (p. 137–152). Springer.

Schumer, M. C., Lindsay, E. K., & Creswell, J. D. (2018). Brief mindfulness training for negative affectivity: A systematic review and meta-analysis. *Journal of Consulting and Clinical Psychology, 86,* 569–583. https://doi.org/10.1037/ccp0000324

Schutte, N. S., Malouff, J. M., & Keng, S. L. (2020). Meditation and telomere length: A meta-analysis. *Psychology & Health, 35*(8), 901–915. https://doi.org/10.1080/08870446.2019.1707827

Scott-Sheldon, L. A., Gathright, E. C., Donahue, M. L., Balletto, B., Feulner, M. M., DeCosta, J., Cruess, D. G., Wing, R. R., Carey, M. P., & Salmoirago-Blotcher, E. (2020). Mindfulness-based interventions for adults with cardiovascular disease: A systematic review and meta-analysis. *Annals of Behavioral Medicine, 54,* 67–73. https://doi.org/10.1093/abm/kaz020

Sedlmeier, P. (2014). Indian psychology and the scientific method. In R. M. M. Cornelissen, G. Misra, & S. Varma (Eds.), *Foundations and applications of Indian psychology* (pp. 53–79). Pearson.

Sedlmeier, P. (2018). Meditation and altered states of consciousness. *Journal of Consciousness Studies, 25,* 73–191.

Sedlmeier, P., Eberth, J., & Puta, M. (2016). Meditation: Future research and theory. In M. A. West (Ed.), *The psychology of meditation: Research and practice* (2nd ed.; pp. 285–310). Oxford University Press.

Sedlmeier, P., Eberth, J., & Schwarz, M. (2014). Meta-analyses and other methodological issues in meditation research: Reply to Orme-Johnson and Dillbeck (2014). *Psychological Bulletin, 140,* 617–622. https://doi.org/10.1037/a0035896

Sedlmeier, P., Eberth, J., Schwarz, M., Zimmermann, D., Haarig, F., Jaeger, S., & Kunze, S. (2012). The psychological effects of meditation: A meta-analysis. *Psychological Bulletin, 138,* 1139–1171. https://doi.org/10.1037/a0028168

Sedlmeier, P., Loße, C., & Quasten, L. C. (2018). Psychological effects of meditation for healthy practitioners: An update. *Mindfulness, 9,* 371–387.

Sedlmeier, P., & Renkewitz, F. (2018). *Forschungsmethoden und Statistik: Ein Lehrbuch für Psychologen und Sozialwissenschaftler* [Research methods and statistics: A textbook for psychologists and social scientists] (3rd rev. ed.). Pearson.

Sedlmeier, P., & Srinivas, K. (2016). How do theories of cognition and consciousness in ancient Indian thought systems relate to current Western theorizing and research? *Frontiers in Psychology, 7,* 343. https://doi.org/10.3389/fpsyg.2016.00343

Sedlmeier, P., & Srinivas, K. (2019). Psychological theories of meditation in early Buddhism and Sāṃkhya/Yoga. In M. Farias, D. Brazier, & L. Mansur (Eds.), *The Oxford handbook of meditation.* Oxford Handbooks Online. https://doi.org/10.1093/oxfordhb/9780198808640.013.27

Sedlmeier, P., & Theumer, J. (2020). Why do people begin to meditate and why do they continue? *Mindfulness, 11,* 1527–1545. https://doi.org/10.1007/s12671-020-01367-w

Sedlmeier, P., Winkler, I., & Lukina, A. (2020). How long did the time spent in meditation feel? "Attention. Attention. Attention." *Psychology of Consciousness: Theory, Research, and Practice.* Advance online publication. https://doi.org/10.1037/cns0000254

Segal, Z. V., Williams, J. M. G., & Teasdale, J. D. (2002). *Mindfulness based cognitive therapy for depression: A new approach to preventing relapse.* Guilford.

Segal, Z. V., Williams, J. M. G., & Teasdale, J. D. (2013). *Mindfulness-based cognitive therapy for depression* (2nd ed). Guilford Press.

Sekida, K. (2005). *Two Zen classics: The gateless gate and the blue cliff records.* Shambala.

Seppälä, E. M., Nitschke, J. B., Tudorascu, D. L., Hayes, A., Goldstein, M. R., Nguyen, D. T., Perlman, D., & Davidson, R. J. (2014). Breathing-based meditation decreases posttraumatic stress disorder symptoms in US Military veterans: A randomized controlled longitudinal study. *Journal of Traumatic Stress, 27,* 397–405.

Shapero, B. G., Greenberg, J., Pedrelli, P., de Jong, M., & Desbordes, G. (2018). Mindfulness-based interventions in psychiatry. *Focus, 16,* 32–39. https://doi.org/10.1176/appi.focus.20170039

Shapiro, D. H., Jr. (1984). Overview: Clinical and physiological comparison of meditation with other self- control strategies." In D. H. Shapiro, Jr., & R. N. Walsh (Eds.), *Meditation: Classic and contemporary perspectives* (pp. 5–12). Aldine.

Shapiro, D. H., Jr. (1992a). A preliminary study of long-term meditators: Goals, effects, religious orientation, cognitions. *Journal of Transpersonal Psychology, 24,* 23–39.

Shapiro, D. H., Jr. (1992b). Adverse effects of meditation: A preliminary investigation of long-term meditators. *International Journal of Psychosomatics, 39,* 62–67.

Shapiro, S. L., Walsh, R., & Britton, W. B. (2003). An analysis of recent meditation research and suggestions for future directions. *Journal for Meditation and Meditation Research, 3,* 69–90. https://doi.org/10.1080/08873267.2003.9986927

Shankman, R. (2008). *The experience of samādhi: An in-depth exploration of Buddhist meditation.* Shambala.

Sharf, R. H. (1995). Sanbōkyōdan: Zen and the way of the new religion. *Japanese Journal of Religious Studies, 22,* 417–458. https://doi.org/10.18874/jjrs.22.3-4.1995.417-458

Sharf, R. (2014). Mindfulness and mindlessness in early Chan. *Philosophy East and West, 64,* 933–964. https://doi.org/10.1353/pew.2014.0074

Sharma, C. (2003). *A critical survey of Indian philosophy.* Motilal Banarsidass. (Original work published 1960)

Shaw, D. (2003). Traumatic abuse in cults: A psychoanalytic perspective. *Cultic Studies Review, 2,* 101–131.

Shaw, S. (2006). *Buddhist meditation: An anthology of texts from the Pali canon.* Routledge.

Shear, J. (Ed.). (2006). *The experience of meditation: Experts introduce major traditions.* Paragon House.

Sheng-Yen. (2002). *Illuminating silence: The practice of Chinese Zen.* Watkins.

Sheng-Yen. (2006). *Dharma drum: The life and heart of Chan practice.* Shambala.

Sherman, S. M., & Grange, J. A. (2020). Exploring the impact of mindfulness on false-memory susceptibility. *Psychological Science, 31,* 968–977. https://doi.org/10.1177/0956797620929302

Shi, L., Zhang, D., Wang, L., Zhuang, J., Cook, R., & Chen, L. (2017). Meditation and blood pressure: A meta-analysis of randomized clinical trials. *Journal of Hypertension, 35,* 696–706. https://doi.org/10.1097/HJH.0000000000001217

Shonin, E., Van Gordon, W., & Griffiths, M. D. (2014a). Do mindfulness-based therapies have a role in the treatment of psychosis? *Australian & New Zealand Journal of Psychiatry, 48,* 124–127. https://doi.org/10.1177/0004867413512688

Shonin, E., Van Gordon, W., & Griffiths, M. D. (2014b). Cognitive behavioral therapy (CBT) and Meditation Awareness Training (MAT) for the treatment of co-occurring schizophrenia and pathological gambling: A case study. *International Journal of Mental Health and Addiction, 12,* 181–196. https://doi.org/10.1007/s11469-013-9460-3

Shonin, E., Van Gordon, W., & Singh, N. N. (Eds.). (2015). *Buddhist foundations of mindfulness.* Springer. https://doi.org/10.1007/978-3-319-18591-0

Simpson, D. (2021). *The truth of yoga: A comprehensive guide to yoga's history, texts, philosophy, and practices.* North Point Press.

Simpson, R., Simpson, S., Ramparsad, N., Lawrence, M., Booth, J., & Mercer, S. W. (2020). Effects of mindfulness-based interventions on physical symptoms in people with multiple sclerosis – a systematic review and meta-analysis. *Multiple Sclerosis and Related Disorders, 38.* https://doi.org/10.1016/j.msard.2019.101493

Singer, T., & Engert, V. (2019). It matters what you practice: Differential training effects on subjective experience, behavior, brain and body in the ReSource Project. *Current Opinion in Psychology, 28,* 151–158. https://doi.org/10.1016/j.copsyc.2018.12.005

Singh, N. N., Lancioni, F. E., Singh, A. D. A., Winton, A. S. W., Singh, A. N. A., & Singh, J. (2011). Adolescents with Asperger syndrome can use a mindfulness-based strategy to control their aggressive behavior. *Research in Autism Spectrum Disorders, 5,* 1103–1109. https://doi.org/10.1016/j.rasd.2010.12.006

Singh, S. K., & Gorey, K. M. (2018). Relative effectiveness of mindfulness and cognitive behavioral interventions for anxiety disorders: Meta-analytic review. *Social Work in Mental Health, 16,* 238–251. https://doi.org/10.1080/15332985.2017.1373266

Singh, U. (2008). *A history of ancient and early medieval India: From the Stone Age to the 12th century.* Pearson Education India.

Sivananda, S. (1945). *Concentration & meditation.* The Divine Life Society.

Slagter, H. A., Davidson, R. J., & Lutz, A. (2011). Mental training as a tool in the neuroscientific study of brain and cognitive plasticity. *Frontiers in Human Neuroscience, 5*, 17. https://doi.org/10.3389/fnhum.2011.00017

Smallwood, J., & Andrews-Hanna, J. (2013). Not all minds that wander are lost: The importance of a balanced perspective on the mind-wandering state. *Frontiers in Psychology, 4*. https://doi.org/10.3389/fpsyg.2013.00441

Smith, J. A. (2003). *Qualitative psychology: A practical guide to research methods*. Sage.

Smith, J. E. H. (2019). *Irrationality: A history of the dark side of reason*. Princeton University Press.

Smith, E. E., & Kosslyn, S. M. (2007). *Cognitive psychology: Mind and brain*. Pearson.

Solé-Leris, A. (1986). *Tranquility and insight: An introduction to the oldest form of Buddhist meditation*. Shambhala.

Soma, T. (1994). *Kalama Sutta: The Buddha's charter of free inquiry*. https://accesstoinsight.org/lib/authors/soma/wheel008.html

Sparby, T., & Ott, U. (2018). A qualitative study of motivations for meditation in anthroposophic practitioners. *PLoS One, 13*(9). https://doi.org/10.1371/journal.pone.0203184

Speck, B. W. (2005). What is spirituality? *New Directions for Teaching and Learning, 104*, 3-13. https://doi.org/10.1002/tl.207

Spijkerman, M., Pots, W., & Bohlmeijer, E. (2016). Effectiveness of online mindfulness-based interventions in improving mental health: A review and meta-analysis of randomized controlled trials. *Clinical Psychology Review, 45*, 102-114. https://doi.org/10.1016/j.cpr.2016.03.009

Spivey, M. (2007). *The continuity of mind*. Oxford University Press.

Staal, F. (1986). The sound of religion. *Numen, 33*(Fasc. 2), 185–224. https://doi.org/10.1163/156852786X00011

Stahl, B., & Goldstein, E. (2019). *A mindfulness-base stress reduction workbook*. New Harbinger Publications.

Starkweather, A. R., Alhaeeri, A. A., Montpetit, A., Brumelle, J., Filler, K., Montpetit, M., Mohnaraj, L., Lyon, D. E., & Jackson-Cook, C. K. (2014). An integrative review of factors associated with telomere length and implications for biobehavioral research. *Nursing Research, 63*, 36-50. https://doi.org/10.1097/NNR.0000000000000009

Stevenson, I. (2006). Half a career with the paranormal. *Journal of Scientific Exploration, 20*, 13-21.

Stone, M. H. (2000). Normal narcissism: An etiological and ethological perspective. In E. F. Ronningstam (Ed.), *Disorders of narcissism* (pp. 7-28). Jason Aronson.

Sumedho, A. (1995). *The mind and the way: Buddhist reflections on life*. Wisdom Publications.

Sumedho, A., & Amaro, A. (2007). *The sound of silence: The selected teachings of Ajahn Sumedho*. Wisdom Publications.

Suzuki, S. (1975). *Zen-Geist, Anfänger-Geist: Unterweisungen in Zen-Meditation* [Zen mind, beginner's mind: Instructions in Zen meditation]. Theseus.

Takano, K., & Tanno, Y. (2011). Diurnal variation in rumination. *Emotion, 11*, 1046-1058. https://doi.org/10.1037/a0022757

Tanahashi, K. (2014). *The heart sutra: A comprehensive guide to the classic of Mahayana Buddhism*. Shambala.

Tanay, G., & Bernstein, A. (2013). State Mindfulness Scale (SMS): Development and initial validation. *Psychological Assessment, 25*, 1286. https://doi.org/10.1037/a0034044

Tang, R., & Braver, T. (2020). Predicting individual preferences in mindfulness techniques using personality traits. *Frontiers in Psychology, 11.* https://doi.org/10.3389/fpsyg.2020.01163

Tang, Y.-Y., Hölzel, B. K., & Posner, M. I. (2015). The neuroscience of mindfulness meditation. *Nature Reviews Neuroscience, 16,* 213–225.

Tanner, M. A., Travis, F., Gaylord-King, C., Haaga, D. A. F., Grosswald, S., & Schneider, R. H. (2009). The effects of the transcendental meditation program on mindfulness. *Journal of Clinical Psychology, 65,* 574–589. https://doi.org/10.1002/jclp.20544

Teresa of Avila. (1904). *The life of St. Teresa of Jesus* (3rd ed.; D. Lewis, Trans.; from the Spanish). Thomas Baker. https://www.catholicspiritualdirection.org/lifeofteresa.pdf

Thanissaro, B. (2004). *Sanditthika Sutta: Visible here-&-now.* https://www.accesstoinsight.org/tipitaka/an/an06/an06.047.than.html [retrieved April 29, 2021]

Thanissaro, B. (2006). *Anapanasati sutta: Mindfulness of breathing.* https://www.accesstoinsight.org/tipitaka/mn/mn.118.than.html

Thanissaro, B. (2011). *Into the stream: A study guide on the first stage of awakening.* https://accesstoinsight.org/lib/study/into_the_stream.pdf

Thompson, B. L., & Waltz, J. (2007). Everyday mindfulness and mindfulness meditation: overlapping constructs or not? *Personality and Individual Differences, 43,* 1875–1885. https://doi.org/10.1016/j.paid.2007.06.017

Thupten, J. (2019). The question of mindfulness' connection with ethics and compassion. *Current Opinion in Psychology, 28,* 71–75. https://doi.org/10.1016/j.copsyc.2018.10.016

Tomasino, B., Chiesa, A., & Fabbro, F. (2014). Disentangling the neural mechanisms involved in Hinduism-and Buddhism-related meditations. *Brain and Cognition, 90,* 32–40. https://doi.org/10.1016/j.bandc.2014.03.013

Trautwein, F. M., Kanske, P., Böckler, A., & Singer, T. (2020). Differential benefits of mental training types for attention, compassion, and theory of mind. *Cognition, 194.* https://doi.org/10.1016/j.cognition.2019.104039

Travis, F. (2020). Temporal and spatial characteristics of meditation EEG. *Psychological Trauma: Theory, Research, Practice, and Policy, 12,* 111–115. https://doi.org/10.1037/tra0000488

Travis, F., & Shear, J. (2010). Focused attention, open monitoring and automatic self-transcending: Categories to organize meditations from Vedic, Buddhist and Chinese traditions. *Consciousness and Cognition, 19,* 1110–1118. https://doi.org/10.1016/j.concog.2010.01.007

Treleaven, D. A. (2018). *Trauma-sensitive mindfulness.* W. W. Norton.

Treves, I. N., Tello, L. Y., Davidson, R. J., & Goldberg, S. B. (2019). The relationship between mindfulness and objective measures of body awareness: A meta-analysis. *Scientific Reports, 9,* 1–12. https://doi.org/10.1038/s41598-019-53978-6

Tromge, J. (1995). *Ngondro commentary: Instructions for the concise preliminary practices of the New Treasure of Dudjom/compiled from the teachings of His Eminence Chagdud Tulku.* Padma.

Tsoknyi, R. (2013). *Talk.* Mind and Life Summer Research Institute – Mapping the Mind, Garrison, NY, USA.

Tsong-Kha-pa. (2000). *The great treatise on the stages of the path to enlightenment* (Vol. 1). J. Cutler & G. Newland (Eds.). Snow Lion Publications.

Trungpa, C. (2002). *Cutting through spiritual materialism.* Shambhala.

Turgon, R., Ruffault, A., Juneau, C., Blatier, C., & Shankland, R. (2019). Eating disorder treatment: A systematic review and meta-analysis of the efficacy of mindfulness-based programs. *Mindfulness, 10,* 2225–2244. https://doi.org/10.1007/s12671-019-01216-5

Turkeltaub, P. E., Eden, G. F., Jones, K. M., & Zeffiro, T. A. (2002). Meta-analysis of the functional neuroanatomy of single-word reading: Method and validation. *Neuroimage, 16,* 765–780. https://doi.org/10.1006/nimg.2002.1131

Uchiyama, K. (2004). The tenzo Kyokun and shikantaza. In J. D. Loori (Ed.), *The art of just sitting: Essential writings on the Zen practice of Shikantaza* (2nd ed.) [eBook]. Wisdom Publications.

Ulrichsen, K. M., Kaufmann, T., Dørum, E. S., Kolskår, K. K., Richard, G., Alnæs, D., Arneberg, T. J., Westlye, L. R., & Nordvik, J. E. (2016). Clinical utility of mindfulness training in the treatment of fatigue after stroke, traumatic brain injury and multiple sclerosis: A systematic literature review and meta-analysis. *Frontiers in Psychology, 7.* https://doi.org/10.3389/fpsyg.2016.00912

Unno, T. (2002). Jesus prayer and the Nembutsu. *Buddhist-Christian Studies, 22,* 93–99. https://doi.org/10.1353/bcs.2002.0032

Upadhaya, K. N. (1968). The impact of early Buddhism on Hindu thought (with special reference to the Bhagavadgita). *Philosophy East and West, 18,* 163–173. https://doi.org/10.2307/1398258

Upatissa, A. (1961). *The path of freedom (Vimuttimagga) of Arahand Upatissa* (translated from the Chinese by Rev. N. R. M. Ehara, Soma Thera, Kheminda Thera). Buddhist Publication Society.

Upton, C. L., & Brent, M. (2019). Meditation and the scope of mental action. *Philosophical Psychology, 32*(1), 52–71. https://doi.org/10.1080/09515089.2018.1514491

Utterback, K. T. (2013). Teaching medieval Christian contemplation: An ethical dilemma? *Buddhist-Christian Studies, 33,* 53–61. https://doi.org/10.1353/bcs.2013.0010

Vago, D. R., Gupta, R. S., & Lazar, S. W. (2019). Measuring cognitive outcomes in mindfulness-based intervention research: A reflection on confounding factors and methodological limitations. *Current Opinion in Psychology, 28,* 143–150. https://doi.org/10.1016/j.copsyc.2018.12.015

Vago, D. R., & Silbersweig, D. A. (2012). Self-awareness, self-regulation, and self-transcendence (S-ART): A framework for understanding the neurobiological mechanisms of mindfulness. *Frontiers in Human Neuroscience, 6,* 296. https://doi.org/10.3389/fnhum.2012.00296

Valentine, E. R., & Sweet, P. L. (1999). Meditation and attention: A comparison of the effects of concentrative and mindfulness meditation on sustained attention. *Mental Health, Religion & Culture, 2,* 59–70. https://doi.org/10.1080/13674679908406332

van Dam, N. T., Brown, A., Mole, T. B., Davis, J. H., Britton, W. B., & Brewer, J. A. (2015). Development and validation of the Behavioral Tendencies Questionnaire. *PLoS One, 10*(11), e0140867. https://doi.org/10.1371/journal.pone.0140867

van Dam, N. T., Hobkirk, A. L., Danoff-Burg, S., & Earleywine, M. (2012). Mind your words: Positive and negative items create method effects on the Five Facet Mindfulness Questionnaire. *Assessment, 19,* 198–204. https://doi.org/10.1177/1073191112438743

van Dam, N. T., van Vugt, M. K., Vago, D. R., Schmalzl, L., Saron, C. D., Olendzki, A., Meissner, T., Lazar, S. W., Kerr, C. E., Gorchow, J., Fox, K. C. R., Field, B. R., Britton, W. B., Brefczynski-Lewis, J. A. & Meyer, D. E. (2018). Mind the hype: A critical evaluation and prescriptive agenda for research on mindfulness and meditation. *Perspectives on Psychological Science, 13,* 36–61.

Vandana, Sr. (1992). *Nama Japa – Das Gebet des Namens in Hinduismus und Christentum. Praktische Anleitung, Ursprünge und Traditionen.* [Nama japa – the prayer of names in Hinduism and Christianity. Practical instructions, origins and traditions.] Matthias-Grünewald-Verlag.

van Gordon, W., & Shonin, E. (2020). Second-generation mindfulness-based interventions: Toward more authentic mindfulness practice and teaching. *Mindfulness, 11,* 1–4. https://doi.org/10.1007/s12671-019-01252-1

van Oosterwijk, R. C. (2012). *Doctrinal backgrounds of Vipassanā-meditation: Insight in current methods and according to canonical sources.* Barkhuis.

van Vugt, M., Moye, A., & Sivakumar, S. (2019). Computational modelling approaches to meditation research: Why should we care? *Current Opinion in Psychology, 28,* 49–53. https://doi.org/10.1016/j.copsyc.2018.10.011

Varela, F. J., & Shear, J. (1999). First-person methodologies: What, why, how? *Journal of Consciousness Studies, 6,* 1–14.

Vaughan-Lee, L. (2006). The Sufi meditation of the heart. In J. Shear (Ed.), *The experience of meditation: Experts introduce major traditions.* (pp. 223–244). Paragon House.

Veehof, M. M., Trompetter, H. R., Bohlmeijer, E. T., & Schreurs, K. M. G. (2016). Acceptance- and mindfulness-based interventions for the treatment of chronic pain: A meta-analytic review. *Cognitive Behaviour Therapy, 45,* 5–31. https://doi.org/10.1080/16506073.2015.1098724

Venditti, S., Verdone, L., Reale, A., Vetriani, V., Caserta, M., & Zampieri, M. (2020). Molecules of silence: Effects of meditation on gene expression and epigenetics. *Frontiers in Psychology, 11.* https://doi.org/10.3389/fpsyg.2020.01767

Verdonk, C., Trousselard, M., Canini, F., Vialatte, F., & Ramdani, C. (2020). Toward a refined mindfulness model related to consciousness and based on ERP. *Perspectives on Psychological Science, 25,* 1095–1112. https://doi.org/10.1177/1745691620906444

Victoria, B. (2020). Meditation to kill and be killed by: The use of samādhi power in imperial Japan. In M. Farias, D. Brazier, & L. Mansur (Eds.), *The Oxford handbook of meditation.* Oxford Handbooks Online. https://doi.org/10.1093/oxfordhb/9780198808640.013.42

Villemure, C., Čeko, M., Cotton, V. A., & Bushnell, M. C. (2015). Neuroprotective effects of yoga practice: Age-, experience-, and frequency-dependent plasticity. *Frontiers in Human Neuroscience, 9,* 281. https://doi.org/10.3389/fnhum.2015.00281

Vishnu-Devananda, S. (1995). *Meditation and mantras.* Motilal Banarsidass.

Visted, E., Vollestad, J., Nielsen, M., & Nielsen, G. (2015). The impact of group-based mindfulness training on self-reported mindfulness: A systematic review and meta-analysis. *Mindfulness, 6,* 501–522. https://doi.org/10.1007/s12671-014-0283-5

Vonk, R., & Visser, A. (2020). An exploration of spiritual superiority: The paradox of self-enhancement. *European Journal of Social Psychology.* Advance online publication. https://doi.org/10.1002/ejsp.2721

Vul, E., Harris, C., Winkielman, P., & Pashler, H. (2009). Puzzlingly high correlations in fMRI studies of emotion, personality, and social cognition. *Perspectives on Psychological Science, 4,* 274–290. https://doi.org/10.1111/j.1745-6924.2009.01125.x

Vul, E., & Pashler, H. (2012). Voodoo and circularity errors. *Neuroimage, 62,* 945–948. https://doi.org/10.1016/j.neuroimage.2012.01.027

Waaijman, K. (2007). What is spirituality? *Acta Theologica, 27,* 1–18. https://doi.org/10.4314/actat.v27i2.52309

Wachholtz, A. B., Malone, C. D., & Pargament, K. I. (2017). Effect of different meditation types on migraine headache medication use. *Behavioral Medicine, 43,* 1–8. https://doi.org/10.1080/08964289.2015.1024601

Wachholtz, A. B., & Pargament, K. I. (2005). Is spirituality a critical ingredient of meditation? Comparing the effects of spiritual meditation, secular meditation, and relaxation on spiritual, psychological, cardiac, and pain outcomes. *Journal of Behavioral Medicine, 28,* 369–384. https://doi.org/10.1007/s10865-005-9008-5

Wachholtz, A. B., & Pargament, K. I. (2008). Migraines and meditation: Does spirituality matter? *Journal of Behavioral Medicine, 31*(4), 351–366. https://doi.org/10.1007/s10865-008-9159-2

Walach, H. (2008). Narcissism – The shadow of transpersonal psychology. *Transpersonal Psychology Review, 12,* 47–59.

Walach, H. (2011). Neuroscience, consciouness, spirituality – questions, problems and potential solutions: An introductory essay. In H. Walach, S. Schmidt, & W. B. Jonas (Eds.), *Neuroscience, consciousness and spirituality* (pp. 1–21). Springer. https://doi.org/10.1007/978-94-007-2079-4_1

Waldron, W. S. (2019). Mindfulness and Indian Buddhist conceptions of unconscious processes. *Current Opinion in Psychology, 28,* 28–31. https://doi.org/10.1016/j.copsyc.2018.09.012

Wallace, B. A. (2006). *The attention revolution: Unlocking the power of the focused mind.* Wisdom Publications.

Wallace, R. K., Benson, H., & Wilson, A. F. (1971). A wakeful hypometabolic physiologic state. *American Journal of Physiology, 221,* 795–799. https://doi.org/10.1152/ajplegacy.1971.221.3.795

Wang, F., Lee, O. E. K., Feng, F., Vitiello, M. V., Wang, W., Benson, H., Fricchione, G. L., & Denninger, J. W. (2016). The effect of meditative movement on sleep quality: A systematic review. *Sleep Medicine Reviews, 30,* 43–52. https://doi.org/10.1016/j.smrv.2015.12.001

Wang, Y. Y., Li, X. H., Zheng, W., Xu, Z. Y., Ng, C. H., Ungvari, G. S., Yuan, Z., & Xiang, Y. T. (2018). Mindfulness-based interventions for major depressive disorder: A comprehensive meta-analysis of randomized controlled trials. *Journal of Affective Disorders, 229,* 429–436. https://doi.org/10.1016/j.jad.2017.12.093

Weber, A. M. (2015a). *Quick overview of Satipaṭṭhāna channels.* Talk given at the Forest Refuge, Insight Meditation Society, Barre, MA, June 25, 2015. https://dharmaseed.org/teacher/360/talk/27954/

Weber, A. M. (2015b). *4 Satipaṭṭhāna channels as a map of experience – identifying them in our experience.* Talk given at the Forest Refuge, Insight Meditation Society, Barre, MA, July 1, 2015. https://dharmaseed.org/teacher/360/talk/28040/

Weber, A. M. (2017). *Re-contextualising mindfulness.* Talk given at the Retreat Center, Insight Meditation Society, Barre, MA, January 9, 2017. https://dharmaseed.org/teacher/360/talk/38676/

Weber, M., Schnorr, T., Morat, M., Morat, T., & Donath, L. (2020). Effects of mind-body interventions involving meditative movements on quality of life, depressive symptoms, fear of falling and sleep quality in older adults: A systematic review with meta-analysis. *International Journal of Environmental Research and Public Health, 17,* 6556. https://doi.org/10.3390/ijerph17186556

Weng, H. Y., Lewis-Peacock, J. A., Hecht, F. M., Uncapher, M. R., Ziegler, D. A., Farb, N. A., Goldman, V., Skinner, S., Duncan, L. G. Chao, M. T., & Gazzaley, A. (2020). Focus on the breath: Brain decoding reveals internal states of attention during meditation. *Frontiers in Human Neuroscience, 14.* https://doi.org/10.3389/fnhum.2020.00336

Werner, C. M., Hecksteden, A., Morsch, A., Zundler, J., Wegmann, M., Kratzsch, J., Thiery, J., Hohl, M., Bittenbring, J. R., Neumann, F., Böhm, M., Meyer, T., & Laufs, U. (2019). Differential effects of endurance, interval, and resistance training on telomerase activity and telomere length in a randomized, controlled study. *European Heart Journal, 40,* 34–46.

West, B. A. (2009). *Encyclopedia of the peoples of Asia and Oceania.* Infobase.

West, M. A. (1980). Meditation and the EEG. *Psychological Medicine, 10,* 369–375. https://doi.org/10.1017/S0033291700044147

West, M. A. (Ed.). (2016). *The psychology of meditation: research and practice.* Oxford University Press. https://doi.org/10.1093/med:psych/9780199688906.001.0001

Whicher, I. (1998). *The integrity of the Yoga Darsana: A reconsideration of classical yoga.* SUNY Press.

Whitaker, J. S., & Smith, D. (2018). Ethics, meditation, and wisdom. In D. Cozort & J. M. Shields (Eds.), *The Oxford handbook of Buddhist ethics.* Oxford University Press. https://doi.org/10.1093/oxfordhb/9780198746140.013.31

Whiteman, J. H. M. (1993). *Aphorisms on spiritual method: The "Yoga Sutras of Patanjali" in the light of mystical experience.* Colin Smythe.

Wick, G. S. (2005). *The book of equanimity: Illuminating classic Zen koans.* Wisdom Publications.

Wilbert, J. (2021). *Analyzing single-case data with R and scan.* https://jazznbass.github.io/scan-Book/index.html

Williams, J. M. G., Crane, C., Barnhofer, T., Brennan, K., Duggan, D. S., Fennell, M. J., Hackmann, A., Krische, A., Muse, K., von Rohr, I. R., Shah, D., Crane, R. S., Eames, C., Jones, M., Radford, S., Silverton, S., Sun, Y., Weatherley-Jones, E., Whitaker, C., ... Russell, I. R. (2014). Mindfulness-based cognitive therapy for preventing relapse in recurrent depression: A randomized dismantling trial. *Journal of Consulting and Clinical Psychology, 82,* 275–286.

Williamson, L. (2010). *Transcendent in America: Hindu-inspired meditation movements as new religion.* New York University Press.

Wink, P. (1991). Two faces of narcissism. *Journal of Personality and Social Psychology, 61,* 590–597. https://doi.org/10.1037/0022-3514.61.4.590

Wink, P., Dillon, M., & Fay, K. (2005). Spiritual seeking, narcissism, and psychotherapy: How are they related? *Journal for the Scientific Study of Religion, 44,* 143–158.

Winning, A. P., & Boag, S. (2015). Does brief mindfulness training increase empathy? The role of personality. *Personality and Individual Differences, 86,* 492–498. https://doi.org/10.1016/j.paid.2015.07.011

Wirth, M. (2006). *Von Gurus, Bollywood und heiligen Kühen.* [Of gurus, Bollywood and holy cows]. Herbig.

Wolf, D. B., & Abell, N. (2003). Examining the effects of meditation techniques on psychosocial functioning. *Research on Social Work Practice, 13*, 27–42. https://doi.org/10.1177/104973102237471

Wong, Fr. J. (2010). The Jesus prayer and inner stillness. *Religion East & West, 10*, 35–48.

Wong, S. Y. S., Chan, J. Y. C., Zhang, D., Lee, E. K. P., & Tsoi, K. K. F. (2018). The safety of mindfulness-based interventions: A systematic review of randomized controlled trials. *Mindfulness, 9*, 1344–1357. https://doi.org/10.1007/s12671-018-0897-0

Woods, J. H. (1998). *The Yoga-system of Patañjali*. Motilal Banarsidass. (Original work published 1914)

Xia, T., Yang, Y., Li, W., Tang, Z., Huang, Q., Li, Z., & Guo, Y. (2020). Meditative movements for patients with type 2 diabetes: A systematic review and meta-analysis. *Evidence-Based Complementary and Alternative Medicine*. https://doi.org/10.1155/2020/5745013

Yamada, K. (2002). *Die Niederschrift vom blauen Fels: Hekiganroku* [The Blue Cliff record] (Vol. 2) (transalted and edited by Peter Lengsfeld). Kösel.

Yamada, K. (2015). *Zen: The authentic gate* [eBook]. Somerville, MA: Wisdom Publications.

Yang, H., Wu, X., & Wang, M. (2017). The effect of three different meditation exercises on hypertension: A network meta-analysis. *Evidence-Based Complementary and Alternative Medicine*. https://doi.org/10.1155/2017/9784271

Yogananda, P. (1950). *Autobiography of a Yogi*. Self-Realization Fellowship.

Zarate, K., Maggin, D. M., & Passmore, A. (2019). Meta-analysis of mindfulness training on teacher well-being. *Psychology in the Schools, 56*, 1700–1715. https://doi.org/10.1002/pits.22308

Zeidan, F., Johnson, S. K., Diamond, B. J., David, Z., & Goolkasian, P. (2010). Mindfulness meditation improves cognition: Evidence of brief mental training. *Consciousness and Cognition, 19*(2), 597–605. https://doi.org/10.1016/j.concog.2010.03.014

Zeidan, F., Martucci, K. T., Kraft, R. A., Gordon, N. S., McHaffie, J. G., & Coghill, R. C. (2011). Brain mechanisms supporting the modulation of pain by mindfulness meditation. *The Journal of Neuroscience, 31*, 5540–5548. https://doi.org/10.1523/JNEUROSCI.5791-10.2011

Zenner, C., Herrnleben-Kurz, S., & Walach, H. (2014). Mindfulness-based interventions in schools – a systematic review and meta-analysis. *Frontiers in Psychology, 5*, 603. https://doi.org/10.3389/fpsyg.2014.00603

Zimmermann, M. (2002). *A Buddha within: The Tathāgatagarbhasūtra*. Bibliotheca Philologica et Philosophica Buddhica VI (PDF). Tokyo, Japan: The International Research Institute for Advanced Buddhology, Soka University. http://iriab.soka.ac.jp/content/pdf/bppb/Vol.%20VI.%20Michael%20Zimmermann,%20A%20Buddha%20Within%20The%20Tathagatagarbhasutra%20...%20ISBN%204-9980622-5-5%20(2002).pdf

Zoogman, S., Goldberg, S. B., Hoyt, W. T., & Miller, L. (2015). Mindfulness interventions with youth: A meta-analysis. *Mindfulness, 6*, 290–302. https://doi.org/10.1007/s12671-013-0260-4

Zou, L., Yeung, A., Li, C., Wei, G. X., Chen, K. W., Kinser, P. A., Chan, J. S. M., & Ren, Z. (2018). Effects of meditative movements on major depressive disorder: A systematic review and meta-analysis of randomized controlled trials. *Journal of Clinical Medicine, 7*(8), 195. https://doi.org/10.3390/jcm7080195

Clear and compact guidance on integrating mindfulness into practice

Katie Witkiewitz / Corey R. Roos /
Dana Dharmakaya Colgan / Sarah Bowen

Mindfulness

Advances in Psychotherapy –
Evidence-Based Practice, vol. 37
2017, viii + 80 pp.
US $29.80 / € 24.95
ISBN 978-0-88937-414-0
Also available as eBook

This clear and concise book provides practical, evidence-based guidance on the use of mindfulness in treatment: its mechanism of action, the disorders for which there is empirical evidence of efficacy, mindfulness practices and techniques, and how to integrate them into clinical practice.

Leading experts describe the concepts and roots of mindfulness, and examine the science that has led to this extraordinarily rich and ancient practice becoming a foundation to many contemporary, evidenced-based approaches in psychotherapy. The efficacy of mindfulness-based interventions in conditions as diverse as borderline personality disorder, posttraumatic stress disorder, depression, alcohol and substance use, emotional dysregulation, attention-deficit hyperactivity disorder, chronic stress, eating disorders, and other medical conditions. The book is invaluable reading for all those curious about the current science around mindfulness and about how and when to incorporate it effectively into clinical practice.

www.hogrefe.com

Start using character strengths today!

"The GO-TO book for building character."

Martin E. P. Seligman, Founder of positive psychology

Ryan M. Niemiec
Character Strengths Interventions
A Field Guide for Practitioners

2018, xx + 300 pp.
US $59.00 / € 46.95
ISBN 978-0-88937-492-8
Also available as eBook

This unique guide brings together the vast experience of the author with the science and the practice of positive psychology. New practitioners will learn about the core concepts of character and signature strengths and how to fine-tune their approach and troubleshoot. Experienced practitioners will deepen their knowledge about advanced topics such as strengths overuse and collisions, hot button issues, morality, and integrating strengths with savouring, flow, and mindfulness. Hands-on practitioner tips throughout the book provide valuable hints on how to take a truly strengths-based approach.

A perfect resource to use with the book: *Character Strengths Intervention Cards*.

www.hogrefe.com

Teach clients the language of character strengths!

Matthijs Steeneveld / Anouk van den Berg

Character Strengths Intervention Cards

50 Cards With Instruction Booklet

2020, 50 cards + 16-page booklet
US $34.80 / € 27.95
ISBN 978-0-88937-566-6

The VIA character strengths look at what positive character traits help us lead fulfilling and happy lives, rather than looking at what is wrong with us. Research has shown that knowing your strengths and using them more often leads to greater well-being, better performance, and more resilience. With these cards, you can help clients learn about their character strengths.

This full-color 50-card set provides cards for each of the 24 VIA character strengths and 6 virtues as well as information cards to hand out in groups and individual sessions. On top of that, 16 ready-to-use, evidence-based intervention cards help clients discover and explore their strengths and practice applying them more often. The cards are a valuable addition to the toolboxes of coaches, trainers, and therapists from any background. The card set is an excellent resource to use with the book *Character Strengths Interventions* by Ryan M. Niemiec.

www.hogrefe.com